Islam :

The Forgotter

Of Foreign

(Iran, Saudi Arabia, Indonesia)

Sugiri

December 2018

About the Author

Born in West Java, Indonesia 1981, the writer continued his education both for High Senior School and undergraduate program in el-Azhar University, Egypt in the field of Islamic Law and Jurisprudence under the full scholarship of Azhar University since 1996 until 2003. While a student in al-Azhar University, he won several writing competencies among both Indonesian students and international students.

In 2009 he got scholarship to continue his education in School of International Relations, Ministry of Foreign Affairs in Iran in the field of Iranian Issues and obtained Master degree in 2010. Since 2011 he studied Ph.D program in Tehran University in the field of Middle East Region (not completed yet). He spent in Iran for around seven years, Saudi Arabia for around five months and in Egypt for seven years.

The author speaks four languages fluently, Indonesia/Malayan, Arabic, English, Persian. He was also official interpreter for Arabic and Persian languages and wrote a novel based on the true events in Iran, Syria and Iraq, which due to the issue sensitivity as the novel talks on human rights issues; he uses a pen name for his novel titled The Man Who Embraced a White Tulip. The novel is also available in Amazon.

He is expert in the issues of Saudi Arabia, Iran and Palestine, Global Terrorism, Political Islam in Indonesia, and Islamic Law and Jurisprudence and writes for Indonesian media on Middle East Affairs.

In 2017 he worked as lecturer in Strategic Intelligent Institution of Indonesian Military Forces for Afghanistan study and its culture. The contact number

Email   josephplara@yahoo.com

Telegram   @gerryplara

FOREWORD

I had privilege that I had stayed for several years in the Middle East region, mainly in Egypt (seven years), Saudi Arabia (five months) then in Iran (seven years). I spent most times there to conduct a thorough research relating to various Middle Eastern issues, not only about Iran. In addition, I have been very lucky to have full ability of understanding four languages, Indonesia/Malaya, English, Arabic and Persian to facilitate the research and add diverse horizons in viewing and analyzing the issue. In fact such ability helped a lot to rely on different written and oral resources in order to make my book more perfect

I wrote the book in English, to be my first English non-fiction book, as I have been eager to share my field research, personal experiences to international readers who are so interested with the issues of Saudi Arabia, Iran as well as Indonesia. Many of Iranian friends have always encouraged me to write on Iran based on my objective standpoints as they did realize I have been to almost all of Iranian cities and villages, and talked to many Iranians from various educational and cultural backgrounds.

I am also interested in Saudi Arabia issues as my field of study in Tehran University was Middle East Regional Study that also covers the country's issues. However I have been to the Kingdom for several months and I had a great chance to talk with the local citizens.

However, as an intellectual and scholar, I would bear a moral responsibility to write on the issues objectively and fairly so the readers will hopefully get more aware to what happened and are happening nowadays in Iran and Saudi Arabia as well as Indonesia. It is open secret, to write something on Saudi Arabia and Iran will bring much sensitivity as they are long viewed as non-democratic states which sometimes attempt at concealing the realities.

In addition, the comparison among Saudi Arabia, Iran and Indonesia in viewing various global issues would be challenging as I do believe there must be few English books discussing on Indonesian foreign policy along with its relation with Islam. In this vein, the book of Mr. Rizal Sukma written in 2003 inspired me a lot that Islam could be an essential element in making and navigating foreign policy. The most recent empirical evidence has shown us the Indonesian society significantly have become more conservative and religiously enthusiastic, some of those even believe that Islam is the only solution for each life aspect, replacing secular and liberal paradigms, which during this time the country has been still upholding. Such an interesting reality, may behoove Indonesian policy makers both internally and externally to take the religious spirit into consideration.

Again, I was given a great opportunity to stay there and see closely the communities of the both states. The countries where their nations are always associated with Islam, might have claimed that their foreign policy takings will be navigated and led to achieve the Islamic goals. In addition, the countries but Indonesia have repeatedly claimed as the most appropriate leading states to the world's Muslims. Yet however, with the passage of time, pragmatism has been always overshadowing their respective foreign policies until now, or perhaps worse, the interests of the rulers may have prevailed over both Islamic and national interests.

Last but not least, among the reasons I wrote the book is that I would like to use some of the royalties of the book selling to be donated to a community in an isolated village in West Java, Indonesia where many of poor, old widows dwell in.

Jakarta, Indonesia

December, 2018

ACKNOWLEDGMENTS

I would like to thank the individuals that relentlessly help me to finally complete the book during my 7 year stay in Iran. There are too many persons to mention, Bastian Juleano (Lecturer in Indonesian University), Siti Fatima (Lecturer in Paramadina University), Bahram Rahbar and Mohammad Kahnoji, etc, all staffs in School of International Relations of Iran and Tehran University.

In addition, I would like also convey my sincere gratitude to my family who kindly supported me to complete the book.

CONTENTS

1. **Introduction** _____ 8

2. **Islam and Society of the Countries at Glance** _____ 25

    Islam and Society in Iran _____ 26
    Islam and Society in Saudi Arabia _____ 35
    Islam and Society in Indonesia _____ 41

3. **The Role of Islamic Ideology in Shaping the Foreign Policy of the Countries** _____ 53

    The Authority of Iranian Supreme Leader and Saudi King in Determining Foreign Policy _____ 77
    Indonesia and How to Shape its Foreign Policy _____ 89

4. **The Implementation of "forgotten Islam" in Foreign Policy** _____ 102

    Palestinian Cause _____ 122
    Iran and the Issue of Palestine _____ 126
    Iran's Relations with Hamas _____ 135
    Iranian Pragmatism in Palestinian cause _____ 141
    Saudi Arabia and Issue of Palestine _____ 144
    Seeds of Relation Normalization of the Kingdom with Israel _____ 152
    Indonesia and the Issue of Palestine _____ 154
    Combating on Global Terrorism _____ 160
    Shia and Roots of Its Extremism _____ 166
    Radicalization of Shia Politics in Iran _____ 172
    Wahhabism and Roots Its Extremism _____ 178
    Iran and Terrorism _____ 182
    Iran and Terrorism, a Victim or Sponsor? _____ 188
    Saudi Arabia and Terrorism, a Victim or Sponsor? _____ 203
    Dilemma of Saudi Commitment on Terrorism Eradication _____ 210
    Indonesia and Terrorism _____ 212
    Strategies of Indonesian Government to Combat Terrorism _____ 216

5. **Soft Power of the Countries** _____ 223

The Importance of Soft Power	223
Islam Nusantara (Islam of the Archipelago)	238
Building Up Capacity of Foreign Students	242
Pesantren and Terrorism	249
The Establishment of Non Governmental Organizations	251
The Allegation of WAMY's Involvement in Terrorism Issue	255
Establishing and Empowering the Functions of Iranian and Saudi Political Lobbies in Abroad	257
Establishing Television and Radio Stations	261
Challenges for Iranian Propagandist Media	263
Challenges for Saudi Arabia's Propagandist Media	270

6. Pragmatism in Foreign Policy in Islamic Sunni Perspective — **274**

7. Conclusion — **283**

Glossary of Terms

Bibiliography

Index

Chapter I: Introduction

It is an unquestionably historical fact that Islam constitutes a key element in help founding and creating modern Iran, Indonesia and Saudi Arabia. Apart from other fact that Islam has become a religion for the vast majority of the people, little wonder to state the founding fathers of the countries were also encouraged to bring Islam into their respective political systems and constitutions. However, the heated debates between Islamists and liberalists chiefly in Indonesia and Iran often took place which in Iran, the revolutionary Islamists eventually succeeded to bring another substantial formula for the state aftermath the 1979 Islamic revolution. Meanwhile in Indonesia, the Islamists had to make compromise in order to avoid disintegration and friction.

In this regard, Islamic Wahhabism's role in taking part to conquer and then unify Arabian peninsula along with various tribes under the al-Saud family flagship in centuries ago could not be overlooked in establishing the monarch Arab Saudi in 1932. Meanwhile Indonesia which until present is constantly considered as the World's most populous Muslim country, strongly believes that Islam was a spiritual inspiration for its people to carry out patriotically physical struggles to expel colonialist powers (Dutch and Japan) from the territory until finally the state was declared its independence officially in 1945 by Soekarno, the first President. In this vein Iran, indicated obviously by renaming the state as Islamic Republic by its founding fathers mainly Grand Ayatollah Imam Khomeini, has always viewed that Islam was the key driver that overthrew one of the world's most powerful monarchy of Pahlavi dynasty in 1979.

Since the phenomenal Revolution of Iran erupted in 1979, the secular monarch state ruled by Pahlavi Dynasty over five decades changed and transformed into the form of Islamic system, which for the first time in modern history, is ruled by an Islamic Jurist often called *Vali Faqih*.[1] It is hardly surprising that the significant impact of such a substantial transformation of becoming an Islamic state, among others is to change the secular nature of Iranian foreign policy into an Islam flavoured one. Putting Islamic principles to its foreign policy agenda has been the most significant manifestation of the regime's extreme self confidence that its people unanimously wanted it, reflected profoundly through the results of the two referenda held in the first months of the Revolution. Since then theoretically Iran has been trying to drive all foreign affairs in seeking and realizing the aspirations of both Islam and *Ummah* interests as both moral and religious obligations from the birth of the newly Islamic state. For Iran, guiding and identifying foreign policy to achieve the goals of broader Islamic interests and Ummah unity must be taken into consideration.

In the early periods of the Revolution, the long term aims of the predominantly Islamic Shia Clerics-ruled state has encompassed the establishment of a universal Islamic government as explicitly cited in its basic constitution by rejecting the world's despotic and

---

[1] Supreme Leader, the highest-ranking official in Iran following the Revolution in 1979. Vali means guardian, faqih means Islamic Jurist. The authority he has is often called Vilayat Faqih which means Guardianship of the Islamic Jurist. The incumbent Supreme Leader or Vali Faqih is Ayatollah Ali Khamene'i. Theoretically, the leader is chosen by the Iranian Council of Expert. For further information, please refer to Iranian basic constitution.

suppressive regimes with its outstanding supports to oppressed nations and liberation movements, and by propagating the newly-invented concept of revolutionary Shiite teachings throughout the world.[2] With the passage of time, these main objectives of the state which have little and deep positive impact on Iranian national interests, were implicitly identified by Imam Khomeini, the main founding father of the Islamic state by noting that the Islamic State of Iran is an ideal form for any global governmental system, in which all types and forms of the world's governments but Islamic Iranian system must be reformed or even deconstructed as they are regarded to have contravened Islamic values and norms. Besides, since its establishment the Islamic Iran has constantly claimed to be leading Islamic world, thus creating considerable rivalry and competition with Saudi Arabia in Muslim world.

In fact such a bombastic, incessant claim to be a leader for all of Islamic nations has been profoundly prompted by other previous claim that the Supreme Leader is a representative of Imam Mahdi, the twelfth infallible Imam for Shia Twelver Imamite adherents, since He has been strongly believed to have occulted in 941 AD.[3] Due to such a controversial claim, then it encouraged Imam Khomeini to introduce the doctrine of *Velayat Faqih* (the guardianship of jurist) that shall be upheld not only by Iranians themselves but also the entire international community, thus adjusting the objectives of Iranian foreign policy under the shadows of the doctrine, that interestingly has been strongly opposed by several other Shia prominent clerics. For Iranian ruling elites, to abide by the doctrine will usher its society into long lasting happiness in hereafter life, thus ignoring to reach happiness in the world. This perception has been simply reflected by issuing numerous unpopular domestic policies. In addition, this political doctrine of Velayat Faqih further implies the central axis of contemporary Shi'a political thought and advocates a guardianship-based political system, which relies upon a just and capable jurist (Faqih) to assume the leadership of the government in the absence of an infallible Imam as cited before. For sure, Iran today constitutes the world's only clerically-ruled government that is unlikely to break up its policies, both domestic and foreign, from Islamic values.

The Iranian rulers have also other spectacular claim of the sole mechanism to garner salvation, that all measures taken by Iran in dealing with regional conflicts are particularly due to Islamic and *Ummah* interests, not even for achieving its national interest, in which Iran would endure moral responsibility to introduce the sacred doctrine to international community by totally exerting the entire possible means, regardless of much objection and disapproval of its suffering people. Iran's continuous involvement in Palestinian cause

---

[2] Bahram Ikhwani Kazemi, *Vagereyaha va Hamgrayeha dar ravabithe Iran va Arabistan*, a three month periodical journal of Middle east, Centre for Research, Science and Strategic Studies of the Middle East, the seventh year, summer edition 1379 page 122

[3] As I will explain later in the next chapter, the vast majority of Iranians are Shia twelver often called Imamiya. They believe in twelve Imams Ali ibn Abi Talib, Hasan ibn Ali, Husayn ibn Ali, Ali ibn Husayn, Muhammad ibn Ali, Ja'far ibn Muhammad, Musa Ibn Ja'far, Ali ibn Musa, Muhammad ibn Ali, Ali ibn Muhammad, Hasan ibn Ali Ibn Muhammad(Al-Askari), Muhammad ibn al-Hasan (Mahdi)

reflected mainly through its significant support to Hamas faction, and helping establish Hezbollah, Lebanese Islamic Shiite radical organization in 1980s were seen as the realization of God's command and Moslems interests alike. Furthermore, these Iranian unique behaviours have been viewed as the manifestation of their basic constitution, particularly in article 154 that urges deeply such massive interventions to help oppressed and ill-fated nations regardless of their religious and national identities.[45] In this vein, Iran's inevitable interventions in the aftermath of Arab spring since 2011 by dispatching its army of Revolutionary Guard to the conflict areas such as Syria, and funnelling financial and logistic supports, have been regarded as effective means to maintain and defence Islamic interests from any existential threat. Moreover most startlingly Iran has viewed that its incredible engagement in fighting with ISIS terrorist group and other radical terrorist groups in Iraq and Syria would aim at eliminating the roots of radical thoughts which would imperil and jeopardize the co-existence of Islamic Ummah.

In nutshell, the whole actions and measures taken by Iran beyond its borders and territory are simply to maintain Islamic interests, and create unity and integration among the world's Moslems amid harsh criticisms of international audience, that in reality, Iran has been practicing partial and imbalanced policies by favouring one group over another, particularly in relation with the Palestinian cause.[6] Not only that, when the nuclear deal was finally reached by Iran and the P5+1 in July 2015, the incumbent Iranian President Hassan Rouhani described it as the greatest diplomatic victory in the history of Islam.[7] Ayatollah Alamul Huda, one of the most prominent Islamic Shia preachers in Iran had once told that Iranian football participation in the World Cup would also mean a pride for Islam.

In fact such a courageous claim to be a leading state for international Muslims is truly made by a state with a Shia as a religion that occupies only 10 to 15 percent of the total number of the world's Muslims who mostly follow Sunni teaching for centuries that theologically and juristically has little difference with Shia, most importantly that Sunni Muslims have never believed the infallibility of twelve Imams who arose after the Prophet,[8] thus never acknowledging the intensively Imam Khomeini-promoted Velayat Faqih doctrine. Nevertheless, Iranian strong claim to be rightful representative of Imam Mahdi as elucidated earlier, has instilled much self-confidence to the Iranian rulers to expand and export its revolutionary values to the regions, implying that Shia, not Sunni, is more appropriate faith to be followed by all Muslims.

---

[4] For further information, please refer to the Iranian Basic Constitution, www.wipo.int (English version)
[5] Ahmad Sadeghi, Genealogy of Iranian Foreign Policy : Identity, Culture and History, the Iranian Journal of International Affairs, IPIS page 5
[6] My interview with Mr. Mahdawi, Palestinian Ambassador in Jakarta took place in 2013. In this interview, he clearly criticized Iranian approach towards the Palestinian issue that Iran is the one which often strives to make political division among Palestinian nation.
[7] www.aawsat.com, 1 June 2018
[8] Juan Cole, Iran and Islam, https://iranprimer.usip.org/resource/iran-and-islam

More interestingly, accommodating and absorbing Islamic ideas and achieving the unity of Islamic Ummah in Iranian foreign policy have been underlined evidently in articles 9 and 10 of the Iran's basic constitution that could be clear justification for extending Iranian interventionist policies in the region whose society are predominantly Sunni Muslims. Once again, Iran with Persian identity seen as an outsider *(Ajami)* by the Arabs for centuries has been largely depicted as a common enemy by several Arab states whose long presence in the region aims at creating chaos and instability in the region instead. Surprisingly, with it deeply understanding the cold and unfriendly behaviour of the Arabs, Iran has never scaled back its "illegal and illegitimate" position in the region despite much internal and international pressures. Rather, given the excessive self confidence, Iran much believes that its revolutionary doctrine of Velayat Faqih shall be enjoyed by all nations with no exception, including the Arabs.

As a matter of fact, this self-claiming to be an Islamic world leader was also prompted robustly by a controversial theory initially introduced by Javad Larijani,[9] a loyal conservative politician in the outset of Revolution. The theory is called Ummul Quro theory which emphasizes on that Iran is an ideal and exemplary state which is likely to represent all Islamic interests. Therefore, due to its significance, the whole Iranian Islamic regime's interests shall be put into the top priority and defended and protected by all Moslems of the world under any circumstances, with no exception. Such theory signifies implicitly an Iran's ambition to be head for all Islamic nations religiously and politically given the fact that the Islamic Iran was not founded only for religious reasons, as some of modern Moslem scholars like Abu Ala Maududi, Pakistani founder of Jamaah Islam political party, and Sayyed Qutb, Egyptian political activist of Ikhwanul Muslimin organization once suggested, rather Islam must be politically inspirational and applied thoroughly into political affairs. The theory also underscores explicitly that expressing formal and conventional submission and loyalty of all world's citizens to Iran is no longer necessary because Islam as a universal religion has never acknowledged such distinction of national borders since 14 decades ago.

More startlingly, the Persian theorist has adopted words of *Ummul Quro* from Arabic which means '*Mother of all villages*,' whose use commonly refers to Mecca city, a central holy place for Moslem pilgrims in Arab Saudi where the Prophet Mohammad was born. Using the Arabic words, rather than Persian, in the theory implies profoundly Arabic language to be more universal and acceptable by Islamic world in order to entice Islamic world's sympathy as the two words (Umm + Qura)[10] are palpably mentioned in Al-Qor'an. In addition, Arabic language, compared to Persian, is commonly taught and learned in Moslem countries even in Iran itself. Therefore, such word using may expose an Iran's religious and political ambition, as mentioned earlier, to replace Saudi Arabia as a traditional leading state for Islamic nations, and even to make Qom city in Iran instead of Mecca and Medina as a

---

[9] He has also two brothers who hold strategic positions in Iranian political system, Ali Larijani's spokesperson of Iranian parliament since 2008, and Sadegh Larijani, currently the head of judiciary since 2009
[10] In Persian means *Madare Dehha*

new centre and headquarter for entire Islamic educational activities around the world, and a central destination for spiritual visit (specifically for Shia Moslems) where the holy site of the shrine of Fatimah bint Musa, Sister of Imam Reza (the 8th Shi'a Imam) is situated.

The idea of revolution export introduced deeply by Imam Khomeini as its main founder in the initial years of the Revolution, would justify issuing Iranian revolutionary foreign policy in order to materialize the aforementioned ambition. Under such a concept, Imam Khomeini further believed that all nations no matter Muslims or not, shall undergo the Iran's astonishing experience so as to bring justice and annihilate all repression and injustice carried out despotic regimes. Islamic revolution, believed to be the greatest achievement of Muslims in modern history, signifies the likelihood of toppling down powerfully repressive regimes like Pahlavi Dynasty, by its oppressed people. Such an amazing success has created the self confidence of Imam Khomeini to further view the world sceptically, thus issuing and guiding foreign policy based on evil and good, black and white description, almost similar with Manichean mindset.

Furthermore, the export revolution concept has also justified trans-border and transnational foreign policies which would seemingly violate the sovereignty of the nations and states based on the Westphalia concept generally long accepted by international community. In consequence, enforcing the revolution export to the globe would eventually deconstruct and rupture the steadily existing secular systems along with diverse forms, replaced by more endurable political system. Therefore, it is hardly surprising that once the Islamic regime was founded, the Arab monarch leaders, mainly Saudi Arabia, displayed their pessimism and antipathy to accept the reality that Imam Khomeini severely opposed monarchic and hereditary succession that contradict Islamic principles on justice and human equality, despite initial sympathetic welcoming of the outbreak of the Revolution by Arab Saudi and the others. Consequently the abolishment of such un-Islamic systems had been central task for the already transformed Iran in 1980s onwards. In addition, a determined decision on resuming military war with Iraq was issued by Imam Khomeini arguably due to his main perspective that the ferocious Saddam Hussein had applied a secular system, instead of Islamic one. Not only that, establishing long standing hostility with US and Israeli Zionism that I will explore more deeply later on, has been the core Iranian foreign policy the state always pursues, although the regime is well aware that normalizing relations with US and Israel would undeniably benefit its national interests.   In this regard, R.K Ramazani, Iranian expert on International Relations, as I quoted from Arshid Mogaddam, further argued that the policies under a Faqih (Islamic jurist) whose authority encompasses whole affairs, will inevitably entail confrontation between that state and the superpowers. Such a conflict is inevitable because the superpowers have arrogated all power to themselves. It is in the context of these basic ideas that the Iranian slogan 'neither East, nor West, only the Islamic republic should be understood, not the irrelevant notions of equidistance or non-alignment. These ideas in effect accept the Western notion of power politics, whereas Khomeini's religious, millenarian, and idealistic view rejects the global role of both superpowers; they are both considered to be illegitimate players in the international system they dominate.[11]

For Imam Khomeini, the universality of Islam shall encompass each territory of the earth, regardless of the applied international laws as the outcome of human's creativity and thought that never require absoluteness. For Imam, the interests of Islamic regime as the solely world's legitimized political system must be prevailed by other Muslim countries over those laws. Accordingly, Imam Khomeini along with his subsequent conservative loyalists would not consider profoundly the side effects of whether his revolutionary foreign policy creates chaos and instability in the region or not. For the charismatic founder, the revolutionary Islam would be the sole, ideal answer for creating justice in any political system of anywhere else.

In addition, guiding Iranian revolutionary foreign policy will inevitably ignore and put aside temporarily, if possible, the realization of its own national interests including the improvement of public welfare in all terrains, as the Islamic regime would challenge, according to its vantage point, any oppressing world's regimes, thus regrettably sacrificing all of Iranian national interests. Thanks to its abundant oil production that made it the second largest oil producer with billion dollars for supporting its national income, Iran has succeeded to extend vehemently its revolutionary influence to many regions without facing any significant obstacles. For the time being, Iranian influence in Arab region for instance, could be seen evidently in four fragile countries namely Iraq, Yemen, Syria and Lebanon, mostly mirrored through helping create and nurture the militant Shia militias with all sorts of support. For Iran, nurturing hostile position with US and Israel and supporting any resistance movements throughout the globe as well as provoking insecurity and disturbance of the regions would pave the ways in accelerating re-emerge of Imam Mahdi, the most waited figure believed by Shia to enforce justice and spread goodness on the earth.

Meanwhile as briefly stated above, the absolute monarchy of Arab Saudi whose power centres significantly controlled by princes (house of Saud), has invariably claimed as a leading state of Islamic nations that is committed to safeguarding and protecting the global Muslim community. Bear in mind that despite large territory, Saudi has only around 30 million populations with many of those are foreign expatriates, yet not discouraging the state for such a claim to lead about 1.5 billion Muslims. For the Kingdom, its claime has risen without no reasons. Saudi Arabia is the location where Islam initially introduced and brought by Prophet Mohammad came into being 14 decades ago with Muslims having the obligation to visit Mecca as pilgrims as regarded the fifth pillar of Islam. As known previously that millions of the world's Muslims would visit Saudi soil of the two holy mosques in Mecca and Medina to make Umroh (lesser pilgrimage) and Hajj (greater pilgrimage), becoming

---

[11] Arshid Adib-Moghaddam, the International Politics of the Persian Gulf, A cultural genealogy, Roudledge Taylor & Francis Group, page 28

obligatory if they can afford to do so as explicitly cited in holy Al-Qor'an, no matter whether they Sunni or Shia followers.

Not surprisingly, since King Fahd had ruled the Kingdom in 1980s, the title of Custodian of the Two Holy Mosques (*Khademul Haramayn*) would be granted automatically to any successive king, meaning that Saudi administration will always be ready to serve pilgrims under no circumstances, regardless of any political clashes that may involve Saudi and the state origin of the pilgrims. Moreover such a titling that interestingly came into revitalization in the initial years of Islamic state of Iran, gives emphasis implicitly on the importance of Saudi Arabia position before the global Muslim community, thus undermining and declining Iran's ambition to be a leader for the world's Muslim community. Saudi further believes that the world's majority Muslims who happen to be Sunnis would prefer Saudi over Iran, thus creating more self-confidence for Saudi rulers to give best service as much as possible to the pilgrims who every day could enter Mecca and Medina cities to carry out Umroh (lesser hajj). In this regard, historically speaking when Hashemian family-ruled Mecca was conquered by first modern Saudi ruler in 1924, the initial measure he did was to attempt attracting sympathy from Islamic world by inviting all representatives of Muslim countries to Mecca to discuss on future of Holy Land.[12] Such an initiative to offer operation and management of the Holy Land to broader world's Muslims, once conveyed by Iran and Qatar, has been discouraged implicitly by current Saudi leaders. Not only that, to reassure Saudi position before international Muslim community as the greatest power in Islamic world, in January 1981, King Khaled bin Abdul Aziz had invited all leaders from Muslim countries to have meetings with him both in Mecca and Taif, often touted as the most costly conference of the world during the time.[13] So it is hardly surprising in this regard. Adel el-Jubair, Saudi Ambassador for UN of the time, had once said that the position of Saudi Arabia to Islamic world is similar to the position of Vatican to Catholic community.[14] In short words, the issue of religiosity for Saudi would constitute a very effective means to entice Muslims sympathy who would gradually perceive it as an ideal leader.

In this regard, most startlingly Iran which seems to be frustrated in replacing the Saudi Kingdom as an attractive location for entire Islamic world for pilgrimage, does not prevent this theocratic state from communicating and transferring its ideology to all Muslims both Sunni and Shia during pilgrimage in Mecca. Even, based on the founding documents of the Office of the Supreme Leader's Representative on Hajj and Pilgrimage

---

[12] Robert Lacey, Kerajaan Petrodollar Saudi Arabia, Pustaka Jaya, first edition, 1986, page 240. The phenomenal book was translated from its English original version titled the Kingdom.
[13] Ibid page 241
[14] Saudi Arabia's Curriculum of Intolerance, With Excerpts from Saudi Ministry of Education Textbooks for Islamic Studies, Center for Religious Freedom of the Hudson Institute, page 31

Affairs, highlights that Iran would use Hajj diplomacy for consolidation of a unified Islamic ummah and to develop strategy and plan policy for the international function of the Hajj. [15]

According to Toby Matthiesen, when ISIS terrorist group declared caliphate in June 2014, Saudi felt intimidated that eventually forced the state to scale back its support from the opposition in Syria, as Saudi territory could be potential target for such ISIS's ambition of expansion by conquering Mecca and Medina, thus threatening the survival of the Kingdom.[16] The claiming of Saudi to be a leading state for Islamic Ummah would be tremendously collided with ISIS interests who often see Saudi Arabia as an illegitimate political system.

Not only that, Saudi views itself as a reference for global Muslim community in all sectors, politically, economically and culturally which drives it to adjust its foreign policy to be compliant with any Islamic and Ummah interests as much evidently seen in king Faisal's ruling in 1970s. In consequence, Saudi is supposed to give much attention and contribution in dealing with a wide array of issues relating to them. In addition the state is supposed to put tremendously the goal of consolidating bilateral and regional cooperation with Muslim states into its top priority. In other words, theoretically the Kingdom shall prefer Islamic and Muslim community's interests over anything else.

Furthermore, due to such an unwavering claim, Saudi has been obliged to spread and develop Islam throughout the world despite of its deep understanding of rigid Islamic uniqueness that may create challenge from global Muslims. In a book titled 'the Looming Tower,' Lawrence Wright had estimated that since 1979 Islamic Revolution Saudi regime has already funded US$ 75 billion only to spread Wahhabi teachings to the entire world, along with a secondary goal, to curb the Iran's religious Shia influences from flourishing. In order to strengthen its agenda and cultivate more sympathy, Saudi, like what Iran has tirelessly done, has much contributed among others by granting educational scholarships to young Moslem students from around the world to study comfortably in Saudi. Additionally, Saudi, akin to Iran, also has actively played a key role in founding and empowering mosques and Islamic centres for religious trainings and educations around the globe. However, as the author of the book stated, Saudi has population no more than 1% of total of world's Muslim population yet its Wahhabi teachings could dominate 90% of all Islamic teachings in the world. [17]

Interestingly, such a claim as leading state to Islamic Ummah has inevitably created rivalry between the countries, not only religiously, but also politically that has lasted since

---

[15] Mehdi Khalaji, Ideology Outweighs Diplomacy in Iran's Hajj Decision,
https://www.washingtoninstitute.org/policy-analysis/view/ideology-outweighs-diplomacy-in-irans-hajj-decision

[16] Toby Matthiesen, the Domestic sources of Saudi Foreign Policy : Islamists and the state in the wake of the Arab Uprisings, Working Paper, August 2015, page 6

[17] Sarah N.Stern, Saudi Arabia and the Global Islamic Terrorist Network, America and The West's Fatal Embrace, Palgrave Macmillan page 13

Islamic Republic establishment in 1979, in which, notwithstanding claim on neutrality in Iran Iraq war, Saudi granted $25 billons and low-interest loan for supporting Saddam Hussein.[18] Furthermore, the Gulf Cooperation Council comprising six Arab states of the Gulf founded in 1981 has been arguably effective way to prevent Iranian influence into the region.

In sum, to realize its ambition to take over the Kingdom's position, Iran identifies various agendas among others by holding international meetings and conferences that involve massive participation from international audience. In some occasions, meetings and seminars are held to express Iran's criticism either implicitly and explicitly over Saudi policies viewed not to be pro Islamic interests. For instance recently, in the first December of 2017, this theocratic state of Iran had convened the 31th international conference of Islamic unity that was amazingly attended by around 220 Islamic Scholars from around the world. The conference itself could be Iranian implicitly reactionary respond to the international Riyadh Summit in Saudi Arabia in May 2017, attended by 55 leaders including President Donald Trump, which deliberately excluded Iran. In sum, many Saudis even believe that Iran's aggressive intervention in the region has been aimed at occupying Islam's Mecca Medina and declaring Shia empire in some parts of the region where the vast majority are Shia, including Bahrain, Iraq and eastern part of Saudi, prompting Saudi monarchy to re-identify and re-formulate its policy towards Iran. [19] Lastly, the assassination of Jamal Kashoggi, Saudi prominent journalist by the Saudi nationals in Saudi Consulate in Istanbul October 2018, according to the CIA's report to be directly ordered by Mohammad bin Salman, the Saudi crown prince, has been an effective opportunity for Iranian media to spread and propagate negative brutal image of the Kingdom to the world.

To seize more sympathy of the world's Moslems, Iran extends much support and endorsement to the holding of annual Shia long march ceremony called Arba'ein (40 days) in Muharram month, in Karbala city, Iraq, among other things by establishing various modern facilities for the visitors. Iranian government, whether it is true or not, has been invariably claiming that the total number of international pilgrims from 60 countries in the Shia ritual ceremony could reach 20 million visitors annually comprising Shia followers of the globe.[20] Certainly such a controversial claim would undermine the Kingdom's effort that serves only 2 million pilgrims each year as by considering the total number, thus creating more self confidence to Iran to be a leading state for Moslem community that will replace the position of the Saudi Kingdom.

---

[18] Tim Niblock, Saudi Arabia, Power, Legitimicay and Survival, Routledge Taylor and Francis Group, 2006, Page 113
[19] Karen Elliott House, Saudi Arabia, Its People, Past, Religion, Fault Lines and Future, Alfred A. Knopf, 2012 page 221
[20] Millions of Shiite Pilgrims in Karbala to Mark Arbaeen, 2 December 2015,
https://www.tasnimnews.com/en/news/2015/12/02/932841/millions-of-shiite-pilgrims-in-karbala-to-mark-arbaeen

In regional conflicts, both states have been embroiled in political and military rivalries, particularly in Middle East region. The issues of Syria, Bahrain, Yemen and Lebanon are the best example for such rivalry, interestingly without taking into account how each of their people oppose vehemently such continuous intervention. Each leader often accuses one another of being sponsor of terrorist groups in the region, or at least of representing evils that mislead and disgrace Islamic unity. For instance, Ayatollah Ali Khamene'i, the incumbent Supreme Leader of Iran has labelled the monarch family as a 'cursed tree' (*Syajarotul Mal'ounah*). A slogan 'Down with Al'Saud' was once yelled by the regime and its staunch supporters when the bilateral relations deteriorated. In turn, in December 2017, Mohammad bin Salman, young crown prince of Saudi, has dubbed Ayatollah Ali Khamene'i, Iranian incumbent Supreme Leader as a reincarnation of new modern Hitler in the Middle East region.

Not only that, Saudi has often accused Iran of supporting Shia minority group in eastern part of the Kingdom to provoke them in making resistance and opposition. In reverse, Iran has also accused Saudi Arabia of being the mastermind for igniting numerous demonstrations and protests carried out by Sunni minority of Kurd and Baluch groups in Iran. Lastly, Iran has accused of Saudi Arabia's role in terrorist attack in a military parade in Ahvaz, Iran, September 2018. In fact, the worst relation of the two states was marked significantly by the rupture of diplomatic relations for twice, in 1988 and 2016 after Militant young Iranians brutally burned the Saudi embassy in Tehran following the execution of a Saudi prominent Shia cleric, Nimr el Bagher Nimr.

With Saudi having cordial relation with Iran under the Shah Pahlavi administration framed profoundly in Richard Nixon's doctrine of two pillars, the founding of Islamic Republic of Iran along with its impact to the region, as elucidated earlier, has successfully created more political suspicions and tensions rather than trust and confidence, best reflected by the Iranian nuclear dossier and its continuous attempt at launching ballistic missile. The both states' sense of hegemonic regional power has made situation much worse which guides and leads them to use significantly their oil national incomes to support and espouse various programs and agenda throughout the world that practically happen to collide with each other, instead of exerting their own abundant oil incomes to support and sustain their national interests.

However Iran and Saudi Arabia have long been admitted as regional powers in Islamic world. Such a fact is not questionable. It is due to that their foreign policies often affect behaviours of other Muslim states, which any political and social event take place in both countries are likely to give influence to the standpoints and perspectives of other Muslim states. There has been strong and systematic willingness of the decision makers of the two countries to evince that the two countries are appropriate to hold Islamic leadership in the globe. In the other hand, in order to consolidate both states' claims as leading states of whole Muslim countries, the policy and strategy to craft a 'hostile' country could be crucial to take as the best effective way to display their undeniable ability politically and economically to vanquish and subjugate the opponent country. Such a way to deliberately creating opponents often tend to fail given the fact that in non-democratic states like Saudi Arabia and Iran, many of their governmental policies don't echo considerably the aspirations of their publics. In addition, both countries are in desperate need to marketing their unique and distinct principles and agenda outside their sovereign borders that necessarily don't reflect their national interests. In this regard, Ora Szekely further believes that successful marketing is about creating a set of publicly accepted norms, according to which, among others, the organization's adversary is viewed as an adversary by the public as well; and the organization is accepted as the right and legitimate party to confront the adversary to address the community's grievances.[21] For instance, US and Israel which Iran considers repeatedly since its initial establishment in 1979 as perennial adversaries not only for Iran but also the world don't necessarily reflect Iranian public opinions. Saudi Arabia which consistently views Iran as a "hostile state" does not necessarily reflect the main aspirations of the Saudi society.

Meanwhile Indonesia has a crucial role in the global dynamics since it has constituted the most populous Muslim country in the world. With its 250 million populations, the fourth largest, the country theoretically is supposed to play active and prominent role in Islamic world, displaying its integrity with Moslems anywhere else. Though since its birth in 1945 Indonesia has never claimed as a leading state for Islamic world, yet it did not prevent it from being proud of moderation and taking middle path in practicing religiosity and tolerance, with a hope to be adopted by other international Muslim societies as way of life to replace radical and extreme interpretation of Islam, particularly when Islam is often associated with global terrorism. No claiming on this, has largely affected guiding its foreign policy not to be taken based on Islamic principles and values. Such a foreign policy taking, interestingly, obtained widespread support of the vast majority of Indonesians which further believe that the foreign policy shall be based on reality that echoes national interests per se. In addition, it would not become its duty to engage more actively in world's Muslim. The country would not have either any moral responsibility to pursue Islamic formalization in various international forums. Even under the framework of ASEAN regional cooperation that significantly considers cultural similarity as the most basic principle of its foundation in 1967, the religious similarity of some member states, would not affect Indonesia to pursue any Islam-flavoured goal in the regional organization. Accordingly, the state, unlike Saudi Arabia and Iran has no further responsibility to establish mosques and Islamic centres in abroad in order to spread and promote the moderation of Islam through the globe. It neither seeks granting numerous scholarships to young Muslim people of the world to study and understand moderate Islam

---

[21] Ora Szekely, The Politics of Militant Group Survival in the Middle East, Resources, Relationships and Resistance, Palgrave macmillan, 2017, page 263

in universities of Indonesia. Furthermore, it is not for the sake of Islam that Indonesia has welcomed enthusiastically the Muslim Rohingya who escaped from Myanmar, and Afghans.

In this vein, the Bebas (free) and Aktif (Active) concept, adopted by its founding fathers in early years of Independence would ostensibly overshadow Indonesian foreign policy for next decades as I will discuss it in detail later. The unchangeable concept would encompass the entire implementation of Indonesian foreign policy that, at the same time, also encourages pragmatism and realistic approach to achieve its national interests. Noteworthy to note, Indonesia's foreign policy, also endeavours to keep implementing "One Thousand Friend Zero Enemy" doctrine to cover up all of its bilateral, regional and multilateral relations despite much harsh criticism of being too slow in taking a decision.

So it is hardly surprising such a doctrine implementation could be the greatest challenge for Indonesia in dealing with particular global issues that may even involve Muslim states, including the long standing rivalry of Saudi Arabia and Iran, which either state has an expectation that Indonesia would stand with them and tilt to one of them. The ongoing shocking conflict between Saudi Arabia coupled with its allied states Bahrain, United Arab Emirates, and Egypt with Qatar since 2017 has implicitly reflected a Saudi willingness that Indonesia with large Moslem population and enormous natural resources, would take side with it as important partner albeit not strategic, to isolate Qatar. In addition, with it considering to maintain good relationship with Iran in 2008, Indonesia was the sole country in the UN Security Council that was abstain in adopting the resolution of 1803 on Iran's nuclear dossier. Indonesia has been reluctant to display its firm stance in condemning and denouncing various human rights violations in Syria, Yemen and Iran reflected evidently by its voting against the alleged Iran's human right abuses at home.

However, in all of its foreign policy guidelines, Middle East region has not been the top priority for Indonesia despite distinct policies taken by each of its president. It is ASEAN (Association of Southeast Asian Nations) organization with its nine other active members that Indonesia is able to play significant role in the region. The separatism case of Mindanao that involved Moslem Moro tribe in Philippines in 1990s and currently Moslem Rohignya issue in Myanmar have exhibited Indonesia's great concern and commitment to actively solve the problems by directly being involved as an inspirational mediator in the negotiations etc.

Therefore, arguably Indonesia's proudly claim as the largest Muslim population state does not necessarily mean the country will be having a strategic partnership with the Saudi Arabia and Iran. In the other hand both countries would also apparently undermine Indonesia's significance by not considering it as their partner state, particularly in economic sector since their establishment in 1932 (Saudi) and Iran (1979) have accentuated the importance of pragmatic approaches in establishing relations with others.

Unlike Saudi and Iran with their constant rivalry that always appear to compete with each other religiously and politically in the globe, Indonesia, as cited earlier, has never shown any willingness for being involved in similar rivalry in the globe, thus favouring neutrality over showing inclination to specific state. Instead, Indonesia would prefer to build image of a tolerant and peace-loving Islam at home, thus not being tempted to concretize promoting moderate Islam in abroad inter alia by establishing particular Islamic buildings etc. In fact, lacking of sense to become hegemonic in Moslem community world has mirrored tremendously the soft stance of Indonesians in viewing the harmonious world. Indonesia still believes that giving priority to develop and grow its domestic economy is inevitable.

Nevertheless, with the passage of time, Indonesia has been a potential target of such religious rivalry of both hegemonic states that are keenly interested in spreading and promoting their uniquely interpreted Islam to Indonesian society. With its huge number of Muslim population, for decades many Indonesian young students have enjoyed full scholarship granted regularly by the states in order to study from its authentic Islamic origin. Several Islamic buildings in Indonesia are well affiliated with the states which support them financially, and managed mostly by those Indonesian alumni.

However, historically speaking the influence of ancient Arabic and Persian traditions to Indonesian Islamic culture has been significantly acknowledged by some Indonesian scholars who presented much evidence that such a cultural influence had took place long before their establishment as modern states. Moreover Nurcholish Madjid, Indonesian prominent scholar, had obviously argued that Islam in Indonesia received the least influence of the Arabisation, compared to other Muslim countries of the world. By further stating Indonesia as Islam *pinggiran* (peripheral Islam), he believed that it was not only due to that Indonesian geographical location is very far from the Middle East region, but also by considering the fact that Indonesian Muslims have adopted a very little Arabic culture and traditions.[22] In this vein, Iran, if compared with Indonesia, had accepted much more Arabic cultural and traditional influence, evidenced simply by the tranformation of Persian alphabet into Arabic following the victory of Arab Muslim troops over Sasanian Persian empire in the 7th century. In reverse, Persian influence to Arab Muslim civilization, chiefly in Abbasid reign (750-1258 CE) couldn't be ignored its reality among other things by adopting the state symbols of Persian Sasanian' such as the throne, the curtain, the royal seal, banners and robes of honour.[23]

As a matter of fact, for decades Indonesia has been a fertile ground for the religious rivalry largely instigated by Iran and Saudi Arabia. Both countries have been trying to expand their influences to Indonesia, that regrettably rather instilled the seeds of radicalism and

---

[22] Jajat Burhanuddin and Kees van Dijk, Islam in Indonesia, Constrasting Images and Interpretations, Amesterdam University Press, page 40
[23] Salam Hawa, The Erasure of Arab Political Identity, Colonialism and Violence, Routledge, 2017, page 101

extremism in Indonesia. Abdullah Sungkar, the founder of Jamaah Islamiah in Indonesia, was heavily influenced by Saudi Wahhabism that he often criticised the obligation of flag raising ceremony at schools on Mondays and the playing of the national anthem, viewing the practices as idolatrous. The Darul Islam movement, an Indonesian Islamic radical movement, started to confront the state in 80s because it was largely influenced by the Iranian Revolution taking place in 1979. Even Abu Bakar Bashir, accused by the Indonesia's intelligence units of being spiritual advisor of radical Jamaah Islamiah organization, said that posters of Khomeini were put up in the Ngruki Islamic boarding school (Pesantren) where he taught, hoping to embolden the students to reach goal of overthrowing the dictator Soeharto, despite the fact that Ngruki Pesantren strongly opposes Shia sect. As matter of fact, the role of Iranian embassy for propagating the revolutionary ideas in Indonesia, among other things by publishing a magazine called Yaum al-Qouds was undeniable.[24] Additionally, since the outbreak of the Iranian revolution, there were roughly 185 books that narrated the phenomenal event, in which about 66 of the books were written by Indonesian authors whereas the remaining ones were the foreign translated books. The books arguably emboldened Islamic activists to make protest over several Soeharto's domestic policies.[25] Therefore, like what much feared also by the Arab leaders during the time, including Arab Saudi, Indonesian government faced sceptically the event of Iranian revolution as it perceived that it would generate militant Muslims in Indonesia to seek the establishment of the Islamic state, as what Imam Khomeini had always pursued profoundly under the framework of Revolution export agenda outside Iranian borders. Moreover, Iranian government has been reluctant to give report to the Indonesian embassy in Tehran regarding the recruitment of new theological Indonesian students by Iranian authority to study in seminary school in Qom and several other cities such as Esfahan and Mashhad in Iran. In this vein, Indonesian government felt afraid that the victory of the revolution which accordingly transformed Iran to be Islamic Republic of Iran would influence Indonesians' vantage point of the likelihood of attributing the Republic of Indonesia with Islamic Republic one. Therefore, it is hardly shocking that for anticipation, Indonesia had made clear crackdowns such as the confiscation of Iranian publications by the Indonesian security apparatus, restrictions for those who wanted to study in Iran; and carrying out a close monitoring to the Iranian embassy in Jakarta established long before the outbreak of the Revolution.[26]

In addition, unlike Iran and Saudi, Indonesia acknowledges a secular Pancasila (five principles)[27] as foundational philosophical theory that shall inspire the entire domestic and

---

[24] Solahudin, The Roots of Terrorism in Indonesia, translated by Dave McRae, Lowy Institute for International Policy, page 102
[25] Ahmdsyarifali.wordpress.com, 13 June 2011
[26] Rizal Sukma, Islam in Indonesian Foreign Policy, Routledge Curzon, London and New York, Page 49
[27] Pancasila comprising two old Sankrit words, panca means five and sila principles as it contains five principles 1. Believe in the one Supreme God 2, Just and Civilized humanity 3, The Unity of Indonesia 4. Democracy led by the wisdom of deliberations among representatives 4. Social justice for the whole of the people of Indonesia.

foreign policy takings, making it much freer to accommodate the smiling face of Islam that is compatible with democracy and plurality. Indonesia does not adopt political Islam nor proclaim Islam as its official religion and has no uniqueness of Islamic interpretation that differs from the others. Most importantly, Indonesia would not have moral duty to spread its moderate Islam to the world by attempting to influence other Muslim countries, and challenge Saudi Arabia and Iran in this field. It is quite true, that guiding its foreign policy of Islamic flavour does not reflect the high aspiration of the vast majority of Indonesians since they prefer to believe that religion is no more than just a personal matter the government shall not intervene to, as most people in Arab Saudi and Iran would also perceive so, in which, according to A.R. Dawoody, most Middle Eastern society oppose the establishment of Islamic Caliphate and the constitutionalization of the Sharia Law that only a few groups attempting to reach the aforementioned goals, may turn into violence if their aspirations have failed to be accommodated by ruling governments.[28] Therefore little wonder to argue that such an agenda in spreading and promoting their religious doctrine through the globe by both Saudi Arabia and Iran has not definitely echoed their national interests.

I would like to kindly divide this book into six main chapters :

Chapter I   : Introduction

Chapter II   : Islam and Society of the Countries at Glance

In this chapter, I would like to describe precisely Islam in the three countries, how they successfully became Shia, Wahhabi and Shafe'i and their differences of interpretation that influence their daily life. As a matter of fact, there are main discrepancies among the Islam that is being followed by the respective societies. In this regard, I shall explain these differences and what impacts could be resulted .

Chapter III   : The Role of Islamic Ideology in Shaping the Foreign Policy of the Countries

In this chapter, I would like to highlight that how Islam could play a tremendous role in identifying and shaping the foreign policy of the three countries. Islam as a philosophy mentioned in their basic institution, specifically Iran and Saudi Arabia, must generate Islamic spirits as what their founding fathers of the countries often looked for.

Chapter IV   : The Implementation of "forgotten Islam" in Foreign Policy

In this chapter, I would like to argue that despite their Islamic nature and claim, Islam does not constitute a significant element in the implementation of foreign policy of the countries. Islam does not give a major effect to their foreign policy shaping despite their pride on Islam given many considerations and logical reasons. Hereby, I would like to focus

---

[28] Alexander R. Dawoody, Eradicating Terrorism from the Middle East, Public Administration, Governance and Globalization, Springer, page 4

on two issues and how the three countries give their different approaches, namely Issue of Palestine long perceived as the most dominant conflict in Islamic world in which the three countries have long been involved in dealing with the case. The comparison of their respective approach toward such a long standing conflict is highly important to make in order to understand deeply what roles they had and have. The Issue would examine how consistent their dealing to defend and support the Palestinian struggles until they reach their basic aspiration which is to become an independent state. The second issue is global terrorism, seen as the most sensitive issue in Islamic world and how their approaches toward such a matter as well as how the issue has influenced the domestic policy takings. In other hand, the states mainly Saudi and Iran have been accused by international community as terrorism sponsors in the region. With Wahhabi as newly born Islam interpretation invariably affiliated to extremism and radicalism, Arab Saudi has been well-known for spreading the seeds of hatred and resentment in international society, including believers and non-believers through Wahhabism. In the other hand, Iran is well known for having hidden political agenda to spread and promote its own revolutionary principles to other states among other things through revolutionary Shia teachings. The existence of Velayat Faqih as most basic political concept of Iran, is deeply known as triggering much fear in the hearts of the global community. Such religiously conflicting phenomena has eventually challenged Indonesia on how it could harness its image as moderate Islam promoter to convince international community that Islam is unlikely to be associated to anarchism, extremism, radicalism and terrorism.

Chapter V   : Soft Power of the Countries

Last but not least, I would like to underline the role of soft power that is being encouraged by the countries, particularly Saudi and Iran. Soft power is a very important means to affect the world's community so that they will embrace their 'new' religious beliefs and faiths. Interestingly, in applying such soft power, the states should compete with each other in such a way that the truth claim of their own beliefs will cloud this rivalry of faith dissemination and propagation. These contradictory natures of such Islamic interpretations have pushed strongly the governments of both states to formulate and identify ways and means so that their religious teachings could be easily accepted by other communities. Most startlingly, the governments even have to allocate special budget to endorse the agenda. Furthermore, in the other hand, the two countries shall be able to convince world's community that their introduced faiths don't teach extremism and radicalism of Islam. In this respect, Indonesia's moderate Moslem society has been the hotbed of their rivalries, not an actor, that affect Indonesia's policy makers to formulate numerous strategies to restrict widely the penetration of their agenda to Indonesia's society thoughts.

Chapter VI : Pragmatism in Foreign Policy in Islamic Sunni Perspective

As the title of the chapter implies, I, who happened to be also expert in Islamic Law and Jurisprudence, would like to shed light to discuss on pragmatic approaches in foreign policy implementation based on Islamic Sunni perspective, chiefly in Sunni world. In this vein, I would like to present various Islamic measures to respond an essential question, whether such foreign policy taken by a Muslim country would be compatible with Islamic teachings or not.

Chapter VII   : Conclusion

Chapter I: Islam and Society of the Countries at Glance

With their large Muslim populations, the three countries could be simply divided into two : Iran and Saudi in the first category that constitute a complex system of theocracy, fully equipped with intensive Islamic role in their political power that are reflected not only by their own Islamic basic constitutions, but also significantly existing Islamic clerics whose roles in the administration shall not be neglected. In this regard, the both states seemingly attempt to accommodate Islamic identity in multiple sectors that total secularization, as some Muslim countries apply like Turkey, is anathema to religious dimension that is significantly thought not to echo the basic interest of their Muslim populations. Meanwhile, Indonesia, like any other Muslim states such as Egypt and Syria, could seemingly be put into the second category of the such a division, tacitly separating politics from religion without any clear official statement from the government, whether Islam would inspire in making regulations and laws at home or not, thus carrying out direct intervention into personal and private matters.[29]

However, Islam constitutes an integral part of the society of the countries that shall not be overlooked. In this regard, the huge impact of Islam is widely believed to be an inspirational force to help create morality and integrity within the society that could give incredible control to all deeds and actions so as not to contravene to what al-Qoran and Sunna have already stipulated. Sometimes, even to some ultra secular individuals either in democratic states or non-democratic, Islam is still recognized to be inseparable identity of the society, meaning that the society is unlikely to be separated totally from religious elements and symbols. Accordingly, the society still tends to express high respect and appreciation to the role and function of Ulama (Islamic cleric) who is strongly believed to own the only authority in articulating and interpreting Islamic laws based on the well-known sources.

However in recent centuries, Muslims of the world generally have been seen as non-active nations who lag behind the non-Muslims, mainly in the technological innovations and breakthroughs. Worse, Muslim world is often associated with multiple uncertain political, social and economic conditions where several bloody conflicts, along with sometimes sectarian background, often transpire. Positivity and lack of initiatives that affect other state's behaviours, due to various factors, are a common nature and character of any Muslim in the world. In this regard, Indonesian society who become so passive in dealing with the global issues, often, is generated by its low profile culture that has long entrenched in their mindset. In the other hand, Saudi Arabia society that is so passive is often caused by

---

[29] Wu Yungui, the Influence of Islam over the Foreign Policies of Contemporary Islamic Countries, Journal of Middle Eastern and Islamic Studies (in Asia) Volume 5, No 3, 2011, page 3

rigid culture and Islamic interpretation, while passivity of Iranian society is due to much fear and lack of mutual trust within the society. In the two latter states, such passivity has been exacerbated by the reality that the governments tend to restrict public participation in political affairs to echo their main aspirations and confine freedom of expression as I will further explore later on.

In the other side, given the fact that Muslims constitute the vast majority of the society, so little wonder political parties both secular and Islamic in Muslim countries often rely on ballots of Muslim majority to enhance their electability prior to the convening of any general election. This thing is well understood by their governments who strive significantly to absorb such an essential aspiration by underpinning both domestic and foreign policies on their interests that may include accommodation of Islamic identity and character. Furthermore, in Indonesia, the roles played by respectful and charismatic clerics have been seen strategic to influence Muslims to vote a presidential candidate.

Islam and Society in Iran

Demographically, Iran with 80 million population, is overwhelmingly Shia rather than Sunni which believe twelve Imams as the rightful rulers of Islam and political successors to prophet Mohammad. According to Shia followers, the last Imam (the twelfth) is called Imam Mahdi[30] is still alive and has been hiding in a cave for the last more than one thousand years since 874 and will reappear in order to bring justice to the world, a doctrine known as the Occultation.[31] Such a doctrine along with doubtless loyalty to their Supreme Leader is repeatedly taught and promoted to Iranian society to cultivate extreme cult in their minds so as they could be handily inserted with the revolutionary concepts.

Historically, Iran society which initially was Sunni followers, had converted into Shia during the Safavid dynasty both persuasively and forcedly that ruled Iran since 16th. Through this period, Shah Ismail, king of Safavid, given the fact that the dynasty was main rival for Ottoman empire in Islamic world, declared that the state religion is Shiism [32] and successfully spread Shia religion into whole parts of Iran. Not only that it is assumed that that some of beliefs that Iranians uphold until now have originated from Safavid period through creative interpretation of official Shia ulemas, many of those derived from Syria,

---

[30] Modern Shia Islam has been divided into three main sects : Twelvers, Ismailis and Zaidis. Shia Twelvers is arguably the most prominent one. The names of twelve Imams are Ali ibn Abi Talib, Hasan ibn Ali, Husayn ibn Ali , Ali ibn Husayn (Sajad), Muhammad ibn Ali (Baghel Ulum), Jafar ibn Muhammad (Sadeq), Musa ibn Jafar (al-Kazim), Ali ibn Musa (Reza), Muhammad ibn Ali (Jawad), Ali ibn Muhammad, Hasan ibn Ali (Askar), Muhammad ibn al-Hasan (Mahdi)
[31] The Mahdi, https://www.globalsecurity.org/military/intro/islam-mahdi.htm
[32] Safavid Empire, (1501-1722), 7 September 2009
http://www.bbc.co.uk/religion/religions/islam/history/safavidempire_1.shtmlwww.bbc.co.uk,

Iraq, Bahrain and Saudi Arabia who were deliberately invited by the King for religious and political purposes to spread Shia Imamate in Iran.[33]

Meanwhile Sunni comprises 10-15% of Iran's total population that mostly are Lor, Kurd, Baloch, Turkmen, some of Azaris and Arabs as well. In sum, Sunni could be also found in southern part of Iran and Khorasan Territory. So it can be said that most Sunnis in Iran live around the Iranian direct borders with Pakistan, Afghanistan, Turkmenistan and Iraq. Additionally, in the Iranian constitution that replaced the previous one issued in 1906 in Qajar Dynasty, further mentions that Iran's government would give respect to the existence of other Sunni followers such as Hanafi, Maliki, Shafe'i and Hanbali as well as Shia Zaydia by granting freedom in applying their own practices based on their sect's interpretations. In this regard, Iran is well aware that Sunni schools particularly Hanafi and Shafe'i are the most minority groups in Iran. However, with Iran's constitution citing obviously Shia Imamate as its formal religion, Saudi constitution does not state explicitly Wahhabism as its own formal religion. It can be said it further, by explicitly mentioning Shia Imamate in Iranian basic constitution would produce significant impacts in both identifying and implementing Iranian domestic policies that could either directly or indirectly create legal justifications for the Iranian regime to apply discriminatory approaches of all dimensions for non-Shia followers, even including Sunni Muslims.

Beside the aforementioned beliefs, the religious minorities of Christian, Jew, Zoroaster, and Baha'i have been living in Iran for years. [34] Attempting to demonstrate equal treatment to the religious groups except to Baha'i community, other minority groups like Zoroastrian, Jewish and Christians would enjoy certain rights including practicing their ritual ceremonies in their own worship places built throughout the country, as they are officially recognized. For instance, the Christian minority has three parliamentary seats – two for Armenians and one for Assyrians and Chaldeans- while Jews and Zoroastrians each have one.[35]

Theoretically Iran shall give protection and guarantee to the minority groups, as reflected explicitly in article 19 of the basic constitution, mentioning that the people of Iran enjoy equal rights, regardless of the tribe or ethnic group to which they belong. Yet in contrast, for years, Iran has been criticized for years as it has applied discriminative approaches to other minority tribes and religions. Much evidence of such discriminatory treatments by the central government in two Sunni provinces where minority Kurds and balochis reside for many years could be easily looked through poor economic infrastructure, employment, public facilities etc. The fact is not limited to economic affairs, the groups have

---

[33] Eram Lapidus, Tarekhe Jawame Islami, Ettelaat publishing, Tehran, 1387, second edition, Page 419
[34] Rainner Brunner, Islamic Ecumenism in the 20th Century, the Azhar and Shiism between Rapprochment and Restraint, diterjemahkan dari bahasa Jerman oleh Joseph Greenman, revised and updated by the author, Brill Leiden Boston 2004.
[35] Shahin Milani, Situation of the Bahá'í Minority in Iran and the Existing Legal Framework, 6 June 2016, https://jia.sipa.columbia.edu/situation-bahai-minority-iran-existing-legal-framework

also been going through political and social discriminations, that all this may lead the groups to inflame their resistance to the central government. In recent years, Baha'is minority implicitly viewed as non- religious group by the constitution and seen as deviant and misleading according the Supreme Leader' fatwa, has emerged to be clear evidence of such discriminatory practices to the minority group,   including confiscation of private property, death execution, imprisonment, arrest, torture, etc taken incessantly by the Iranian government. For the time being, the case of Sepanta Niknam, a Zoroastrian member of Yazd city council due to his suspension from his position, and ill-fated Gonabadi Daravish (Sufi) minority group that represents the largest of Iran's Sufi order, had much attracted international attention. Above all, with its diversity of its minority groups of tribes and religions, Iran's criminal statute, known as the Islamic Penal Code to impose the death penalty on anyone who murders a Muslim, but if a Muslim murders a non-Muslim, he or she will not be put to death, has been deeply criticized to be a discriminatory one. [36] Therefore little wonder, according to Annual Report issued by US Commission on International Religious Freedom in 2018 by considering the aforementioned facts, Iran is still classified in tier I as a country of particular concern.[37]

Unlike Wahhabism in Saudi Arabia which proved to have established a passive society, Shia followed by most Iranians requires the society to actively actualize and express their aspirations through among others protests and demonstrations. Shia has been commonly viewed an Islamic sect which ceaselessly promotes liberation for all oppressed nations, and denounces all suppressive regimes. Yet in Iran, the Shia society has been significantly harnessed by its elite rulers to espouse accomplishing their revolutionary agenda as a manifestation of the concept of Guardianship of the Jurist (Velayat Faqih). The significance of the Shiite of Iranians has been understood quite well by the government as it would give much effort for brainwashing since their childhood. However, in Iran activities to express freedom and liberty that any Shia follower should enjoy, must be undermined and downplayed through the securitization of the internal situation intentionally carried out by the government. Meaning that the government will support any activity that seemingly aligns with its ultimate goals of preserving the sustainability and continuality of the doctrine of Velayat Faqih. In the other hand, the government will easily dissuade and curb each activity deemed contradictory to the goals.

In fact, since decades ago Iranians have been suffering, generated significantly by state mismanagement that has been caused by incapable clerical ruling elites, thus making them subject to resentment and hatred among society. Their predominant political power is seen profoundly as an inappropriate measure that blends political man-made affairs with holy religion, thus instead generating the state to be a theocratic state. Such a combination could be simply seen in Friday sermons commonly held in centralized public areas that, rather than focusing to talk on behavioural and ethical matters, the preachers would focus

---

[36] ibid
[37] Annual Report of 2018 issued by US Commission on International Religious Freedom, page 44

on political and global affairs along with emphasis on long running hostility against America and Israel.

As a matter of fact, unlike in Indonesia where Islamists often seek the implementation of Sharia to the law and sometimes the establishment of Caliphate, in Iran, many efforts of coerced Islamization have already overshadowed numerous fields of Iranian life that include laws and political institutions, and educational systems. Little wonder to note, forcing Iranian publics to apply strict Islamic standards in dress (wearing veils/headscarves for women) and other Islamic social behaviours could be a common reality. As conservative Supreme Leader has final say for domestic decisions, no wonder that many policies issued would be in favour of Iranian radical conservative clerics.

In this vein, the clerical rulers seem to control the system of education and enforce their ideas to educational curricula. In fact the Islamization of the educational system for instance has been effect from cultural revolution since the early days of Islamic Revolution through Khomeini's Nouroz message emphasizing that university must be a healthy environment for the teaching of Islamic sciences.[38] At that time, in order to purify the educational system which Imam thought to have been polluted by western systems, all schools and universities were closed down. As many 40.000 teachers were expelled or forced to retire. Second textbooks and education materials were collected in order to be purified from un-Islamic values.[39] Unfortunately such an effort has been sustained under the presidency of the conservative Mahmoud Ahmadinejad in 2005. During his tenure, he intensively continued transforming humanities science into revolution-flavoured ones. The president replaced many academic staffs with conservative ones who deeply believed in the Islamisation of universities. Similarly, student admissions were similarly centralized, and the admission of doctoral students came under the control of the ministry of science, research and technology. This control helped the government prevent politically active students from continuing their education and facilitated the access of pro-regime students to postgraduate studies. As mentioned before, universities also lost their autonomy to design and prepare their curricula. Such a fact could be one of the outstanding reasons for many talented Iranians who are forced to leave the country in order to grab better future in abroad. According to governmental statistics, each year around 60.000 Iranians would immigrate, whereas the United Nations and International Monetary Fund organizations estimate the number to be 150.000-180.000, in which 70 or 80 percent of whom are the educated and skilled ones.[40]

---

[38] Peyman Vahabzadeh, Iran' struggle for Social Justice, Economics, Agency, Justice and Activism, Palgrave Macmillan, 2017, page 137
[39] Yasin Tamer, Basic Changes in Iranian Education System Before and After Islamic Revolution, December 2010, page 67
[40] 11 keshvar ba bishtarin mizan farar maghzaha, 1 August 2017, http://www.tabnak.ir/fa/news/717591/١١-ها‎C8%‎80%‎E2%کشور-با-بیشترین-میزان-فرار-مغز

Based on my personal observation, then as time when on, Iranian's great respect to those clerics whom they deeply view to be obsessed to political power by manipulating the religion and often combining true religion with superstitions and illogical narratives, began to decline and disappear. Furthermore, Iranian society has begun deeply realizing the government has exploited Shia Islam for its own service, making the clerics to be tremendously dependent on the state as it grants them multiple privileges politically and economically, giving rise to oligarchy and increasing corruption cases in governmental bureaucracy.

Iranian public no longer trusts not only in its government but also among itself, exacerbated by governmental mismanagement and repeatedly malign behaviours of the clerical rulers. Such frustration and sceptical attitude of Iranians generated particularly by economic matters has given rise to a wide range of mistrusts and suspicions in the society. In this vein, the Iranian regime's efforts to securitize the atmosphere of public areas have helped mushroom suspicious feelings among Iranians. I can dare say that the people have been living in fear of unclear future and embedded in insecure feeling within securitized atmosphere although they keep concealing such a feeling by enjoying anything available and highly limited.

With the passage of time, ironically the bitter reality led them to blame the religion as a main factor of backwardness and political and economic stagnations. The more frustrated and dissatisfied they become, the more impetus they would have for leaving out the country as they tremendously believe that the state has failed to provide facilities, alongside with much restriction, to articulate and express their skills and talents.

Interestingly, Iranian society has been conditioned to face multiple economic sanctions imposed by US and other countries since the Islamic republic's birth as if the sanctions could no longer affect its economy. They do realise about the mushrooming of the bureaucratic and financial corruptions made systematically by their political elites. Yet they would decide to be silent as they deeply apprehend risks they have to face. Rather, they endeavour acutely to hide their political and economic misery by undergoing their usual life, not attempting at carrying out street protests and demonstrations given their deep understanding that such efforts would be useless and, instead, could even put their life and their families into peril. Yet in recent years as we have already witnessed, they eventually embarked on having more courage to risking their life by conducting various massive and intensive demonstrations, protesting unpopular policies and sometimes yelling out on regime's dictatorship, which they believe to be a significant factor for economy to worsen. Such a continuously deteriorating economic and political situations have prevented gradually Iranians from owning a proud feeling as Muslims. Indoctrinating the society since its childhood to shape a mindset of being more patient in dealing with multi-dimensional predicaments as the world is only a transit location for temporary life, has already been a backlash against the regime which has failed to realize the promised justice and welfare within the society. Therefore small wonder Sayyed Shahaboddi Chaposi, political governor deputy of Tehran once said that in May 2016 that 90 percent of Iranian youths kept distance from Islam as a result of internal (bad) politics. [41]

It is no longer secret that such their disappointment and hatred of the Iranian public are also stirred by the fact that the clerics were attempting to misuse religion, just to get them much wealthier and pursue their vested interests. In other words, clerics have failed to be exemplary figures for the deceived and suffering society. Therefore, it is hardly surprising that suspicious feeling and mutual distrust have already became rampant in society as the people attempt to maintain their life survival by permitting and allowing all types of illegal measures. Clerics have proven to have precluded society significantly from religiosity and Islamic ethics, creating heretic interpretations and narratives. Worse, it seems that maintaining and defending the theocratic regime's survival is above all, the most priority of all, rather than building Islamic capacity and ethics of the secularized society, as the regime invariably believes that defending it would equal to defending Islam. Apparently in order to realize such a goal, the regime would prefer the Iranian society to be revolutionary over religious one. As the agenda and programs have failed to meet the public expectations, little wonder that it has lost its trust to the clerics along with their revolutionary propaganda.

Accordingly In 2017 alone, several abusive actions and harassment to the clerics took place. For instance In last October 2017 a clergyman was under attack in Shokofe Square in Soutehast Tehran, and the same day, other clergyman was also attacked in subway station in Tehran. [42] Some months earlier in mid 2017, an assault to one clergyman also occurred in the subway station of Shahare Ray, in Tehran. Such an attack to a clergyman carried out by a group also took place in Nishapur in Khorasan Province, in mid 2017.[43]

Thanks to the role of information access provided by restricted Internet and satellite, Iranians no longer experience any difficulty to get such an access despite using anti filter proxies, thus creating much trouble for Iranian regime that highly attempts to block the penetration of any information access from outside.

I could dare say, due to multiple political, social, economic problems, most Iranian people started to blame religion of Islam as the most propelling factor for the creation of the economic backwardness and misery. Like Saudis, Iranians comprising 60 percent of the total population as young age with under 30, would prefer to have common life that shall be avoided from any political and social restrictions despite their great participation in several Shia ritual ceremonies. The long running securitized atmosphere has prompted them to find

---

[41] 90 darsad Javonan Ma Emroz az Islam Fashila Gereftan, 21 May 2016, http://www.trt.net.tr/persian/yrn/2016/05/21/90-drsd-jwnn-m-mrwz-bh-wsth-rftrhy-sysy-m-z-slm-fslh-grfthnd-495105
[42] www.kayhan.ir, 23 October 2017
[43] www.ilna.ir, 19 July 2017

ways to the access of freedom and liberty while blaming and denouncing the roles of the clerics seen as bringing misfortune and hardship to the society. Like many Indonesians, Iranians would prefer that Islamic laws could be only implemented in specific personal matters. For this reason, they would regret such a 1979 Revolution that totally changed political structure to take place while reminiscing the great power of Pahlavi dynasty. Such deteriorating political and economic situations in Iran could be well reiterated by Mousavi Chalak, the Head of Iranian Social Workers Association in November 2016 by acknowledging that among 185 countries, Iran was the bottom of the list behind Iraq regarding the world's unhappiest countries.[44] More ominously in July 2018 Iranian Ministry of Health has noted that one fourth of the society, in some areas one third, are stricken with symptoms of mental illness that require medical treatment.[45]

Force and coercion in religiosity often carried out by Iranian Islamic government particularly in headscarf wearing (*hijab*) for Iranian women has gradually generated continuous resistance of the people, reflected evidently by a recent phenomenon of some Iranian girls who intentionally and courageously took off their headscarves on crowded streets. A very interesting report by Iranian parliament in July 2018 stated that based on various polling conducted within Iranian society, that only 35 % of Iranians including both citizens in urban and rural areas still believe that wearing a headscarf is valuable and only 40% who tolerate governmental intervention in promoting Islamic ethics to the society. The report also simply notes that 50 % of the people perceive that headscarf wearing is a tradition, which means it is no longer a religious duty.[46]

In this regard, the government, rather than promoting personal morality to its society, has been endeavouring to introduce revolutionary values through any possible means and tools. As elucidated earlier, it seems that the government prefers to have more revolutionary society than more religious one, so it could shape easily loyalty and allegiance to the society. Therefore, countless national budgets are always allocated to endorse such an effort in shaping revolutionary society, downgrading the importance and significance of other fields that absorb more national interests. In addition the government has always been preoccupied with its significant undertakings in formalizing Islamic identity rather than developing any domestic policies to form more virtuous and pious society. Therefore, preserving Islamic appearance is paramount in Iranian societal life as a form of revolutionary articulation on loyalty and submission to the government.

The coercion of headscarf wearing is one of the best descriptions on how displaying Islamic identity on the public area is excessively essential. Therefore, amid critical situations in Iran politically and economically, the society is often taught how to pretend holding the revolutionary principles in order to keep its survival. For instance, many young people felt

---

[44] www.irannewsupdate.com, Iran : Saddest Country in the World, November 8, 2016
[45] www.irna.ir, 25 July 2018
[46] Markaze Pazoheshaye Majlis : Kahesh 50 darsad afradi ke Hejabi ra Arzoshman midonan, 28 July 2018, https://www.radiofarda.com/a/iran-women-obligatory-hijab/29395884.html

compelled to let their beards grow in order to show their own sympathy to the regime, thus becoming advantageous point for applying jobs in government institutions. My personal experience further demonstrated how preserving a idelogical revolutionary appearance is quite important when Iran's Imigration police rejected my resident permit application just because I attached the form with a picture of myself with a necktie.

In this case, the government successfully established the society that is too much dependent on the governmental supports by creating an atmosphere that differs from any other else in the world. The deteriorating economic situation could be blessing in disguise in order to help shape revolutionary character of Iranian society due to its significant dependency on the government. Above all, traditional mindset of Iranian society could smoothen and facilitate process of indoctrination by the regime. In sum, sensitiveness of Iranians has been harnessed well by the government to buy their loyalty and allegiance.

More ominously, Iranian government always believes that the more revolutionary the society is, the more religious and pious it would be. Such a conclusion has been kept repeatedly by Iranian rulers since the establishment of the Islamic state in 1979, prompting them to create the securitization of the public areas. As a tremendous outcome of such a securitized atmosphere in the society systematically, the life of the society is always haunted by fear and worry. For ordinary Iranians, being completely attached with the government is the only way and option to salvage and guaranty their future. Some of my Iranian friends were urged enormously, alongside growing their beards, to hang the pictures of Iranian Supreme Leaders on the house wall on the sidelines of job process in the government institutions. According to their confessions, the more revolutionary appearance they have, the more chance they would get to be accepted for jobs.

The people are so scared and look very careful if they want to express their sensitive political and religious opinions, thus spreading mistrusts and suspicions among the members of the society. Not only that the youths don't feel free to exhibit their talents and skills in public areas. The feeling of such a fear and worry would gradually kill intellectuality and creativity of the youths as they would feel hopeless that their government will not accommodate and absorb their basic expressions. Interestingly, existing mistrust and suspicion are the two dominant characters of many Iranian political oppositions living in abroad who find it hard to unify and synchronize their various ideas and perspectives towards their willingness to change their governments at home.

According to Iranian government, the more people are involved in various revolutionary agenda held routinely, the more economic advantage and higher position they would obtain, further undermining and eliminating sincerity from the society. Therefore little wonder in Iranian society wearing a headscarf would constitute the preservation of traditionalism and a form of its submission and loyalty to the government, rather than a religious duty, prompting Iranian women to remove their headscarves unflinchingly while they are not in Iran, or they will not practice obligatory prayers when they are no longer in government institutions.

I can further argue based on my thorough observation while travelling almost all parts of Iran between 2009-2017, that Iranian Muslim society in the term of religious devotion could be divided into four categories, secular liberal, conservative moderate, conservative revolutionary, conservative revolutionary.

In Iran, four categories are found anywhere around the country both urban and rural areas. Meaning that the society living in cities and towns does not necessarily represent people with secular liberal thoughts. In reverse, the society living in villages does not necessarily represent those with religious revolutionary thoughts. In addition, such a categorization is not driven simply by considering both educational background or literacy and economic situations, which means that economic and educational sectors are not the main factors determining level of their religiosity, as since their childhood, like any other Muslim nation, they would be raised and introduced with Islam as their religion. Therefore, it is a little bit hard to make generalization on which one of the society's domicile is more religious and in the mean time, more secular. In addition, Iranian society is very complicated and needs years to understand more deeply their characters. Persian language seems to be a must for anybody who conducts a significant research on Iran by making direct interviews with the people and studying a wide range of books written in Persian. Most challengingly, Iranian society would not simply tell their opinions on various political issues until they get fully trust to whom they speak. Above all, I can say that most of the Iranian society has lost their hopes, expressing their frustration with distinct ways.

Based on my observation while travelling to almost all of the country, I would argue that, if some other Muslim countries like Indonesia has trend of being more conservative in society I would like to elaborate further, in Iran conversely, the society gets more secular. Meaning that, Iranian society would keep their distance gradually from religiosity. As elucidated previously, they prefer to view religious symbols like wearing a headscarf as not a religious obligation but rather a long entrenched tradition. For them, growing beards is no longer a Prophet's Sunna but rather a loyalty expression to the state. In addition, they would eschew discussing religious matters in anywhere else; their respectful attitudes to the clerics tend to decline. No doubt, it can't be generalized that each individual would be the same, yet such a trend of being more secular in Iran in recent years could be felt and seen.

Startlingly, Iranian society always believes that being non-Shia is not a big deal. They are so tolerant that they accept various beliefs and faiths of the others well despite their deep curiosity to know religious identity of somebody else. Nevertheless, there is another minor group within Iranian society yet its broader influence can be felt evidently in different aspects of life, which is a revolutionary radical group. The role and function played by the group can't be simply ignored as they are supported significantly by the government. Bear in mind too, the group is not necessarily conservative religious. Perhaps, their appearance looks revolutionary but their ways of thinking is secular. As mentioned before, preserving revolutionary symbols is extremely important to sustain their survival politically, economically and socially. Interestingly, Shiite rituals like 10 Moharram involves participation not only the group but also all dimensions of Iranian society including the secular ones. However the motivations for taking part in such traditions are diverse from one to another. For the secular ones, the motivation was only to escape from boredom and monotony, not because they have robust faith on historical traces of such tradition. Little wonder, in order to galvanize their enthusiasm to take part, Iranian government usually allocates special enormous budgets to support the programs including facilitating and giving privileges to the participants such as giving a minimum price for anybody who is interested in conducting pilgrimage to Karbala for *Arba'ien* commemoration. Preserving and maintaining holy shrines of Imamzade (immediate descendant of a Shi'a Imam) scattered around the country has constituted a great concern for Iranian government.

In addition, I can argue further that Iranian society has potentialities to be a democratic nation. They will return into religiosity and conservatism if their political system turns into democratic as however Iranian society can't be easily separated from traditionalism which is inspired among other things by the religion. Not only that, having commitment to strongly preserving family ties and owning emotional sensitiveness would be good capital for Iranian society to become more religious if the state turns into more democratic one. Little wonder, I can argue that the more revolutionary Iranian regime is, the more secular Iranian society would be.

Islam and Society In Saudi Arabia

As mentioned earlier, the kingdom is the location of the main Saudi cities of Mecca and Medina, where Prophet Mohammad had lived and passed away. These two locations are routinely visited by millions pilgrims every year both Sunni and Shia Muslims, and became famous places for studying Islam alongside with al-Azhar university in Cairo.

Islam is an integral part of Saudi community's identity that may affect the behaviours of their horizontal interaction within the society. Little wonder, the government has considerably attempted to identify and issue many popular domestic policies based on such a fact, like what it has made when the Saudi Council of Economic Affairs and Development identified one of the eleven programs for Vision 2030 in 2017 to achieve is to develop and strengthen individual's national identity based on Islamic and national values. [47]

As a result it is not exaggeration to note that daily life in Arab Saudi including its educational curricula and broadcast programs on the state television will not be obviously

---

[47] David Cowan, the Coming Economic Implosion of Saudi Arabia, A Behavioural Perspective, Palgrave Macmillan, 2018, page 40

separated from religious matters.[48] However, according to Mansor Moaddel and Julie De Jong in their collaborative article, noted that despite the fact that Saudi Arabia constitutes a bastion of conservative Islam, the country is more identified with the nation rather than with their religion. They even further argued that most Saudis (68%) believe that the implementation of Sharia law in very important or important. [49]

Demographically, Saudi Arabia with 33 million population, comprises mostly Sunni (20 million) who follow Hambali fiqh school that gives more emphasis on interpretation of Al-Qor'an and Sunna literally. This school arguably has inspired Wahhabism principles that was founded and spread by Mohammad bin Abdul Wahab in 18th century, with help of Mohammad bin Saud, the founder of first Saudi Kingdom. Nevertheless, despite the fact that majority of Sunni Muslims in Saudi Arabia follow Hambali school in fiqh (Islamic jurisprudence), yet Wahhabism teaching is not a dominant faith of most Saudis as they believe that Wahhabism is always affiliated with violent acts. As a matter of fact , young Osama bin Laden, the main founder of al-Qaeda terrorist group, reportedly did not find any conformity with the type of radicalism of Wahhabism that grew amazingly inside the Kingdom during the time. Rather, he was interested in understanding Islamic thoughts introduced by Ikhwanul Muslimin organization in Egypt.[50] According to Michael Azadi, the Wahhabi thoughts that have dominated many Saudi ulemas, is followed only by 22 % of Saudis.[51] The small number further displays how recent Saudis themselves have believed that rigid Wahhabism could not be adopted as way of life and pattern of perception to solve their religious and social problems. The long running efforts of the Kingdom-supported Clerical Sheikhs in bringing society to be more Wahhabi seems to have failed given much objection and opposition from ordinary Saudis particularly the young generation, who prefer to have more open society despite their unwillingness to be totally secularized. Furthermore based on the survey of Arab's opinion in 2017-2018 conducted by Arab Centre Washington DC, as many 43% of Saudis agree that no religious authority is entitled to declare followers of other religions to be infidels, while the rest of 34% expresses disagreement. [52]

Therefore arguably the estimated number above (22%) may decrease in the future as much information on other Islamic interpretation could be provided significantly to Saudis through internet and satellite access, gradually undermining the credibility of governmental Wahhabi clerics whose roles and decrees would depend on the monarch's point of view.

---

[48] Medea Benjamin, The Unjust Kingdom, Behind the US-Saudi Connection, OR books 2016, page 21
[49] Mansor Moaddel and Julie De Jong, Values, Political Action, and Change in the Middle East and the Arab Spring, Oxford University Press, 2017, page 41-43
[50] Lawrence Wright, the Looming Tower, al-Qaeda and the Road to 9/11, Alfred A. Knopt, New York 2006, page 79
[51] Dr. Michael Azady, Religius Composition of Persian Gulf States www. Gulf2000.columbia.edu
[52] For further information, please see Arab Opinion Index 2017-2018, www.arabcenterdc.org

Nevertheless, it has been unwritten practice that Saudi elite rulers have established Wahhabism as their official political ideology without explicitly mentioning it in its own basic constitution, unlike Iranian constitution with specific Shia Imamate. Most startlingly, however despite of Islamic identity in Saudi's basic constitution, Arabs in general, based on the same survey, aspirations for having a government based on Islamic Sharia is only 31%. Still, more Arabs believe (38%) that carrying out religious obligations/ritual would define individual as religious. [53] In fact according to Ellen R. Wald, while Saudi Arabia was undergoing general liberalization in the 1960s and 1970s, the ruling elites decided to make a very fundamental change which was choosing traditionalism (conservatism) for its societal life to counter the negative impacts caused by the Iranian revolution in 1979.[54] Saudi Arabia believed that to counterweight Imam Khomeini's acute ambition to spread his influence to the region shall be faced by more religious and pious Saudi society.

In addition, despite no official data on the total number of Shia population in Saudi, yet it is estimated that 10% or 15% of Saudis are Shia (3.3 million) who are predominantly Shia Imamate. Interestingly, the Shia population concentrated in the eastern part of Saudi which luckily has been blessed with the enormous natural resources of oil and gas that contribute 60 % of GDP to Saudi national economy. Some of those live in Medina city (commonly called Nakhawila society) and the southern border territory with Yemen. Like Shia minor community, no official data of other religious communities has been issued. Other religions such as Hinduism and Christianity may be applied by foreign expatriates who work and stay in the Kingdom. However, religious freedom is denied even for the Shia minority; and conversion from Islam to another religion, like in Iran, is a crime. [55] In Saudi it has been estimated that 1.5 million Christians (almost all foreign workers) live inside the territory, yet they are still not allowed to worship publicly, thus contradicting implicitly the Saudi diplomatic efforts to encourage interfaith dialogue in the United Nations several years ago. Even bible is very hard to find in bookstores,[56] and importing it may be subject to legal punishment since such an act has been viewed as proselytizing into Christianity. However according to Sherifa Zuhur, most of the time, Saudi authorities permit non-Muslims to worship in private homes, preventing Sharia policemen often called Mothawe from disturbing them.[57] According to Annual Report issued by US Commission on International Religious Freedom in 2018, the Saudi government has not implemented total reforms to textbooks that propagate intolerance and violence including some of the horrible contents of the books used during the current school year, as deeply acknowledged by a Saudi senior businessman that Saudi educational curricula still continue propagating Wahhabi hatred of

---

[53] Ibid
[54] Ellen R.Wald, Saudi Inc, the Arabian Kingdom's Pursuit of Profit and Power, Pegasus Book, New York London, page 143
[55] Saudi Arabia Country Handbook, the Marine Corps Intelligence Arctivity, Page 46
[56] Karen Elliott House, Saudi Arabia, Its People, Past, Religion, Fault Lines and Future, Alfred A. Knopf, 2012 page 218
[57] Sherifa Zuhur, Saudi Arabia, Greenwood Publishing Group, 2011, page 176

Jews, Christians, and Shia Muslims.[58] Therefore little wonder, by considering the aforementioned facts, Saudi Arabia like Iran, is still classified in tier I as a country of particular concern.[59]

Saudis, as observed well by Karen Elliott House, a US former prominent journalist in her book On Saudi Arabia, Its People, Past, Religion, Fault Lines and Future, have undergone their life amid various restrictions of religious rules, government authority with its skill in spending the income of abundant natural sources, and cultural traditions, leaving them in passivity and thus guiding a few of whom, including independent modernist and conservative Muslims, to seek new alternative for their static and stagnant life, thanks to effective use of internet that provides them much filtered and blocked information.[60] Under the shadow of the securitized atmosphere, coupled with numerous political and social restrictions and constraints and intensive human right violations in Saudi, she also argued that many Saudi citizens expect a more open society, yet devoutly Islamic but free of some of the restraints imposed by religious conservative police who put "terror' on them if seen to be acting in un-Islamic way, often called *Mothawe*.[61] According to Medea Benjamin, there are about four thousand religious police, patrolling the streets enforcing the strictness of the Sharia own interpretation such as dress codes, the strict separation of unrelated men and women, and observance of prayers.[62] To some extent, such expectation was the case with Iranians who mostly fear on the harassment carried out by the religious Sharia police in public areas. Most startlingly, the implementation of strict function of *Mothawe* /Sharia police in Saudi Arabia and Iran as well would much depend on who the king is and who the president is. She further notes that under the King Abdullah in 2013, *Mothawe* was no longer supposed to detain people, make arrests, conduct interrogations, guard the entrances to shopping malls to enforce proper dress code and forbid women from entering malls if they were not accompanied by a male guardian. [63]

Nevertheless, according to the author, seeking for justice, rather than freedom, has proven to be an important element that unites conservatives and modernizers, young and old who deeply demand the government to be transparent and accountable, as well as ability to provide standard services such as good education, jobs, affordable housing and decent health care. [64] She further believed that Saudi youth who became less patient and more demanding, despite their diverse vantage point, could be shared with three fundamental characters: alienated, underducated, and underemployed,[65] who have lost their trust to the government that failed to act in accordance with the Prophet's teachings

---

[58] Karen Elliot House, Saudi Arabia in Transition, From Defense to Offense, but How to Score, Belfer Center for Science and International Affairs, page 20
[59] Annual Report issued by US Commission on International Religious Freedom in 2018, page 82
[60] Ibid page 9
[61] Ibid page 18
[62] Medea Benjamin, Kingdom of the Unjust, Behind the US-Saudi Connection, OR books 2016, page 21
[63] Ibid page 21
[64] opcit page 18
[65] Ibid page 108

in humbleness and modesty. Therefore unsurprisingly, based on the same survey, shows that definition of democracy for Saudis shall be given more emphasis on preservation of civil/public liberties (19%). Yet, weirdly as reflected by the same survey, 40% of Saudis admitted to be able to criticize government, while only 33% are not.[66] In practice criticizing governmental policies through media social in recent years rather than using Saudi media as it is highly controlled by the government, is likely to bring negative consequences to the Saudi writers, even for any foreign citizen (the latest shocking cases are the expulsion of Canada's ambassador from Riyadh as Canada's government expressed its concern over the arrest of women's rights activists in August 2018, and the assassination of Jamal Kashoggi, a Saudi prominent writer, in Turkey in October 2018)

Furthermore, it seems that economic problem has been core for ordinary Saudis particularly unemployment problem among the youths comprising 60% of the total population. Such a long lasting problem has been created as the youths were failed to be prepared as skilled workers or as they were willing to work for higher income with less working hours if compared with foreign workers who are estimated to reach 10 millions. Little wonder that unemployment has already become the most crucial problem in the Kingdom. Therefore, the program of Saudization introduced in past decade has been posing indirect threats to multinational and franchise companies in Saudi Arabia willingly or unwillingly to employ Saudi youths by taking multiple factors into consideration including labour cost, social and cultural perceptions, control over process of production, lack of social integration in multicultural work environment, job tenure, inadequate qualifications and mobility.[67] For instance, in order to decrease the unemployment number in the Kingdom, in 2000 under the framework of Saudization, the *Nitaqat* program has been introduced stipulating that any business with more than 20 employees must employ at least 25 percent Saudis.[68] Based on my personal observation within the Kingdom, the managers of the companies actually are not eager offering jobs to those Saudis by considering the aforementioned reasons. As Mohamed Ramady further argues that such a program could be curse for the society since it would behove young Saudis to do jobs they are not really willing to do because of social values and status.[69]

Therefore, in order to lessen their social grievances, the elite ruler would issue various popular domestic policies by exerting and allocating its abundant oil income. Such popular policies would be regarded strategic to muffle their vigorous restlessness especially following the scary event of Arab Spring that took place in adjacent Arab states. The Kingdom did realise that peoples' power could topple overthrow it as several Arab countries including Egypt, Tunisia, Libya etc have already gone through. In this vein little wonder King

---

[66] For further information, please see Arab Opinion Index 2017-2018, www.arabcenterdc.org
[67] Mohamed A.Ramady, The Saudi Arabian Economy, Policies, Achievements, and Challenges, Springer, 2010, page 369
[68] Medea Benjamin, the Kingdom of the Unjust, Behind the US-Saudi Connection, OR books 2016 page 68
[69] Opcit page 365

Abdullah in 2012 issued plans spending an additional US$37 billion on housing, wage increases, unemployment benefits, etc. Not only that, such an attractive policy has also been implemented by King Salman when in 2015, announced a two month bonus of salaries for all government workers, pensioners, soldiers and students under Saudi scholarship.[70] Yet with the passage of time, to deal with Saudi budget deficit, the government in recent years has begun to audaciously take unpopular decisions including reducing subsidies for energy, water and electricity, and increasing gasoline price to 96 cents from 64 cents.[71] In addition, the unpopular policy also encompasses imposing taxation, suspending giant infrastructures, cutting ministers' salaries and freezing salaries for government employees.[72] All of this absolutely has engendered restlessness and discontent among Saudis who eventually give much more focus on economic affairs, rather than political and human rights issues.

On the other hand, issues such as freedom of expression, freedom of assembly, independent judiciary, political participation, and human right enforcement have been main concerns for Saudi civil society. It is well known that Saudi political activists often urge royal family to implement the entire reform for all aspects mentioned earlier, sometimes leading them into arrest and imprisonment.

In addition, most Saudis, like in Iran and other states, apparently do not view the absolute monarch character of the Kingdom along with the matters of separation of powers and hereditary rule as a big and crucial problem, as long as the government is able to provide basic economic needs to its people. In sum, Saudi society became used to accept puritanical Wahhabi approach in dealing with social norms as they deeply understand that those Saudi clerics don't see a big deal with modern innovations and political issues.[73] However, despite restricted social atmosphere where rigidness of Islamic interpretation often prevails, thus limiting all sorts of entertainment and fraternisation inside the Kingdom, most startlingly a survey conducted by Gallup in 2015 that Saudi society occupied the most third country which feel happy about their lives after Colombia and Fiji. [74]

In fact, Saudi women, as a result of inflexible interpretation of the religion and cultural practices, experience much more restrictions that men do, thus making Saudi Arabia is the world's most gender-segregated nation.[75] Therefore little wonder, in recent years the Kingdom while promoting its ambitious 2030 vision, has issued some favourable policies for women rights including allowing women to join Saudi official foreign visit and vote in *Majlis Shura* (consultative council) election in 2015 and last but not least lifting ban for women's

---

[70] Ibid page 21
[71] Karen Elliot House, Saudi Arabia in Transition, From Defence to Offense, but How to Score, Belfour Centre for Science and International Affairs, page 11
[72] www.forbes.com, 1 January 2018
[73] Muhammad Al-Atawneh, Wahhabi Islam Facing the Challenges of Modernity, Leiden, Boston, 2010, page xvi
[74] Gallup-international-bg
[75] www.theweek.co.uk, 5 June 2018

driving and allowing them to go to sport stadiums and music concerts.[76] According to Karen Elliot House, within the past year, a Saudi chairwoman of the Saudi stock exchange has been appointed, and a woman has also been appointed to lead women's sports.[77] However, such significant steps and reforms carried out by the Kingdom in involving more active roles for Saudi women in the society have been often resisted by some of the Saudis in the name of traditions and values, as Prince Khaled al Faisal once stated that Saudi Arabia is probably the only country in the world where the government is pushing for reforms and the people are pulling back.[78]

Islam and Society in Indonesia

Talking on Islam in Indonesia, what crosses to international community's mind is that Indonesia constitutes the largest Muslim population of all countries in the world, approximately 207 million of 250 million of total population, along with its Islam moderation. Indonesia significantly contributes 13% of total Muslim population of the world.[79] Similar to Iranians and Saudis, Islam could be immediately associated to Indonesians. Interestingly in Indonesia, in practicing and applying Islam as a pattern of life has already led Clifford Geerz, American anthropologist who made research in Java island in 1952-1954, to take into conclusion on the contentious division of Indonesians mainly Javanese people into Abangan representing a stress on the animistic aspects of the overall Javanese syncretism and broadly related to the peasant element in the population, Santri representing a stress on the Islamic aspects of the syncretism and generally related to the trading element (and to certain elements in the peasantry as well), and Priyayi stressing the Hinduist aspects and related to the bureaucratic element.[80]

However, Islam in Indonesia has not been well known for its contribution to the entire Islamic world and has never desired to build its own culture-based Islamic civilization that might promote the moderate Islam to the world. Nurcholish majid further believed that for centuries, Islam was mainly used as ideological tool to oppose the foreign colonial domination[81] that sought to insert its influence to Indonesian Muslims, without attempting to harness Islam as the inspiration for civilization. The same condition could be applied currently that Islam in Indonesia has not played significant role in any Islamic world dynamics, maintaining its low profile with limited contribution to the Islamic world, mainly

---

[76] Ibid page 13
[77] Karen Elliot House, Saudi Arabia in Transition, From Defense to Offense, but How to Score, Belfer Center for Science and International Affairs, page 15
[78] Mohamed A.Ramady, The Saudi Arabian Economy, Policies, Achievements, and Challenges, Springer, 2010, page 389
[79] www.indonesia-investments.com
[80] Clifford Geertz, the Religion of Java, the University of Chicago Press, p age 6
[81] Jajat Burhanuddin and Kees van Dijk, Islam in Indonesia, Contrasting Images and Interpretations, Amesterdam University Press, page 41

to Middle Eastern issues. Indonesia has remained aloof from any Islamic world – related concerns, particularly in intellectual terrains. However, history notes that Jihad resolution once issued and promoted by Indonesian clerics in the initial years of Indonesian independence in 1945 to mobilize Indonesian Muslims to fight against colonialist powers has had a very significant impact to awaken Muslims throughout the world in fighting and struggling to gain their independent and sovereign states.[82] Not only that, if compared with Islamic Arab and Persian civilizations, Indonesia has enjoyed little the intellectual tradition that made the state not famous among the Islamic world. Most ominously, Islam in Indonesia has often been viewed as not genuine and original given that Islam was not given to rise initially in Southeast Asian territory.

As Abdurrahman Wahid (Gus Dur), prominent scholar and also former Indonesian president, and Nurcholis Majid much believed that Islam is unlikely to be separable component of Indonesian identity that occupies the most important element in Indonesians' practical life, religiously, socially, culturally and politically. Furthermore Abdurrahman Wahid once noted that despite the fact that Indonesia is not an Islamic state, it does not mean that Islamic law can't be enforced, which Indonesian society got used to applying Islam without any state intervention. Even the scholar maintained a view that establishing an Islamic state is not obligatory to Muslims, but establishing the (Muslim) society that sticks to Islamic teaching is obligatory.[83] Meanwhile Nurcholis Majid underscored primarily that the role of Muslims in expulsing the foreign colonialists from the territory shall not be downplayed.[84] Interestingly, while the fact that each national achievement of the nations (Arab and Persian) in both regions, Arab Saudi and Iran, could be immediately associated with Islamic achievements, rather than their national identity, yet In Indonesia, such achievement would not be simply associated with Islamic accomplishment notwithstanding Indonesian Muslim.

Apart from Islam that covers 87% of its total population, Christian (Protestant and Catholic), Hindu, Buddha, and Kong Hu Cu are minor religions of the people. In recent years, Kong Hu Cu alone has been officially recognized by Indonesian government as a formal religion in Indonesia following the period of reformation in 1998 based on presidential decree no. 6/2000 as a democratization process that was trying incredibly to revitalize the freedom of expression of the entire Indonesian elements, revoking the Presidential Instruction no.14/1967 that forbad any traditions and religions related to Chinese ethnic, starting to acknowledge Chinese New Year as national holiday. Meanwhile in Saudi Arabia and Iran, the holy days for non-Muslims are not public and national holidays.

Generally speaking, the minority groups are able to practice their religious faiths comfortably as a positive result of applied democratic values which emphasize on mutual respect and understanding. In Indonesia, unlike Saudi and Iran, conversion from Islam to

---

[82] Abdullah Ubaid & Mohammad Bakir, Nasionalisme dan Islam Nusantara, Kompas, 2015, page 11
[83] Ibid page 115
[84] Ibid page 44

another religion is not a crime, driving incredibly the country to be the best exemplar of growing democracy in Southeast Asia, as according to the Freedom House, Indonesia in 2007 was the only country in the region categorised as free. [85] Arguably if compared with Iran and Saudi Arabia, democracy in Indonesia would be the most appreciated, which in the two states, the freedom of expression and opinion, often seen by the regimes as political and religious dissent that could stir domestic instability, has been often associated with threats of imprisonment, torturing, exiling, and even death penalty sentencing. In this vein, Robert Hefner even further believed that Islam was the force that facilitated Indonesia's transition to democracy, inspiring to create the foundation of civil society that enables democracy in Indonesia to be more effective, unlike Islam in the Middle East that has proven to have simply dissuaded democratization process. However, according to the survey on Democracy Index issued by Economist in 2014, Indonesia was categorized as flawed democracy, not yet full democracy.[86]

Despite this reality, Indonesia, mostly Sunni with Shafe'e school well known for its moderation in making *ijtihad* (independent reasoning in seeking Islamic laws) does not constitute an Islamic state which underpins his laws and regulations to be based on Islamic values. Rather, Indonesia is a secular democratic country that practically would accept some of Islamic influences, meaning that the state is not totally separated from Islamic characters by attempting to accommodate Islamic laws if deemed necessary. Soekarno, the Indonesian first President, influenced partly by the secularist ideas of Mostafa Kemal Attaturk, the founder of modern Turkey in the 20th century, believed that religion and state could be united in practical life, but not in official, meaning that he advocated further the development of people's life with the quality of Islam. Soekarno even believed that the qualified Muslims could be eligible to fill in official positions including the membership of the House of Representative, who later would issue numerous policies based on Islam including Islamic political aspirations.[87]

Nevertheless, with the passage of time, the facts had revealed that Moslem members of the House of Representative have not necessarily struggled and given much effort for reviving Islamic political aspirations to be implemented, yet some of them, mainly represented by the Islamic parties, have been trying significantly to revive the implementation of Islamic Sharia into the basic constitution by amending it. However their unwavering attempts did not yield any positive result when their proposal of adopting

---

[85] Greg Fealy and Sally White, Expressing Islam, Religious Life and Politics in Indonesia, Institute of Southeast Asian Studies, Singapore, Seng Lee Press Pte Ltd, Page 174
[86] Mohamad Guntur Romli and Ciputat School Team, Islam Kita Islam Nusantara, Ciputat School, first edition February 2016, page 119
[87] Faisal Ismail, Islam, Politics and Ideology in Indonesia : A Study of The Process of Muslim Acceptance of the Pancasila, a doctoral dissertation for Institute of Islamic Studies in McGill University Montreal in December 1995, page 39

Islamic Sharia to the annual meeting of the People's Consultative Assembly in August 2002 was rejected after long debate.[88]

According to Luthfi Assyaukanie, the defeat of the Islamic political parties in the debate has already displayed the failure of much effort to revive the formalization of Islamic state with Sharia implementation that started since the early years of the Indonesian independence. As information to share, the vote share of parties that clearly campaigned for the implementation of Islamic Sharia had declined from 14 percent in 1999 to 11 percent in 2004 and then to 7 percent in 2009.[89] In nutshell, it can be argued for the time being that most Indonesians are not interested in formalizing Islam as the state form, and Indonesia has always avoided self-identification as an Islamic state despite Muslim majority. For many Indonesians who view that the religion is solely a personal affair the state could not interfere to, Islamic law has to be applied only to the personal matters including marriage and inheritance, thus not necessarily becoming a basis of Indonesian statehood. However little wonder Indonesian Muslims would be angry and offended if Islam is subject to demonization and humiliation. In addition, they would deeply demonstrate and display the feeling of sympathy to any humanitarian tragedies that involve Muslim community in the globe.

Therefore, it is hardly surprising then; one of the largest Islamic political parties named PKS (Welfare and Justice Party) was trying to be more inclusive to include all religious followers, attempting to find out appropriate alternative formula that is compatible with current socio-political situation and dynamics.[90]

In special case like in Aceh province of Sumatera Island, historically the local people had played a major role in contributing in struggles to gain Indonesian independence in 1945 with mobilization of Islamic identity expression controlled significantly by their own ulemas.[91] Therefore little wonder that Islamic laws based on al-Qor'an and Sunna (Prophet's tradition) have been implemented since decades regularly until today, despite much objection and opposition by non-governmental organizations on the implementation of Qanun Jinayah (criminal laws), particularly since the province gained its special autonomy in 2001, thus changing its province old name into Naggroe Aceh Darussalam (NAD).[92]

However, this secular character of the state does not encourage the state to spread its moderate Islam to the world, unlike Saudi Arabia and Iran, as mentioned earlier. Yet, Indonesia by exerting its own soft power, continuously would introduce and propagate a

---

[88] Luthfi Assyaukanie, Ideologi Islam dan Utopia, TIga Model Negara Demokrasi di Indoesia, Freedom Institute, first edition, August 2011, page 204
[89] Mirjam Kunkler and Alfred Stepan, Democratization and Islam in Indonesia, Columbia University Press, New York, page 25
[90] Ibid page 246
[91] Arskal Salim, Challenging the Secular State, the Islamization of Law in Modern Indonesia, University of Hawa'i Press, Honolulu, page 143
[92] www.downtoearth-indonesia.org

moderate Islam to the world, hoping that such type of Islam is able to inspire other Muslim communities as antithesis for radical and extreme Islamic thoughts, thus preventing them to act against Islamic laws. In fact this moderate Islam that Indonesia upholds has already became inspirational privilege for identification of its foreign policy on how to enhance bilateral and multilateral relationships with Moslem countries based on the perception.

Though Indonesia is not definitely an Islamic state as cited earlier, yet many Indonesians still seem to support institutionalizing the religion by the State including the establishment of the Ministry of Religious Affairs and Indonesian Ulema Council. Furthermore they also support the religious court, institutionalizing the marriage, and teaching religious subjects in schools which, according to Ahmad Syafii Maarif, an Indonesian prominent scholar, would be obligatory for the state to interfere with the matter, because it reflects its basic constitution implementation.[93] However in Indonesia, pro-Islamic legislation and regulations could restrict some personal freedom as John Bowen, a prominent anthropologist, argues. He greatly further concluded that about 10 percent of total Indonesia's 495 regions, Sharia-based laws have been introduced, some of which were indicated to be incompatible with national law. John Bowen later gave some examples, in South Sulawesi, some laws require both male and female civil servants to wear Islamic dress and to be able to recite some verses of Al-Qor'an before he or she is accepted to hold public employment; the obligation to recite from memory the first seven lines of Al-Qor'an before marriage ceremony and etc.[94] More interestingly, all Sharia laws and regulations issued between 1998 and 2013 were applied in provinces and districts where secular parties had controlled local parliaments, and the few Islamist party members that won local elections mostly refrained from adopting Sharia laws, that rather were pursued by the local government who had no affiliations with Islamist parties. [95] Not only decentralization that prompted the issuance of pro Sharia regulations, at national level mainly in 2008, an anti pornography bill was ratified by the Parliament, stirring much controversy among the society. Anti Ahmadiya and Shia campaign has been the main factor that triggered demonstrations and protests carried out by the Muslim activists, urging the government to display firmer stance to the minority religious groups such as in the case of Shia minority group in Sampang, East Java, yet at the same time, undermining profoundly the principles of democracy itself.

As a matter of fact, before Dutch entered Indonesia as colonial power, for many decades, Islamic law was partially implemented by Indonesian community. For instance, Sultan Malikul Zahir, king of Samudera Pasai, was considered one of the prominent Islamic jurists in 14th century. Not only that, he also played significant role by introducing moderate

---

[93] Luthfi Assyaukanie, Ideologi Islam dan Utopia, TIga Model Negara Demokrasi di Indoesia, Freedom Institute, first edition, August 2011, page 22
[94] Mirjam Kunkler and Alfred Stepan, Democratization and Islam in Indonesia, Columbia University Press, New York, page 36
[95] Michael Buehler, the Politics of Shari'a Law, Islamist Activists and the State in Democratizing Indonesia, Cambridge University Press, first published in 2016, page 10

Shafe'i school to other regions in Nusantara (Indonesian archipelago), even some jurists from Malaka Kingdom often paid visit to Samudera Pasai, only to consult Islam-related many issues. Putting tittles for kings in Nusantara such as adipati, in alogo, saayadin and padotongomo is clear evidence how Islam had obviously affected the communities in that period.[96][97]

Most interestingly, cognizant deeply of the existing Indonesian Muslim majority, the implementation of Islamic law in Indonesia was once adopted by colonial Dutch jurists such as Solomon Keyzer (1823-1868) and then approved by Lodewijk Willem Christian van den Berg (1847-1927) by stating that Indonesian Muslim community had implemented Islamic laws as a whole. For this reason, VOC government asked D.W. Freijer to draft summary that contained both marriage and inheritance laws. After having been reviewed by Islamic jurists, the law book was then used by VOC in 1760 to settle disputes among Indonesian Muslims in the territories that it had already conquered and ruled. The book was often called compendium freijer. By emerging Christian Snouck Hurgroney as a colonial Dutch adviser, the implementation of Islamic law gradually was kept in distance. Having his hidden agenda to impose divide et impera strategy, with his profound knowledge on Islamic law, he later

---

[96] Andi Sunarto, Hukum Islam di Indonesia, Fakultas Hukum Universitas Hassanudin, Makassar 2011

[97] Nevertheless, there are three theories regarding the first period of entrance of Islam to Indonesia. All do much believe that the spread of Islam in the archipelago was not carried out through the use of force, in which Azyumardi Azra has preferred to call the process of the Islamisation of indigenous peoples as adhesion, rather than conversion, which 'conversion' may imply that the indigenous society, before deciding to follow Islam, were following the revealed religions such as Judaism and Christianity, in which they were required to leave the old beliefs thoroughly.[97] First theory called Mekkah theory, in 7th century, Islam was brought and introduced by Muslim Arab traders who came to Indonesia through Sumatera Island with aim at spreading Islam to other parts of the world as their main goal. Furthermore, King Sriwijaya in Jambi, Sumatera Island, named Srindravarman sent a letter to Caliph Umar bin Abdul Aziz (717-720 M) of Umayyad dynasty, asking him to send somebody to Sumatera to teach him Islam and explain him Islamic laws.[97] Such a theory was developed by Hamka, Indonesian prominent scholar. The second theory called Gujarat theory in which in 13th century many Arab Moslem Shafe'i traders who settled in Gujarat and Malabar (western part of India) since 7th century came to eastern part of the world, including Indonesia. This theory was introduced by the western scholars. The last theory is Persian theory, stating that Islam to Indonesia was brought by Muslim Persians due to some similarities of tradition that has grown both in Indonesian and Persian societies such as commemorating the mourning day of 10 Moharram or Asshura, usually held by Shia Persians, in Pariaman, west Sumatera. Another evidence of the theory is the existing similarity of Calligraphic art of gravestones in Indonesia and Persia.[97] The theory has been developed by Hoesein Djajadiningrat, Indonesian history expert. In Java Island, it was well-known that Walisongo (nine saints) played influential roles to introduce Islam to the society of Java in 14th century, by gradually diminishing the domination of Hindu Buddha cultures that persisted for many years in Indonesia. The aforementioned theories have generated many observers to believe that Islam came to Indonesia peacefully and such a penetration even was integrated with the local culture and wisdom that inspired identification of democratic principles under the framework of Pancasila (five principles) as Indonesian state ideology and philosophy. In sum, through intensive trading between those Muslim Arabs and indigenous societies, scholars further believed Islam has been successfully spread in Indonesia through marriage, education, political approach and art.

advocated customary laws rather than prevailing Islamic laws.[98] The colonial Dutch had proven to have intervened in Islamic affairs by scaling back the laws of inheritance from the religious court in 1931, thus prompting harsh protest from Hasyim Ash'ary, the NU organization founder who then asked for the establishment of the *Islamic ummah* unity of Indonesia.

With the passage of time, the existing strong aspiration on Islamic expression among Indonesians also was understood well by the Japanese colonist that came later after the expulsion of the colonial Dutch in 1942, in which it created Madjlis Syuro Muslimin Indonesia (Masyumi/Council of Indonesian Muslim Associations), the largest Islamic political party during the time, following the dispersing of Majlis Islam Ala Indonesia (Indonesian high Islamic Council) in 1943.[99] Due to much awareness of the fact that Islam was the religion that vast majority of Indonesians believed, the Japanese colonist also issued a policy called as Nippon's Islamic Grass Root Policy which aimed at exploiting the ulemas' potentialities of the villages. Furthermore, the Japanese colonist also founded Shumubu (religious affairs office) in Jakarta and in 1944 opened its branch in many parts of Indonesia, named Shumuka.[100] Not only that, the Japanese colonist, based on Kyai Wahid Hasyim's request, son of Hasyim Ash'ari, granted special military training for Santris (Pesantren students) and allowed them to establish their own defence front, Hezbollah and Sabillilah.[101]

As a matter of fact, since early years of Indonesian independence in 1945, the efforts to materialize Islamic state in Indonesia were taken by several Islamist political elites of the time, specifically by Kartosoewirjo who advocated the establishment of Islamic state and Moslem representatives such as Ki Bagus Hadikusumo and Kiai Ahmad Sanusi after Japan had promised to grant Indonesian independence. In this vein, based on Kartosoewiryo's idea, Jakarta charter that was made initially contained words "the duty of applying Islamic Sharia to all of its adherents." In fact, three days before the independence proclamation, and three years afterward, Kartosoewiryo then deeply urged Kiai Joesoef Taudjiri to proclaim immediately Indonesia as Islamic state. Yet he refused. Accordingly in Tasikmalaya region, West Java in 7 August 1947, Kartosuwiryo himself proclaimed a Islamic state, along with the adoption of ten articles explaining that newly established Islamic state would encompass whole Indonesian territories and nations. Kartosowiryo also began to prepare governmental concepts and structures like any other governmental systems did. Several Islamist movements in Java, Sulawesi and Sumatera started to emerge, advocating the same goal of Kartosuwiryo, while Indonesian government regarded them as separatist and destructive. With the passage of time, in order to curtail mutual allegation among clerics who were accused of protecting these movements, an institution named Badan

---

[98] Persis.or.id, 28 February 2017
[99] Mohammad Guntur Romli and Tim Ciputat School, Islam Kita Islam Nusantara, first edition in February 2016, Ciputat School, Page 57
[100] Islamcendekia.com, 9 January 2016
[101] opcit

Musyawarah Alim Ulama (Shura Board of Ulemas) then-Majelis Ulama Indonesia (Indonesian Ulema council) was founded that obviously aimed at monitoring these movements and help the government curb them.[102]

Furthermore, adopting Pancasila[103] as basic philosophy of the Indonesian state has given much influence to the religious practices at home, which mostly believe that five principles of Pancasila would not contravene the Islamic essences that emphasizes on religiosity, humanity, justice, equality etc. Furthermore, Pancasila shall be regarded to be stirring mutual tolerance and respect under the unity of the state, that accordingly denies any godless ideologies. Furthermore democracy values reflected prominently by Pancasila has driven the ruling elites mainly in the aftermath of Soeharto's dictatorship collapse in 1998 to give much effort in absorbing public aspirations on freedom of speech and expression under the framework of mutual respect and understanding. Many Indonesians who became more aware on the importance of national integrity and unity, not necessarily adopting it as way of life, believe a religion does not constitute any constraint and restriction in undergoing their life, and appear satisfied that the state is not built on the specific religion, yet still absorb their religious aspirations particularly to their civic right laws.

Such a fact has been once asserted by Kyai Mashkur, the former Minister of Religious Affairs in the early years of Indonesian independence who further stated that Pancasila, is an essence and substance of Islamic teachings, thus signifying the consent among the Moslem prominent figures during the time.[104] Pancasila itself for Indonesians, developed aggressively by President Soeharto, poses best example of how the Indonesian Moslem founding fathers were attempting to compromise the heated debate that might lead to disintegration of the nation, by deleting 7 sensitive words of *'dengan menjalankan syariat Islam bagi pemeluk-pemeluknya'* (with implementing Islamic Sharia for its adherents) and replacing them with Ketuhanan Yang Maha Esa (Belief in the one and only God) in the meeting of PPKI (Preparatory Committee for Indonesian Independence) members, then becoming a first principle of Pancasila.

To the date, Pancasila, albeit being not completely accepted by some conservative Islamic figures, has been believed as an effective tool to unite Indonesian nation with different backgrounds of ethnicity, religion, tradition and language, certainly along with an open criticism that Indonesia will not accept atheism anyway and explicitly has to support religious communities, rather than irreligious ones, differently from liberal democracy the West upholds. Religion in Indonesian occupies a very significant place that look impossible to be separated from their daily life. However, as best shown by the 2007 survey carried out

---

[102] Sammy Mantolas, Kartosowiryo, Proklamator Negara Islam Indonesia, 24 October 2016, https://tirto.id/kartosoewirjo-proklamator-negara-islam-indonesia-bXqX

[104] Mohamad Guntur Romli and Ciputat School Team, Islam Kita Islam Nusantara, Ciputat School, first edition February 2016, page 100

by LSI, it unsurprisingly had displayed that 90 percent preferred a Pancasila state to any alternative (Islam-based state), emphasizing on the percentage of Indonesian voters who since 1999 have not voted for the political parties, either strict or moderate Islamist nature.[105]

In past several years, Indonesian Muslim society despite their zealous religiosity and perception that Islam encompasses all aspects of human life including political matters, yet they prefer to highlight that Islam shall not be mixed with politics, thus driving the religion into politicization, not because that Islam is no longer compatible with political dynamics, but it would be based on bitter experience of some political Islamic parties which have involved with several scandalous un-Islamic issues, mostly financial and bureaucratic corruption. Indonesian Muslims further believe that Islam has been used to be an effective tool and means to create electability in general elections, undermining and downplaying other non-Muslim political candidates, yet at the same time, they feel disappointed with un-Islamic ethics shown unflinchingly by some of the Islamic political parties. Seemingly, in Indonesia, due to their tremendous disappointment to un-Islamic ethics and behaviours shown unabashedly by some Islamic political parties or politicians has already drove their religious standpoints to be more moderate and tolerant as previously they had much expectation that emerging Islamic political parties in 1998 transitional period could resonate Islamic voices, thus leading them given their frustration to vote for national and secular political parties. They did realise that during the time Islam has been misused and manipulated by some politicians to attract a large number of voters and smoothen their ambitious power. As a matter of fact, Islamic clerics in Indonesia reportedly often enter political affairs and further issue legal opinions/fatwa to influence Moslems. Yet, unlike in Iran, their fatwas will not have significant influence to determine the government to take both domestic and foreign policies. In fact, fatwa is not binding legal opinion that may distinct from one to another.

In addition, the politicians also often carry out other political manoeuvres before the holding of general elections to increase electability among other things by approaching non-state Islamic organizations with large number of membership. They harness the function of mosques to deliver campaign and propaganda, somehow threatening the Muslims to enter the hell if they vote for undesired candidate. The case of Basuki Tjahaya Purnama, often called Pak Ahok, the first non-Moslem candidate for local leader election of Jakarta in 2017 and candidacy of Megawati, first female political figure and Soekarno's daughter for presidential election in 2009 have best described how religious sentiment had overwhelmed political situation in those days.

Recent years have witnessed the more growth of Islamic spirit and conservatism of Indonesian Muslims, evidenced tremendously by women's more willingness to wear Hejab

---

[105] Jajat Burhanuddin and Kees van Dijk, Islam in Indonesia, Constrasting Images and Interpretations, Amsterdam University Press, page 60

(Islamic headscarf) and Television stations that broadcast various Islamic programs which always emphasize the moderateness of Islam and tolerance among religious adherents. The 2013 Miss world pageant held in Indonesia cancelled including the swimming suit competition for the first time, and in the opening ceremony of Asian Games of 2018 in Jakarta, the Indonesian traditional dancers said the phrase *'Assalamualaikum'* to welcome all of the international audiences before starting the entire programs, etc. Last but not least, Indonesian government as the host, has deliberately introduced Sharia economy including the discussions on Waqf (a voluntary, permanent, irrevocable dedication of a portion of one's wealth) and Zakat (obligatory form of giving, determined by the taxation of wealth and income) to be discussed in the annual meeting of International Monetary Fund and World Bank in October 2018 in Bali Island, Indonesia.[106]

Such a more conservative standpoint of Indonesian Muslims could be indirect outcome of their dissatisfaction and disappointment over liberal and profane culture which was tied up with unclear ideal values and consumerism that made significant gap between patterns of life and religiosity and spirituality, the condition that may apply in other nations.

One most recent survey published by ISEAS-Yusof Ishak Institute in Singapore has demonstrated a shocking fact that 82% of Indonesians support an assumption that women must wear hejab as part of Sharia implementation. Not only that, the survey has also indicated that 67% of Indonesians believe that Sharia implementation could be able to keep and maintain social morality.[107]

Indonesian society that grows more religious and conservative in recent years is also evidenced by a very startling national survey conducted by the Centre of Islamic Studies and Society, Islamic State University in August-September 2018, showing that almost 83% of Indonesian teachers from kindergarten level until High Senior School would agree that Islam is the only solution to solve the entire problem in the society. The shocking survey also displayed that around 40 percent of the surveyed teachers would agree that all sciences are already existed in al-Qoran, so there is no necessity to study any science originating from the West.[108]

Additionally, people's more growing participation in several protests and demonstrations for the issues of Palestine must be good evidence how Indonesians would like to express and speak out their Islamic identity by presenting solidarity for Palestinians as integral part of Islam Ummah. The society looks more eager to extend its support to the issue by collecting all sorts of donations sent to the Palestinians in the area conflict. Most

---

[106] Rina Anggraeni, 18 September 2018, https://ekbis.sindonews.com/read/1339028/33/bi-sertakan-pembahasan-ekonomi-syariah-di-pertemuan-imf-world-bank-1537203057
[107] Survey: Muslim Indonesia Semakin Konservatif, 8 September 2017, https://www.dw.com/id/survey-muslim-indonesia-semakin-konservatif/a-40410411
[108] Muhammad Nur Rochmi, 18 October 2018, https://beritagar.id/artikel/berita/6-dari-10-guru-punya-sikap-intoleran

startlingly, they seem ready to be dispatched to carry out Jihad to help Palestinians' struggles in expelling Israeli Zionists from Palestinian territory.

Interestingly, Indonesian society becoming more conservative was realised well by former US President Barrack Obama when he compared Indonesian Muslim society while spending his time in Jakarta who were relaxed and syncretistic Islam to a more fundamentalist and unforgiving interpretation. Most startlingly in this regard, Barrack Obama obviously pointed out Saudi Arabia (Wahhabism) influence that has already shaped Indonesian conservatism and fundamentalism. [109]

Unsurprisingly, more conservative Indonesian society, not only well harnessed politically by Islamic politicians to generate more electability, but also has been used to generate larger opportunity and benefit in economic sector including establishment more Sharia-flavoured banks in past two decades, endorsed legally by the government since 1998 through the law number 10, affirming that there are two sorts of Indonesian banking system, conventional and Sharia. In recent years various product companies often use the girls wearing hejabs to be models for their advertisements and brand ambassadors, attempting to attract Indonesian *hijabers* (girls or women who wear Islamic headscarves) and implicitly re-emphasizing that the products have already obtained Islamic permission that are safe to consume. In recent years, I can argue that Indonesian society has become more conservative in religiosity and more liberal in politics.

However, according to an annual report issued by US Commission on International Religious Freedom in 2018, Indonesia is still classified in tier 2, occupying better position than that of Saudi Arabia and Iran, as a country of particular concern given the fact that Indonesia engages in or tolerate religious freedom violations.[110] In sum, such an assumption could be raised by the shocking fact that Indonesia still implement the law on religious desecration adopted in 1965 view largely as effective legal mechanism to curb any minor religious groups like Shia and Ahmadiya from expressing and practicing their own rituals, particularly in the aftermath of reformation era in 1998. The article that was initially aimed at curbing Kebatinan (mysticism) sect, stipulates that each person is banned intentionally in public area to tell, advocate and give effort to obtain public support, in order to carry out interpretation on a religion adhered in Indonesia or make religious activities that resemble religious activities of that religion's essences.[111]

However, the culture/character of succumbing still overwhelms the nature of Indonesian society deeply, trying to persuade reconciliatory approach rather than confrontational. Such a perception would be the prominent and unique element for any Indonesianist to understand and identify Indonesian cultures, which according to them, all

---

[109] Medea Benjamin, the Kingdom of the Unjust, Behind the US-Saudi Connection, OR books 2016 page 73
[110] Annual Report issued by US Commission on International Religious Freedom in 2018, page 169
[111] Sebelum 1998, Ahmadiyah dan Syiah Tak Disebut Melakukan Penodaan Agama, nasional.kompas.com, 20 February 2018

matters and conflicts shall be dealt and settled by using the family (friendly) approaches. The general Muslims are easily provoked by the issues related to the dishonouring of the religious symbols. Most startlingly, even the worst criminals will attempt to defend Islam when sensing Islam is already insulted and disgraced. However, a wide range of both vertical and horizontal conflicts that may interrupt at home are usually solved easily and quickly as the society, as intimated previously, always pursues reconciliatory approach, plus by giving more emphasis on unity in state and nation.

II. The Role of Islamic Ideology in Shaping The Foreign Policy of the Countries

It is unquestionable and worth mentioning that foreign policy in any country would mirror a combination of its long entrenched ideology and perceived national interests.[112]

---

[112] Gawdat Bahgat, Anoushiravan Ehteshami & Neil Quilliam, Security and Bilateral Issues Between Iran and Its Arab Neighbours, Palgrave Macmillan, page 6

Meaning that this integral element could not been simply overlooked by any stakeholder to navigate and guide foreign policy that reflects realisation of all values and principles that ideology pursues to achieve its national interest. With the passage of time, accomplishing national interests must vary its methods and mechanisms, depending on how open and close/strict ideology a state upholds.

However, an ideology brought tightly by a country often differ with that of the others, even among Muslim countries which mostly don't take Islam as its ideology that would affect domestic and foreign policies. In the other hand, many Moslem countries are not too comfortable to be seen that they ignore and neglect altogether Islamic character and identity in their foreign policy taking. According to them, keeping Islam out of their life totally and being too secular in every aspect is not praiseworthy.

Furthermore, as elucidated earlier taking Islam as basic foundation of the constitution does not necessarily that Islam would be reflected in foreign policy making. More often, it would hinge on leaders' willingness and commitment, thus implementing pragmatic and more realistic approaches as I would like to explore further in another chapter. Interestingly, governments sometimes are eager to put ideology in their foreign policy in a bid to obtain more legitimization from vast majority of Muslim society as Islam becomes an integral part and identity of the society.

Since long times ago, Islam has been assumed by Islamic political scholars as an effective cure for solving the entire problems that failed to have been solved by liberal secular ideologies. The function of religion has been long perceived to be helpful and alternative solution that could respond to each human curiosity and inquisitiveness given its comprehensiveness of whole aspects, not solely practical religiosity. In this regard, Islam as ideology that differs from other sorts of ideologies as it derives from God's revelation, not an outcome of human creativity and innovation, is simply believed to have broader scope, encompassing faith and Sharia, dealing with relations between God and individuals vertically and among individuals in society horizontally.

The last *samawi* (abrahamic) religion of Islam is deeply believed by Islamists to be a proper alternative that could replace all sorts of existing ideologies. Owing to its character as directly emanating from God's guidance, Islam is further believed to be the only answer for any changing political and social situations which Western utopian visions have failed to respond prevailing socio-political challenges in the Muslim countries. The emerging of incessant frustration from Muslims is plausible since their own governments have failed to bring in economic welfare and prosperity to the nations despite all the western/non Islamic ideologies. Therefore, with the passage of time, the slogan that Islam is the solution or the only solution came to surface as a sympathetic and reactionary respond to each matter of human's life, promising the followers a better future.[113] In this regard, the societies in several countries even became more conservative to counterweigh the growing liberal and secular tendency.

Indeed, little wonder to say, Islam has put some very basic guidelines how foreign policy shall be conducted by the Islamic states including through acknowledging the universality of Islam that promotes goods and prevents evils, and establishing ties and relations with unbelievers in the case of emergency, etc. With its crystal clear characters, Islam as political ideology would confine significantly the behaviours of the ruling elites, not to choose and pursue internal and external policies based on their convenience and sole willingness. Instead, they have to deeply absorb rules laid down based on Islamic frameworks, by guiding and navigating their foreign policy to be compatible with Islamic values and principles.[114]

According to Taqiyuddin an-Nabhani, a prominent ulema from Palestine who also established radical Hizbut Tahrir movement in 1953, an ideology attempts to create a state that hopefully could accommodate the implementation of that ideology following its foundation. Meaning that there are numerous figures or organizations bearing the same assumption on comprehensiveness of Islam who then give significant efforts to establish a political state that is much hoped that Islamic Sharia could be realized completely and implemented altogether, and could inspire the governing system. In the modern history, particularly after the second world war, Arab Saudi and Iran are the best examples of the implementation of Islamic ideology at home and how both states have been attempting tremendously to influence other communities in many countries to take and follow such offered distinctive ideologies.

Before going to deeper analysis, it is worth understanding that in the aftermath of the abolishment of last Ottoman Caliph by Turkish Grand National Assembly in March 1924, due to much difficulty and significant obstacles, none of the Muslim countries has appeared to rekindle and revive such a caliphate for Islamic world, thus refraining from even talking on the issue in bilateral and multilateral discussions. Furthermore, Muslim leaders even believe, apart from its unlikelihood in this modern world, building Caliphate does not constitute a moral and religious obligation.

Therefore it is not surprising that the only effort following such an abolition was taken by non-state actor/Islamic educational institution which was al-Azhar University in Cairo in 1926 to attempt at appointing a new Caliph over the world of Islam and establishing the Islamic public order, later proved to be failed. In fact the agenda of rebuilding caliphate has left controversy among Muslim nations. Most interestingly, Wahhabi developed by

---

[113] John L. Esposito, Lily Zubaidah Rahim, Naser Ghobadzadeh, The Politics of Islamism, Diverging Visions and Trajectories, Palgrave Macmillan, 2018, page 8
[114] Ayatollah Ibrahim Amini, Foreign Policy of an Islamic State, Islam and Muslims, el-Tauhid Islamic Journal volume 2 no.4 page 2

Saudi Arab, believes that Caliphate after four Rashidoon Caliphate is invalid as it is no longer compatible with Sharia implementation.[115] Even Shia Iranians are reported not to attend the meeting as it absolutely has believed that Caliphate is Sunni- characterized concept.[116] In Indonesian context, except Hizbut Tahrir Indonesia banned officially in July 2017, the two Indonesia's largest Islamic organizations, Nahdatul Ulama and Muhammadiyah, have barely talked on the Caliphate concept.[117]

Historically, both Saudi Arabia and Iran did not meet any significant obstacles and real impediments in adopting their basic constitutions which are based on Islamic principles and characters. Furthermore, it is worth mentioning that Islamic constitution of Iran alone was approved by 99,5% voters in a referendum held on 2 and 3 December 1979 in which some months before, 98.2 % of Iranian voters decided to have Islamic Republic as a new system for their state.[118] In such a democratic referendum has shown evidently main aspiration of most Iranians in the early years of the revolution that Islam was much expected to be generating political stability and economic welfare for them.

In Saudi Arabia since the Kingdom has invariably applied an absolute monarchy in its political system, governmental policies are believed to be echoing Saudi society interests and aspirations interestingly without any necessity to further involve any role and participation of the Saudi society. In fact, the cultural passivity of Saudi society as alluded earlier would be also a prominent factor propelling sustainability of the Kingdom and guaranty its survival, thus the society would not see a big deal for the rulers to become authoritarians in guiding both domestic and foreign policies. However, the Kingdom has never overlooked acutely how for many centuries religion of Islam has become an integral part and inseparable identity of Saudi society. Therefore little wonder the government put the first priority on safeguarding Islamic values in conformity with Sharia to its national five-year development plans. [119]

For Indonesia alone, as explained previously, some political elites who at first successfully brought Islamic ideas to a charter called Piagam Jakarta that was drafted and adopted by nine members of BPUPKI (Investigating Committee for Preparatory Work for Independence) in June 1945, had finally failed to maintain their basic aspiration that seven words *"dengan kewajiban menjalankan syariat Islam bagi pemeluknya"* (with a duty to implement Islamic Sharia for its adherents) were eliminated in 18 August 1945, one day after the independence declaration, and further replaced with words *"Ketuhanan yang Maha Esa"* (Belief in the One and Only God). During the time, the step was eventually taken

---

[115] Imran N.Hosein, the Caliphate the Hejaz and the Saudi-Wahhabi Nation-State, Masjid Darul Qur'an, Long Islam, New York, page 24
[116] Ibid page 38
[117] Reno Muhammad, ISIS Mengungkap Fakta Terorisme Berlabel Islam, Noura Books, 2015, page 71
[118] Look at the Basic Constitution of Islamic Iran page 3, www.wipo.int.
[119] Mohamed A.Ramady, The Saudi Arabian Economy, Policies, Achievements, and Challenges, Springer, 2010, page 26

as a main compromise between nationalists and Islamists who preferred unity and integrity among the sensitivity of diverse ethnics and nations that had already shown legitimacy to newly-proclaimed state.[120] In this regard, Indonesia sadly had missed chance to formalize Islam as a basis of the state, in order to pursue the greater purpose and paramount goal of the founding fathers who were deeply cognizant of existing distinct interests of the nations. Nevertheless, Indonesian Muslims have never lost Islam to be inspiring the legal adoption of Islam in identifying personal (private) matters and civic laws (*Akhwal Shakhsiya*). For most Indonesian Muslims, Islamic law shall play prominent role in legally determining the laws and regulations of marriage, inheritance, etc, which put aside secular opinions.

Furthermore, due to general scope of the semi-secular Pancasila (five principles) particularly in the first principle, Indonesia will not be obliged to underpin its own foreign policy based on specific religion that is Islam. Moreover by understanding Pancasila also would not behove identifying foreign policy to pursue world's Islamic and Muslim interests in global context. In addition, adopting open ideology of Pancasila, Indonesia is not obliged to absorb and involve participation of non-state Muslim organizations to identify and guide both Indonesian domestic and foreign policies. In nutshell Indonesia would identify and formulize its foreign policy under the framework of only–national interest pursuit. However Indonesian government deeply realize and understand that Islam poses an integral part of Indonesian identity that can't be overlooked, which eventually drives it to identify and guide foreign policy with Islamic flavour. Therefore little wonder that Indonesia proves to be actively contributing in seeking political settlements to resolve various conflicts in Muslim world, and enthusiastically be involved in numerous international organizations with Islamic characters.

As elucidated earlier, both countries, Iran and Saudi Arabia often claim to be leading states for Islamic world, triggered significantly by their own basic constitutions that evidently adopted Islam. In Saudi basic law of particularly in article 7, it has been emphasized explicitly that Islamic Shari'a is a foundation of the state of 99 percent Muslims. Furthermore, the 1992 adopted constitution following first gulf war, also palpably stated that Saudi Kingdom is a sovereign Islamic Arab state whose constitution is Al-Qor'an and Sunna of the Prophet. In this regard, in undergoing its governmental system, Saudi elites would refer to the interpretations of the appointed Ulemas, based on these two Islamic Hojjahs (divine reasoning). Meaning that every single decision and policy taken by the ruling elites are supposed to contain Islamic flavours; and every disputable case must be referred into these two divine resources for getting solutions. Furthermore the basic law that consists of nine chapters and 83 articles was made circumspectly so as not to contradict Sharia.[121] Not only that, the basic constitution also re-emphasizes on the Kingdom's responsibility and obligation to defend and maintain Islam and the holy places as well as to

---

[120] Pancasila sebagaik Kalimatun Sawa, 2 Juni 2016 https://www.republika.co.id/berita/al-Qor'an/opini al-Qor'an/16/06/02/o84u466-pancasila-sebagai-kalimatun-sawa
[121] Sherifa Zuhur, Saudi Arabia, Greenwood Publishing Group, 2011, page 80

strengthen Islamic and Arabic values. According to Mohamed A. Ramady, on the broader international stage, the Kingdom will continue to direct its foreign policy to be acting as a mediator and arbitrator in inter-Arab and Muslim national affairs.[122] Yet interestingly, it further underscores that members of the family should be brought up in accordance with the teachings of Islam,[123] thus automatically rejecting secular hedonistic lifestyle for years some of whom take on.

Meanwhile, in Iran with 99 percent of Muslims, the basic constitution of article 1 notes that the form of Iran's government is Islamic Republic, while article 5 evidently mentions that the responsibility of governing would be granted to a jurist during the occultation of Imam Mahdi.[124] In the introduction of the constitution, it has been also obviously highlighted that the constitution is a declaration of the social, cultural, political, and economic foundations of the Iranian society would be based on Islamic principles and norms that reflect the heartfelt desire of the Islamic community.

As cited earlier, given the fact that both countries have seen formalization of Islam in their basic constitutions, the implications would be very definite, not only in foreign policy identification and implementation that I would like to explore later, but also in identifying domestic policies. The ruling elites of each state are accordingly obliged to formulate, implement and monitor as well the implementation of Islamic ethics within their own societies, in which apart from adopting legal system, the governments would seek establishing official apparatus to sanction the agenda of monitoring, surveillance and vigilance of the society so as not to be contravening Islamic principles. Violence and anarchy in implementing such agenda sometimes apparatus take prove to have stirred fear and objection from society in respective countries. In foreign policy affairs, Islamic ideology would automatically narrow and widen both states in taking their respective foreign policy as it will give restrictions and draw boundaries as well as it would grant another agenda that is distinct from other states. Such uniqueness and distinction would be great impediment and challenge for both states in establishing international relations. Furthermore because of such an ideology, both states often pursue their foreign policies which are not transactional and reciprocal that would not bring any political and economic benefits to their people.

Meanwhile, one of the greatest implications of such a claim to be leader for Islamic world, is that for many years, both states have been centres and magnet of international students for studying Islam. For those with Sunni background, besides al-Azhar university in Cairo, a lot of Muslim youths throughout the world appear to be interested in continuing their studies in the holy two cities, Mecca and Medina. In the other hand, those with Shia background would prefer to study in Shia seminary school in holy city Qom city in Iran, along with Najaf city in Iraq. In this vein, reportedly in the wake of Islamic Revolution in Iran in

---

[122] Mohamed A.Ramady, The Saudi Arabian Economy, Policies, Achievements, and Challenges, Springer, 2010, page 485
[123] Madawi el-Rasheed, a History of Saudi Arabia, Cambridge University Press, Second Edition, page 167
[124] For further information, please see the Iranian basic constitution

1979, Indonesian young students vigorously were attracted to study Islam in Qom city, Iran as they were truly amazed with the fact that Islam, based on Iran's experience, could finally inspire political matters on the ground. Meanwhile, even since 17th century, Mecca and Medina were chosen by Indonesian students as main destinations for studying on Islam who successfully transmitted Islamic intellectuality to Malayan-Indonesia, particularly in relation with reformation of Islamic teachings, reconciliation and rapprochement between Sufism and Fiqh (Islamic law and jurisprudence).[125]

With Islam as an inseparable identity of the Kingdom and where Wahhabism ideology rose to prominence, Arab Saudi grants wider authorities to its Wahhabi clerics in some specific domestic affairs, in which the ruling elites will not able to intervene with. Yet in the other hand, the ruling political elites would have special authority and power which deny Wahhabi's intervention in identifying and guiding governmental policies. In fact, tradition to dividing and sharing power and authority into two, political and religious authorities, largely was practiced by both the first Saudi Kingdom founder and Wahhabism founder, and has been sustained until current days under the pledge of loyalty and allegiance of Wahhabi adherents to the King. The kingdom is always in dire need of the existence of Wahhabi to consolidate and strengthen its position as the government that is eager to accommodate Islamic interests and maintain its central position as the Custodian of two holy mosques, thus significantly avoiding the Kingdom from labelling secular and liberal state, and muffling much accusation and disappointment from Islamic world of having cordial relations with non- Muslim states. In turn Wahhabi would need the Kingdom's political support to disseminate and propagate its own unique teachings both at home and abroad despite long standing objection of international community. In this vein, the Kingdom is much convinced that Wahhabi would never seek regime change of monarchy, and require its loyalists to carry out resistance and opposition against the Kingdom's interests. Instead, the loyalists would endorse and support the Kingdom's sustainability and survival as long as it does not violate God's commands, even if the Kingdom strives to make reforms in social and cultural fields as we are inevitably witnessing nowadays carried out by Mohammad bin Salman, Saudi crown prince. Such a fact has been further asserted by more than eight fatwas and statements issued by Abdul Aziz Al ash-Sheikh Grand Mufti in 2017 that warn against disobeying the legitimate ruler, and preaching the virtues of allegiance to the current ruler. Additionally, one fatwa in March 2016 was issued by Grand Mufti stating it is binding upon the believer to love the ruler, defend him, and not to insult him.[126]

---

[125] Oman Fathurrahman, book review on Jaringan Ulama : Pembaharuan dan Rekonsiliasi dalam Tradisi Intelektual Islam di Dunia-Melayu-Indonesia by DR. Azyumardi Azra, Studia Islamika, Volume 11, No.2, 2004, page 372
[126] Abdullah Alaoudh, State-Sponsored Fatwas in Saudi Arabia, 3 April 2018, http://carnegieendowment.org/sada/75971

Moreover, the Saudi monarchy would never ignore the importance of (Wahhabism) Islamic identity in society as a pillar of stability and steadiness as Wahhabism always requires its followers to obey all rules and regulations the Kingdom issues, with no exception, despite Kingdom's tacit objection to the rigidity and inflexibility of the ideology that often prevents it from smoothening its diplomatic efforts on counter global terrorism and defending human rights issues before international community, thus justifying its rule by claiming to protect and propagate Islam, as the one true religion to the mankind. In this regard, it seems weird that Saudi Wahhabi clerics have no direct involvement in taking and identifying Saudi foreign policy when one of the main concerns of its foreign policy is to spread and facilitate such a ideological concept throughout the world, while identifying and monitoring substance of the concept shall be vested in those clerics.

Karen Elliot even further believed that such a perception on Islam is interestingly also asserted by Saudis given limited access to information, who see that al Saudi monarchy also constitutes the religious exemplar of an Islamic community of believers, [127] despite the fact that such perception may tremendously shrink at any given time depending on how much the Kingdom could create social and economic welfares to the society.

Yet, as a matter of fact, the Kingdom would provide their ulemas' special authorities as cited earlier for only three scopes: controlling the functions and roles of mosques widely founded in the entire Saudi territory; owning active roles in numerous cultural agendas, and educational sectors. Meaning that Islamic extremism of Wahhabism would be definitely reflected in social fields of Saudi by much inserting its Islamic knowledge and values into three aforementioned sectors. The ruling elites seem not to have right to make direct intervention to define Islam-nuanced programs of cultural and educational sectors since Kingdom significantly accentuates and upholds such substantial dividing between political and religious terrains. For instance, in the field of education, large intervention and authority of Wahhabi clerics could be evidently framed in identifying and guiding Saudi educational curricula, which Head of the Ministry of Education, a grandson of Wahhabism founder, has further Islamized university curricula and expanded religious faculties in Saudi.[128] In this vein, the royal Kingdom has never feared that one day Wahabbism could be propelling factor of any popular revolution that overthrows the regime as it believe that the ideology, unlike Shia along with active and confrontational contours, Wahabbism promotes to its adherents further passivity and blind allegiance to political rulers, in which they would never have any courage to question the legitimacy of those rulers.

As a consequence of the sharing powers between the dominant two houses/ families, el-Saud and el-Sheikh (often referred to the offshoots of Mohammad bin Abdul Wahab), it is hardly surprising that the King would not grant more authority to those clerics

---

[127] Karen Elliott House, Saudi Arabia, Its People, Past, Religion, Fault Lines and Future, Alfred A. Knopf, 2012 page 30
[128] Robert Lacey, Inside the Kingdom, Kings, Clerics, Modernists, Terrorists, and the Struggle for Saudi Arabia, Viking, page 52

out of the aforementioned ones. In this vein, the clerics would be viewed as non competent and right individuals to carry out any intervention to some specific issues and policies. Moreover such an argumentation was heavily endorsed by one famous Prophetic hadist, stating that " *You know more about your world*," implying that prophet's knowledge was limited too, and not necessarily covering all matters. For instance domestic political, economy and trade-related policies usually become a domain for the ruling elites to decide and determine, thus negating further any clerical intervention and contribution. It would also encompass the whole vital strategies and policies that relate to the survival of Kingdom and its sustainability such as succession issue among princes, foreign policy taking, and military field. In this vein, keeping away those fields from any clerical intervention has been taken as an effective strategy even during the initial years of modern Saudi by King Abdul Aziz, its founding father. [129]

According to McMillan, tradition of power and authority sharing between political and religious individuals has deeply overshadowed Saudi governmental system and structure to date, interestingly accepted unanimously by Saudi society that prefers to more focus on dealing with economic and social issues. However, despite having huge authority, apparently the Kingdom would have any right to control social issues whose authority is exclusively given to Wahhabi clerics in interpreting and adopting Islamic laws (often called Ijtihad) from the two divine sources, al Qoran and Sunnah of the Prophet. The creation and empowerment of the most -feared Sharia police or Mothawe in Arabic definition has been reflecting such an explicit control.[130]

Once again it would further showcase that Wahhabi clerics own definitely special status that could not be ignored by the Kingdom as the ideology had played a very prominent role to legitimize spiritually the conquering attempts carried out by the first Saudi founder, thus ushering him to successfully unify it under the el-Saud family, which in turn, giving much freedom and latitude for Wahhabi clerics to spread the ideology throughout the country. In its modern history. such robust and cordial relationships could be simply framed inter alia by the marriage between the two families of Ibnu Saud and Ibnu Abdul Wahab (Sheikh),[131] well evidenced by the marriage of King Abdul Aziz, the founder of modern Saudi with Tarf bin Abdullah el Sheikh, a descendant of Wahhabi founder, also a mother of King Faisal, the third Saudi king. Not only that, with the passage of time, despite no direct intervention with the succession of the kings, a clerical opinion constitutes a very important element in daily life of royal family. For instance, King Faisal still considered a clerical fatwa in transitioning the throne from Saud to him. King Khaled, king Faisal's

---

[129] Ellen R.Wald, Saudi Inc, the Arabian Kingdom's Pursuit of Profit and Power, Pegasus Book, New York London, page 136
[130] M.E.McMillan, From the First World War to the Arab Spring, Palgrave Macmillan page 197
[131] *Lindholm, Charles (2002) [1996]. The Islamic Middle East: Tradition and Change. John Wiley & Sons. hal 196*

successor is reported to have met the state religious authority every Tuesday, and his brother Fahd and his successor as well, continued that tradition.[132]

Therefore, it can be argued succinctly that Saudi foreign policy, like other state's common practice, would be identified and implemented based on genuinely strategic interests with a deep look to any regional and global dynamics. As such, it is undeniable that such a policy taken by the Kingdom would not take clerical opinions and decrees into consideration, although in both theory and practice, it is likely to collide with any Islamic and *Ummah* interests, or according to the clerical interpretations, it would even violate religious principles and values. As Karen Elliot further argued that princes of the kingdom significantly prefer to co-opt rather than to confront, to buy rather than to bully, to deflect rather to directly deny.[133] More interestingly, such perception has also affected issuing and identifying foreign policy that stands on reconciliation rather than confrontation, accommodation rather than isolation, soft diplomacy rather than hard diplomacy. Even with Iran, the main rival of the region, Arab Saudi has often preferred to solve its bilateral problems by exerting political and diplomatic ways and mechanisms, rather than taking hard approaches.

Furthermore, the Wahhabi governmental clerics are required deeply to display their loyalty to all royal decrees. Any decree issued by the King as the most authoritative political figure in Saudi, shall not be contested and objected by them under no circumstances, thus making the absoluteness of the Kingdom's authority more evident, as suggested by a Quranic verse of an-Nisa number 59 " *O you who believe! Obey God and obey the Messenger and those in authority among you.* Historically speaking, such blind loyalty of Wahhabi ardent followers has been the most effective component the Saudi founders fully harnessed in order to smoothen their political agenda to conquer territories and took power from local tribe leaders.

However, Islamic identity is totally inseparable from policies taken by the Kingdom. The prominent roles played by the clerics are reflected among others through issuing fatwas (clerical edicts) to endorse and espouse King's decisions, particularly to any case relating to foreign policy identification. Such Islamic legal opinions are issued to obtain spiritual dimension that any Saudi foreign policy taken would be justified and condoned automatically by the Islamic laws despite opposition and disapproval from other clerics who are apparently independent.

In addition, the issuance of clerical fatwas is necessary to carry out to endorse governmental measures towards any sensitive domestic issues that could endanger the existence of Saudi ruling. For instance, in further engaging with the dramatic event of holy

---

[132] Ellen R.Wald, Saudi Inc, the Arabian Kingdom's Pursuit of Profit and Power, Pegasus Book, New York London, page 138
[133] Karen Elliott House, Saudi Arabia, Its People, Past, Religion, Fault Lines and Future, Alfred A. Knopf, 2012 page 27

Mosque occupation dramatically perpetrated by hundreds of Islam militants led by fundamentalist Juhayman al-Otaybi in Mecca in November 1979, the Kingdom had to wait to take action until a fatwa legalizing for cracking down was issued.[134] Not only that, a King would like to deliberately use religious fatwas to encounter any critical opinions of Islamists and liberals at home. For instance, in 60s when the King assumed that pan- Arab Nationalism brought up vehemently by Egypt's leader, Gamal Abdul Naser posed an existential threat for the survival of kingdom and viewed the concept as a significant rival for Pan-Islamism built by Saudi Arabia, the King would support the clerics' initiative to counter such a revolutionary idea by financing the writing of a book named Critique of Arab Nationalism in the Light of Islam and Reality. The book alone had been distributed considerably into many Arab's states in the region.[135] Not only pan Arab Nationalism, such countering fatwas were needed to respond and counter aggressively the revolutionary ideas and principles prominently brought by Imam Khomeini in 1980s that affected perception and perspective of Shia minority group inside the Kingdom against the government's policies.

With the passage of time particularly in the aftermath of 9/11 tragedy and several terror acts at home, the Wahhabi clerics were inclined to support governmental policies regarding counterterrorism by condemning al-Qaeda terrorist network.

In the other hand, based on written agreement on mutual support, all ruling Kings would be demanded to accommodate numerous radical Wahhabi Fatwas, thus formulizing them as domestic policies that must be implemented within the society. Discriminative policies of Saudi toward Shia minority group during 20th century are arguably the implication of Wahhabi Ulema intervention to the policies by issuing fatwas which discredited Shia's existence in the eastern part of Saudi Arabia. For instance, the latest fatwa of 2017 announced by Saleh Fauzan, a member of the Council of Senior Scholars stated that anyone who doubts that the Shia followers are infidels would be considered an infidel. [136]

Nevertheless, when a king needs to accomplish the national interests and maintains the state's survival which appear to contravene the Islamic laws according to radical interpretation, such fatwas are eventually necessary to be issued flexibly in accordance with the Kingdom's policies. Such a fact has shown more precisely that the clerical positions and authorities must be inferior by putting them under the Kingdom's authority and control.

More interestingly, the validity and relevance of fatwas would be applied publicly if they are approved by the Council of Ministers or even by King himself. It means that such

---

[134] Marissa Allison, Militants Seize Mecca : The Effects of the 1979 Siege of Mecca Revisited, University of Mary Washington, page 3

[135] Nabil Mouline, The Clerics of Islam Religious Authority And Political Power in Saudi Arabia, Yale University Press page 126

[136] Abdullah Alaoudh, 3 April 2018, State-sponsored Fatwas in Saudi Arabia
http://carnegieendowment.org/sada/75971

fatwas are unlikely to have coercive power without prior State's approval[137] that would carry out further assessment and evaluation, thus perhaps including the kingdom's interest. No doubt, such a prior assessment would automatically undermine the objectivity and honesty of fatwas, thus gradually diminishing people's reliance to the respectable position of Ulemas.

Little wonder in fact, King would have a special privilege not always to abide by the fatwas and follow the religious advices. Indeed such a privilege could enable King to seek more appropriate fatwas issued by other Islamic clerics who perhaps live abroad whose fatwas would grant a legal justification to King to implement his domestic policies that are disapproved and discouraged by the Saudi clerics at home. For instance, in 2006 when king Abdullah had an intention to expand the capacity of Haram mosque in Mecca so as to accommodate more international pilgrims, he failed to find any fatwa from domestic Islamic clerics to justify his domestic measure. The King became disappointed, then asked for a fatwa from non-Saudi ulemas would give justification to such a decision. In 80s particularly in King Fahd's ruling, the Kingdom has been giving much effort to establish more cordial and friendly relations with USA. Such a strategy was pursued amid harsh criticism given by Abdul Aziz bin Baz, Saudi Grand Mufti who reportedly had issued a fatwa denouncing it because of the US firm stances in helping Israeli interests against Palestinians.[138]

Due to the significant role played by Saudi ulemas, in 1971 King Faisal initiated to found the Council of Senior Scholars that comprises seventeen senior ulemas and is headed by a senior Mufti. This institution constitutes the most vital institution which plays a role of being the main legislative board, besides the council of ministers, in addition to ideological reference for the kingdom family. In sum, to display Kingdom's desire to control more its ulemas, the government also established the Ministry of Justice and High Court Council at the same time.[139] Several decades later, in order to showcase the Kingdom's superiority over the position of Ulemas, the King also founded the High Council for Islamic Affairs in 1994 that functions to deal with numeral matters that require ulema's opinion. The institution has also authority to make review on many death penalty -related cases and other major crimes. The Ministry for Islamic Affairs, Endowment, Dawa and Guidance have been reportedly dominated by thousands ulemas who certainly own shared perspectives and missions with the Kingdom's.[140]

Not surprisingly, such institutionalization carried by the Kingdom, has a very significant impact to the objectivity of those co-opted clerics. Accordingly, they have to think twice before issuing any opinions/fatwas that seem critical to kingdom family's behaviours that may contradict Islam, particularly relating to the kingdom's lavish lifestyle. In this regard, the function of the ulemas is only limited to delivering their religious advices to the

---

[137] Opcit page 160
[138] Fatemeh Shayan, Security in the Persian Gulf Region, Palgrave Macmillan, page 91
[139] Ibid page 153
[140] Sherifa Zuhur, Saudi Arabia, Greenwood Publishing Group, page 96

elites. For instance, in 60s when the Kingdom decided to open a school for Saudi girls, Wahhabi ulemas severely defied such a decision, viewing that the school would certainly spread fitna (defamation) within the society. Then the ulemas had to approve the decision reluctantly, along with some conditions which included the accommodation of Wahhabi teaching into educational curricula, segregation based on gender status, appropriateness of clothing for the girls in the schools.[141]

As a matter of fact due to the consequence of power sharing between ruling elites and ulemas, in general the identification and implementation of Saudi foreign policy does not necessarily wait for any approval of Ulemas that accordingly could change substance of the policy. In the matters of foreign policy, separation between genuine political consideration and religious contemplation becomes more evident. Furthermore, the role of Ulema hereby is restricted only to endorse and support state's foreign policy by presenting legal argumentations so that the issuing of policies would have their spiritual legitimacy, thus eschewing secularization. In Islam such a policy making is well- known to be a legal concept named *Siyasah Syar'iya* (legal politics) postulating the allowance for a ruler to identify, formulate and issue his own decisions based on his genuine opinions, as long as they are not against with Islamic values. [142]

In other words, Saudi foreign policy frames a strategic outcome of the genuine assessment of the Kingdom without necessity to further consultation with the clerics. Therefore it is hardly surprising the foreign policy sometimes prompts profoundly a wide range of censures and criticisms addressed particularly by Saudi independent Islamists, due to their view on incompatibility of such policies to Islam. For instance, during the first gulf war in 1990, Saudi had initiative to ask the US to station its military personnel of around a half million in its territory due to the existential threat posed by Iraq that was likely to invade militaryly the Saudi territory after Kuwait, thus generating inevitable controversy among Islamists who viewed that such a decision would disgrace the holiness of Mecca and Medina cities. Apart from this, according to the Islamists, asking help and assistance from unbelievers to contain Iraq which is a Muslim country despite Shia majority (60%), is not religiously praiseworthy. In this long standing polemic and public perplexity, Wahhabi ulemas emerged and played a very significant role to issue a fatwa justifying and supporting the contraversial policy.

The principle of non-intervention of the governmental ulemas in identifying foreign policy does not mean necessarily diminish Islamic spirits completely from its foreign policy. Yet however, Islam has been inspiration for Saudi's global interaction that makes it unique and different from other Muslim Arab countries. It is unique given the fact that its neighbouring Arab states don't put Islamic interest as their basis for determining their own foreign policies, but rather national interests although Islam is the religion for the vast

---

[141] Fatemeh Shayan, Security in the Persian Gulf Region, Palgrave Macmillan, page 211
[142] David Commins, The Wahhabi Mission and Arab Saudi, IB Tauris, page 117

majority. Saudi, unlike Iran, has never "compelled" those countries to adopt Islam as identity for their states. Rather several Arab states have tended to give more emphasis on Arab nationalism/Pan Arabism or secular concept rather than Islamic one. However, Saudi has been very unique country and pragmatic which eventually harnessed Arab nationalism for engaging with two issues, Palestine against Israeli occupation and Iran against regional Arab states.

As elucidated earlier several times, Saudi Arabia has given emphasis on Islamic interest and Muslim countries as top priority of its foreign policy implementation. In fact, this Saudi approach has been taken since the first years of modern Saudi establishment in 1932 noting further that Islam has been among the most important elements in inspiring the creation of the country, not only that because the country is the cradle of Islamic civilization. As a matter of fact, before bin Saud the founder of modern Saudi, came back home from his exile in Kuwait in 1902, he had a steady communication with both the offshoots of the founder of Wahhabism and numerous Hambali school scholars. Obviously such intensive communications affected Ibn Saud's attitudes towards establishing solidarity and cooperation among Muslim countries. [143]

Little wonder the extreme loyalty and subjugation of those Wahhabi clerics have become the main concern of the criticism of the independent Islamic scholars who believe that some of the religious fatwas have been politicized and manipulated to be compatible with the kingdom's interests and aspirations in a bid to accomodate them. In this vein, Sa'ad al-Faqih, a Saudi prominent opposition living in exile, the clerics have lost their autonomy as they became a rubber stamp to royal decisions, thus calling for independent ulama whose authority derives from social base that negates the kingdom's interference.[144] As time went on, this phenomenon was sadly exacerbated by the royal decree in 2010 that the Council of Senior Scholars fully sponsored by Saudi government constitutes the only body that has permission to issue public fatwas, downgrading gradually the existing fatwas formulated by the independently competent ulemas who appear to be more moderate, democratic and friendly in interpretating Islam.[145] In addition, the royal decree could implicitly signify a legal justification to arrest those independent Islamic scholars, if regarded that their legal opinions, often called *Nasiha* (advice), would stir instability and insecurity in the region. Moreover in order to portray the significance and sacredness of the Council of Senior Ulemas in dealing with domestic affairs, in 2011 a Royal Decree has been issued

---

[143] Gregorry Kusach, Yelena Milkomian, *Tathawwaru Siyasate al-Kharijiye Saudiya Min Tasis daulat ila bidayatil islahat,* revised by Dr. Majid bin Abdul Majid Turki, Riyadh 1426 H/ 2005 M, page 27
[144] Madawi Al-Rasheed, Constesting the Saudi State, Islamic Voices from a New Generation, Cambridge University Press, page 244
[145] Abdullah Alaoudh, 3 April 2018, State-Sponsored Fatwas in Saudi Arabia
http://carnegieendowment.org/sada/75971

amending the press law to criminalize any criticism of Saudi Grand Mufti along with the Council.[146]

Furthermore according to Dr. Madhawi Rashed, an expert on Saudi history and sociology, such opposition brought by Islamist group in Saudi who often voices reforms inside the kingdom,[147] has its own uniqueness due to that it has grown amid the warm relations between the political elites and Wahhabi group who invariably claim on Shari'a implementation,[148] making it harder to synchronize perspectives on any issue among Islamic preachers and scholars (ulemas) who are supposed to be neutral. Moreover due to politically different vantage point, it further demonstrates clash of authority in issuing fatwas between the independent and dependent ulemas which accordingly would perplex Saudis to choose and follow.

Arguably, the role of Islam as ideology in determining Saudi foreign policy has been very significant, particularly when Saudi was ruled by King Faisal between (1964-1975), well known for being a descendant of main founder of Wahhabism. In addition, the King was deeply known for having more experience and familiarity with dealing and interaction with foreign states, even since his childhood, than the two former kings did. Although the duration of his tenure was very short (11 years), yet he obviously had initiated multiple unprecedented breakthroughs, even since he held position as crown prince in 1950s when he strongly proposed in 1956 that Islam shall play more prominent role in world's politics. The crown prince Faisal had always further believed that Islam as basis for Saudi state could also be applied in other states as Islam promised stability, security, discipline in Saudi Arabia.[149] Nevertheless such a proposal to prioritizing Islamic identity was not greatly welcomed by Muslim states which were inclined to accentuate the concepts of nationalism and socialism to be an effective panacea for their own problems, and not religion.[150]

With the passage of time, visionary Islamic views of the King successfully led him to accommodate more Islamic flavours and identities in his foreign policy when he ascended the throne in 1964. His position was able to render him much opportunity to explore and realize his long standing dreams when he was a crown prince. However, it does not mean the two former Kings did not accommodate and absorb Islamic interests to their own policies, mirrored evidently in defending Palestinian issues, etc, yet in the era of the Faisal's ruling, Islamic interest appeared more obvious, and was the main pillar in determining his

---

[146] Medea Benjamin, The Unjust Kingdom, Behind the US-Saudi Connection, OR books 2016, page 36
[147] Some of independent critical Islamists whose views often contravene the government ideas such as Shekh Safar ibnu Abdurrahman alHaqli, Salman al-Audah and Nasser bin Sulaiman al Umar have been put to Saudi jails. Their critics to the elite rules in 90s were reflected into two petitions, called Petition of religiosity and petition of advice.
[148] Madawi Al-Rasheed, Muted Modernist, the Struggle Over Divine Politics in Saudi Arabia, Oxford University Press, page 4
[149] Robert Lacey, Kerajaan Petrodollar Saudi Arabia, Pustaka Jaya, first edition, 1986, translated from its English original version the Kingdom, page 457
[150] ibid page 456

foreign policy. The King had given rise to more concrete Islamic breakthroughs and initiatives in politics and diplomacy, supported significantly by the kingdom's abundant oil income. For instance, it took only 6 months (December 1965-September 1966) that the King paid official visits to nine Muslim countries, including Iran, Jordanian, Sudan, Pakistan, Turkey, Morocco and Egypt.[151] Issues like Israel-Palestine conflict, arising of pan Arab Nationalism brought deeply by Gamal Abdul Naser, rivalry (cold war) between the two super powers of US and Soviet, and facing the fact that many Muslim countries were seeking and demanding their independence from colonial powers, were among the factors triggering King Faisal to engage more with Islam.

So by taking the aforementioned facts into consideration, one of the most considerable approaches that the King took was reviving the concept on Islamic insurgence (Pan-Islam) along with its spirits that could reach all Muslim societies throughout the world. Bearing in mind that his strong ambition was deeply encouraged by the abundant oil sale with remarkable price and later the passing away of his main regional rival, President Gamal Abdul Naser in September 1970, granting more space to the King to materialize his dream to become a leader for both Arab and Islamic world.[152] Pan Islam reintroduced by the King, had imbued Islamic world to get more conscious and sensitive towards unity and solidarity among Muslim states in dealing with myriad political, economic and social issues that afflicted Muslims during the time.

Therefore, in order to awake and generate Islamic spirit and prevent un-Islamic thoughts and ideologies from arising in international arena, in 1960s and 1970s several wider strategies and steps were taken by the King including co-establishing several national and international Islamic institutions such as Muslim World League (WML) in May 1962 and OIC (Organization of the Islamic Conference in 1969 that aimed to promote cooperation, solidarity and consciousness among the members, politically, socially and economically. OIC alone eventually had generated the birth of Islam Development Bank (IDB), multilaterally based financial institution in 1974 with its headquarter, like OIC, also in Jeddah city, Saudi Arabia.[153]

The WML, later explained in more detail, constitutes a non-state institution which is actively involved in cultural and educational programs and fund collection, that has been an umbrella for other small organizations. Its headquarter is in Mecca city, and interestingly many strategic positions were occupied by Ikhwanul Muslimin organization activists who once escaped from Egypt and Syria, attempting to preclude themselves from harsh repression and oppression conducted by despotic ruling regimes of the two states. Meanwhile the OIC poses a multilateral organization established to become a forum for foreign policy and political coordination among the Muslim countries members. Indeed the

---

[151] Ibid page 458
[152] Madawi el-Rasheed, a History of Saudi Arabia, Cambridge University Press, Second Edition, page 126
[153] Thomas Hegghammer, Jihad in Saudi Arabia, Violence and Pan-Islamism since 1979, Cambridge Middle East Studies 33 page 19

creation of the mentioned institutions endowed with Saudi financial support further proved that Wahhabism sect of Saudi has constituted an integral part of Islamic world that should be accepted by world's Muslim majority, and no longer an existential threat to other Sunni communities. Moreover, bringing Iran into membership of the OIC had further demonstrated the acceptance of Shia minority also as an integral part of the whole Islamic Ummah.

As time went on, since their establishments, both organizations have undergone disseminating information through media, in a bid to awake Islamic world's consciousness on Muslims' conditions in many parts of the world who had to face political and social pressures. Via magazines like *Akhbar al-Alam al-Islami* (Islamic World News) and *Majallat Rabithat al-Alam al-Islami (*Muslim World League Magazine*)*, Muslims in Morocco could get access to understand assorted situations and conditions of other Muslim people in Balkan, or in Southeast Asia. In reverse, through the publishing of such media, Indonesian Muslims could get an access to information to what was happening in Middle East region.[154] So it is hardly surprising, in King Faisal's leadership, Saudi Arabia has been home for around 250.000 Rohingya Muslims who fled Myanmar in 1960s, to avoid repressive and oppressive treatments from their own government. [155]

Another effort of Saudi that reflected Islamic interest accommodation globally is securitization of pan-Islam. For instance, in February 1979, Islamic Institute of Defence Technology in London, sponsored by OIC, held a conference with a title *"Security with focus on identification of methods and mechanisms in strengthening defence field in Islamic world."* In the same year, the Institute had also published a monthly magazine, named Islamic Defence Review. In 1980, OIC also adopted a resolution on security and solidarity in Islamic states stating for the first time that any security of each Muslim state would be main concern for all the members. In the next year, under the framework of OIC, the Committee of Islamic Security was founded. Not only theoretically, as a matter of fact, OIC had practically expressed its solidarity to any struggle carried out by Muslims to resist the colonial and imperialist powers and to fight against aggression including giving its unwavering supports to the Lebanese army against Israeli aggression in 1982, Muslim Somalia versus Ethiopia in 1984, Comoro against French colonialism in 1980s, Muslim Azerbaijan against Armenians in Nagorno Karabakh conflict in 1988 etc. Furthermore, in Afghanistan and Bosnia's conflicts, the state members of OIC had dispatched their military troops massively to both states to help them fight against alien power aggression.[156] Saudi Arabia, along with Pakistan and United Arabic Emirates, officially recognized the Taliban regime in Afghanistan, viewed as genuine Islamist group which sought promoting Islamic

---

[154] Ibid page 20
[155] Aya Batrawy, Rohingya crisis: Saudi Arabia stays silent on growing humanitarian disaster despite oil interests and historic ties, 21 September 2017, https://www.independent.co.uk/news/world/middle-east/rohingya-crisis-latest-saudi-arabia-burma-muslim-refugees-persecution-rakhine-oil-bangladesh-china-a7958716.html
[156] Opcit, page 21

Salafiya movement and countering communism in the region.[157] In addition, in order to prevent spreading the godless communism ideology profoundly brought by Soviet Union in some regions including South Yemen, Horn of Africa and Soviet's naval presence in the Indian ocean in 1980, Saudi Arabia had viewed necessary to establish an alliance with the US.[158]

Saudi Arabia, if compared with Iran and Indonesia, has given more concrete contributions in making mediation and reconciliation of several conflicts that involve Muslim nations. For instance, the monarch state had initiated the Taif Agreement signed in Taif, Saudi Arabia in 1989 to end civil war in Lebanon. Saudi Arabia also had initiated the Mecca agreement in 2007 to bring Hamas and Fatah political parties into internal reconciliation.

Still in most recent years, in security field, in order to prevent terrorism from spilling over into the region much prompted by terrorist groups such as ISIS and al-Qaeda, and curb Iranian influence in the region, in 2015, Mohammad bin Salman, Saudi Minister of Defence Affairs and also Crown Prince, had announced the creation of the Islamic Military Alliance to Fight Terrorism (the Islamic NATO/ Islamic Military Alliance). Such an alliance of defence has opened a joint operation centre in Riyadh, capital of Saudi Arabia that has already been joined by 36 members.[159] Besides, a strong initiative to launch military attacks by King Salman to curb Houthi rebellion in Yemen in March 2015 was profoundly supported and endorsed by the Kingdom's Islamists, inevitably viewed to be bringing Islamic interests, in which even Salman al-Awda, the most prominent Saudi Islamist preacher currently jailed due to his political opposition to the kingdom, gave religious justification for the killing of Shia Houthis, largely supported by Iran.[160] Suddenly Arab Saudi has already transformed to become Sunni community patron in engaging with some clashes tremendously provoked by Shia militias who receive Iran's long running financial and military supports.[161] It has been also reported that Saudi Arabia has continued providing the material and political supports to the Syrian rebels who oppose Bashar Assad administration vehemently supported by Iran. Arab Saudi is much aware that Iran poses an existential threat, not only for Arab's region, but also world's Islam community.

In earlier years in November 2008, in order to promote Saudi tolerance and inclusivity to other different religious followers before international community, Saudi had initiated Interfaith Dialogue in the UN building in New York, believed to be presenting itself

---

[157] Wu Yungui, The Influence of Islami Over the Foreign Policies of Contemporary Islamic Countries, Journal of Middle Eastern and Islamic Studies (in Asia) Volume 5, No.3, 2011, page 4
[158] Tim Niblock, Saudi Arabia, Power, Legitimicay and Survival, Routledge Taylor and Francis Group, 2006, Page 112
[159] Fadi A.Haddadian, the Future of the Islamic NATO, 13 Juni 2017, foreignpolicyblogs.com
[160] Toby Matthiesen, the Domestic sources of Saudi Foreign Policy : Islamists and the state in the wake of the Arab Uprisings, Working Paper, August 2015, page 8
[161] David Schenker, The Shift in Saudi Policy, 10 February 2016, https://www.washingtoninstitute.org/policy-analysis/view/the-shift-in-saudi-foreign-policy

as the leader of all muslim community, [162] that largely promotes tolerance and moderation to the world, repudiating the long standing assumption that Saudi has been intentionally spreading its extreme Wahhabi ideology around the world.

In addition to the abovementioned steps, in order to halt more aggressive Arab nationalism ideas by Egypt and communism brought by Soviet Union that presumably influenced many Saudi civilians, king Faisal had allowed many members of Ikhwanul Muslimin organization activists who fled Syria and Egypt to live in Saudi. During their stays in Saudi, they were empowered and absorbed as religious teachers by the Kingdom in which accidentally was lack of competent human resources. Not surprisingly, they succeeded to insert the radical ideas of Ikhwhanul Muslimin group to the already-modernized educational curricula in 1970s. In result, such radicalized curricula succeded to some extent in shaping radical and fundamentalist young Saudis to be provoked by the Kingdom itself easily to carry out Jihad in several countries. According to Stephanie Lacroix, the first generation of extremist group in Saudi was the result of the mixture between Ikhwanul Muslimin and Wahhabi ideas. Moreover, in order to showcase sympathetic attitude to the Islamists' struggles, the King once asked President Gamal Abdul Nasser to grant his amnesty to Sayyed Qotb, a prominent activist of Ikhwanul Muslimin, so that he could circumvent the execution.[163]

In short words, King Faisal significantly succeeded to found multilateral institutions that aim at reviving and reinvigorating Islamic spirits that would awaken Muslim society's consciousness and understanding on numerous world's issues, ranging from Palestinian cause until Kashmir polemic that involved Pakistan and Afghanistan as well, and Apartheid implementation in South Africa which definitely hampered Muslim minority group. Not only that, under the Faisal's leadership, the kingdom had successfully become an important player both regionally and internationally, even prior to the rising up of world's oil price in 1973-1974. Furthermore, based on Newsweek report in 1977, Saudi Arabia was estimated to have granted financial contributions of millions dollars to several Muslim states including Egypt, Jordan, Syria, Pakistan, Sudan etc...[164]

Nevertheless, the King's efforts to revive Islamic spirits and identities in international politics have been facing challenges and obstacles. Saudi, always associated with its attempts to spreading radical Wahhabism that differs theologically from that of the vast majority of world's Muslims, has to convince the others and prove them that Wahhabism rigid ideology poses one of the numerous Islamic Sunni theologies that will never try to create chaos and instability within society.

---

[162] Karen Elliott House, Saudi Arabia, Its People, Past, Religion, Fault Lines and Future, Alfred A. Knopf, 2012 page 218
[163] M.E.McMillan, From the First World War to the Arab Spring, Palgrave Macmillan page 197
[164] Rachel Bronson, Thicker Than Oil, America's Uneasy Partnership with Saudi Arabia, Oxford University Press, 2006 page 128

As a matter of fact, with the passage of time, because of the advance and cutting-edge technology and penetration of globalization as well as existing demands, Wahhabi Ulemas were eventually compelled to be more flexible in behaviour by opening their interaction with other World's ulemas; and gradually started to accept other 'different' Sunni thoughts. Even since 1950s the Wahhabi Ulemas had a positive perception that other Sunni societies would be considered 'believers' that deserve support and protection from the Kingdom. In 1954, for the first time in Saudi modern history, such a formal recognition was obviously shown when Senior Mufti Mohammad bin Ibrahim convened a formal meeting with other Sunni ulemas such as Mufti of Egypt, Hasanyn Mohammad Makhluf and Tunisian scholar from Maliki school, Mohammad Taher Ashur. [165]

As concrete evidence of pro-Islamic interest in Saudi foreign policy, since the creation of modern kingdom until current days, its foreign policy has been focused on the establishment of relations with Muslim Arab states in Gulf territory, then with Arab States in middle east and North Africa, and then with Muslim states of the world.[166] As such in theory, opening cordial relations with other states bilaterally and regionally for Saudi must contain Islamic basis that Islam would be paramount component to be Saudi consideration in guiding and driving its foreign policy.

In reality, due to political dynamics of the region, Saudi has also proved that it also keeps establishing and maintaining good relations with non-Muslim countries.[167] Yet in theory, such a relationship has a secondary nature, not a priority, and would occupy its short term goal achievement, that as long as Saudi interests persist, relationship with those non Muslim countries would be pursued. In this regard, Saudi rulers have always believed that Islam poses an inseparable identity for Saudi society and a unifying force of various tribes and clans in Saudi peninsula. Therefore, the accomplishment of Islamic interest in its foreign policy would equally mean the implementation of basic Saudi nation's aspiration.

Meanwhile, the priority circle of Iran's foreign policy would encompass neighbouring countries, then Middle East region, then Islamic world, then the third world and remaining countries.[168] For Iran, such a concentrated foreign policy practically would not negate and overlook three ultimate goals that Iran has always pursued since its creation in 1979, namely internal consolidation of power, export of Islamic revolution, and proposing pan-Islamism[169] promoted vehemently by the main founding father, Imam Khomeini in 1980s. For Iran, the existence of neighbouring states, particularly the ones whose populations are mostly Shia adherents, could be effective gateways in spreading its revolutionary Shia

---

[165] Thomas Hegghammer, Jihad in Saudi Arabia, Violence and Pan-Islamism since 1979, Cambridge Middle East Studies page 33

[166] The Foreign Policy of the Kingdom of Saudi Arabia, www.mofa.gov.sa,

[167] Ibid page 25

[168] Dr, Manocheher Mohammadi, *Ayendeye Nezame Baynal Melali Va Siyasate Khareji Jomhoriye Islami Iran*, Ministry of Foreign Affairs, Tehran, Summer 1387, page 184

[169] Karl Yambert, the Contemporary Middle East, A Westview Reader, Third Edition, Westview Press, 2013, Page 346

ideology throughout the world as what we have been witnessing nowadays. The two latter priorities further signify an Islamic identity to become Iran's high concern in defining and identifying its foreign policy, particularly with Muslim states, despite the fact that following Imam Khomeini's death in June 1989, such prioritizing has little faded.

Since four decades ago, Iran has been attempting to give its contribution politically and economically in Islamic world. The Islam–nuanced characteristics such as Islamic culture, Islamic regulations, Islamic laws and ethics are among the important elements that determine the identification of its ideological foreign policy. An aggressive and frontal Iran's foreign policy driven significantly by Imam Khomeini's guidelines, was trying to obtain Islamic world's legitimacy as a manifestation of the most important political Shia doctrine of Imam Mahdi occultation. [170] Under the concept of Revolution Export, Iran has had a full ambition to share its own sacred experience to other states that would achieve the implementation of justice and the annihilation of injustice.[171]

When most governments in Muslim countries in co-opting the prominent Islamic clerics attempt at subjugating their authority and function before the authority of their governments, thus issuing legal opinions confirming and supporting governmental policies, the Islamic Republic of Iran is perhaps the only state in the world that tries to put the religious authority proportionally since Iran has never acknowledged partition between politics and religion in daily aspects. Therefore, it is not surprising that Islamic identity in each of its foreign policy taking would be always embedded, claiming that its foreign policy taken for achieving Islamic and Muslim interest would be tremendously inherent. All this in fact has given more self confidence to Iran to propagate and spread its unique values and principles throughout the world, even by using any mechanisms that practically would contradict the international laws, and prompt worsening its bilateral relations with other states.

As cited earlier, constantly hostile attitude of Iran towards US and Israel constitutes strong evidence on implementation of Islamic-nuanced foreign policy since Muslim countries have shared vision and vantage point that Israel is an illegal occupying power to Palestinian land. In this vein, Iran has invariably supported Palestinian struggles in order to gain their independence, and routinely granted its financial assistance to a handful of Palestinian militant movements like Hamas and Jihad Islam. Palestinian issue for Iran has been a crucial issue that can't be separated from its foreign policy, which it seems ready to sacrifice anything else to help those oppressed people nonetheless sharp criticisms and objections from Iranians. Most startlingly, this matter of how Iran is much willing to embroil itself in Palestinian cause, thus sacrificing its own national interest was actually reaffirmed by one lecture delivered in 2015 by Hassan Nasrullah, the incumbent leader of Lebanese

---

[170] Fakhreddin Soltani dan Reza Ekhtiari Amiri, Foreign Policy of Iran after Islamic Revolution, research gate Januari 2010 page 199

[171] Vahid Noori, Status Seeking and Iranian Foreing Policy : The Speeches of the President at the United Nations, Iranian Review of Foreign Affairs, Volume 3 No 1 edisi musim semi tahun 2012 page 132

Hezbollah organization, pointed out that Iranian rulers have already sacrificed their national interests for the sake of Islam Ummah.[172]

Not only that, Iran has highly kept an assumption that Islamic Ummah which surpasses any restriction and constrain resulted by the creation of national borders of the states, shall be given priority over the concept of modern states introduced by the secular Westphalia Treaty in 17th century. For Iran, Islamic Ummah would never acknowledge the borders of the states' territories given the fact that Islam seen as a universal religion, shall be a force to unite multiple ethnics and nations in this world. Islamic Ummah is the entity par excellence that would guaranty welfare and bring in stability and peace in the world. Furthermore, Iran has often criticized that the West-made treaty as it clearly has ignored the main elements of Islamic ethics such as justice, truth, discrepancy between good and evil manners, etc.[173] So little wonder, Iran has had a strong perception that all treaties and agreements signed and adopted by Iran prior to the Islamic Revolution had embodied Zionism's vicious conspiracy against Islam.[174]

Islamic idea and aim at reaching to the Islamic unity in all aspects that are underlined evidently in article number 9 and 10 of the basic constitution, has a tremendous impact to the identification of Iran's foreign policy that is demanded to realizing Islamic unity *(Vehdat Ummat Islamiah)*. The significance of Islamic unity in Iranian foreign policy taking was once affirmed by Imam Khomeini implicitly that disunity and schism of Islamic world between Sunni and Shi would be more dangerous than nationalism.[175] As a matter of fact, the aspect of justice enforcement in Iran's foreign policy as reflected in article number 154 has been also inspired by Islamic Shia traditions and cultures, particularly under the framework of the support of oppressed people.[176] Therefore it is not surprising that Iran, like Saudi Arabia, significantly would put much attention towards numerous international issues that involve the interests of Islamic Ummah.

In Iran's diplomatic world, particularly under Ahmadinejad leadership (2005-2013), the establishment of bilateral relations with Asian and African states which have huge number of Muslim community was preferred and tremendously pursued. The foreign strategy taken by this ultra conservative president ostensibly differs from that of under Mohammad Khatami leadership era (1997-2005) from reformist faction who tried to drive its foreign policy in a rational way.

---

[172] Please look at to the Arabic lecture given by Hassan Nasrollah in 24 October 2015 broadcasted by Press TV, Iran's national media.
[173] Ahmad Sadeghi, Genealogy of Iranian Foreign Policy : Identity, Culture and History, the Iranian Journal of International Affairs, IPIS, page 10
[174] www.m.awsat.com, 27 Juli 2018
[175] Frederic Wehrey, Beyond Sunni and Shia, the Roots of Sectarianism in a Changing Middle East, Oxford University Press, 2107, page 96
[176] Alireza Firozi dan Sayyed Jalal Dehgani Firozabadi, Diplomasi Umumi Jumhuri Islami Iran dar Dorene Usulgharayi, Jurnal Ravabethe Khareji, tahun ke-4 nomor 2 edisi musim panas 1391, page 87

Furthermore, establishing better relations with African and Latin America states was also materialized by Ahmadinejad who sought those countries to be the potential targets for spreading Iranian and Shia revolutionary influence among the societies. The shared visions of anti US were the main consideration for Iranian foreign policy under Ahmadinejad to grant more focus on those Latin America states despite far distance. In addition, Iran under the Ahmadinejad's presidency proved to have had a confrontational approach towards West that was accused of having interfered with Islamic Ummah affairs. Ahmadinejad often used the podium of United Nations General Assembly held annually in September to voice Islamic principles, cultures and Iranian revolution, as well as persuade the world's community to isolate Israel from international arena.[177]

However, unlike Saudi Arabia, Iran has not yet been considered as initiator state in establishing Islam-nuanced organizations with Muslim state members. The limitation of movement of Iran arguably due to Shia ideology that most Muslim countries do not believe and instead accuse it for having covert agenda to convert their own societies into Shia. In sum, Iranian frontal and confrontational approaches that may drive Iran to be isolated politically and economically before international community could also pose a main obstacle for establishing such organizations. For instance, Iran is not a member of World Trade Organization to date despite its vehement desire. In some peaceful negotiations, Iran's participation for mediating has been rejected. In contrast, Iran is an active member in D-8 Organization for Economic Cooperation since its establishment in 1996 in Turkey, along with other members of Muslim countries with large populations and economy such as Bangladesh, Egypt, Nigeria, Indonesia, Malaysia, Pakistan and surely Turkey as its initiator of the organization.

Yet, Iran like Saudi Arabia, has been actively hosting many international Islamic events in the fields of politics, economy and socio-culture by inviting largely foreign participants who mostly have the shared vision and view with Iran on the issues. For any international event, Iran would mobilize its fully controlled national media as well as Iran-affiliated foreign media to blow up and cover significantly those events so as the results and conclusions to be heard by international community. For instance, Iran holds annually the international competition of al-Qor'an recital that is usually joined by hundreds of Muslims coming from numerous countries. For Iran, along with the support of enormous budget allocation, such an event is extremely crucial to be held in order to avert Muslims' perception that al-Qoran of Shia version is different from that of in Sunni world. As a matter of fact, some of Shia clerics further believe that current holy Qoran that Muslims recite is not yet complete. Not only that, Iran proved to have often hosted various international conferences to support Palestinians by inviting many Palestinian politicians and scholars, along with the emphasis on "one state solution" for solving the issue, that I would like to explore more in another chapter. Several conferences and seminars on counter-terrorism

---

[177] Fakhreddin Soltani dan Reza Ekhtiari Amiri, Foreign Policy of Iran after Islamic Revolution, research gate Januari 2010 page 204

are regularly held, in order to reaffirm assumption that peaceful Islam is not associated with terrorism, thus strongly condemning radicalism and extremism in religiosity that may inspire justifying the terrorist acts, as well as to reassure that Iran is not like what western countries view negatively that Iran is supporting global terrorism.

Faced with the fact that both countries annually allocate their special budget only to materialize and accomplish Islamic interests in which they also actively give their financial supports under the framework of full scholarships to young Muslims of the world, and to build specific places in large scale for developing Islamic activities throughout the world like building Islamic schools, mosques, charitable institutions, centres for Islamic culture and education. In Sum, they have also employed and offered jobs in both states-affiliated institutions to multiple foreign student graduates of their Islamic universities. Besides, since many years Iran and Saudi Arabia have also granted intensively financial contributions to Muslim countries struck by natural disasters and humanitarian tragedies.

Iran's sincere intention to give more contribution to Islamic world has also been realized through its proposal to create camps which reflect the united Islam Ummah. In reality, the idea alone had constituted one of the most important pillars of Iranian foreign policy during Iran-Iraq war in 1980-1988 as Iran was greatly worried of polarization of Muslim states as ramification of existing sharp ideological rivalry between American and Soviet Union. The unification of Islamic *Ummah* was regarded an effective means as alternative to synchronize and coordinate various perspectives of world's Muslims in engaging negative implications of such a rivalry. The almost impossible idea was certainly endorsed by Imam Khomeini by promising to driving Iran to initiate the realization of the mentioned camp,[178] triggered by consequences of its self-claim of being a leading state for Islamic world.

Apart from this, as a matter of fact, the Islamic resurrection was long developed by Imam in 1960s when he overtly defined himself as a Muslim, rather than an Iranian, implying that he was preferred to be religious instead of being a nationalist with significant pride of Persian empire and ethnicity. He himself, despite much curiosity of the scholars on his originality, often mentioned Iranian society as 'Muslim people' instead of 'Iranian / Persian people' while advocating them to preserve Islamic traditions and cultures.[179]

One of the greatest contributions that has been deeply claimed to be given for Islamic world' interests in early years of the establishment of Islam Republic was its strong depiction on the military war between Iran and Iraq in 1980s as a holy war carried out by Iran against the unbelievers of secular Baath party in Iraq, assumed by Iran to have acted repressively to Iraqi Shia community group. Iran further believed that Saddam Hussein had a

---

[178] DR Sayyed Jalal Dehgani Firozabadi, Siyasat Khareji Jomhori Islam Iran, Markaz tahqeq va to'see olome insane page 352
[179] Christin Marchall, Iran's Persian Gulf Policy, From Khomeini to Khatami, Routledge Curzon Taylor and Francis Group, page 12

vicious plan to topple down the newly born Islamic government. Therefore, following the recapturing of Khoramshar town of Iran from Iraqi military force after two year tireless fighting since 1980, thus leading Saddam Hussein to announce ceasefire, Imam Khomeini decided to resume the war by the reason of defending on and preserving Islam from Saddam Hussein's ambition who, based on Imam Khomeini's assumption, intended to decline Islamic values and downgrade the Islamic Republic before international arena, by replacing them with un-Islamic liberal and secular systems.[180] Furthermore such a controversial decision was the reflection of Supreme Leader's view that waging war against unbelievers is totally legitimate as he further believed that conquering non-Islamic territories would equal to defending the principle of God's unity and Islam, thus categorizing the war as defensive war.[181] Even Imam Khomeini himself had once stated that the war along with all sacrifice was a grace of God.[182]

In recent years, Iran often has claimed that its military intervention and operation in some countries of the region has been propelled by heartfelt and noble goal of the founding fathers of Islamic regime as a mechanism to defend and maintain the Islam world's interests from any forms of global arrogance and imperialism. Furthermore, Iran also has been convinced that the implementation of its foreign policy would absolutely bring in benefits and goodness for Islamic world. In this vein, in each single step in international political arena, this theocratic state would be eager to associate its entire measures with goal accomplishment of Islamic interests. In the other hand, United States as well as Israel would be inevitably assumed as political enemies, not only for Iran, but also for entire Muslim world, or any world's state which shares the vision and perspective.

For Iran, its undeniable achievement of nuclear energy technology constitutes a great achievement, not only for Iran, but also for entire Islamic world which mirrors Moslem's competition and capability in parallel with the West in the field of technologic development. For Iran its constant military intervention in the region equipped with sophisticated weaponry and huge budget allocation constitutes strategic mechanisms to take leadership of the Islamic world.[183] Furthermore, Iran, as what President Ahmadinezhad had once stated, believes that its nuclear program has spiritual dimension as it operates under the control of the Hidden Imam Mehdi who has full control over the world.[184] In

---

[180] Ibid page 150, interestingly at the same time, Saddam Hussein also portrayed Imam Khomeini as unbeliever and despotic leader who did not deserve preaching on Islam to Arab people. Furthermore, Saddam also likened Iran-Iraq war as Qadisiyah war that occurred in 637 AC when Muslim Arab troops led by Saad Abi Waqqas succeeded to defeat Zoroastrian Persian troops led by General Roustam. Please for further information, refer to Arshin Adib Mogahaddam, the International Politics of the Persian Gulf, Routledge Taylor & Francis Group page 36

[181] Mehdi Khalaji, Apocyptic Politics, on the Rationality of Iranian Policy, the Washington Institute for Near East Policy, January 2008, page viii

[182] www.imam-khomeini.ir

[183] Frederic Wehrey, Beyond Sunni and Shia, the Roots of Sectarianism in a Changing Middle East, Oxford University Press, 2107, page 104

[184] Ibid page 26

addition, Iran has also simply claimed that any measure or action which harms Iran's reputation, automatically it will disgrace all Islamic world's reputation.[185] Even in the official website of Ayatollah Ali Khamene'i, he is referred to not as the Supreme Leader of Iran, but more widely as the Supreme Leader of all Muslims. [186]

The Authority of Iranian Supreme Leader and Saudi King in Determining Foreign Policy

In the theocratic state like Iran, Supreme Leader (a competent figure who functions as Vali Faqih), has the most central role in taking and determining each policy, both domestically and internationally. Such a measure in fact has been underpinned by Shia Imamate faith that stipulates any governance that exists after the death of Prophet (Peace be upon Him) and the twelve Infallible Imams would unlikely have legality and religious justification. Yet for Shia followers particularly the Twelvers, the absence of Imams in the wake of the major occultation of Imam Mahdi as the last Imam, does not necessarily eliminate obligation to establish an ideal state that could be created by only several competent and eligible Islamic jurists *(Fuqaha)*. Therefore, unsurprisingly the function of Vali Faqih will cover all human's life dimensions with no exception whose authority would include domestic and foreign affairs.

In Iran, similar to any practice of other countries, several government institutions to deal with foreign affairs have been founded, in which the only main difference with that of in other states lies on the existence of Vali Faqih or Supreme Leader. Supreme Leader in Shia political doctrine functions as a representative of the occulting last Imam until He re-emerge in the world. For this reason, Supreme Leader would be automatically given prerogative rights under the shadow of his power absoluteness that can't be owned by other clerical rulers, even by *Marja'e taqleed* (source of emulation). Under this concept, it is asserted obviously that there is no separation between religious and profane affairs due to comprehensive authority of Supreme Leader, in which Arabic word 'Fiqh' taken from 'Vali Faqih' implies the understanding of both religious and non-religious affairs based on the interpretation of al-Qoran and Hadits.

Arising from such a belief of the Occultation, the concept of Velayat Faqih (authority/guardianship of the jurist) that inspired the establishment of Islamic Iran emerged as an inevitable force for Iranian political system in 1979 following the outbreak of revolution that unseated Pahlavi dynasty. The doctrine of *Velayat Faqih,* developed first by Imam Khomeini and long inspired by reformists of Sunni movements in other countries like Mohammad Rashid Ridha (1865-1935) and later Abu Ala Maududi (1904 – 1979) who proposed Islamic government instead of secular form, has been the most strong evidence of combination of Islamic ideology and political system of governance. It obviously constitutes

---

[185] Karim Sadjadpour, Reading Khamenei : The World View of Iran's Most Powerful Leader, Carnegie Endowment for International Peace, page 21
[186] Ibid page 22

the central axis of contemporary Shi'a political thought, particularly to Shi'a Imamite, that succeeded to render theocratic character to the newly born state.[187]

Most startlingly, Vali Faqih/Supreme Leader, the figure who holds the authority of Velayat Faqih, is often believed to be the only representative of Imam Mahdi during His major occultation on the earth as it is highly believed that all rulers in the world are considered illegitimate, thus leading a shocking perception that even establishing interaction with those leaders/rulers could be deemed forbidden.[188] Accordingly a competent Faqih both religiously and politically shall be introduced to rule people until He re-emerges to rule the world justly as Shia followers hope to accelerate his arrival to take over all of the existing political systems. As a matter of fact, since its establishment four decades ago, Iran has been ruled by two Supreme Leaders, Imam Khomeini (the founding father of Islamic Republic) and Ali Khamene'i (incumbent one), contentious figure seen as far less capable than the former one, particularly in religious affairs.

Practically the concept regarded as an ideology of the state profoundly initiated two decades prior to the Revolution, had constituted the core system of clerical rulers in such a way that changing it, will change automatically the entire political system of Islamic Republic of Iran.[189] In fact, the doctrine that seemingly is anathema to any external criticisms, particularly those related to questioning his absolute authority, the principles of the revolution, and even non-elected bodies under his control that might have its legal consequences,[190] implies more power absoluteness than the Prophet did who still kindly accepted criticisms from His companions. However, Ali Khameini once issued a fatwa noting that there is no any difference between acknowledging the ruling jurist's authority and that of the authority of the Prophet and infallible Shiite Imams. [191] In this vein, according to Naser Ghobadzadeh, Velayat Faqih is something created by Almighty God, although his appointment should be determined through an election held by the Assembly of Experts. Therefore, little surprising as he noted, that all government officials must get his approval to avoid them from labelling as *Taghut* (oppressive government). [192]

---

[187] ,According to Shia's faith, there are two times of His occultation, first, small occultation occurred from 874 till 941 AC after the death of His father. While He was in minor occultation, four deputies of him were appointed to become bridge of communication with Imam Mahdi. They are Usman bin Said Al-Amri Samman, Mohammad ibn Usman ibn Said al-Amiri, Husayn ibn Ruh and Ali ibn Mohammad al-Samuri. The second major occultation was estimated to have happened in 941 AC. https://www.al-islam.org/shia-political-thought-ahmed-vaezi/what-wilayat-al-faqih

[188] John L. Esposito, Lily Zubaidah Rahim, Naser Ghobadzadeh, The Politics of Islamism, Diverging Visions and Trajectories, Palgrave Macmillan, 2018, page 53

[189] The case of Hasheem Aghajari in November 2002 sentenced to death due to his indirect criticism to the absolute power of Velayat Faqih is a good example.

[190] En.radiofarda.com, 11 September 2017

[191] Mehdi Khalaji, The Future of Leadership in the Shiite Community, the Washington Institute For Near East Policy, year 2017, page 55

[192] John L. Esposito, Lily Zubaidah Rahim, Naser Ghobadzadeh, The Politics of Islamism, Diverging Visions and Trajectories, Palgrave Macmillan, 2018, page 56

Furthermore, as Imam Khomeini had explicitly stated in a letter openly addressed to Ali Khamene'i in 1988 one year prior to his death, that the establishment of the government based on Velayat Faqih is on the top priority over any other Islamic obligations, such as prayers, fasting and pilgrimage to Mecca and constitutes the most important divine rule prior to all divine legal rules.[193] In sum, he has special authority to change the legality of Islamic Pillars if they are regarded against with the Islamic interests.[194] Even the loyalists further believe that any violation and infringement to the laws issued by Velayat Faqih would be automatically equal to the violation of God's laws and Imam Mahdi.[195]

The implementation of the doctrine has influenced significantly a wide range of Iranian life matters politically, socially and economically. The doctrine implies that the authority of Supreme Leader will include all matters related to religion (Ibadah and Moamala/Following Islamic Beliefs and Practises- its commands, prohibitions, halal and haram), and non-related religious matters including many issues not mentioned explicitly in al-Qoran and Sunna[196] such as identification of foreign and economic policies etc. The absolute power of Supreme Leader, despite amid sharp criticism by scholars,[197] is legally justified by the basic constitution, particularly in article 5 stating evidently that during the absence (ghayba) of his holiness, the Lord of the Age, May God all mighty hasten his appearance, the sovereignty of the command [of God] and religious leadership of the community [of believers] in the Islamic Republic of Iran is the responsibility of the faqīh who is just, pious, knowledgeable about his era, courageous, and a capable and efficient administrator, as indicated in Article 107.[198] Not only this, his absolute authority is often regarded equal to that of the Prophet or 12 Imams in which his decrees are binding on everyone and have coercive power that must prevail over any other subsidiary Islamic standards or laws. Even Imam Khomeini himself further believed that his theory that implies such large authority to the ruling jurists, goes beyond any law.[199] Therefore, it is not

---

[193] Ibid page 37

[194] Imam Khameyni' letter addressed to Imam Khamenei in 1988. For further content, please visit www.khameini,ir, Shahife Imam, volume 20 page 452.

[195] *Takhalofe az Farmane Vali Faqih Mokhalafet ba Farman Khoda va Imam zamane ast*, 27 April 2011, http://aftabnews.ir/vdccepqsi2bqio8.ala2.html

[196] (the way of life prescribed as normative for Muslims on the basis of the teachings and practices of Muhammad and interpretations of the Al-Qor'an)

[197] Among critical scholars are   Ezzatollah Sahabi, Ayatollah Na'ini, Hojjati Kermani who implied that impossibility of Supreme leader's knowledge to cover all the human being matters. Neil Shelvin, Velayat Faqih in the Constitution of Iran : the Implementation of Theocracy page 370

[198] For further information, please refer to Iranian basic constitution that has been adopted in 1979 and later amended in 1989

[199] Mehdi Khalaji, Tightening the Reinns, How Khamenei Makes Decisions, the Washington Institute for Near East Policy, March 2014, page 14

surprising that the judiciary, legislative and executive branches of government, armed forces and media are under the control of his authority. [200]

In this regard, Mehdi Khaleji further argued that the doctrine of Velayat Faqih endowed with absolute authority, both theoretically and practically contradicts the changeable Islamic Jurisprudence (fiqh) itself since the doctrine would negate and rebut any other Islamic law interpretation and other Islamic jurists authority, as the only Supreme Leader's opinion could prevail. Such a doctrine as mentioned previously, also sparked oppositions and objection among Shia clerics since Imam Khomeini had tried to create a religious justification for putting aside Islamic law (Fiqh). Therefore, little wonder, Mehdi Khaleji believed that the regime's interest is much preferred to even all of the Islamic laws[201] as Imam himself once stated that safeguarding the regime is a religious duty above all duties.[202] Such a shocking fact was also confirmed by speech of General Mohammad Ali Jafari saying that Islamic Republic is a divine sacred government that safeguarding it is prior even to performed prayer.[203]

In short words, a Supreme Leader shall function as both political and spiritual leader whose power absoluteness would silence his dissidents as a result of the claim of being a representative of Imam Mahdi on the earth during his occultation. So opposing the concept, according to his radical loyalists such as Ayatollah Mesbah Yazdi, would be equal to idolatry or polytheism, biggest sin according to Islam, as Supreme Leader represents the highest God's grace to humankind.[204] Even furthermore, Deputy of Socio-cultural affairs of Iranian Revolutionary Guard, Mohammad Reza Naghdi once highlighted that the concept of Iranian Velayat Faqih constitutes the most succesful human government after the Prophet ever.[205]

In this regard, John L. Esposito, International relations expert, further had revealed that the absoluteness of Vali Faqih's authority has dated back into 2500 years ago when ancient Iran (Persia) was ruled by Sasanian empire in which the Kings were claimed as a shadow of God on the earth whose authority included religious matters. [206]

---

[200] Mohsen Kadivar, Wilayat Alfaqih and Democracy, The first draft of this paper was presented in 36th Annual Conference of Middle East Studies Association of North America (MESA), Washington DC, November 2002. This article is a chapter of this book: *Islam, the State, and Authority: Medieval Concerns and Modern Issues*, Asma Afsaruddin (editor), Palgrave Macmillan, Dec. 2011
[201] Mehdi Khalji, Nazhme Novin Rouhaniyat Dar Iran, Aida Orient Book, first edition 2010, page 67
[202] Mehdi Khalaji, Apocyptic Politics, on the Rationality of Iranian Policy, the Washington Institute for Near East Policy, January 2008, page 28
[203] Mehdi Khalaji, The Dilemma of Pan Islamic Unity, 27 November 2009, https://www.hudson.org/research/9859-the-dilemmas-of-pan-islamic-unity-
[204] Ayatollah Mohammad Taqhi Mesbah Yazdi : Mokhalafat be Velayat Faqih Be Mana Shirk be Khodast, 6 February 2017, https://www.radiofarda.com/a/1135628.html
[205] Sardare Naghdi : Velayat Faqih Pasaz Hokomate Rasulullah Movagtarin Hokomate Bashari ast, 8 October 2018, http://www.asriran.com/fa/news/635038/سردار-نقدی-ولایت-فقیه-پس-از-حکومت-رسول-الله-موفق‎%80%E2‎%8Cترین-حکومت-بشری-است
[206] John L. Esposito, Islam and Democracy after the Arab Spring, Oxford University Press, page 51

Nevertheless in practice, Imam Khomeini and his successor Ayatollah Ali Khamenei have never overtly claimed themselves as the representatives of Imam Mahdi. In the other hand, they neither denied such a claiming mostly addressed by loyalists. In return, Supreme Leader would have the most strategic role in identifying and determining crucial policies, including foreign policy. Supreme Leader would always be putting red lines and specific rules that are not allowed to be surpassed by any governmental officials of legislative, executive and judicative institutions. Moreover he often gives his intervention to issues of appointment of specific individuals for strategic positions in governmental and religious institutions. Not only that, he could unseat anyone from their positions, who proved to have violated these "red lines" sketched by him.

As a matter of fact, the absoluteness power of Supreme Leader has been reflected in its basic constitution, particularly in article number 5 that states "During the absence of his holiness, the Lord of the Age, May God all mighty hasten his appearance, the sovereignty of the command (of God) and religious leadership of the community (of believers) in the Islamic Republic of Iran is the responsibility of the faqih who is just, pious, knowledgeable about his era, courageous, and a capable and efficient administrator, as indicated in Article 107. [207] In this article, it is mentioned explicitly that Supreme Leader would function as a guardian of God's commands and spiritual leader. In reality the use of words "God's commands" could be interpreted widely and ambiguously to cover all human's affairs including foreign policy. In this vein, Supreme Leader would have right to impose his intervention to foreign policy if it deems necessary, thus guaranteeing its implementations and practices so as not to violate the "red lines" determined evidently by the Supreme Leader. In this vein, his decisions are believed largely to have sacred values and spirituality, thus simply denying any objections from other decision makers in foreign policy.

In discussion on the absoluteness of Supreme Leader's power, in a letter written by Imam Khomeini to his successor, Ayatollah Ali Khameini in 1988 before the former passed away, had implied that the establishment of the state based on Velayat Faqih doctrine is the top priority of any Islamic duties else such as prayers, fasting and going for pilgrimage. Even furthermore, Supreme Leader has an authority to change the Islamic laws if they deemed to have already violated Islamic interests.[208] Imam Khomeini also assured that safeguarding the Islamic regime of Velayat Faqih for Muslims is more important than applying the obligation of five time prayers.[209] It is arguably that any action, legally or illegally, that aims to preserving the survival of Islamic regime would be endorsed by the laws. Therefore, it is not surprising as cited earlier that rejection of Velayat Faqih concept has the same implication to the rejection of God's laws that deserves severe punishments such as death penalty or at least expulsion to other countries. Ironically, as a reflection of absolute power of Supreme Leader, all failures created by the government must be addressed to the responsibility of

---

[207] For further information, please refer to the Iran's basic constitution
[208] Sahife Imam, volume 20 halaman 452, www.khamenei.i
[209] www.mashreghnews.com, 16 February 2014

other policy makers but Supreme Leader as he would be unlikely to make any mistake in managing and guarding the state.

Yet it does not necessarily mean that Supreme Leader will not make any consultation with the concerned institutions to determine state policies. He would also accept advices and ideas from other competent figures so that the outcomes will not collide with other more crucial interests. Yet it is worthy to keep in mind that the decisions taken by him would be regarded as final decision that may affect to change any policy taken by more eligible institutions such as President along with Minister of Foreign Affairs, or pro-national interest policy that according to His perception, contradicts Islamic revolutionary ideology.

In fact Supreme Leader's absolute right of intervention in determining foreign policy has created uniqueness of Iran's foreign policy, obviously undermining the function of the related ministry that in contrast, based on my observation in the field, has much preferred to accommodate and absorb national interests rather than ideological ones, and circumvent foreign policy from revolutionary characters as most countries commonly practice. Meaning that authority of the concerned institutes, particularly the Ministry of Foreign Affairs must be overshadowed significantly by Supreme Leader's authority that represents final says to all foreign matters.

Practically, the definition of national interest in Iran's foreign policy as logic consequence of being revolutionary state, is extremely ambiguous and obscure, in which the Iranian principlists or hardliners (*Osholgharayan*) including Supreme Leader himself, would define it more presumably to the regime interests, rather than people's interests. As such Iranian government institutions such as Presidency, Ministry, Parliament, Council of Guardian, Assembly of Experts, Supreme National Security Council have also significant roles to determine and identify foreign policy. Little wonder due to various policy makers who often undoubtedly also reflect multiple interests, determining Iran's foreign policy would likely trigger long debate among the factions. In this case, the intervention of Supreme Leader is in dire need in mediating such a debate that usually stands on the hardliner voices, other than the reformist ones.[210] Besides, according to Rejai Khorasani, former Iran's representative in UN, the unofficial voices such as statements issued by conservative Friday prayer leaders appointed by Supreme Leader who mostly have no competency altogether in analyzing global dynamics, sometimes have significant negative impacts and implications to the Iran's constructive foreign policy.[211] More ominously, no synchronization and coordination in issuing foreign policy among Iranian government officials sometimes take

---

[210] Amy Thomsoon, The Ties that Bind Iran and Hamas Principal Agent Relationship, a thesis written as precondition to obtain master degree in Masey University New Zealand, 2012 page 67
[211] Christin Marchall, Iran's Persian Gulf Policy, From Khomeini to Khatami, Routledge Curzon Taylor and Francis Group, page 16. For instance the statement of Ayatolla Hossein Sadeghi, prominent Iran's Shia cleric that Bahrain is part of Iranian territory had sparked critics from the Iran's Ministry of Foreign Affairs in which obviously it could not counter such a controversial statement

place, as what it has been shown most recently by Shabani, Commander-in-chief of Revolutionary Guards by saying that Yemeni Houthi rebels bombing on two Saudi oil tankers in Bab el Mandab strait of Red Sea was under Iran's military instruction. As matter of fact, Iranian officials to date, have repeatedly confirmed that Iranian support to Yemeni Houthi rebellion is limited to non-tangible, immaterial and spiritual one.[212]

Yet the uniqueness of Iranian foreign policy also lies on the implementation and execution of foreign policy that is not monopolized only by the Ministry of Foreign Affairs. In this vein, the Ministry of Intelligence and Security, Islamic Revolutionary Guard Corps as well as Office of Special Consultation on International Affairs for Velayat Faqih are sometimes involved in accomplishing and realizing foreign policy taken, often generating public controversy and perplexity.

Not only that, its uniqueness also persists on the authority of Supreme Leader to appoint directly Shia loyal clerics in order to hold positions in several target countries as His representatives as well as directors of cultural affairs who are usually assigned in Iranian embassies abroad. Indeed these special positions have a very significant impact in directing Iran's foreign policy, even further their positions would prevail over that of Minister or Ambassadors as they constitute direct representatives of Supreme Leader.[213] Once again it has shown clearly that the position of Velayat Faqih in political system is higher than that of President and lower government officials.

As mentioned earlier, such a conclusion could be reflected by a fact that the authority of President and his Minister of Foreign Affairs would be overshadowed by the absolute power of Supreme Leader that often leads to frustration of those government officials. In practice, both officials are no more than just the executive powers who must comply with Supreme Leader's directions and guidelines. Such an interesting fact has been once unfolded evidently by Mohammad Ali Abtahi, Vice President of former reformist President Mohammad Khatami, in his interview with As-Sharg Iranian Newspaper that he acknowledged very deeply that there is a high wall which has restricted President Khatami's policy making due to it has been tremendously overshadowed by the authority of Supreme Leader. He also advocated that presidential candidates shall not make tantalizing promises to people on change for better life given that such promises are hard to be materialized later.[214] Furthermore, Akbar Ganji, an Iranian opposition journalist, assumed implicitly that all deterioration and slowdown caused by mismanagement of President Ahmadinejad's administration should not be addressed only to him, but to Supreme Leader's central

---

[212] Sardare Shabani : Hosiha be Khaste Ma do Naftekesh Saudi ra zadan, 7 August 2018, https://www.dw.com/fa-ir/iran/a-44987962
[213] opcit page 68
[214] Iranian-american forum youtube channel, *Namayesh Entekhabat Dar Nezame Wilayat Faqih*, 18 Februari 2016

role.[215] In nutshell it can be said that change in presidency after four year administration, does not necessarily change fundamental economic and political situations.

There are so many examples of how the authority of Supreme Leader proves to be more effective than other Iranian officials in determining Iran's foreign policy. One example, any constructive policy on normalizing relations with US taken by Iranian President and his Minister of Foreign Affairs in order to lift economic sanctions etc, would be objected obviously by Supreme Leader in which anti-American policy has been inseparable principle of Islamic regime since its establishment in 1979. Another example is the building of nuclear reactor. Many observers believe that its implementation won't bring any benefit for Iranian economy, neither for short term goal nor long term. Yet the hardliners who ostensibly dominate various spheres of Iranian political system, succeeded to realize the program by insisting, despite lack of Uranium natural source at home, that owning nuclear reactor is realization of identity and credibility of an Islamic state in the advance of technology field.[216]

Nevertheless, Ayatollah Ali Khamene'i often grants the Ministry of Foreign Affairs to determine diplomatic mechanisms and methods based on international practices. In fact despite having final decisions on all fundamental domestic and diplomatic issues as manifestation of his power absoluteness, Supreme Leader would give authority for decision making process to other concerned officials.[217] For instance, he won't further intervene with the identification of right mechanisms and methods taken by Iranian Foreign Ministry, including convening negotiations and bilateral and multilateral talks etc based on international practices, as long as that final result of such mechanisms would be compatible with his inclination and guideline. Interestingly, non intervention principle of Supreme Leader in dealing with foreign affairs, could also be framed in some unique ways carried out by Presidents when deciding for some of critical international issues. In this vein, Mehdi Khalaji even believes that since taking the presidential power in 2005, in critical situations, Mahmoud Ahmadinezhad preferred divine consultation to human decision by making Estakharah prayer (special prayer for seeking guidance of God). In addition, the President was deeply accused of relying on divination with regard to destruction of Israel and its exact date. Rather than relying on comprehensive analysis and thorough observation, the President was also accused of not taking seriously US military threats as some arcane scientists told him there would be any attack on Iran.[218]

As elucidated previously, furthermore, if Ali Khamenei's decision in foreign policy seems to contradict the international practices and traditions as he is vehemently believed

---

[215] Akbar Ganji, Foreign Affairs, the Latter Day Sultan, translated from Persian into English by Farhad Abdolian, www.abdolian.com, 19 November 2008
[216] www.forbes.com, 23 February 2013
[217] Mehdi Khalaji, Apocyptic Politics, on the Rationality of Iranian Policy, the Washington Institute for Near East Policy, January 2008, page viii
[218] Mehdi Khalaji, Apocyptic Politics, on the Rationality of Iranian Policy, the Washington Institute for Near East Policy, January 2008, page 16

not to have such a competency and knowledge on international relations and laws, yet ironically President along with his Minister could hardly object and criticize such decisions. Whether they like or not, they have to obey the decisions and final says taken by Supreme Leader under no circumstances although such decisions will probably give negative impacts to the national interests. The examples of such an interesting phenomena are so many, including posing ceaseless hostility and confrontation against US interests that definitely affects political and economical situations at home. Other instance, when Hassan Rouhani, incumbent President, just came back home after delivering his lecture about Iranian moderate attitude to the world and its preparedness to abide by laws as a member of UN in the meeting of General Assembly of UN held in September 2017, was in contrast followed by the measure of ballistic missile launching in Gulf territory that sparked much controversy internationally, particularly America by eventually imposing another economic sanction to Iran as well as stating that such an action has already tainted the spirits of JCPOA (Joint Comprehensive Plan of Action) signed in July 2015 in Vienna. This case once again had shown ineffectiveness of Iran's foreign policy that as usually involves many players in determining its foreign policy, as suggested above.

Because of no trust even among the government officials, in several cases specifically those related to regional issues, identification and realization of policy, the authority would be vested in an institution called *Bayt Rahbar* (Supreme Leader's Mansion) that indirectly undermine the authority of President and his Minister, thus granting the latter as protocol for ceremonial state agenda. Regrettably the significance of the exceptional revolutionary institution is often ignored by political observers on Iranian foreign policy. *Bayt Rahbar* led by the Supreme Leader would be a special channel to identify and implement its radical foreign policy, often challenging the foreign policies taken by the traditional government institution such as Ministry of Foreign Affairs. Therefore it is hardly surprising that all Iranian ambassadors assigned to strategic and sensitive Arab countries, would be appointed by Qods Force, a special forces of Iran's Revolutionary Guards that is responsible for trans-border military operations which has direct responsibility to *Bayt Rahbar*. Another example showing that how *Bayt Rahbar* would be viewed more reliable than any other government institution is when Vladimir Puttin, Russian President, met face to face with Supreme Leader without any single participation of President Hassan Rouhani in 2017.[219] Not only that, in recent years, Ali Akbar Velayati, former Iran's Foreign Minister, currently serves as international affairs consultant for Ali Khamene'i, had been engaged in foreign missions instead of Javad Zarif as Iran's incumbent Foreign Minister, including conducting official visits to Lebanon and Iraq as well as Russia (July 2018). Ironically almost at the same time in October 2017, the Foreign Minister instead was officially assigned to pay visit to African countries that seem not to have much interest with Iran, including South Africa and Uganda to inaugurate a hospital founded under the

---

[219] Amir Taheri, Khamenei Orders New Supervisory Body to Curtail Government, www.awsat.com, 25 September 2017

auspice of Iranian government. In April 2018, Dr. Javad Zarif, like previous years, also paid official visits to some countries in African continent and Latin America, strongly evidencing more that the role of Iranian Foreign Minister deal only with countries that have secondary priority to Iran. However, due to lack of technically diplomatic skills of *Bayt Rahbar* to deal with Iranian nuclear deal negotiations with states of 5+1 and Supreme Leader's reluctance, complete authority was then granted to Iranian foreign Ministry. Lastly, while joining FATF (The Financial Action Task Force) seems beneficial to avoid Iranian economy from total collapse according to the Iranian Ministry of Foreign Affairs and parliament, yet such a joining FATF was still deemed a significant obstacle by the Guardian Council whose half of its members are appointed directly by Supreme Leader, to extend relentless financial support to the militant groups in the region. [220]

Despite much criticism on countries visited by the Iranian high officials that would not bring in any benefits for Iran's economy, many analysts have speculated that such efforts granted to and taken by the Minister, have displayed more distrust and scepticism of Supreme Leader to the roles and functions played recently by the Ministry that appears to take reasonable and more flexible measures in realizing foreign policy rather than revolutionary and frontal ones. Arguably, Bayt Rahbar knows little on art of diplomacy as it will act without further respect to the prevailing international laws and systems. Such little understanding could be the greatest challenge for other states to found amicable relations with Iran because the ambivalence of Iranian foreign policy taking would confuse them to which approach and mechanism they should adopt. Worse, *Bayt Rahbar* keeps assuming that its real divine mission is to change world's existing political systems, thus making it comply with the system it promotes and propagates. In this vein, all efforts of Iranian diplomats to attract sympathy from international audience and call for better diplomatic ties would be fruitless as they must be overshadowed inherently by the general outlines determined by Bayt Rahbar which is regrettably still dominated by conservative and fundamentalist political wing.

Based on my observation which I happened to study in the School where future Iranian diplomats are trained, most of them definitely did realize that the authority of Supreme Leader would significantly overshadow Iranian foreign policy despite their complete understanding on diplomatic ethics and international laws. Meaning that subjects of their study could be meaningless since they already knew that the subjects are almost inapplicable in establishing international relations and implement them under the framework of general international laws. As future diplomats they would be demanded to creating hopes for the nation by realizing its expectations in international arena amid their deep awareness that Supreme Leader would act otherwise.

---

[220] Shura Negahban Mohemtarin Layehe mortabete ba FATF ra rad kard, 4 November 2018
https://www.radiofarda.com/a/the-guardian-council-dismissed-the-fatf-realated-bill/29581533.html

Most interestingly, among the prominent officials from the same reformist group, it sometimes happens that the opinion of the Minister of Foreign Affairs would not be compatible with that of the President. For instance the firing of Manouchehr Mottaki, Iranian foreign minister during his official visit in Senegal in December 2010 by President Ahmadiniezad had once tremendously shocked domestic politics. In this regard, Keyhan newspaper, Iranian most conservative newspaper, had proved it well in June 2018 when Mr. Rouhani once said that the nuclear deal of JCPOA will be able to lift the sanctions from Iranian banks whereas Mr. Zareef has noted that the deal will not necessarily lift the sanctions.[221]

Considering such facts on how complicate Iranian foreign policy taking is, it would be understood well that having good relations with Iran based on internationally acknowledged mechanisms does not necessarily mean that one country would have deeper ties with Iran. Meaning that it is highly recommended for any country to establish bilateral relations with Iran by considering significant role of Supreme Leader (*Baytul-Rahbar*) rather than President and his Foreign Ministry as he has already had a final say for all Iranian foreign policy. Therefore, it can be said that understanding an Iranian foreign policy must be challenging as it must be always overshadowed by other interest that constitutes the most important element in Iranian politics which is revolutionary one.

Meanwhile in Saudi Arabia, just like Vali Faqih of Iran, King has a very central role in issuing policies related to the international relations. Although his authority is not mentioned explicitly in Saudi basic constitution 1992, later amended in 2005 on the absoluteness of power of the King, yet several articles in the Constitution implicitly stipulates the absoluteness of Kings' authority, particularly in articles number 44, 55, 56, 57, 58 and 60. In article 44 for instance, it has been clearly stated that the Kings shall be their final authority (judicial authority, executive authority, regulatory authority).[222] Even King has an authority to appoint all Saudi diplomats and ambassadors under no circumstances.[223] Furthermore the power absoluteness King always enjoys would be simply negating and rejecting any objections emanating from critical Saudis who fear to express their diverse opinions due to existential threats of severe unpredictable punishments. As mentioned earlier, such phenomenon has been exacerbated by the fact that passivity of Saudis generated by strongly considering cultures and traditions could dissuade those objections and criticisms from arising, prompting the Kingdom to aggressively buy their loyalty by putting priority to progress a plethora of popular policies by harnessing its oil production in order to accomplish and realize its national interests particularly in economic sector.

Nevertheless, some of pro-regime scholars have denied the absolute power of King by considering a fact that the authority of King is also limited through strong control

---

[221] Please refer to Persian Keyhan newspaper, published in 25 June 2018
[222] For further information, please refer to the basic constitution of the Kingdom
[223] Sherifa Zuhur, Saudi Arabia, Greenwood Publishing Group, 2011, page 85

imposed by members of royal family. Those scholars have argued that in practice, determining the Saudi foreign policy would be carried out by King alone if he was well-known as capable king in identifying and taking such policies, like what was once implemented by King Abdul Aziz (1932-1952) and King Faisal (1964-1975).[224] In the other side, if King has no capability to do so due to his lack of competency, theoretically he has to make further consultation with the other members of royal family who are believed to understand the issue more deeply. Uniquely in Saudi, each senior prince would be given responsibility and authority to study more deeply one strategic country. For example, King Abdullah was well known as specialist for Syrian issue, while Prince Sultan has been expert on Yemen, etc. Therefore, when the King needs any review and analysis regarding one country, he will consult on it with the concerned expert prince.[225] In the Kingdom, as the Foreign Ministry is seen to be very strategic, the highest authority would be usually given to the Royal Family, just like the Ministry of Defence and the Ministry of Interior.[226]

According to Dr. Madani, former Saudi Minister of Foreign Affairs, the King would like to invariably open consultation with the Crown Prince, vice of Crown Prince and other members of royal family. In addition, King often consults with various government institutions such as Ministry of Foreign Affairs, Ministry of Defence, Ministry of Internal Affairs, National Security Council, Intelligent unit and Parliament before making any strategic policy. King also often makes consultation privately with Islamic scholars and political, economic as well as military experts, etc.[227] However, akin to the central role of Iranian Supreme Leader along with all types of consultations and coordination, this fact would not eschew the function of Saudi King to issue final say for various matters, both internally and externally.

Therefore, according to Wahhabi clerics, identifying and implementing foreign policies that are not Islamic in nature, are regarded as reflection on legal politics (*Siyasah Sharia*) which allows King to issue decisions with no need to contain Islamic values and principles as long as they don't contradict Sharia laws. As a matter of fact, the concept of Siyasah Sharia is often adopted by the King by relying only to reasoning, to identify many domestic and foreign policies which have not been discussed yet in Sharia previously, under the framework of national interest pursuit.[228]

However, before concluding the aforementioned comparison of the authorities of the Saudi King and Iranian Supreme Leader, often called Vali Faqih, it is worthwhile to note that despite all absoluteness of the authority they enjoy which negates further questioning,

---

[224] Fahad M. Alsultan, the Saudi King : Power and Limitation in the Saudi Arabian Foregin Policy Making, International Journal of Social Science and Humanity, Volume 3, No. 5 September 2013 page 459
[225] Raymond Hinnesbuch & Anoushirvan Ehteshami, translate by Dr. Mohammad Qahremenpour dan Morteza Mesah, Siyasate Khareji Keshvarhaye Khavarmiyane, Tarbiyat Islami Marjeyeat ilmi, tahun 2002, page 371
[226] Medea Benjamin, the Unjust Kingdom, Behind the US-Saudi Connection, OR Books, 2016, page 13
[227] Ibid
[228] David Commins, The Wahhabi Mission and Saudi Arabia, IB Taurus London New York page 117

degree of loyalty of the clerics in each state can't be likened. Iranian Shia loyalist clerics are inclined to regard a Supreme Leader as a cult, whose position is arguably divine due to being representative of the Occulted Imam, whereas degree of loyalty of the Saudi Wahhabi clerics to a King is much less than that of those Shia clerics.

Indonesia and How to Shape Its Foreign Policy

As non Islamic state mostly whose laws and regulations are simply based on secular ones, and not on God's revelations, Indonesia would arguably determine and apply its foreign policy on pragmatism and flexibility more than Arab Saudi and Iran do. Theoretically for Indonesia, Islam that vast majority holds as faith, would not become significant consideration and component in taking and determining its foreign policy, which means all of its active and free foreign policy would be realized and accomplished only as reflection of national interest that must be achieved through diplomatic efforts and mechanisms. Therefore in this vein, Indonesia while attempting to apply the concept of thousand friends and zero enemy, will not necessarily put its top priority to embrace Muslim and Islamic countries. It might pursue closer relations with those assumed to tremendously bring political and economic benefits to the country. Apart from this, the old adage of 'the enemy of my enemy is my friend' that is often applied by Saudi Arabia and Iran in developing ties and interactions in the region, would not be used by Indonesia as it strives to maintain good bilateral relations with all countries.

Besides, moderation of Islam promoted proudly through Indonesian foreign policy emphasizing on the domination of moderate Muslim nation in Indonesia does not necessarily give influence to other countries to follow such a pattern since moderation of Islam has acknowledged no uniqueness which other Muslim countries also develop. Meaning that the commonality of moderate Islam is not monopolized merely by Indonesia, which in the other hand, revolutionary Shia and Wahhabi are strongly believed to be the outcomes of creative interpretation of their founders as reaction and protest to the ongoing events in the communities during the time. Therefore, such a fact profoundly further generates the low profile of Indonesian foreign policy among Islamic world, which differs from ideological Shia and Wahhabi brought constantly by Iran and Saudi Arabia that aim at changing and influencing other states' behaviours and perspectives. Moreover, psychological expansionism has been the core element of both Saudi Arabia and Iran foreign policy that compete each other in order to entice Islamic world's attention.

In fact, such approach has been pursued by Indonesia since the early years of Indonesia's independence in 1945 which attempted to guide its foreign policy to be more realistic and compatible with global political dynamics during the time along with the only purpose, in seeking international support and recognition to the newly born Indonesia. For instance 8 (eight) main point strategies for Indonesian foreign policy that shall be achieved in 2015 - 2019 simply mirror the perspective that Indonesia would pursue the same objectives and goals as what it did in the previous decades, always giving emphasis more on cooperation under the ASEAN framework.[229]

In this regard, pragmatism and realistic approach of Indonesian foreign policy taken to realize the cited points mainly with regard to putting its top priority for regional cooperation, as Saudi Arabia and Iran also apply with their respective neighbouring states as explained evidently earlier, will dominate the identification and determination of its policies on bilateral, regional and multilateral issues. In nutshell, Indonesia would direct its foreign policy by giving more concentration on developing and consolidating bilateral relations with neighbouring countries which are also the members of ASEAN organization, as even explicitly underlined by the Broad Guidelines of state policy in 1973 and the President Soeharto's Instruction concerning the implementation of the People' Consultative Assembly (MPR) in 1973.[230]

Additionally, Indonesian foreign policy that rests heavily on Bebas Aktif (free and active) concept initiated for the first time by Mohammad Hatta, former Indonesian vice President in Soekarno era, to respond cold war rivalry brought primarily by US and USSR, has strengthened perception that Indonesian foreign policy would be free in action and independent in judgement as long as the coveted domestic goals encompassing sovereignty, defence, Indonesian citizens protection and economic sectors, would be heavily achieved and realized regardless whether they would be good for Islamic principles or not and irrespective of whether they would bring up Islamic identity or not.

Under Bebas Aktif formula, Indonesia has also officially pledged to play an active role, mostly by harnessing functions of existing regional and multilateral forums in order to create peace and stability of the world, reflected by its active participation in peace keeping force under the framework of United Nations. In this regard, Indonesia will appear to be neutral in engaging international conflicts regardless of whether they take place in Moslem countries or not, or whether the conflict might bring Islamic identity (sectarian issues) or not. For example since 1957 Indonesia has dispatched roughly 40.000 personnel in 28 peace

---

[229] The 8 (eight) points include 1. Strong diplomacy for maritime and border 2. More increasing Indonesia's leadership in ASEAN 3. More increasing Indonesia's role in international arena 4. Strong economic diplomacy 5. Prime service and protection for Indonesian citizens/Indonesian legal entities. 6. Qualified foreign policy 7. Highly national support and commitment to the foreign policy and international agreements 8. Effective monitoring of diplomatic results. www.kemlu.go.id
[230] Asep Setiawan, Politik Luar Negeri Indonesia, www.academia.edu

keeping mission of UN, in addition to another plan to send military troops in Congo and police force in South Sudan in this year.[231]

In fact since Soesilo Bambang Yudhoyono came into power as the 6th president in 2004, the jargon of one thousand friends, zero enemy has significantly overshadowed Indonesian foreign policy taking to date.[232] In this regard by wielding such jargon, Indonesia has been striving to establish and maintain good relations with other states and settle all strife and dissension through diplomatic channels. Ironically the jargon which rather stresses Indonesia's low profile position before international community and asserts reluctance and hesitation in determining and guiding its foreign policy eventually sparks controversy and debate among scholars as it often precludes Indonesia from achieving the ultimate goal of national interest. Under the framework of such a jargon, Indonesia will have no significant courage to take decisive decision and evince critical position on many happenings and events carried out by the countries that evidently contravene the universalism of human rights and humanity. Therefore, little wonder that Indonesia attempts not to display critical gestures on military manoeuvres that some Moslem states have held that often prompt humanitarian tragedies to occur.

In this vein, Indonesia along with its foreign policy that emphasizes on reconciliation and neutrality could be an effective mechanism to carry out diplomatic mediation among feuding Muslim countries. However, good intention and neutrality are not sufficient to endorse Indonesia's efforts to mediate. Its vague stance and slight role before Islamic world has precluded it from developing mediation. In addition, Indonesian reluctance to play more significant role, along with limited financial support and lack of human resources in dealing with the matters of Islamic world have been tremendous factor and reason why Indonesia's position is ceaselessly overlooked. In addition, the strength of moderate Islam concept Indonesia always promotes to entice Islamic world would be meaningless if Indonesia fails to consolidate its domestic economy at first, thus assisting other developing Muslim states which are still tied with economic and investment problems. In this vein, it is hard for Indonesia to take the same steps and strategies that Saudi Arabia and Iran do which always allocate special national budget resulted from oil and gas sale for improving and maintaining their respective good images before Muslim community, which ironically often sacrifice their own domestic economic development programs.

Nevertheless, with the passage of time, the accentuation of Bebas Aktif formula for Indonesian foreign policy has stirred much controversy and debate, often viewed as the

---

[231] Swedia Apresiasi Komitmen Indonesia dalam Pasukan Perdamaian PBB 14 April 2018, https://internasional.kompas.com/read/2018/04/14/11242381/swedia-apresiasi-komitmen-indonesia-dalam-pasukan-perdamaian-pbb

[232] Ihsanuddin, CSIS Minta Jokowi Tak Lanjutkan Politik "One Thousand Friends Zero Enemy" SBY, 21 October 2014, https://nasional.kompas.com/read/2014/10/21/21422271/CSIS.Minta.Jokowi.Tak.Lanjutkan.Politik.One.Thousand.Friends.Zero.Enemy.SBY

major obstacle for the government to take immediate position and stance concerning several international issues, further creating an assumption that Indonesia has been under pressure from other countries. For instance, Indonesian support to the UN Security Council resolution on Iranian nuclear in 2007 was seen as the inevitable result of US intervention to Indonesia following the direct talk between the two Presidents SBY and George Bush.[233] In one hand, such a formula could give Indonesia more latitude to identify and implement its foreign policy, yet on the other hand, Indonesia would be compelled to take much consideration before issuing policies that fix with the framework of Bebas Aktif formula. Not only that, the implementation of the formula could undermine and put aside Islamic identity of Indonesians as the world's largest Muslim country given that its foreign policy shall be driven and guided to accomplish national interests as much as possible that may persist within non-Muslim countries.

Furthermore, unlike Saudi and Iran, both water and land borders, surrounded by mostly Muslim countries, Indonesia is geographically surrounded by many states where Islam is not the majority religion for their societies. Therefore it is hardly surprising to note that numerous goals to be achieved within ASEAN framework often do not promote and bring any Islamic issues and characters, at least not in top priority of bilateral discussions and meetings, since ASEAN establishment itself in 1967 was further generated vehemently by strong commitments of the leaders in having shared vision and position to create Southeast Asian region more peaceful and stable, and to deal with political rivalry between two ideologies brought by US and Soviet Union.[234] In this vein, as cited earlier, when Arab Saudi was trying to bring Islamic identity of Pan-Islam to prevent communism from spreading into region, ASEAN leaders had attempted at promoting more general ways and principles to deal with the issue.

In addition, unlike Iran with unclear and ambiguous foreign policy makers as elucidated earlier given its revolutionary character and distrust among government officials, in Indonesia the issuing and identifying of foreign affairs- related policies would be rendered solely to the Ministry of Foreign Affairs, founded in August 1945 in the wake of Indonesian independence proclamation, mostly headed by professional and career diplomats[235] which in identifying and determining foreign policy would also definitely consider contributions and aspirations from concerned stakeholders. However, being Moslems of those Indonesian stakeholders even when intellectual Muslims were able to occupy strategic positions in bureaucracy mainly in the last years of Soeharto's collapse,[236] does not necessarily mean they would drive and guide Indonesian foreign policy based on Islamic identity and character. However the marginalization of Indonesian Muslims in political sector generally

---

[233] www.bbc.co.uk, 26 March 2007
[234] Setnas-asean.id
[235] ibid
[236] Yudi Latif, Inteligensia Muslim dan Kuasa, Democracy Project, Yayasan Abad Demokrasi, Jakarta 2012, page2

could be reflected as dominant practices for many centuries in which that they have been consistently viewed as outsiders, rather than insiders.[237] In nutshell, compromising attitude that shall encompass each aspiration of all national elements has been an effective means to put aside Islam in making and determining whole Indonesian political policies, including foreign policy.

Yet, in the other side with the state always claiming to be a democratic, Indonesia shall not curtail the rise of Islamic civil society, political parties and social movements which may seek profoundly that the government is able to accommodate more Islamic identity in its foreign policy as reasonable actualization of being the majority group. In sum, as logic consequence of being a democratic state, Indonesia can't avert Islamic minority groups from expressing their aspiration of Sharia implementation in the constitution. In this vein, Indonesia could only offer understanding on the importance of Pancasila and the 1945 Constitution, with a large support of prominent clerics, that they do not contradict Sharia substantially. Therefore, the significant role played by Indonesian clerics to convince those minor groups would prevail and can't be overlooked.

However, Indonesia shall not ignore the very significant roles played by the Moslem Arab countries which sincerely had recognized Indonesia as an independent state right after its proclamation in 17 August 1945. Rizal Sukma, Indonesian prominent scholar, significantly has viewed that the co-religionist factor that Indonesia constitutes Muslim country, might have played a contributing role in persuading Arab governments to extend their diplomatic support to it who apparently knew Muslim Indonesians through tremendous interaction with Indonesian pilgrims and existing large numbers of Indonesian students in Arab states. In addition, Indonesia cannot undermine how much Arab state supported Indonesian position during the debate at the UN Security Council in August 1947 on the Indonesian question following the first Dutch military aggression one month earlier. Even such cordial diplomatic relations between Indonesia and Muslim states have lasted since Ottoman Caliphate emerged, particularly in 16th century when Aceh sultanate under Sultan Alaudin Riayat Shah dispatch his representative to Istanbul, Turkey, to recognize Ottoman as caliphate for Muslims as well as ask for military assistance to resist Portugal colonialist who also plundered Acehnese merchant ships. In addition, the diplomatic relations were also well developed by Mataram and Banten sultanates with Mecca ruler of Sharief in order to gain the caliphate title.[238]

To consolidate and crystallize such robust and long standing supports, Egypt was the first country that did it by concluding the Treaty of Friendship between Indonesian and Egypt in June 1947. Other Arab states including Lebanon, Syria, Saudi Arabia and Yemen began to follow suit. Even Egyptian government further believed as what its Prime Minister

---

[237] Ibid page 12
[238] Oman Fathurrahman, book review on Jaringan Ulama : Pembaharuan dan Rekonsiliasi dalam Tradisi Intelektual Islam di Dunia-Melayu-Indonesia by DR. Azyumardi Azra, Studia Islamika, Volume 11, No.2, 2004, page 369

Mahmoud el-Nokrashi Pasha in King Farouk period once stated frankly to Indonesia's diplomatic mission to Egypt in April 1947 that Islam was the main factor for Egypt to support Indonesian struggles to gain its total independence.[239] In sum, in order to display and concrete their solidarity to Indonesia, It has proved that several Arab countries gave respond to the Dutch second military aggression in December 1948 by closing their ports and airfields to Dutch ships and planes.[240] Nevertheless, the role of Indonesian students in al-Azhar Islamic university in Cairo who have lived in Egypt for studying since mid-19th century,[241] could not be overlooked for their spectacular roles in urging Egyptian government and Arab League to grant official recognition to Indonesia right after Indonesia's independence declaration.[242]

In fact as mentioned briefly above, the 'secular' nature of Indonesian foreign policy was constantly pursued even by the Islamic leaders of Masyumi (Majelis Syuro Muslimin Indonesia/Council of Indonesian Muslim Associations), the later- banned largest Islamic party which tirelessly pursued Sharia implementation and establishment Islamic state, that succeeded to take power during the parliamentary democracy period in 1950-1957 as Rizal Sukma noted that Indonesian foreign policy was not expressed in terms of Islamic language, nor did it reflect an Islamic agenda. Instead of voicing establishment of world Islamic Caliphate following the dismissal of last Ottoman Caliphate in 1920s, the party had only attempted that Indonesia be accepted as a member of the UN, and at restructuring the Indonesian's representative offices abroad and assigning skilled and capable officials to engage with internationalized-domestic issues mainly the west Irian case, and giving much effort to maintain world peace as logical implications of ideological rivalry between US liberalism and USSR communism and of the people's struggles of the developing countries in gaining their independence.[243]

Logically, when Indonesian was once ruled by the Muslim leaders of Masyumi who often sought for the implementation of Islamic Sharia laws in Indonesia yet in the meantime never looked at Islamic agenda for the basis of Indonesian foreign policy, would assert an assumption that Indonesia will never seek to pursue any Islamic agenda, mirrored more concretely on the categorization of the international community as believers and unbelievers or between *Dar al-harb* (a territory whose political system is still yet to be based on Islamic law), *Dar-al- Islam* (a territory whose political system is based on Islamic law) *and Dar-assulh* (neutral area which initiates peaceful agreement with dar-el Islam*)* or perception of a worldwide Ummah under Caliphate concept, thus putting it on the top priority, for its foreign policy as significantly reflected in past six decades. During the time, the Indonesian Muslim leaders strongly believed that before voicing Islamic identity and

---

[239] Rizal Sukma, Islam in Indonesian Foreign Policy, Routledge Curzon, London and New York, Page 27
[240] Ibid page 28
[241] http://kabar24.bisnis.com/read/20160223/255/521946/5.000-mahasiswa-indonesia-belajar-di-al-azhar-kairo
[242] www.waag-azhar.or.id
[243] Opcit page 28

character to international community, they had to deal first with a plethora of internal problems since Indonesia was very susceptible to any existential threats, both internally and externally. As such putting priority on engaging with internal matters did not necessarily ignore their basic aspiration to further echo Islamic agenda to international community.

Instead, since early years of Indonesian independence, Indonesia would certainly underpin its foreign policy on principles laid in Pancasila and messages cited explicitly in the 1945 basic constitution that put aside formalization of Islam as basis of the state and premier legal resource. The consensus of Muslim leaders with other prominent secular and liberal figures in adopting Pancasila as philosophy basis for the state did not necessarily mean that Indonesia has to lose its spiritual and religious dimensions, given the fact that Pancasila has been severely believed to contain the basic principles that do not contradict Islamic values.

Therefore little wonder that in 1960s by taking political dynamics into consideration, rather than improving bilateral relations with Moslem countries, Soekarno regime heavily advocated the creation of the Jakarta-Phnom Penh-Beijing-Pyongyang Axis to resist west domination in the region as the manifestation of neo- colonialism and imperialism politically and economically. Additionally, Soekarno opposed vehemently the creation of the Malay Federation which also had Islam as religion for majority population. Such opposing stance of Indonesia once again had shown that Islam was not significant element to be considered, thus reaffirming assumption that what Soekarno did was genuinely political. Interestingly such an Indonesian confrontational position was not approved by many Arab countries that rather granted Malaysia observer status in the second Non Aligned Movement conference in Cairo. In addition, Indonesian alliance with those countries was in fact not shared by Arab-Muslim countries which in contrast preferred to have a moderate approach.[244] It once again had shown that Indonesia did not have sufficient leverage to affect behaviour change of those countries despite the fact that Indonesia has been the most populous Moslem country of the world that came into being not long after their independence.

As a matter of fact, not only did international dynamics affect heavily on 'more secular' of the foreign policy, but the preferably domestic Issues also had influenced the issuing of Indonesian foreign policy, reflected significantly in Soeharto era. In the so-called new order era that began in 1967, President Soeharto gave much focus on developing economy at home that accordingly eliminated its frontal positions against west including relation improvement with Malaysia, highly implemented by the previous government. Soeharto viewed that West was the main source of financing for Indonesian economic growth as developing country.[245] Despite his authoritarian ruling and dictatorship, Soeharto also enormously dealt with other very strategic issues such as national unity and territorial integrity that definitely drove him to apply more pragmatic and realistic approaches, once

---

[244] Ibid page 35
[245] www.indonesia-investments.com

again not giving priority to open closer relationship with other Muslim countries. It has been well evidenced by among other things, despite active participation due to the common sense on inseparable part of Muslim countries that led it into participation in the first meeting of the organization in Morocco, its rejection to seek formal membership in OIC (Organization of Islamic Country) established in 1969 by refraining from signing the charter in 1972, simply because that Indonesia, based on its 1945 basic constitution was not an Islamic state, and its foreign policy shall be based on Bebas Aktif concept, not Islamic principle one.[246] Nevertheless, Indonesia's participation in the organization did not help consolidate its position in that multilateral organization although since 1990s it has been very active in taking prominent roles in OIC including as chairman for Committee of Six which aimed at facilitating the peace process between Moro National Liberation Front (MNLF) with Philippines government, chairman of the organization in 1993,[247] and host for the OIC's ministerial level meeting in Jakarta in 1996.[248] Indonesia's membership in the D-8 organization established one year prior to Soeharto's collapse, simply exhibited Indonesia's willingness to be more active among Muslim communities particularly in economic and development sectors.

As Riza Sukma argued that under the Soeharto's New Order era, determining and identifying the foreign policy has been the domain of a few government officials and small national elite, especially those of the Ministry of Foreign Affairs and ABRI (Indonesian Army Force) which did a little to guide the foreign policy to be based on Islamic principles. They further believed that foreign policy conduct must reflect no more than Indonesia's national interest, not which of any specific religion adherent, [249] despite interesting fact that most of those were Muslims. Therefore, it is hardly surprising that while Malaysia demanded Serbia be called as aggressor in the Bosnian conflict during the Tenth Non Aligned Summit held in Jakarta in 1992, Indonesia instead strongly rejected it. In addition, Indonesia had never shown any prominent role to participate in resolving the conflict, but through diplomatic settlement and further rejected Bosnian President to dispatch its armed forces to the conflict area. After much pressure from the Moslem community including from MUI (Indonesian Council of Ulama), Indonesia decided to send a 200 medical detachment as part of the UN peacekeeping force in July 1994, later sent its troops under the auspice of OIC.[250]

Therefore it is hardly surprising that MUI, in Soeharto era, was highly regarded as bridge connecting Soeharto's policy to the religious matters, displaying his strong commitment to the people and Islamist groups that he was not implementing fully secularized policies in Indonesia.

---

[246] Politik.lipi.go.id
[247] Rizal Sukma, Islam in Indonesian Foreign Policy, Routledge Curzon, London and New York, Page 52
[248] ibid
[249] Opcit page 52
[250] Ibid page 77

Soeharto's claim was shown evidently by issuing laws and regulations that brought Islamic identity and character including obtaining formal recognition of a marriage act, the law on religious courts of 1989 and the Islam Law Compilation issued in 1991. Not only that, in the last years of his administration, in order to attract sympathy from Indonesian Muslims, Mr. President eventually had attempted to accommodate and absorb more Islamic interests and identities such as increase of public displays of religiosity, starting to speak Arabic, going for Hajj to Mecca, and promoting 'greenization/Islamization' to some strategic governmental positions. More interestingly, between 1988-1993, Soeharto was seeking to ally with Islamist Hardliners like Sumargono to counter the growing demands for democratization from the people. In economic sector Soeharto gave permission for the founding of the first Sharia bank in Indonesia, named Bank Muamalat Indonesia in 1991. He also enhanced the authority of Islamic courts; increased Islamic TV programming and funding for Islamic schools; annulled the sport lottery; and, last but not least created a new state- controlled Ikatan Cendekiawan Muslim Indonesia (Union of Muslim Intellectuals of Indonesians) in December 1990. [251] When wearing a headscarf in Saudi Arabia and Iran has been obliged under any circumstances in public area, Indonesia had once banned the wearing for female students in state-owned schools and later made it optional under the Soeharto's administration, also in 1990. Whether he had other intention or not, such intensive efforts were made some years before he was forced to step out of the administration in 1998, often called as reform era. Therefore little wonder that Soeharto even ostensibly believed that in order to maintain constantly his long standing executive power, Soeharto was in dire need of adopting such policies that seemed to be pro-Islamic interests. The President was believed that his repressive and oppressive approaches to Islamist groups in 80s due to his excessive fear on Islamic insurgency influenced among other things by Islamic Revolution in Iran, had already dismayed and hurt Muslims's feelings, that instead, paved ways for Muslim youths to attempt more deeply at finding their Islamic identity.

In foreign relations and international affairs, Soeharto had an official meeting with Yasser Arafat, PLO leader, in 1984 emphasizing Indonesian support to the Palestinians' struggle in obtaining independence state status. In the Non-Alignment Movement meeting hosted by Indonesia in September 1992, the support of the members for Palestinian independence also emerged. The first time Soeharto's presence in Organization of Islamic Countries (OIC) meeting held in Dakar, Senegal in 1991 carried out not long after it was accepted as full member of the organization, signified evidently his willingness to incite much sympathy from Indonesian Moslems at home.[252] In addition, Soeharto also paid official visits to several Arab and Muslim countries including Iran, Tunisia and Jordan, and also attended the Developing-8 (D-8) Summit in Turkey.[253] Furthermore, it may be said that

---

[251] Zachary Abuza, Political Islam and Violence in Indonesia, Routldge Taylor and Francis Group, first published in 2007, Page 19
[252] Politik.lipi.go.id
[253] Rizal Sukma, Islam in Indonesian Foreign Policy, Routledge Curzon, London and New York, Page 71

the year of 1990s had witnessed the gradual New Order's inclination to "Islamic" foreign policy and took courage to tremendously display Islam as largest religious identity of Indonesians, despite the fact that Indonesia has been still considered as peripheral state whose influence to the Islamic world was not significant enough and was never shown as initiator for establishment of any Islamic regional and international organizations. All this, as cited earlier, is due arguably to the combination of numerous major obstacles including its political geography, lack of human resources, and reluctant willingness of Indonesian government to be dominant power in world's Islamic community.

In reformation era following Soeharto's fall, the role of MUI/Indonesian Ulema Council itself has become more central to grant an Islamic label on religious and moral issues, in which, albeit nonbinding, it occupies a very strategic position that most Indonesian lawmakers don't dare to ignore and undermine.[254] In that period, the Council also started to act more independently from the government particularly in the Abdurrahman Wahid's (Gusdur) administration (1999-2001) after he opened a little space for the likelihood of having non-diplomatic commercial relation with Israel that undoubtedly sparked much controversy and debate.[255] In the former era mainly in the very short President Habibie's administration (1998-1999), as Carool Kersten elaborated, the independence of the Council is also shown by issuing some tausiyahs (non-legal recommendations and admonitions, spiritual non-binding advice) to the government.[256]

In short words, I can further argue that guiding Indonesian foreign policy based on un-Islamic principle and identity was also the case of post-Soeharto administrations as what Rizal Sukma once suggested that role of Islam in Indonesian foreign policy has always been a secondary one. Even he concluded in his phenomenal book "Islam in Indonesian Foreign Policy," that Islam has entered Indonesian foreign policy only in form rather than substance.[257] Moreover several positions and policies taken by each President often stirred discontent and anger among Moslem communities at home, and prompted controversy among them. It can be said that nonetheless entering reform period that would probably absorb more Islamic aspirations, yet practically it hasn't affected to be substantially accommodated by Indonesian foreign policy. The more concrete rise of Islamic movements and political parties significantly resulted from its transitional period into more democratic state, proved to be failing to bring Islamic characters as substantial inspiration for driving and guiding the foreign policy, although more active and aggressive approach has been shown by Jokowi's administration, particularly in Palestinian cause, as I will explore in more detail in next chapter.

---

[254] Mirjam Kunkler and Alfred Stepan, Democratization and Islam in Indonesia, Columbia University Press, New York, page 39
[255] Carool Kersten, Islam in Indonesia the Contest for Society, Ideas and Values, Oxford University Press, page 191,
[256] Ibid page 192
[257] Rizal Sukma, Islam in Indonesian Foreign Policy, Routledge Curzon, London and New York, Page 140

The Indonesian cautious reactions, making it very late to issue its decisive policies for supporting Muslims that have undergone several bloody clashes and tragedies in Muslim countries carried out by non Muslim countries often sparked disappointment of the Indonesian Muslim society. For this reason, the government faced dilemma that it has had to accommodate the interests of the contradictory entities at parallel time, between secular pragmatists and Islamists. The case of US military aggression to Afghanistan in the early 2000s proved it with Indonesia under Megawati's administration having to take soft position, implicitly approving the aggression under the framework of war on global terrorism. However, with the passage of time, Megawati's position had reversed as she argued that no state have right to launch any military aggression towards other states under the pretext of war on terrorism. She even further advocated that US not launch its military attack to Afghanistan in Ramadhan month as such an act would hurt all Muslims of the world.[258]

In addition, arguably Indonesian foreign policy has been guided to accentuate mostly in declaratory forms, coupled with condemnation and criticizing, rather than implementing concrete actions to deal with the ongoing conflicts in Muslim countries. In fact the non conducive situation in economic and political terrains including devastating financial crisis at home and separatism efforts, mainly in the transitional administration of the reformation period starting after Soeharto administration collapse were likely to become the biggest obstacle why Indonesia had to put priority on recovery at home. Unlike Saudi Arabia and Iran, such traditional practice to oversee and overcome domestic economic problems first, rather than engaging more in world's Muslim issues has overwhelmed Indonesian decision makers to put priority at home. Therefore it is hardly surprising to note that Indonesian foreign policy has been driven to find good friendly states as much as possible rather than antagonist ones in establishing foreign relations with significant hopes that they could contribute to improve Indonesian economic recovery and reach other important goals.

To date, Indonesia has been attempting to be inclusive state that could be accepted by all states under no circumstances with it trying to formulate some initiatives that may differ from their predecessors and successors alike. Most startlingly, Indonesian trying to become more open and neutral in applying its foreign policy has often negatively backfired to Indonesian interest itself. For example, Indonesia would not been viewed as a perennial allied state by each Arab Saudi and Iran within constant political rivalry in the region despite Indonesia's much need to their oil supply and foreign investments, as Indonesia has invariably heralded both Islamic countries as brotherly and friendly countries in many bilateral occasions. Other instance, in Gusdur presidency era initially expected to bring more Islamic aspirations as he was the leader of NU, the largest Muslim organization in the world, he stressed the importance to the establishment of a coalition comprising China and India

---

[258] Ikrar Nusa Bakti, Politik Luar Negeri di Bawah Presiden Megawati Soekarnoputri, perpustakaan. Bappenas.go.id

(Asia's Central Axis). In addition, in his administration era, much closer ties with Middle Eastern states was accentuated through the appointment of Alwi Shihab who spent some years in the region as foreign Minister with significant hope that they could give financial contributions, particularly to the rentier states to re-normalize Indonesian unstable economy. Gusdur policy towards Middle East was not definitely encouraged by religious impetus, but rather economic.

However, in contrast with former presidents, in Megawati presidency that lasted from 2001-2004, approaching the region was extremely not at her foreign policy agenda.[259] Yet it doesn't mean that her presidential administration ignored completely the importance of Middle East regions to help investing in Indonesia and undermined the solidarity for Palestinian struggles.

Under the SBY's administration (2004-2014) that was dogged by the most tremendous event of Arab Spring in 2011, while significantly applying the same concept of thousand friends and zero enemy in foreign policy, SBY was trying to bring Indonesian neutrality in taking stances towards the popular uprisings that succeeded to overthrew the despotic Arab regimes. He further hoped that Indonesian experience of becoming a democratic state, could be deeply adopted by the conflicting Arab countries to overcome the issue.[260] Like his predecessors, SBY also paid official visits to several Arab countries in May 2006.[261]

Most currently in President Jokowi's era, he also continued Indonesian foreign policy to open relationships with all countries. His robust willingness to establish closer ties with the Middle East region was shown by his visit to the region in the first years of his administration and by his other official visits to the region during his tenure. In this vein, Jokowi, the president who is well know with *blusukan*[262] agenda has believed that his visit was expected to be able to create the balance of western core-perceived policy. in addition, most startlingly Jokowi endowed with a courageous heart also paid official visit to some other Muslim countries in south Asia, Afghanistan and Pakistan, two countries where terrorist attacks are likely to occur.[263] Also keeping in mind, in his administration, the humanitarian issues of Rohingya, Myanmar and Palestine have often occupied the directing of his foreign policy, that I would like to highlight more obviously in another chapter. Indonesia has also significantly offered to mediate the two feuding countries, Saudi Arabia and Iran following their diplomatic relations rupture in 2016. President Jokowi could be the first Indonesian president who stated explicitly that Islam and brotherhood constitute an

---

[259] Ibid page 130
[260] Dunia.tempo.co, 1 March 2014
[261] M.merdeka, 25 April 2006
[262] A strategy of emphasizing direct contacts by eschewing tight presidential protocol, with people to listen and observe what they really hope and aspire from the government.
[263] Jokowi: Timur Tengah dan Asia Selatan Jadi Perhatian, 28 January 2018,
https://www.republika.co.id/berita/nasional/umum/18/01/28/p38ojw382-jokowi-timur-tengah-dan-asia-selatan-jadi-perhatian-ri

unifying element for enhancing bilateral relations with Saudi Arabia when he officially received King Salman's visit in Indonesia in March 2017.[264]

---

[264]RAJA SALMAN: Hubungan Indonesia-Arab Saudi Dipersatukan oleh Islam, 1 March 2017, https://news.okezone.com/read/2017/03/01/337/1631500/raja-salman-hubungan-indonesia-arab-saudi-dipersatukan-oleh-islam

Chapter IV : The Implementation of "Forgotten Islam" in Foreign Policy

In reality, as frequently mentioned earlier, almost all political analysts and thinkers believe that foreign policy shall reflect national interest of the countries, meaning that foreign policy of one state shall be compatible with its own national interest that mostly encompasses deepest aspirations of its nation. Yet in practice, to profoundly objectify it, states even including Islamic states with their Islamic- flavoured basic constitutions such as Iran and Saudi Arabia, would usually feel compelled to take more flexible foreign policy that responds such demands. Despite predominantly Muslim population in the three countries under discussion, yet however their foreign policy implementations would not necessarily mirror Islamic aspirations given the fact that such policies shall be guided and driven by taking their national interests into consideration, the interests which fit the aspirations of all, not for a specific group. Therefore in reality, too often, achieving national interest will not necessarily reflect the achievement of Islamic identity and Muslim world's goals. In contrast, the achievement of Islamic interest will not necessarily echo the accomplishment of the national interests.

Most startlingly if we take a deeper look to recent international relation history, pragmatic approach was often taken by Mohammad Morsi, the fifth President of Egypt from 2012-July 2013 who is tightly affiliated with Muslim Brotherhood (Ikhwanul Muslimin), a militant group designated as terrorist by some states. Observers did assume once he took power from the previous secular one, many changes towards the Islamization of all life aspects of Egyptians would take place, yet the reality on the ground didn't prove it as the President often took pragmatic approaches to deal with various domestic and international issues. For instance, in his ruling, bilateral relation between Egypt and Israel was not much affected, pledging his commitment to the Camp David peace agreements. He attempted to be in neutral position to solve the military clash between Hamas and Israel, but he decided to destroy the tunnels used to smuggle goods and weapons into Gaza strip as he saw the tunnel has been used by radical and criminal individuals.[265]

In nutshell pragmatic and realistic approaches constitute integral part of foreign policy taking in these countries, and would repeatedly overshadow identifying it by exerting any means and mechanisms in order to accomplish their respective short term and mid-term goals which eventually lead into realization of national interests as their long term goal that includes security and prosperity, as what Hans J.Morgenthau believes that national interest constitutes a main pillar for foreign policy. The countries are in dire need to

---

[265] David D. Kirkpatrick, Into the Hands of the Soldiers, Viking, 2018, Page 183

guaranty their survivals in all aspects as each of these countries would acknowledge the limitations of their multiple elements that prop up their sustainability, chiefly the ones that relate to its declining natural resources and lacking of competent human capitals. Small wonder, in order to reach the goals, foreign policy taking in countries like Saudi Arabia and Iran will accept flexibility in building up their global interactions by putting aside for temporary unalterable values and principles of the countries.

In this vein for sure, in understanding more profoundly the pragmatic behaviours of the states due to their uniqueness, would require a deeper analysis and thorough assessment by taking multifaceted aspects into consideration. Having deep and comprehensive analysis to understand such 'deviated' policies of the countries will finally reveal various plausible impetuses that navigate them to take and implement policies that differ from general outlines and principles firmly sketched by of the countries. It is not the case with Indonesia which always places national interest as its ultimate goal, thus flexibility by exerting all means and mechanisms would be an inseparable element in taking its foreign policy. Therefore, it could be much easier for scholars to understand behavioural changes in Indonesian foreign policy which never claims as an Islamic state and whose basic constitution is not based on Sharia. Conversely as cited earlier, in non-democratic states with long entrenched claim as Islamic states like Saudi Arabia and Iran, any scholar must give much effort to render more comprehensive understanding on the impetuses and motivations that lead their policy makers to put aside considering Islamic ideology and identity as well as Muslim world's ultimate goals in their foreign policy taking.

In addition, national interests of both states are least likely to be fully accomplished as their domestic policies are often regarded to be discriminatory to minority groups in their respective countries which are obviously reflected by imposing much restriction to the groups to take part in political affairs for instance. It is worth mentioning that national interest shall encompass interests of all groups and communities by further eschewing and avoiding discriminatory treatments and giving access as many as possible to minority groups to express their political and social aspirations.

In result, both countries would unflinchingly label any criticism or opposition against the governments as betrayal to the nations. Ominously, the Iranian government may designate him/her as traitor of Islamic interest, much wider than just being as traitor of the country due to Iran's constant claim as the leading state for Islamic world, which perceives that betraying the state is equivalent to betrayal to Islamic ummah.

Furthermore, taking pragmatic approaches evidently reflected in Saudi and Iran's relentless meddling in numerous issues of Middle East Region such as Syria and Yemen often risk life of other Muslims they are supposed to avoid. Regrettably, all this comes as justification to launch military attacks and support several Muslim militia radical groups to accomplish political goals in spite of annihilation of Muslim's life and harsh criticism from other Muslim countries.

Although Saudi Arabia and Iran often give emphasis on cementing bilateral relations with Muslim countries, yet like any other states including Indonesia, priority still would be given into strengthening relations with their neighbouring states which by chance whose populations are dominated by Muslims, as a outcome of such pragmatism. Bearing this in mind, in this vein Iran also demonstrates its uniqueness and distinction in driving its foreign policy with it seemingly establishing cordial relations with non-Muslim states calculatedly would not lead into achieving its national interest, but rather the regime's interest. Establishing good relations with states such as Venezuela, Cuba and North Korea wouldn't bring something beneficial economically to the state, yet however maintaining such relations with these countries has been obviously generated by Iran's constant assumption that the countries proved to have similar global perspective with Iran in castigating and censuring several American policies. As a state underpinned coherently by revolutionary principles and values, expressing and announcing formally that America represents global arrogance and big Satan would be the best modality for enhancing its bilateral relations with other states which have the similar standpoints, despite the fact the countries may have crucially distinct positions with Iran, among other things, by expressing their official recognitions on Israel as an independent and sovereign state. In consequence, any Moslem country which proved to have shown its resistance and protest overtly against US policy would be simply approached and preferred by Iran in establishing more cordial and friendly relations.

However, with Iran incessantly implementing its foreign policy based on its own Islamic interpretation that sometimes prompts inevitable sectarian conflicts and clashes in the region, Saudi Arabia, to some extent, would still significantly consider rationality in taking its foreign policy by considering its behaviour to comply with the corridors of the international law. In other words It would mean that elements of rigid, extreme Wahhabism doctrine is overlooked in building up its interactions with other states, but rather the doctrine itself would often get more apparent domestically rather than externally, except the one relating to the realization of its religious duty of Islamic Wahhabism propagation and promotion.

In addition, in order to accomplish their foreign policy goals that lead into the realization of their respective national interests under the shadows of pragmatism, their diplomats are not in necessity to be equipped with Islamic knowledge since their policy makers have been well aware that their foreign policies would be taken to achieve goals beyond accomplishing Islamic interests. Meaning that all this time, it implies more deeply that foreign policy of the countries has been associated to Islam as an inspirational component, not a substantial determiner. Moreover, Islam in foreign policy would be taken to promote its identity, not in substance and essence. Little wonder the countries have never talked and discussed on the establishment of universal Caliphate for all Muslim countries, division of the world into *Darul Harb and Darul Islam*,[266] promotion of *Hudud*[267] punishment in bilateral and international treaties, etc. Even the states believe that as long as national interest is achieved, so religious aspiration of their people would be automatically accomplished, thus no longer necessary to pursue accomplishing Islamic substance and essence. Generally Muslim states are likely to understand that however, their respective foreign policies must be driven through rational and practical mechanisms in order to achieve their realistic goals and objectives.

In addition, as I would elaborate later, foreign policy itself requires wider space of Ijtihad[268] as it shall comply with domestic, regional and international dynamics. In this regard, when Muslim states began to declare their formal existence, so struggling for achieving substantial Islam would be automatically faded away. Meaning that struggling for realizing Islamic national interests in global context would be prevailing as it deals with more tangible and concrete ideas such as poverty and hunger eradication, economic, education and health affairs strengthening, etc. Interestingly such a fact is implicitly affirmed by Islamists in the Muslim states who tend to give more focus through their incessant struggles to formalize Islam in domestic politics, rather than formalizing it within global context.

Interestingly some countries like Saudi and Iran would not necessarily associate its foreign policy goals with the achievement of the national interests, but rather to maintain and sustain their regime survival. In fact, it is too hard to distinguish and differentiate between national and regime interests in ideological and undemocratic states like Iran and Saudi Arabia, as the ruling elites would claim that two sorts of interest are practically no difference. Moreover this assumption could be seen in the very early years of creation of the states which Saudi Arabia, in order to safeguard the monarchy's sustainability, had to adopt exceptional policies to establish cordial relations with US government since Saudi Arabia was in dire need of economic and military assistance from US during the time. In addition as time went on, Saudi Arabia which usually took firm stances towards Israeli aggression and occupation of Palestinian territory mainly in King Faisal's leadership, has to adjust its foreign policy in absorbing softer and more accommodative stances to Israeli interests and apparent got more dependent to the US whose foreign policy implementation is often not compatible with Islamic ummah interests.

In contrast, as many may know, Iran has been taking several antagonist and hostile stances towards US policies mainly reflected by stirring hostage crisis of US embassy in Tehran in the aftermath of Revolution outbreak in November 1979 as political manifestation

---

[266] Dar al-Islam is defined as the land which is governed by the laws of Islam. In opposite, Dar al-harb which is ruled not by Islamic laws.
[267] The set of laws and punishments specified by God in Al-Qor'an such as stoning and hand cutting www.collinsdictionary.com.
[268] Ijtihad is a technical term of Islam law that describes the process of making a legal decision by independent interpretation of the legal sources, the Qur'an and the Sunnah.

of revolutionary propaganda in resisting and opposing Great Satan, leaving Iran more economically and politically isolated before international community.[269] No doubt, Iran also decided to cut diplomatic relation with Israel as a revolutionary manifestation of its constant support to Palestinian struggles, thus handing the Israeli embassy in Tehran to Palestinians. Resuming war against Iraq under the religiously ambitious initiative of Godfather Imam Khomeini who strongly believed that Saddam was no more than a notorious unbeliever politician, simply reflected the obscurity of Iranian national and regime interests. Yet however, Iran is reported to have established economic and trade cooperation with US and Israel in 1980s in a world's shocking case called Contra Affair despite its significant effort to conceal such transactions from media coverage.

And Indonesia, due to the state's vulnerability and fragility emanating from colonialist power's pressure in the early years of its independence proclamation in 1945, had to take obviously pragmatic and flexible approaches in its foreign policy including revolutionary measures greatly brought up by first President Sukarno. In Sukarno's administration era, it seems that Indonesian foreign policy was tremendously directed into establishing much closer relationship with the US- feared states including Soviet Union and China. Certainly for Indonesia, due to its basic constitution that grants much flexibility in foreign policy taking, pragmatism is somewhat inevitable and almost compulsory as long as it could lead into realization of its own national interest. Little wonder, in the aftermath of Sukarno leadership in 1967, Indonesia under Suharto regime was significantly guided to putting high priority to look West/USA. Pragmatism was later applied by President Abdurrahman Wahid (1999-2001) by giving emphasis in foreign policy on Asia first including Middle East region, simply reflected in advocating Jakarta-Beijing-New Delhi axis as emerging new economic giant.

In other words, arguably the implementation of the countries' foreign policy following their formative period as consequence of pragmatic practices did not bear and pursue any Islamic identity and character although during the time Islam had posed a majority's religion; and the composition of political elite rulers of the respective countries was certainly dominated by politician Muslims. They have to put aside Islamic identity and interest in foreign policy for a while, only to guaranty survival and sustainability of the regimes or realize public interests at home. Pragmatic approach is a strategic step that is commonly taken by almost all states of the world, including Iran, Arab Saudi and Indonesia. Such a pragmatism aims at guarantying the survival of their existence as a nation and a state, in which practically their foreign policies would be directed to reach the goal. Meaning that, as cited earlier, Islamic interest shall be put aside for a while in order to materialize the countries' survival. In this vein, according to Akbarzadeh, pragmatism will automatically restrict absoluteness of the Supreme Leader's rule which he would try to

---

[269] Karl Yambert, the Contemporary Middle East, A Westview Reader, Third Edition, Westview Press, 2013, Page 338

develop the concept of Fiqh Maslahah (Fiqh of interests) that allows him to ignore Islamic principles for temporary.[270]

For Indonesia, the pragmatism could be taken more widely as it never claimed as an Islamic state. Indonesia, like most countries of the world, would determine its foreign policy based on national interest pursuit, accommodating all aspirations of various religions and ethnics which factually seem more complex and complicated than those of Saudi Arabia and Iran. The country which looks more democratic than the two states, invariably believes that realization of its own national interest would grant survival of the country, not merely the state administration. This fact obviously differs to what Iran and Saudi Arabia have long assumed that the interests of the regimes would be more important than those of their peoples, thus putting the regimes 'interests on the top priority. Even furthermore, as mentioned earlier, the two countries shall be giving their priority to safeguard and protect the regime, other than preserving Islamic ideology despite their ceaseless claiming as both Islamic states and leading states for international Muslims community. In this regard, the naming of Saudi Arabia suggests that country is defined through the name of Saud family, whereas the naming of Islamic Republic for Iran would suggest that clerical rulers shall be dominant in Iranian political administration.

For Iran, the ideology of Shia Islam in determining and formulizing its foreign policy would have a significant impact due to that with such an ideology, identity and role of Iranian nation could be simply defined in order to reach the goal of the establishment of Islamic government. In practice, by taking the significance of Islamic ideology in Iranian foreign policy into account, even before recruitment, anyone who is interested to become future Iranian diplomats, have to pass exams on the religious issues and be assured that they will keep in the straight lines of revolutionary principles and values. In addition, Iranian diplomats assigned in overseas would have to bear practically uncommon and revolutionary duties, which make Iranian embassies abroad a place for making coordination and arrangement pertaining to the propagation and promotion of its revolutionary principles. Under any circumstances, Islamic identity based on their revolutionary clerical and political interpretation is unlikely to be separated from taking its foreign policy. Iranian embassies abroad would operate under the shadows of revolutionary guidelines that could affect the staffs to act uncommonly. Furthermore, Ayatollah Ali Khamenei, current Iranian Supreme Leader gave empashis that Iranian national interest should be based on both national and revolutionary identity.[271]

The principles such as defending on Islam and Shia, promoting anti-imperialism, global arrogance, anti-Zionism jargons, being a fortress for revolution and protector for oppressed nations, claiming of its Supreme Leader as a leader for Islamic world dubbed as

---

[270] John L. Esposito, Lily Zubaidah Rahim, Naser Ghobadzadeh, The Politics of Islamism, Diverging Visions and Trajectories, Palgrave Macmillan, 2018, page 162
[271] www.pishkhaan.net, 13 June 2017

Amirul Muslimin [272]that is obliged to enforce justice and resist any tyranny and oppression etc would be integral principles for making its foreign policy.[273] Even Imam Khomeini himself once stated that Iranian foreign policy could not ignore and put aside Muslim world's problems including hunger and deprivation problem.[274]

Hence, such principles obviously make Iranian foreign policy to be unique and different from that of other states. The principles precisely also imply a duty for Iran's political elites to introduce, promote, propagate those principles to outside the world with a great hope that the target countries would be eager to apply them in various fields due to their holiness and sanctity, that in fact most Islamic states prefer to tackle their own internal matters to external ones. Such principles inevitably also imply on excessive self-confidence of Iran that continuously believes the sole duty of the world's society is annihilation of despotically oppressive regimes.

In sum, principle of Iran's neutrality described explicitly in a phenomenal jargon *"La Sharqi wala la Gharbi, Jomhorriye Islam Iran"* (Not East nor West, only Islamic Republic of Iran) has indicated the presence of independency and neutrality in foreign policy taking, in which based on the principle, Iran would exert different mechanisms in dealing with both Western and Eastern countries. The principle also implies any negation and rejection to foreign intervention in formulizing the basis and foundation of Iran's foreign policy. Not only that, the principle that has already become a jargon for the Iran's Ministry of Foreign Affairs, has exposed a radical, hostile approach of the regime to keep distance with superpowers USA and Soviet Union; and Its unwillingness to join any bloc of the states' influences, rather resisting them, chiefly the US. In fact, such principle has been applied following the outbreak of Revolution 1979. Interestingly in practice, Iran has not held consistently such fundamental principle by ignoring it in its interactions with other states, in which in several cases, Iran has opened its alliance with Russia, [275] and even developed good relations with several communist states.

For sure, ironically, such unique principles when applied on the ground both regionally and internationally, often contradict the interests or principles of other concerned states, mainly Arab states in Gulf territory. The principles, assumed by the regime as divine truth and absoluteness, are not necessarily believed by the others. Hence, those countries often have not welcomed sincerely the Iran's 'good intentions,' even responding them negatively and suspiciously due to in fact that the principles brought by Islamic regime for almost four decades proved to have generated chaos and insecurity within the territory.

---

[272] Leader of all Muslims
[273] Dr. Sayyed Jalal Dehgani Firozabadi, *Siyasate Khareji jomhorriye Islami* Iran, Centre for Research and Development of Human science, Tehran 1389
[274] www.imam-khomeini.ir
[275] Many facts in the field have already indicated that how well Iran's bilateral relationship with Russia is. For several times, Vladimir Putin has paid an official visit to Iran including his last visit in November 2017. In tripartite meeting with Turkey, both presidents of Russia and Iran had a meeting held in Ankara, April 2018 amid the main discussion on Syrian conflict

The principle of the only truth of Shiism when applied to affect the feelings of Shia minority groups living in Sunni majority countries, certainly would spark much fear and worry of the host countries. No doubt, the radical revolutionary Shia interpretation propagated intensively by Iran would give influence to Shia minority to carry out resistance and opposition towards their legal governments, yet illegal according to them as a logic consequence of long drawn political and social oppression taken by the governments. Furthermore Iran has always believed that all types of government on the earth to be illegal that must be changed by revolutionary ways, in order to be legal one. So it is not surprising that Iran posses an existential threat for the survival of other states as Iran has been trying to distract loyalty of Shia minority groups from their elite rulers by propagating and disseminating tremendously such divine principles through all possible mechanisms.

The Iranian principle as a pioneer in resisting global arrogance would like also to affect and disrupt its bilateral, regional and multilateral relations that are supposed to be established well in order to obtain the final goal of its own foreign policy. This fact indeed implicitly has confirmed a prevailing opinion within Iranian society that the goal of the outbreak of Islamic Revolution was not economical.[276] According to Iran's perspective, global arrogance brought by USA in dealing with regional dynamics reflected mainly by its partially biased approach to the Palestinian cause, must be resisted by all countries given the fact that it has created successfully global injustice and imbalance. Iran believes that USA constitutes a pioneer of oppressive regime that intensively attempts at spreading its hegemony into the rest of the world, and significantly interferes with Iranian domestic affairs until the change of the Islamic regime is materialized.

In international forums, Iran has often brought the anti-USA related topics along with its famous jargon "Down with America" without realizing deeply that most audiences may have conducive relations with USA. Not only that, within Iran alone, all government officials and society of Iran despite their scepticism, have been mobilized massively to institutionalize and popularize jargons like anti US imperialism and anti-Israeli aggression. In fact, this unique principle, along with other revolutionary policies, has been main factor propelling Iran's isolation from international community that surely harms its own national interest, reflected among other things by the imposing of the repeatedly military and economic sanctions mostly by western countries that also include the restrictions to enter the European and US territories.

However the revolutionary Iran, due to capacity limitation and lack of ability in dealing with various issues, has also applied strategic and pragmatic approaches in implementing and realizing its foreign policy goals, thus putting aside revolutionary and ideological characters for certain periods, in order to accomplish greater and more urgent benefits and advantages for its national interests, or regime's survival. Arguably Iranian ideological and revolutionary interests appear to be very flexible, not rigid and absolute, in

---

[276] www.khorasantime.ir, 4 February 2017

contrast to what other countries may have ever imagined that Iranian foreign policy must reflect rigidity, confrontation, and source of political and sectarian tensions. As mentioned earlier, this theocratic state would use strategic approach if felt to be more beneficial for the survival of Islamic regime, meaning that ideological interest will be put aside for a while until the long-term goal is obtained. Hereby, even for an only purpose of maintaining the survival of the regime, any approach including changing Islamic laws and regulations could be unflinchingly taken. Interestingly, such flexibility was demonstrated obviously by the pragmatic approach taken by Hassan ibn Ali, the second Imam in Shia Twelver, when he preferred peace through negotiation rather than resistance and confrontation with Muawiyah bin Abu Sufyan, first Chaliph of Umayyid Dynasty in 7th century. Interestingly, the story was translated by incumbent Supreme Leader, Ayatollah Ali Khamene'i, from Arabic book into Persian long before he was appointed as a Vali Faqih in 1989 and even some years before the founding of Islamic Republic of Iran in 1979, implying further that flexibility in Iranian foreign policy taking is somewhat praiseworthy and necessary according to the Supreme Leader's guidelines. [277]

In addition, Iran would be eventually compelled to loosen its strict foreign policy when imminent internal and external threats to the survival of its ruling appear. In this vein, Iran well understands that sustainability of regime and nation shall be put into the top priority despite the fact ignoring and overlooking revolutionary actions and agenda would often spark harsh criticism from the conservative hardliners at home. It means that if strategic and ideological interests were collided with each other in dealing with one external issue, then strategic interest by applying the necessary and required steps would prevail. Iranian approach to such threatening measures will be automatically flexible by stressing that such an approach would never constitute its total submission, but for realizing its short-term goal.

This is what actually once emphasized by Mehdi Khalaji, a prominent Iranian expert of Shiism, Iranian political elites both theoretically and practically have demonstrated that if the two interests were not met with each other, the strategic one must be preferred.[278] Kenneth Pollack, a prominent US scholar, did believe that the current Iranian Supreme Leader Ali Khamenei, despite his strong hostility and opposition to US policies, has pursued such an antagonism in a calculated, pragmatic fashion, which according to David Menashri, an Israeli scholar, the state's interests must be preferred over revolutionary dogma in both foreign and domestic policies.[279]

Nevertheless, as cited before, in Iran the interest of the regime does not necessarily reflect Iranian national interest, whereas interestingly the Iranian regime attempts

---

[277] Trita Parsi, Losing an Enemy, Obama, Iran, and the Triumph of Diplomacy, Yale University Press/New Haven & London, 2017, page 201
[278] Mehdi Khalaji, Apocalyptic Politics, On the Rationality of Iranian Policy, the Washington Institute for Near East Policy, page 29
[279] Kenneth M. Pollack, Unthinkable, Iran, the Bomb, and American Streagy, Simon & Schuster, Page 24

significantly to blur and obscure discrepancy of the two sorts of interest, strongly advocating that the regime's interest as the best pattern for all political systems on the earth would automatically echo public aspirations and interests, or even to entire Islamic world.

As a matter of fact, such Iranian pragmatism and flexibility in foreign policy have been applied even since the early years of creation of Islamic state, emphasizing more evidence that Islamic Republic, even since its founding, could not be totally independent from international community albeit much effort to accomplish independency and self-sufficiency. It proved once again that the more Iran tries to achieve such a goal of being total independent, the more dependent Iran would be, which Iran has often admitted its limitedness in various terrains, mainly in supporting and disseminating its revolutionary agenda in the globe. For instance in the middle of 1980s, Imam Khomeini had refused the radical shia clerics' advice that Iran keep distance with Turkey which had already recognized Israel as an independent state right after some years of Israeli independency declaration in 1948. It seems that according to those ulemas, establishing bilateral relations with Muslim countries which recognize the state of Israel would certainly tarnish its own revolutionary principles and even constitute ignominious setback. In this vein, Imam rather argued that Prophet (PBUH) reportedly dispatched His ambassadors to some territories.[280]

In fact, applying pragmatism in Iran's foreign policy has been more reflected following the death of Imam Khomeini in 1989 one year prior to his highly pragmatic stand of accepting the UNSC resolution of 598 to end long running war with Iraq.[281] As elucidated previously that Iranian Supreme Leader has final says and draws guidelines in many sensitive issues including foreign policy. Iran under the spiritual leadership of Ayatollah Ali Khamene'i to date has been practicing strategic approaches to gain and accomplish its short-term goals. However, less charismatic Ali Khamene'i along with his less- understanding to Islamic Shia laws as stated by many prominent Shia clerics, if compared to Imam Khomeini, has been one of the most significant factors in giving less influence to Iranian society, thus making its foreign policy more flexible and adaptable.[282] However with the passage of time,

---

[280] Rouhollah K. Ramezani, Reflections of Iran's Foreign Policy : Spiritual Pragmatism, Journal of Iranian Review of Foreign Affairs, Volume 1 No.1, spring edition year 2010, page 59
[281] www.en.imam-khomeini.ir, 19 July 2017
[282] In this regard, Iran's foreign policy could be divided into seven phases. First, the phase from February until November 1979 when Iran entered provisional government period under the leadership of Mehdi Bazargan who led coalition between Liberal Islamic Freedom Movement and Secular National Front. Second, from November 1979 until 1984 that was overshadowed strongly by Islamic ideology of imam Khomeini. Third, from 1984 until 1989, in which there was little shift towards pragmatism when Iran felt on extremely bad impact of Iran-Iraq war. Fourth, from the death of Imam Khomeini until the period of reformist President Khatami in 1997 that was filled with much pragmatism to normalization of Iran's economy. Fifth, from Khatami's period to Ahmadinejad presidencty in 2005 that emphasized more on gaining national interest. Sixth, from Ahmadinejad's until 2013 that was engulfed by controversial rhetoric of Ahmadinejad towards West and Israel. Seventh, from 2013 until today when Hassan Rouhani emerged as reformist President which has been trying to depict a well-moderate Iran to the world's communities. For further information, please refer to Christin Marchall, Iran's Persian Gulf Policy, From Khomeini to Khatami, Routledge Curzon Taylor and Francis Group, page 23

such an assumption has failed to prevent Ali Khamene'i from resuming revolutionary agenda in the globe. Some of consistent foreign policy that reflect largely ideological and revolutionary Iran such as keeping hostile positions with US and Israel, and spreading Islamic fundamentalism to the globe are not fully declined.

It is noteworthy to note that pragmatism practiced by Imam Khomeini has been a significant guideline and direction for many Iranian political rulers that could be legal justification to do so in latter days. More importantly, it has implied that taking such an approach does not mean that it would violate Islamic principles and spirits, which once inspired tremendously the creation of the Islamic state in 1979. For these clerical rulers, the purpose of gaining and achieving short term goals in order to reach long term goals is, in fact, endorsed and encouraged by Shia religion, much evidenced by Imam Khomeini himself. Accordingly this notion was once noted by Hashemi Rafsanjani in 1990s, former Iranian President, that the ideological principles in Iranian governmental system would be flexible obviously reflected by denying the rigid foreign policy along with its ideological revolutionary characters. He also suggested that laying down a state into perils and risks that may lead into its complete annihilation due to taking ideological policy will not be viewed to be reflecting an Islamic spirit.[283] Furthermore he analogized Iran's pragmatism to his own phenomenal statement *"We can't build dams with slogans"* that implied his more pragmatic approach in endorsing and supporting his own economic programs of infrastructure reconstruction as negatively far-reaching consequence of its long standing military conflict with Iraq.[284] In short words, the aim of Iran's foreign policy could be elaborated into three phases, namely short-term goal, mid-term goal and long term goal, that shall complement each other in order to achieve long term goal which is the survival of Islamic Republic.[285]

In fact as time went on, the peak of Iran's pragmatic foreign policy occurred more evidently when Mohammad Khatami came into power as a new President in 1997 to replace Hashemi Rafsanjani. The moderate-reformist President had given much effort to normalize Iran's relations with western countries even including with the US, mirrored by issuing a controversial decision that rejected imposing a death penalty to Salman Rushdi, UK's citizen and author of a contentious novel titled Satanic Verses. In sum, despite consistent antagonist attitude taken by Ali Khamene'i to US as symbol of global arrogance, Khatami was the first political leader and cleric who advocated the Islamic world to implement sacred war against terrorism following tragedy 9/11.[286] Interestingly, in Iranian political system, such moderate stances of Mohammad Khatami could be also indicative of the more

---

[283] Trita Parsi, Treacherous Alliance, The Secret dealings of Israel, Iran and the US, Yale University Press/New Haven London, page 263.
[284] Christin Marchall, Iran's Persian Gulf Policy, From Khomeini to Khatami, Routledge Curzon Taylor and Francis Group, page 23
[285] Fakhreddin Soltani dan Reza Ekhtiari Amiri, Foreign Policy of Iran after Islamic Revolution, Research Gate Januari 2010 page 202
[286] Opcit page 62

moderate Supreme Leader's approach in dealing with global affairs although he was reluctant to explicitly express it due to his unwavering willingness to maintain long lasting hostility to US and other 'enemy of Islam and Islamic *Ummah'*.

Moreover, based on the strategic considerations of pursuing regime's revolutionary interests, that is no doubt why Iran has had so much willingness to open very cordial relation with secular socialist Syria with a very small Shia community, rather than with other states that own large community Shia such as Azerbaijan and Bahrain regardless of how Syria could much benefit to Iranian economy. In addition, despite widespread public objection, it is no longer a secret that Iran looks eager to support President Bashar Asad with various means and methods. Worse, when international community denounced the brutality of the President to his civilians in Syria conflict, Ali Khamene'i has instead praised Mr. President as honourable figure in hosting the delegation of the Ministry of Religious Affairs in March 2018.[287] As such Iranian significant military intervention in Syrian crisis since 2013 has further signified the regime's intention to obscure and blur its interest with national interests. A 'pragmatic' approach taken by Iran in the conflict would further show that revolutionary agenda in Iranian foreign policy must prevail over others, thus sacrificing and undermining national basic aspirations. Most startlingly, history once noted that Iran's support to Syria was also mirrored through Imam Khomeini's stance while condemning bloody genocide targeting fundamentalist political activists of Ikhwanul Muslimin group carried out by President Hafed al Asad, father of Bashar Asad, in 1982, in Homa, Syria yet such a massacre has never had affected the bilateral relations between Iran and Syria. Ironically, while the massacre was occurring in Syria, Khomeini ceaselessly advocated world community to defend oppressed nations from their own repressive regimes.[288] In the other hand, when in 1980s a bloody conflict between Shia Amal movement and Palestinian Liberation Organization/PLO in Lebanon took place, Iran staunchly backed PLO, not Amal movement with Shia clear affiliation. Iranian position looked weird as Iran constitutes the world's largest Shia population. However shortly after it proved that PLO supported Saddam Hossein in Iran-Iraq war, Iran immediately scaled back its relation with the organization.[289]

In addition, Iran reportedly did not support Muslim Chechnya's struggle in obtaining its independence from Russia despite many other Muslim countries condemned Russian aggression to Chechnya as Iran has had a very strategic interest with Russia. More interestingly, Iran even declared that the conflict was a Russian internal matter which Iran never expressed willingness to make intervention with the conflict.[290] In the case of Nagorno Karabakh that has involved Azerbaijan and Armenia, Iran surprisingly stood with

---

[287] www.leader.ir, 1 March 2018
[288] Mohsen Milani, Why Tehran Won't Abandon Assad (ism), the Washington Quarterly, Fall season 2013 page 80
[289] Frederic Wehrey, Beyond Sunni and Shia, the Roots of Sectarianism in a Changing Middle East, Oxford University Press, 2107, page 97
[290] Bledar Prifti, US Foreign Policy in the Middle East, the Case for Continuity, Palgrave Macmillan, 2017, page 164

Armenian with its Christian majority, whereas Azerbaijan constitutes mostly large Shia population albeit secular in nature. Last but not least, Mike Pompeo, US secretary of state in September 2018 in his official tweeter account had criticized Ali Khamene'i, Iranian Supreme Leader, for his total silence on persecution and detaining of hundreds of thousands Uighur Muslim citizens of China, a state which for many years has constituted the top buyer of Iranian oil.[291]

As a matter of fact, with Iran always promoting and developing unity among Muslims of the world particularly between Sunni and Shia materialized among other things by holding several international conferences and meetings on Islamic unity, stipulating article 12 of Iranian basic constitution on affirming such tolerance to Sunni followers in Iran and holding annually an unity week of Sunni and Shia in addition to dubbing year 2009 as the year of Sunni and Shia solidarity, yet sad facts often occur at home concerning intensive discriminatory treatments carried out by Iran to Sunni adherents. To date, Sunnis have never been granted permission to build Sunni mosque in Tehran, compelling them to rent large apartments to conduct Jum'e, Eid Fithr and Adh prayers which regrettably are often subject to shutting down and destruction from security apparatus. Sunnis feel much on discriminations in politics, economic and social fields. For instance, strategic government positions shall be given into Shias nonetheless for Sunni majority towns/cities. According to Moulavi Abdul Hamid, Sunni Prominent preacher in Zahedan city who also enjoys travel restriction, in some Sunni areas, of 300 and 400 of institutional staffs, only 15 Sunnis are employed.[292] Since the creation of Islamic Republic of Iran until the President Rouhani's administration that started in 2017, there has been no Sunni minister appointed. The only highest governmental position ever granted to Sunnis is the position for a vice of Minister of Oil Affairs. In addition, Iran had only one Sunni ambassador, Saleh Adebi, ambassador for Cambodia and Vietnam.[293] It is no longer secret, the Sunni-dominated provinces like Kurdistan and Sistani Baluchistan have being undergoing backwardness and stagnation in economic and social matters, if compared with other provinces where Shias are predominant. Culturally, Sunni followers in Iran still face restriction that reflects in their limited presence in Iranian national media and strict censorship of books written by Sunni authors. In addition, dozens of Sunni followers accused for creating internal instability and chaos have been imprisoned and sentenced into death, a harsh and baseless accusation that they have always denied.

In addition to politic and security issues, the Iran's pragmatic approaches have also appeared in economic and trade sectors. For instance, other than with Muslim states, Iran reportedly has developed its deeper economic and trade relations with three non-Muslim

---

[291] Please refer to Mike Pompeo's tweeting in 14 September 2018
[292] Molana Abdul Hamed Ahlusunnat ba ghozashte 40 sal az Omr Enghelab Hamchenin az Tabez ranj mibarand, 4 June 2018,https://www.radiofarda.com/a/f4_abdulhamid_slam_discrimination_sunni_minority/29270604.html
[293] www.iranhumanrights.org

states namely India, China and South Korea. Most importers of Iranian oil are dominated by non-Muslim countries. Even furthermore Iran reportedly has opened its close relations with Communist North Korea since 1979 that was tremendously shown by delivering congratulatory remark by its leader to Imam Khomeini on the success of the establishment of new state, [294] while in parallel its bilateral relations with several Muslim countries was declining, triggered by fear of the impacts of revolution export. As time went on, under Ahmadinejad administration (2005-2013), Iranian foreign policy was driven significantly to deepen its economic relations with Latin American states.

Despite holding a unwavering hostile stance to USA since its formation, it proved that Iran had established an unimaginably closer cooperation and collaboration with US particularly in Afghanistan conflict in 2001 with Iranian officials offering the country as temporary military base for coalition troops to US government in launching effective and efficient attacks to topple down Taliban's government in Afghanistan. In addition, Iran had offered its good intention to America to link it with Northern Alliance group that by chance opposed Taliban, and was supported by Iran. Above all, the most important pragmatic approach that Iran has ever had taken along its modern history was the scandal of Iran Contra/ Iran Gate in 1985 to 1987 in Ronald Reagen's administration in which, based on Israeli advice, America succeeded to sell military weaponry to Iran covertly when Iran was in desperate need of a huge number of cutting-edge military weaponry and equipments in facing the largely Arab-supported Iraq. Most amazingly such a contentious transaction and deal was reached in tandem with the moment of the imposing of the military sanction by the US given an allegation of Iran's role in supporting terrorism in the region. As a matter of fact, the large amounts of money resulted from the transaction was used by US to fund anti-Sandinista fighters, known as Contras, against the socialist government of Nicaragua. Last but not least, the two feuding states had held secret talks between US and Iranian governments before US pre-emptive strike to Iraqi territory in 2003 as revealed by Zalmay Khalilzad, US former ambassador for Iraq[295] that accordingly allowed around 160.000 US troops to across the Iran's border. [296] Iran also rejected Iraqi requests to get its support in the strike.[297] Both US and Iran ware also reported to convene secret talks in Muscat, Oman, prior to adoption of JCPOA (Joint Comprehensive Plan of Action) nuclear deal in 2015. In fact, despite much hostile and antagonist stance of Iranian rulers, it is no longer a secret that thousands of Iranians who are the families and relatives of those political elites have been residing in USA for working, investing and studying. According to Steven Mnuchin, current US Secretary of the Treasury, has stated that currently there are 5.432 of Iranian

---

[294] Amir Taheri, man el moalim Haqiqhi Khamene'i, al Khomeini am Kim? M.aawsat.com, 1 September 2017
[295] Michael R Gordon, US Conferred with Iran Before Iraq Invasion, Book says, 6 March 2016, https://www.nytimes.com/2016/03/07/world/middleeast/us-conferred-with-iran-before-iraq-invasion-book-says.html
[296] Gawdat Bahgat, Anoushiravan Ehteshami & Neil Quilliam, Security and Bilateral Issues Between Iran and Its Arab Neighbours, Palgrave Macmillan, page 98
[297] Trita Parsi, Losing an Enemy, Obama, Iran, and the Triumph of Diplomacy, Yale University Press/New Haven & London, 2017, page 27

elites' children in US, owning property and personal assets around 148 billion dollars in their bank accounts. Interestingly such a phenomenon was explicitly confirmed by Mahmoud Bahmani, former head of Iranian central bank.[298] Not only that, an Iranian parliament member, Mojtaba Zonon has admitted that one of the positive outcomes of JCPOA deal signed in 2015 was the granting of 2500 green cards by the US under Obama's administration, a shocking statement that was also implicitly confirmed by President Donald Trump tweeting in July 2018.[299] Even Mashomeh Ibtikari, current vice President for women affairs who had a prominent role in US embassy occupation in Tehran right after the outbreak of Islamic Revolution in November 1979, is reported to send his son to America for studying.[300] My personal experience has also shown that one of my lecturers in the university also my thesis supervisor, well known for being ultra conservative as he often displayed his harsh criticisms to the US and UK, yet in fact he already sent his son to UK for studying.

Above all, one of the most significant proofs on such a pragmatic approach taken by Iran is its relation with Saudi Arabia. Furthermore establishing bilateral relationship between the two states could be regarded as an actualization of their respective claims to their capability as regional power, rather than an expression of national interests. Anti monarchy jargon and critical gestures shown considerably by Imam Khomeini toward the Kingdom in the first years of the Revolution had once generated fears and worries among Arab leaders, mainly Saudi Arabia, which succeeded to ignite massive protests carried out by the Shia minority group in eastern part of the Kingdom and provoke Iranian pilgrims to yell out anti-American and Israel slogans during Hajj. However with the passage of time, the bilateral ties have gone through ebbs and flows reflected by two times of diplomatic relation rupture in 1988 and 2016 and tremendous military involvement in proxy wars in the region. While almost all of the Iranian presidents have already visited the kingdom for bilateral talks, crown prince Abdullah is recorded to have official visit to take part in OIC summit meeting held in Tehran in 1997 during Khatami's presidential administration.[301]

As mentioned earlier that flexibility and pragmatism in foreign policy are commonly applied by almost all states in order to achieve their real long-term goals, even including ideological states like Kingdom of Saudi Arabia. Such a pragmatic approach taken by Saudi could be traced back into Kingdom's modern history while it established close relations with western countries such as America and Britain in a bid to consolidate and maintain King's power while King Abdul Aziz, the main founder of the modern state in 1932, was attempting at vanquishing numerous territories in Arab peninsula that he much claimed to be ruled

---

[298] Hesab 148 miliar dollar Aghazadeha dar Amrika tayed shod, 6 July 2018, https://tahririeh.com/-148-حساب/میلیارد-دلاری-آقازاده-هادر-آمری/

[299] Ryan Pickerell, trump: obama gave us citizenship to 2,500 iranians during nuke deal negotiations, 3 July 2018, https://dailycaller.com/2018/07/03/trump-obama-citizenship-iranians/

[300] Mashome Ibtikari, Pesaram dar Amerikas, https://www.fardanews.com/fa/news/586968/-معصومه-ابتکار-پسرم-آمریکا-است

[301] Banafsheh Keynoush, Saudi Arabia and Iran, Friend or Foes, Palgrave macmillan, page 140-145

once by his ancestors, and unifying them into one entity under his ruling family. Interestingly Saudi's efforts to grab political and economic supports from those countries were taken within the shadows of brutal and radical Islamic Wahhabi group often called al-Ikhwan that was intensely exploited by the King to smoothen his agenda in conquering and unification. The group was reported to have severely opposed and objected such close ties, believing that establishing relations with unbelievers' powers would tarnish purification attempts of Islam. As such, since its establishment, it is worthwhile to note that pragmatism in foreign policy has been taken by the Kingdom to guaranty and maintain the sustainability of its monarchy in the region.

In the other hand, the royal family has been fully aware that geographically and geopolitically, Saudi territory has been flanked by states with overlapping different interests that may have threatened its fragile existence, particularly from Hashemite family, former ruler of Hejaz who was expelled from his ruling in 1924/1925. In addition, Saudi domestic security has been often vulnerable to the existential threats imposed by local and global terrorism as well as recent military assaults carried out by Yemeni Houthi rebels. Not only that, despite having enormous natural resources of oil and gas first found and explored by Standard Oil of California 1938 along with its large territory, yet however its total population is just around 30 million whereas in the early years of its state founding, the population was no more than 3 millions. Karen Elliot further argued that despite richness in natural resources often spent to buy loyalty and allegiance, Saudi is a weak country that owns spectacular modern military equipment, yet it does not reflect military might. [302]

Therefore, by taking such facts into consideration, apart from being a state with multiple nations and diverse cultures given pilgrimage and foreign expatriates, the Kingdom has given its top priority to security issues by strengthening its intelligence functions, and implementing the flexibility of its foreign policy in a bid to prevent the threats from emerging.

However, historically speaking those potential threats were generated much by Saudi citizens who were arguably the outcomes of the radical and extreme Saudi educational curricula, rather than external ones that eventually led the state to intensify cooperation on counter-terrorism as well as purchasing cutting edge military equipments from other countries, particularly US. Interestingly the Saudi pragmatic approach by prioritizing partnership relations with USA to date has tremendously prompted much objection and opposition at home, as many Saudi militant Islamists view that US government with its contentious foreign policy intensively engages in the issues that harm Muslim interests. In addition, they further believe that asking unbelievers for help is strongly dissuaded by the religion.

---

[302] Karen Elliott House, Saudi Arabia, Its People, Past, Religion, Fault Lines and Future, Alfred A. Knopf, 2012 page 214

In fact the cordial relations between the two states have been established when King Abdul Aziz, main founder of Saudi, met with US President Franklin Roosevelt aboard the USS Quincy off Cairo in 1943, making him to be the first leader whom Abdul Aziz officially had ever met. Above all, Saudi's policy to allow US presence in Saudi territory in order to confront Saddam Hussein in gulf war in 1990 under any circumstances, supported significantly by religious fatwas issued by the government clerics, had sparked much controversy and anger among Saudi conservative and fundamentalist Muslims who viewed that such a policy was religiously illegal and not congruent with Qoranic teachings. More interestingly "un-Islamic" Saudi foreign policy had led many critical Saudi independent ulemas to write a petition to the Kingdom in early 90s called Letter of Demands (*Khitab al-Matalib*) which contained among others to establish an advisory council ruling on domestic and foreign affairs on the basis of Islamic Shari'a; and build a foreign policy that preserves the interests of the *Ummah*. Furthermore, the petition also highlighted that the situation of (Saudi) embassies should be rectified so that they reflect the Islamic character of this country.[303]

In sum, Saudi has intentionally labelled Islamic group of Ikhwanul Muslimin as terrorist group and sources of evil, in contrast with the fact that many Muslims of the world for years have believed the group to be a moderate Islamist group who never advocated and justified violence and terrorism in spreading religion. Even former US Secretary of State Rex Tillerson seemed reluctant to designate the group as terrorist group since some of its activists have already become parts of Bahraini and Turkish governments. Therefore due to such a designating taken in the wake of Arab Spring in 2012, Saudi played significant role by helping Secular Abdel Fatah Sisi topple down President Mohammed Morsi, also a prominent Ikhwanul Muslimin (Muslim Brotherhood) activist, from his presidential position through military Coup in 2014.[304] Since mid- 2017, along with the three other Arab states namely Egypt, Uni Emirates Arab and Bahrain, Saudi cut its diplomatic relation with Qatar due to its accusation of Qatari role in supporting terrorism in region and its relation closeness with Iran. Saudi also did not display any condemning gesture to Israeli occupation and opposing reaction to many US policies that are very detrimental for Palestinian interests. Even Saudi did not explicitly express its support to militant Hamas organization.

With the passage of time, the pragmatism of Saudi has also been implemented during 1960s when King Faisal reportedly extended his support to Shia Yemeni monarch other than republican socialist rebels who had support from Gamal Naser, President of

---

[303] See the contents of the Letter of Demands point 1 and 9, Stephane Lacroix, Awakening Islam, the Politics of Religious Dissent in Contemporary Saudi Arabia, translated from French to English by George Holoch, Harvard University Press, 2011, page 179
[304] What is the Moslem Brotherhood, 19 June 2017,
https://www.aljazeera.com/indepth/features/2017/06/muslim-brotherhood-explained-170608091709865.html

Egypt, further implying that sectarian solidarity based on Sunni character has not been Saudi interest.[305]

In current days, we have been witnessing reforms intensively conducted by a young Crown Prince, Mohammad bin Salman in a bid to realize his ambitious agenda VISION 2030, targeting to limit the Wahhabi religious authority domestically. Once again, pursuing the agenda has pushed the Kingdom to develop more cordial relations with the US whose policies, mainly under the administration of Donald Trump, have created controversy and disagreement among world's Muslims, including US official recognition on Jerusalem as new capital for Israel state.

Moreover, the flexibility of Saudi foreign policy could be also reflected in economic and trade sectors, meaning that by tremendously considering many factors, Saudi has to establish deeper relations with non-Muslim states rather than Muslim ones. In this vein, as scholars argue that the Kingdom, in business and economic affairs, is driven by western economic dynamics, principally profit maximization, rather than Islamic prescriptions,[306] despite the significant establishment of several Sharia banks at home. For instance, in 2016 alone, of six main import partners of Saudi, UEA is the only Muslim country. The remaining states are China, United States, Germany, Japan and South Korea.[307] While the top export countries of Saudi are China, Japan, India, US and South Korea.[308] In sum, the Kingdom will continue to "look East " in its international trade relations, most importantly China and India, to some extent Malaysia. It is also expanding good relations and trade ties with Brazil and Russia.[309] Such facts have already shown more deeply that Saudi economic and business sectors would be significantly underpinned by merely its pragmatic foreign policy that would bring more economic benefits to the state.

However Saudi further believes that in order to gain stronger legitimacy from its people, it has to create popular strategies and policies to attract foreign investments from those target countries in a bid to reduce the increasing number of unemployment as well as to diversify Saudi export dominated much by oil production during the time. Therefore, it is no longer secret that Saudi Arabia which puts the economic and development programs into its top priority, has had already developed close trade and investment interests with a number of non-Muslim countries. Such a fact could be well echoed that right after his appointment as a new King in 2005, King Abdullah's first foreign official visit was China. In return, the Kingdom was also chosen as President Donald Trump's first foreign trip in May 2017.

---

[305] Nader Hasehmi & Danny Postel, Sectarianization, Mapping the New Politics of the Middle East, Oxford University Press, page 156
[306] David Cowan, the Coming Economic Implosion of Saudi Arabia, A Behavioural Perspective, Palgrave Macmillan, 2018, page 96
[307] www.statistia.com
[308] Atlas.media.mit.edu
[309] Mohamed A.Ramady, The Saudi Arabian Economy, Policies, Achievements, and Challenges, Springer, 2010, page 485

This ironic fact could be seen in, among other things, economic and investment bilateral relationship of Saudi and Indonesia in which, based on statistical data issued by the Investment Coordinating Board of the Republic of Indonesia, the Saudi investment in Indonesia in year 2016 ranked 57 of all states of the world, with only less than one million dollars.[310] On the other hand, the official visit of King Salman to Indonesia in 2016 that was expected at first to be able to attract investment US$ 25 billion, only succeeded to bring roughly US$ 6 billion, if compared to Saudi investment in China that reached US$ 65 billion, tenfold total investment of Saudi in Indonesia.[311]

As a matter of fact, the Kingdom's emphasis on unity among Muslim countries has been obviously tarnished by its discriminatory treatments to Shia minority group despite various efforts given by the Kingdom to reduce negative sense of such a treatment such as holding first dialogue national involving Shia minority group in 2003 and other subsequent similar conferences, in addition to book publishing of sectarian dialogue written by a Shia scholar in 2007.[312] Wahhabi's teaching adopted by the Kingdom which believes Shia is not part of Islam, has created legal justification to carry out repression and restriction of the Shia religious practices, and even attack them through Saudi national media. Promoting Shia education and culture is officially banned, including history and tradition of Shia in schools and universities. Teacher position would not be given to Shia followers.[313] In addition, Shias are not given high positions both in government and private institutions. They are also not offered ministerial positions (only one Shia Minister of State appointed by King Abdullah in 2014).[314] As a matter of fact since its establishment in 1932, the Kingdom has assigned no more than two Shia ambassadors namely Jamil al-Jishi for Iran (1999-2003) and Hamzah Ghoush.[315]

Unlike Arab Saudi and Iran's foreign policies which have other objectives apart from achieving their own national interests as consequence of being Islamic constitution-based states, Indonesia, as explicitly cited in its law no 37 year 1999 on foreign relations, has specified its foreign policy taking to limit the goals into the achievement of its national interest. Meaning that, Indonesia would have legal justification that pursuing Islam-characterized foreign policy does not constitute the top priority, but rather to certainly achieve national interest that does not necessarily echo Islamic identity of most Indonesians.

---

[310] Soedjatmiko, Investasi Arab Saudi di Indonesia Urutan ke -57, 25 February 2017, https://www.jawapos.com/ekonomi/25/02/2017/investasi-arab-saudi-di-indonesia-urutan-ke-57
[311] Jokowi Kecewa Investasi Arab, Ini Penanaman Modal Saudi di Cina, 13 April 2017, https://bisnis.tempo.co/read/865881/jokowi-kecewa-investasi-arab-ini-penanaman-modal-saudi-di-cina
[312] A report compiled by National Security Research Division on Saudi-Iranian Relations Since the Fall of Saddam, Rivalry, Cooperation, and Implications for U.S Policy, page 37
[313] Raihan Ismail, Saudi Clerics and Shia Islam, Oxford University Press, halaman 104
[314] Medea Benjamin, The Unjust Kingdom, Behind the US-Saudi Connection, OR books 2016, page 31
[315] Badar Ibrahim, Muhammad Sadeq, Al-Harake Syi'i Fi Saudiyah Tasisel Mazhab wa Mazhabate Siyasi, Arab Network For Research and Publishing, halaman 75

Little wonder for instance promoting and developing cultural and traditional diversity would overwhelm and overshadow Indonesia's foreign policy taking in abroad, only giving a little portion to the promotion of Islam as an inseparable element of Indonesian society. However for Indonesia, being well-known for moderate Islam it always highly accentuates before international community would be diplomatic effective tool for dealing with various global issues such as promoting the discussions on counter-terrorism issues along with interfaith dialogue. In this vein, Indonesia would attempt to make balance by not ignoring altogether the importance of Islam as the largest identity and a unifying force of Indonesian nation even since the state's foundation in 1945. Apparently Indonesia would adopt Islamic spirit into its foreign policy if it is still relevant to the discourse and leads into the realization of national interest. As such, instead of being inspirational force that shall drive and guide Its foreign policy due to the adoption of Pancasila (five principles/basics) as open ideology and the absence of the achievement of Islamic purpose in its laws and basic constitution, Islamic element under the framework of pragmatic approach is used to be effective means to accomplish Indonesia's national interest, particularly the issues that relate to moderate Islam. As a matter of fact, Indonesia always considerably perceives that realizing the goal would implicitly mean realizing Indonesian Muslims' aspiration.

With the passage of time, the two issues of Palestine and counter-global terrorism are seemingly the most important reflections on Islam-spirited foreign policy of the three countries. The issues could be simply associated with the states even during the early years of their official foundation. Palestinian cause has enticed attraction their respective leaders to identify and guide foreign policy in order to comply with Palestinians' struggles by supporting them with all sorts of means and mechanisms, thus putting aside their ultimate goals of realizing their national interests. Meanwhile, radicalism and extremism in Islamic interpretation that are likely to lead emerging terrorism could be also seen as inseparable factor that have overwhelmed domestic security and stability of the countries. Ironically, Wahhabism/Salafism has been largely viewed by international community to have produced 95 % of the Islamist terrorists despite the fact that fewer than 5 percent of world Muslims follow such an ideology. [316]

Yet historically speaking, King Abdul Aziz, the founder of Saudi modern in 1932, had to deal with radical, extreme Wahhabi Ikhwan group by getting rid it before his successful unifying effort. Meanwhile, four years after its independence declaration, Indonesia also had to engage with radical Islamic movement led by Kartosoerwiryo who highly proposed founding an Islamic state of the newly-born Indonesia. Republic Islam of Iran founded right after the breaking out of Islamic revolution in 1979, also had to deal with terror activities carried out by the frustrated members of Mojaheden el-Khalg organization that still exists to date, urging actively the overthrowing of the Islamic Iranian regime. In truth, for many decades, the three countries have also gone through a wide range of destructive terror acts

---

[316] Opinion.bdnews24.com, 23 May 2018

sometimes carried out by the like-minded terrorist global networking which underpins terror acts in the name of Islam, making it great challenge for the policymakers of the states to counter it by more deeply presenting moderate and middle path Islam.

In the other hand, both aforementioned issues undoubtedly would draw world's Muslims to further assess and judge whether Arab Saudi, Iran and Indonesia would be consistent on supporting Palestinians and giving much effort to annihilate global terrorism, in which all of their respective attempts in engaging with such issues could be implicitly reflecting Islamic and Muslims interests, internally and externally. Each state would repeatedly claim that it always promotes moderate and tolerate Islam in opening and establishing relations with international community as it deeply understands that radicalism and extremism are anathema to the cultivation of such bilateral, regional and multilateral ties. Furthermore, the three countries often discuss and give emphasis on counter terrorism efforts in their respective bilateral talks.

In reverse, failures in dealing with both issues reflected by imposing a plethora of accusations mainly to Arab Saudi and Iran for supporting global terrorism by financing radical movements and dispatching militant fighters to outside borders, would significantly tarnish their image and reputation before world Muslim community, with some terror acts being often associated to both states particularly in the aftermath of 9/11 tragedy.

I. Palestine Cause

In fact, Palestinian cause has emerged several decades ago long before the issue of global terrorism becomes more concern of international community following the tragedy 9/11. The issue that began to arise internationally after Israeli independence declaration has generated Muslim countries to drive and guide foreign policy to extend political and economic supports to Palestinians. The conflict that has lasted since more than 7 decades ago has pointed out lack of coordination and synchronization as well as friction among Muslim nations that proved to have failed in finding out a more politically appropriate solution.

In addition, the issue has already become special as the states are yet to have diplomatic relations with Israel, in which opposing the founding of Israeli state vehemently would not create controversy and objection within Islamic world, arguably viewed Israel as the public enemy by most Muslim nations. In nutshell, to reject Israel by not recognizing it diplomatically as an independent state is regarded to be one of the safest conduct of foreign policy, mainly for Indonesia and Iran whose long standing antipathy would not give ramification to their relations with the US, seen as important ally for Israel since both countries have not been much overshadowed by the US interest. It is worthwhile mentioning that Saudi Arabia and Indonesia view the Palestinian dossier as a merely political that may accept flexibility and elasticity in taking political solutions. in this regard, Indonesia and Saudi Arabia always believe that pursuing two-state solution to the issue constitutes the framework of their respective foreign policy, even since its initial founding, Saudi Arabia has been well known for its moderate stance towards the issue when King Abdul Aziz, the Saudi founder, did not object to the establishment of a Jewish entity (state) in Palestine. As Ellen R. Wald further notes that the King's concern was that if a Jewish state encompassed most of Palestine, Jews would eventually expand beyond the border of the British mandate into other parts of the Middle East. [317]

In the other side, Iran always believes that the issue of Palestine further constitutes the combination between politics and religion. Iran perceives politics is an integral part of the Shia religion, which leadership (*Imamah*)[318] constitutes one of the main pillars of Shia faith. The long entrenched perception has encouraged Iran to take a very distinct approach in dealing with the issue, which is to prefer taking a revolutionary approach through Jihad implementation against Jews (Zionists).

However, Islamic Republic of Iran born later after Saudi and Indonesia, has missed several significant events of the conflict starting from happenings in the wake of contentious declaration of Israeli independent state in 1948 that consequently resulted in Palestinian refugees often called *al-Nakbah*, and numerous Arab wars against Israel significantly supported by the Superpower, etc.

Furthermore interestingly it can be argued that moderate and soft approach towards the conflict has began to be applied by the Kingdom in parallel with the birth of Islamic Republic state of Iran which has often suggested revolutionary approaches in dealing with the conflict including elimination of Israeli state from the map. This fact would give emphasis on the reality that Saudi approach in giving its substantial support to the cause could be flexible depending on regional and global dynamics, and perhaps personal characters of the Kings.

Yet, such a fact did not affect softening Iranian foreign policy towards the conflict, and preclude Iran from putting priority of its foreign policy on Palestine Issue albeit along with different and unique approaches as I would like to highlight further. In this vein Iran furthermore believes that Palestine issue would be very effective tool to display and exhibit tangible contribution more evidently as a leading state of world's Muslims, indirectly undermining and replacing Saudi role.

As a matter of fact, when President Donald Trump announced Jerusalem city as new capital for Israel in December 2017 thus implying official rejection on the city to become Palestine's future capital, international community particularly Islamic world got devastated

---

[317] Ellen R.Wald, Saudi Inc, the Arabian Kingdom's Pursuit of Profit and Power, Pegasus Book, New York London, page 39
[318] Shia Islam, countrystudies.us

and angry. Such a contentious decision planned long before since 1995, once again has proven to have created frictions among world's community including Muslim/Arab states in giving perspectives in relation with the conflict resolving. As it was issued by the superpower, little wonder the policy turned to have its global implication, mainly to those Muslim countries that have developed special relations with the US. In addition, unrelenting US supports to Israel largely viewed as 'common diplomatic enemy' reflected among others by vetoing 43 drafts of UN Security Council Resolution against Israel since 1972 would examine the three countries' commitments in extending supports to Palestinians, thus perhaps leading them to take more pragmatic approaches to deal with the issue.

As a direct response for such a worry and anxiety on future peace process under the framework of the two state settlement, an emergency meeting of OIC was held and hosted by Turkish government, joined by dozens Muslim state leaders including Indonesia and Iran who vehemently opposed and condemned the US policy, reflected by the presence of Presidents Joko Widodo and Hasan Rouhani in the summit meeting. However, it has been reported that Saudi Kingdom sent only his ministry official, not its ruling leaders, King Salman, nor Mohammad bin Salman, the Crown Prince that inevitably sparked much speculation among international Muslims on Saudi's strong and firm commitment for the issue. In addition, in responding such Donald Trump's decision, Iran made further concrete step which is the ratification of the law by the parliament on its official re-emphasis on Jerusalem as the immortal capital of Palestinian territory.

On the other side, with Saudi having more moderate and softer stance against Israel interest, reportedly that in 2017 Saudi has granted free opportunities of pilgrimage (hajj) under the annual routine programme initiated since 2009 for Palestinians whose families already died in fighting against Israeli occupation, thus strengthening positive image and reputation of Saudi. This kind of Saudi contribution unfortunately lacked international media coverage.

Not only that, to show its solidarity on Palestinian's struggle, in December 2017 Saudi had refused the participation of Israeli chess delegation in the World's championship of chess held in Riyadh. Adel Jubeir, Saudi Minister of Foreign Affairs once refuted to be interviewed by Israeli television network. In April 2018, King Salman even renamed the Arab Summit held in Riyadh Jerusalem Summit, expressing Arab leaders' solidarity over Palestinian struggles.

Yet in contrast, September 2017, Crown Prince Mohammad bin Salman was rumoured to have paid a secret visit to Israel, having a meeting with Israeli Prime Minister Benyamin Netanyahu, that certainly was denied by the Saudi government officials. Also reportedly, there was meeting held between Prince Turki bin Faisal, former head of Saudi Intelligence unit with Israeli Major General Yaakov Amidror, Israeili former National Security

Advisor in May 2016 in Washington.[319] Furthermore, an openly aknowledged meeting was arranged between Saudi retired major general, Anwar Eshki and Dore Gold, a senior Israeili Foreign Ministry official in 2016 in Jerussalem.[320]

Meanwhile in Iran, also reportedly in October 2017 there was a meeting between Saleh al-Arouri, Head Deputy of radical Hamas Organization with numerous Iran's high officials in Tehran, Iran. In the same year, it is reported that several Hamas officials entered the Iranian territory, only to attend the funeral ceremony of Ghasem Soleymani's father, the Commander of Qods force.[321] Good relation between Iran and Hamas was asserted strongly by Hamas representative in Tehran, Khaled al-Qoddomi 2017 stating that Iran has resumed funding and giving weaponry to Hamas after 5 year of stagnant relationship.[322]

Historically since early 20th century, Palestine had never become an independent state, in which in 1918 Palestine was a part of South Syria under the rule of Ottoman Empire. In 1920, League of Nations granted Britain mandate over Palestine and Transjordan in which previously in 1917 Britain had promised Jewish community the foundation of a state under Balfour Declaration. A resolution 181 issued by General Assembly of the UN on partition plan, while regarded unjust by Palestinians was a golden opportunity for Jewish community to unilaterally declare the creation of Israeli state in 1948 that eventually has been followed by the expansion of the territory and building of illegal settlement as well as other human rights abuses.

Until now, various steps and strategies of International diplomacy including the issuance of dozens UN's Resolutions have been made to resolve the conflict. Despite the fact that Palestinians have failed to reach their long standing dreams to be gain a status of independent state, yet some achievements in international arena shall not be overlooked and ignored, attesting much contribution of the three countries which pledged to espouse Palestinian interests through their respective foreign policy implementations. Among those achievements, the state has been recognized as an observer member – non state in General Assembly of UN in 2012 and a member in International Criminal Court in 2015. However the endless-seemingly conflict has been often exacerbated by numerous internal rifts between Hamas and Fatah political parties, and overshadowed by the ceaseless biased mediation of the US.

---

[319] Mohammade Abdelaziz, Media Analysis of the Meeting Between Prince Turki Al-Faisal and General Amidror, 20 May 2016, https://www.washingtoninstitute.org/fikraforum/view/media-analysis-of-the-meeting-between-prince-turki-al-faisal-and-general-am

[320] Can Israel and the Arab States Be Friends? 27 August 2016, https://www.nytimes.com/2016/08/28/opinion/sunday/can-israel-and-the-arab-states-be-friends.html

[321] Khaled Abo Toameh, The Iran-Hamas-Hezbollah Connection, 8 November 2017, https://www.gatestoneinstitute.org/11330/iran-hamas-hezbollah

[322] Hazem Balousha, Why Hamas resumed ties with Iran, 29 June 2016, https://www.al-monitor.com/pulse/originals/2016/06/gaza-hamas-resume-relations-iran.html

Iran and the Issue of Palestine

For Iran, Palestinian issue posses two of four basic principles of its foreign policy since Imam Khomeini's ruling era in the aftermath of Islamic Revolution in 1979, that include fighting against Zionist enemy and liberation of Jerusalem city, as well as giving support to oppressed Muslim nations.[323] Palestinian nation regarded as both Muslim nation and oppressed people (*Mustaz'afin*), has constituted an Iranian political strategy.

Its incessant support that has became integral part of its foreign policy would further navigate the government to maximize its contribution until the Palestinians' long waited aspiration to have an independent and sovereign state comes into realization. In this regard, the initial strong support of Iranian government was reflected in the convening of first Congress for Liberation of the Quds, joined by members of various liberal movements in Tehran one year after the Islamic state was born. Even furthermore, the Iranian founding fathers truly believed that the victory of the Revolution wouldn't be perfect if Palestinian territory was still under Israeli occupation.[324] Therefore with the passage of time, guidelines of Ayatollah Ali Khamenei as the incumbent Supreme Leader on his unquestionable support to Palestinians by taking revolutionary mechanisms and ways that pursue the conflict settlement with military approach was immediately reflected by the signing of a statement of emphasis on the need for the annihilation of Israel from the world map by the majority of Iranian parliament members in March 1994.[325] However, as Trita Parsi once stated, Ayatollah Khomeini, the main founder of Islamic Republic of Iran declared that Iran should provide only ideological support for the Palestinians and avoid any direct entanglement with Israel.[326]

As a matter of fact, the Issue has created not only a golden opportunity for Iran to prove itself as a leading state for Islamic world, but also has made a great challenge for identifying its foreign policy which is often at odds with its goal achievement of national interest. In this vein, Iran feels obliged to articulate its incessant supports to the Palestinian cause, both at home and abroad, that gave us initial conclusion that such an intensive support of Palestine cause could be the first target of Iranian revolutionary export to the region, that I would like to shed light further. In this vein, Grand Ayatollah Montazeri, onetime designated successor of Imam Khomeini, once stated in the first years of Islamic

---

[323] Gawdat Bahgat, Israel and the Persian Gulf, Retrospect and Prospect, University Press of Florida, page 18
[324] Ali Alfoneh, Iran Unveiled, How the Revolutionary Guards is Turning Theocracy Into Military Dictatorship, the AEI Press, 2013, page 216. In this vein, Akbar Hashemi Rafsanjani once given a phenomenal inauguration speech before the congress, 'Until the victory of the revolution of Palestine and until Israel has left the occupied territories, our revolution will not have reached its total victory'
[325] Trita Parsi, Losing an Enemy, Obama, Iran, and the Triumph of Diplomacy, Yale University Press/New Haven & London, 2017, page 38
[326] Trita Parsi, Losing an Enemy, Obama, Iran, and the Triumph of Diplomacy, Yale University Press/New Haven & London, 2017, page 39

Iranian establishment, "I hope that our slogan of Today Iran, Tomorrow Palestine is not only a slogan.'[327]

Nevertheless, geographically Iran does not possess direct borders with Israel/Palestine's territory that might require Iran's more involvement and embroilment in engaging the conflict. Consequently Iran neither had Palestinian refugees case nor military clashes with Israel in since Israeli creation in 1948, even historically speaking for thousand years ancient Persian empires have never had any political disputes with Jews, instead help free them when they were forcibly brought to Babylon. Yet in fact, following the creation of Islamic Republic of Iran in 1979, a huge number of Iranian Jews are reported to have left out for Israeli territory. Above all, Palestinian Muslims are mostly Sunnis.

Despite the aforementioned facts, since its establishment, Iran has constituted the most confronting state towards the Israeli occupation if compared even with any Arab states in the region, viewing sceptically Israel as cancerous tumour that must be eradicated from the earth. So, it is not astonishing that the repetitive rhetoric on annihilation of Israeli state has been often delivered by Iranian officials, including by Supreme Leader himself that Israel won't survive another 25 years as of 2015, who strongly view the military resistance is the only option must be taken to engage with Israeli legal actions, not by holding diplomatic negotiations under the framework of two state solution that proved to have given more chance for Israel to materialize its illegal decision and brutality.[328] Furthermore Iran has been confident that each country directly involved in peace process negotiations with Israel, could be said automatically it recognizes the creation of Israeli state. [329]

In this vein, practically with various courageous and dauntless anti-Israel jargons, Iran definitely succeeded to shock the world and accordingly draw Islamic world's sympathy through a controversial Ahmadinejad's remark in the United Nations in September 2005 by reaffirming that Israel must be wiped off the map. In an international conference called the World Without Zionism, this ultra-conservative President delivered a harsh criticism towards Muslim states leaders who have already recognized officially the Israeli existence, stating that such a decision of recognition reflected Muslim's submission and defeat against Israel.[330] Even to show his resentful feeling towards the Zionism, Mr. President who did not

---

[327] Ibid, page 217
[328] Historically speaking, in seeking peaceful solutions for the conflict, several international deals have been achieved including most importantly Camp David Accords in 1987, Madrid Conference 1991, Oslo Accords 1993, Israeil-Jordan Peace Treaty 1994, Camp David 2000 Summit
[329] Abbas Imanpour, Jayegeye Farayandeye Solhe Khavarmiyane dar Siyasate Khareji Iran va Amrika, jurnal Khavarmiyane tiga bulanan, Pusat Riset Keilmuan dan Studi Strategis Timur Tengah tahun 11 nomor 2 Musim Panas 1383 page 63
[330] Ewen MacAskill dan Chris McGreal, Israel Should be wiped off map,say Iran's president, 27 Oktober 2005, www.theguardian.com

stem from clerical realm, had ever overtly denied the Holocaust tragedy in a summit meeting held in Mecca in 2003 and through several interviews in media. [331]

Both Ayatollah Ali Khemene'i and former President Hashemi Rafshanjani through their remarks have been well known for being the most radical figures in Iranian modern history of Islamic Republic following Imam Khomeini's death, well echoed in delivering their strong denunciation on Israeli policy.[332] Not only that, the Iranian conservative politicians often prefer using 'word' *Sahyounist* (Zionist) to the word of Israel to bring its negative implication. Overshadowed by its revolutionary characters, Iran has also often hosted a plethora of national and international meetings and conferences with the topic on support to Palestine and resistance against Israel held routinely since 1990s.[333] In addition, Israeli office that was established during Dynasty Pahlavi in 1957 in Tehran to reflect Iran's de-facto recognition of Israel, has been transformed into Palestinian embassy right after the victory of the revolution. The street where the embassy is situated was also changed into *Kheyabon Filistin* (Palestine Street). Within Iranian territory, in order to expose more solidarity and support of Iranians to Palestinian struggles as a manifestation of Imam Khomeini's declaration in early years of the Revolution, Qods day is commemorated and celebrated massively by the people annually, sponsored incredibly by Iranian government held on Fridays of the last week of Ramadan month.

It is also worth to note that in dealing with the issue, Iran has not been an active player in seeking a political solution of the conflict both regionally and multilaterally since Iran along with unique approach in foreign policy, has always believed that revolutionary solution shall resolve the conflict, further creating political gaps and discrepancies in perspective and point of view with most states which seemingly prefer two state solution to one state solution. In addition, being *Ajami* (non-Arabs) of Iranians is likely to have created a great obstacle that the country will not be invited by the conflicting parties and Arab states to join the peace process. Most probably Arabic feature of Palestinian case constitutes one of the most important elements that prevented Iran's involvement to directly resolve the conflict. In addition, Iran has been accused by the Arab states of possessing a hidden agenda in the region of the expansion of its revolutionary Shia principle, instead of having a sincere intention to support Palestinians. Arabs seemingly have been much aware that despite of Imam Khomeini's death, yet his famous jargon *"the path to Qods goes through Karbala in Iraq"* does not necessarily fade away. However, according to Barry Rubin, the author of the

---

[331] National Security Research Division, Saudi-Iranian Relations Since the Fall of Saddam, Rivalry, Cooperation, and Implications for U.S Policy, page 24
[332] Hashemi Rafsanjani az Nabudi Israel ta najati Iran, 6 February, 2013, https://www.radiofarda.com/a/f7-commentary-on-rafsanjani-role-in-iran-current-era/24894991.html
[333] Among the conferences held by Iran are International Conference on the Islamic Revolution's Support for People of Palestine 1991, International Conference on Supporting Palestine Intifadha 2001, International Conference on Qods and Supporting Palestinian Rights 2006, a two day conference on the International Conference to Review the Global Vision of the Holocaust in Tehran, in 2006 . International Conference of Islamic World Scholars in Defense of Palestine Resistance in 2013, and International Conference in Support of the Palestinian Intifadha in 2017

Arab States and the Palestine Conflict, Palestine has been a central element in the rise of Arab Nationalism and Pan-Arabism which examined conventional wisdom and ruling ideology of the Arab world on its solidarity and oneness.[334] In nutshell, Palestine issue represents more deeply political divergence between Arab leaders and Iran which consistently believes that Palestine is an international issue, neither a bilateral nor regional one.

For example, when Madrid conference hosted by Spain aiming to reinvigorate and rekindle peace process held in October 1991 to include participation of several Arab countries, Iran was not invited deliberately by the US. According to Iran, such a conference had failed to bear positive outcomes for Palestinians, thus becoming a golden opportunity for Iran to prove once again to the Islamic world that such a peace process held through diplomatic negotiations and talks would not yield any favourable result for Palestine's interests. In addition, as an implicit counter for Madrid conference, Iran then decided to host an international conference by inviting Palestinian figures who appeared much disappointed and sceptical to the zero result of the conference. For this theocratic state, such a rival conference would be indicative on the first realization of Iran's seriousness to encompass participation of Palestinian rejectionist groups despite dissimilar Sunni and Shia ideologies, with Iran reducing its funding to Lebanese Hezbollah organization one year earlier.[335] As it was predicted earlier, the conference once again stipulated one state solution rather than two state solution as a political spirit brought significantly in the Madrid conference. In sum, the conference also reasserted its support to other radical Palestinian organization called the Islamic Jihad.[336]

As a matter of fact, Iran's interaction with the conflict has been made mainly under the Pahlavi ruling since Israel had declared itself as an independent and sovereign state in 1948 in which initially Iran did not recognize the state. Yet at that time, Iranian monarch government did not put the Palestinian issue on the top priority of its foreign policy due its pragmatic closeness to the US. In this regard, according to Trita Parsi, Iranian prominent scholar and author of a phenomenal book Treacherous Alliance, the Secret Dealings, Iran and the US, Pahlavi dynasty had attempted to hide much bilateral cooperation with Israel including technology and military cooperation, intelligent information exchange that aimed at curbing political and religious oppositions inside the country.[337] In sum, as an expression of solidarity for Palestinian struggle, Pahlavi dynasty had objected the partition plan suggested by UN in 1947. Not only that, the King of Pahlavi proved that it had opposed Israel to be accepted as new UN member two years afterward. However as time went on, such a pro- Palestine policy had changed 180 degree in which in 1950 the Iranian monarchy

---

[334] Barry Rubin, the Arab States and the Palestine Conflict, Syracuse University Press, first edition, page 1
[335] Trita Parsi, Losing an Enemy, Obama, Iran, and the Triumph of Diplomacy, Yale University Press/New Haven & London, 2017, page 30
[336] Banafsheh Keynoush, Saudi Arabia and Iran, Friend or Foes, Palgrave macmillan, page 132
[337] Trita Parsi, Treacherous Alliance, the Secret Dealings of Israel, Iran and the US,yale university press/new haven and london page 25

took decision to be the second majority Muslim country after Turkey to recognize Israeli state albeit de facto recognition.[338] Moreover, to concretize Pahlavi's support to the newly born Israel, the Consulate General of Iran had opened in Jerusalem city, later dissolved in the revolutionary era.[339]

In contrast, the Palestine Issue has been a main concern of Iranian Shia clerics for many decades long before the outbreak of Revolution in 1979. For instance in 1940, Ayatollah Abdul Qaem Kashani urged Iranians to organize a long march in protesting the event of massive immigration of Jews to Palestine land, and to be volunteers in Palestine. In addition, those Shia clerics, particularly those residing in Qom city including Imam Khomeini himself often delivered the sermons that condemned the Israeli creation, calling for boycotting Israeli products as well as censuring cordial relation between the two countries much described as relations of love without a marriage contract.[340]

Furthermore Imam Khomeini stated firmly that Israel is enemy for Islam that reflected the biggest creation of West's crime in which political and economic embargo must be carried out more effectively by Muslims. Additionally, Imam had also issued a fatwa/legal opinion that part of *Khums*[341] must be paid to help Palestinian struggle.[342] Not only that, Imam Khomeini had also criticized the egoism of several Arab's leaders, under the influence of West, who prevented millions Arabs to spread Jihad to liberate Palestinian land from Israeli occupation.

Following the revolution, the Palestine cause has been challenge that examines Iran's foreign policy whether its approach and mechanism taken would stand on Palestinian side or not. Iran directly has duty to make the issue on its top priority that can't be changed as long as Islamic feature of the state persists. So it is not surprising, Iran has been demanded to express more firmly its position on several ramifications caused by the conflict such as oppressive measures taken ceaselessly by Israel, refugee problem, racist treatment, building separating wall and illegal settlement until Palestinians could achieve their own goals, which is the Palestine state creation. Hence, this is why Imam Khomeini, along with the Arab's leaders, had denounced the Camp David deal in 1978 between Israel and Egypt that prompted Egypt to become the first Arab country which recognized the Israeli existence by noting that such a deal would harm not only the Palestinian interest, but also the states in the region. The deal would obviously generate all forces to counter such a

---

[338] Lior Sternfield, Zionism and the Shah : on the Iranian elite's evolving perceptions of Israel
[339] www.veteranstoday.com
[340] www.iranicaonline.org
[341] The obligation for Shia followers to pay one fifth of the annual surplus income, or of mine and treasure, taking into account the required conditions in fiqh. In the verse of Khums, the people who are rightful to receive khums are divided into six: God God's Messenger Dhi l-qurba (close relatives of the prophet), Orphans Miskin (those who are very poor), Ibn al-sabil (those who are in trouble financially while traveling)
[342] Ray Takeyh, Guardian of the Revolution, Iran and The World in the Age of the Ayatollahs, A Council on Foreign Relations Book, Oxford University Press 2009, page 62

phenomenon.[343] Interestingly, Imam also pointed out that it is necessary to distinguish between Jewish community and Zionism, which he criticized the latter harshly by saying that Zionism has no religion. [344] Hence, Iran has cut its diplomatic relations with Egypt as expression of its objection to the deal, [345]which later on he welcomed Palestinian PLO's visit conducted by Yasser Arafat-led delegation to Tehran to deliver congratulatory message and Palestinian support on the newly-born Islamic Republic of Iran in which during the meeting Imam failed to convince Yaser Arafat to take more revolutionary approach against Israeli occupation.[346]

For Iran the conflict mainly has mirrored many principles and goals of its own foreign policy that complement one another including the establishment of Islam unity on the earth, support to any struggle of weekly marginalized nations and any world's liberation movements, respect to sovereignty of one country's territory along with no recognition to unbelievers occupation to Muslims.[347] This is also reasserted by Iran's former Foreign Minister Ali Akbar Salehi that Palestine can't be divided into two parts, depicting two state solution often brought by many state leaders is not a best option. Therefore according to him, with Iran not recognizing Zionist state, it also emphasizes on no recognition to a divided Palestinian land. Salehi advocated for holding a free and active referendum joined by all Palestine nation as the sole solution to deal with the conflict, assuring that such an Iranian policy toward Palestine is absolutely unchangeable and would be endorsed endlessly by Iranian regime. [348]

Despite Khomeini's passing away in 1989, the spirit of anti Zionism and support for Palestinian struggle has not decreased significantly. The Khomeini's guidelines have still been maintained in shaping Iran's foreign policy. In this vein, Iranian parliament immediately ratified a political, social and economic – dimensioned law to show its official support to the resistance of Palestinians against the Zionists. Besides, such a ratified law has mirrored coordination efforts of Iranian government institutions to numerous

---

[343] Trita Parsi, Treacherous Alliance, the Secret Dealings of Israel, Iran and the US,yale university press/new haven and london page 27
[344] Ibid page 29
[345] Later on diplomatic relation between the two countries was resumed when Egypt was ruled by Mohammad Morsi the fifth President of Egypt who came from Ikhwanul Muslimin group. Historically speaking, Ahmadinejad and Mohammad Morsi were the state leaders to pay official visits each other in 2012. Yet, such relations became stagnant when Morsi was unseated by Coup conducted by then-President Abdul Fatah Sisi in June 2013. Until now relations of both countries are tackled by interest section.
[346] Rachel Brandenburg, Iran and the Paletinians, www.iranprimer.usip.org. PLO with pan-Nationalism and pan-Arab agenda failed to attract sympathy of Imam Khomeini beside the fact that PLO's support to Iraqi regime rather than Iran, thus prompting Islamic regime has never granted its financial assistance to the organization, other rather to Hamas and Islamic Jihad movements. According to Iran, moderate position of PLO had successfully led to the recognition of Israel by many. In 1989, Ayatollah Ali Khamene'i, the successor of Khoemini mentioned Yasser Arafat as an idiot and traitor.
[347] Ali Akbar Velayati, Jomhoriye Islami Iran va Tahavolat Palestin (1979-2006), markaze esnade va tarekhe diplomasi, Tehran 1386, page 12
[348] Ashgabat.mfa.ir

supportive activities to Palestine including granting assistance to Palestinian family who are suffering and living in uncertainty.

Iran has often argued that the resurrection of resistance movements in West Bank and Gaza have been inspired mainly by Iranian revolution. The absolute victory of Revolution had affected psychologically to Palestinians to keep resisting against Zionist's occupation. Not only that, Iran was so much confident that the rising of Islamic Jihad movement that constituted a branch of Ikhwanul Muslimin movement, and of Tahrirul Islam party in early 1980 were inspired obviously by Imam Khomeini's revolutionary thoughts. In this regard, Dr. Fathi Syaqaqi, leader of Jihad Islami once said that Iranian Revolution had surprised emotionally Palestinians that succeeded to bring hopes and inspirations to defeat Israel in the near future. Not only that, Iran claimed that the creation of the Centre for Palestine Jihad Islam in Gaza strip in 1980s was inspired by Iranian revolution that also inspired deeply the political role played intensively by Palestinian young students. Moreover, this theocratic state often has claimed that the radical and militant leaders of resistance movements started to accept the reality that due to Iranian revolution victory, Palestinian issue is no longer a domestic and Arab's issue but an international Islamic issue with no exception.[349] Therefore, by considering such facts, Yitchak Rabin, Israeil Prime Minister in that time once acknowledged well that revolutionary Iran, even without any presence of Imam Khomeini, has sought to annihilation of Israel.[350]

From the aforementioned facts, it can be concluded that Iranian political elites will shape Iran's foreign policy that includes among others the support to Palestinian struggles in liberating their occupied territory, in which Iran will never open its diplomatic relation with Israel as it never believes that the two state solution would be the best option. Furthermore, Supreme Leader has often asked Palestinian people to resume Inthifada (uprising) efforts against Israeli military aggression that has been viewed by himself as a cancer that should be eliminated immediately. As a matter of fact, his strong and constant objection to Israeli occupation is often followed by its military manuevers both at home and abroad, displaying its cutting-edge technological ability crafted to annihilate Israeili existence.

Indeed, in dealing with the Palestinian conflict, the Iranian ideological interest would be preferred over its strategic and national interests. It would mean that the conflict posses clear evidence that Iran, due to its claim as leader for Muslim states, has to involve itself to carry out any pro-Palestinian measures. The issue, as mentioned earlier would be both an opportunity and challenge for Iranian revolutionary ideology. A challenge, due to Sunni majority of Palestinians would not accept easily and welcomingly Shia ideology that Iran invariably would pursue in the region. In contrast, "good intention" presented by Iran

---

[349] Trita Parsi, Treacherous Alliance, the Secret Dealings of Israel, Iran and the US,yale university press/new haven and london page 38
[350] Ibid page 33

would be often regarded suspiciously and sceptically by Palestinians who believe to bring a hidden agenda.

Therefore, Iran with its diverse ethnics, regardless its format as ideological state, is likely to be more welcomed in Israel, rather than in Palestine. It is estimated there are around 200.000 Iranian Jews are currently residing in Israel. Some of those even hold most strategic positions in Israeli government that could not be given if they were in Iran. The Israeli important figures like former President Moshe Katsav and former Minister of Defence, Shaul Mofaz were born in Persian land. Meanwhile Dan Halutz, head of Israel Defence Forces is an Iranian Jew who immigrated to Israel. [351]

Apart from its distinct Shia ideology, the Iranian non-Arab identity would be the biggest challenge for Iran to convince Arab Palestinians. The difference of culture and ethnicity is probably the most leading obstacle for Iran to actualize its good intention to Palestinians. Palestinians as Arabs, may understand precisely that thousand year historical relations between Arab and Persian nations were rife with political clashes and disputes, rather than establishing cooperation and building trust. Therefore, little wonder Saudi Arabia has persuaded multilateral supports from other Arab leaders mainly Egypt and Jordan to keep Hamas out from Iran's hands significantly viewed as an existential threat for the Arab's region.[352]

Nevertheless, Iran has been well-aware of such apathetic approach of Palestinians. It has not been easy for Iran to open closer relations with them despite the fact that Palestinians have been in dire need to any foreign assistance, including Iran. In contrast, such restrictions must be changed to open opportunity for exporting of Iranian revolutionary principles to other regions including Palestine. Therefore, it is not surprising that Iran has been attempting to find political slots so that this ideological interest could be accepted by Palestinians; and the fruits of the Islamic revolutionary would be enjoyed together by oppressed nations on the earth, including Palestinians. Iran has hoped that the revolutionary principles could be inspiring Palestinians to eliminate and annihilate Israeli state from political map. Iran has never sought to lose its own expectations. There have been strategies offered to display Iranian solidarity to Palestinian struggle, for instance in international forums where Iran has tried significantly to ask other UN members to simultaneously expel Israeli membership from UN. In cultural field, Iran had sponsored painting competition for children in several Muslim states with title "Israel must be wipe off the earth." Furthermore, in the field of strategic security, Iran had pledged to dispatch Iraqi

---

[351] Trita Parsi, Treacherous Alliance, the Secret Dealings of Israel, Iran and the US, yale university press/new haven and london page 8

[352] A report compilation by National Security Research Division on Saudi-Iranian Relations Since the Fall of Saddam, 2009, page 86

fighters detained in Iranian prisons, to combat against Israel in Lebanon, besides advocating the establishment of Islamic troops to expel Israelis from Arab region. [353]

Not only politically and culturally, the Iranian hostility and antagonism towards Israel have been also shown in sport sector. We may still remember that in August 2017, two Iranian football players who played for Panionis Club of Greek have been punished by Iran's Football Union by banning them to play for lifetime, only because they reportedly played for the Club against Maccabi Club of Tel Aviv, Israel.[354] In November 2017, Iranian wrestler Alireza Karimi pretended to lost the game, in order to avoid competing with an Israeli wrestler in the next round.[355] Such an action has been praised ultimately by political elites of Iran.

In addition, since 2013, Iranian Red Cross Organization has a routine agenda which is to provide *Efthar* (fast breaking) for roughly 250.000 Gazans during Ramadan month, as its material support for people who are being blockaded and suffering.[356]

As a matter of fact, Palestinian case has reflected an approach incompatibility between Iran and Arab Saudi. It proves once again that Islamic world issues don't necessarily mirror the similarity of vision and perspective of both Islamic states. For instance in August 1981, when Prince Fahd, Saudi Crown Prince of the time, proposed 8 points[357] of the conflict resolving, Imam Khomeini criticized decisively the proposed points as they implied the acceptance of Israeli existence by taking more tolerant approach to this colonialist regime. He himself labelled any political figure who had ratified such a proposal as traitor for Islam. Not only Khomeini, Hashemi Rafsanjani like other sceptical Iranian leaders, had asked Arabs to resist politically, economically and militarily against American and Israeli interests in the region. Previously, the former President in a Friday prayer sermon, once addressed an idea to create a Qods division army. [358]

---

[353] Ibid page 101

[354] Barney Henderson, Iran bans two footballers for life for playing against Israel's Maccabi Tel Aviv, 11 August 2017, https://www.telegraph.co.uk/news/2017/08/10/iran-bans-two-footballers-life-playing-against-israels-maccabi/

[356] www.al-bayader.org, 27 May 2017

[357] The eight points were Israel to withdraw from all Arab territory occupied in 1967, including Arab Jerusalem; Israeli settlements built on Arab land after 1967 to be dismantled, including those in Arab Jerusalem; A guarantee of freedom of worship for all religions in the Holy Places; An affirmation of the right of the Palestinian Arab people to return to their homes and compensation for those who do not wish to return; The West Bank and the Gaza Strip to have a transitional period under the auspices of the United Nations for a period not exceeding several months; An independent Palestinian State should be set up with Jerusalem as its capital; All States in the region should be able to live in peace in the region; The United Nations or Member States of the United Nations to guarantee the carrying out of these provisions.

[358] Trita Parsi, Treacherous Alliance, the Secret Dealings of Israel, Iran and the US, Yale university press/new haven and london page 81

However, with the passage of time, according to Trita Parsi, Iranian long entrenched position to view a radical pattern to solve the conflict by acknowledging one state solution to be the only solution, has already softened with Iran accepting the adoption of the Saudi Arabia peace plan in the Beirut Declaration of the Arab League in March 2002 suggesting the Arab leaders' readiness to live in harmony with Israel as long as Israel could fulfil several pre-conditions presented in the summit that included both withdrawal of Israeli military troops from all occupied territory and recognizing Palestinian state.[359] Seemingly, such an Iranian softened position wouldn't be maintained for much longer which radical view of Ayatollah Ali Khamene'i would still dominate taking Iranian foreign policy against the total annihilation of Israeli existence in spite of desperate willingness of Iranian Ministry of Foreign Affairs to take moderate approach towards the conflict.

Iran's Relations with Hamas

Due to that Iran has been well aware of such religious, huge cultural and social constraints mentioned previously, the Mullah state shall find other political mechanisms that enable the theocratic state to accommodate its vision and mission in Palestine cause. Such Iranian distinct approach to the case has eventually navigated it to take distinct measures that tremendously differ from those of many countries. For instance, with many Muslim countries often relying on granting their donations to UNRWA as mandated by the General Assembly of the United Nations to carry out relief and works programmes for Palestine refugee since 1950, Iran is reported to contribute nothing to the agency in the year of 2017 as once stated by Nikki Haley, US ambassador to the UN.[360] In this regard, as will be explored later, Iran would prefer to extend its financial assistance to Hamas and other radical Palestinian organizations.

Of the great importance and effective significance is to establish good relations with militant Islamic organizations which echo Iranian revolutionary agenda. Iran further believes that militancy of the Palestinian rejectionist groups was inspired by the principles of Iranian Revolution which Iran accordingly shall support by all means. As time went on, Iran finally could find some of commonalities and compatibilities of standpoint with Hamas *(Harakatul Muqawwamatul Islamiyah/* Islamic Resistance Movement) organization and Jihad Islam movements despite different substantial ideologies of Shia and Sunni. Their militancy in fighting and Jihad accentuation towards Israeli lawful occupation has enticed attention of the Iranian regime to extend its constant supports to the organizations, mainly with Hamas and its radical military wing of Izz-el-Dien alQassam, as one of the two largest political parties in Palestine beside Fatah political party. In this vein, with Iran giving ceaseless support to such militant organizations and movements, such a thing would automatically

---

[359] Trita Parsi, Losing an Enemy, Obama, Iran, and the Triumph of Diplomacy, Yale University Press/New Haven & London, 2017, page 54

[360] Despite US cuts, Haley accuses world of failing to fund Palestinians, 24 July 2018, www. timesofisrael.com

undermine and downplay the central roles of other reconciliatory groups chiefly Fatah which looks to be never compatible with Iran's strategy and goal. Therefore, in order to exhibit Iranian seriousness to engage with the issue by exerting confrontational and radical approaches, its foreign ministry even publicly announced its encouragement to form a new Palestinian rejection front that aims at isolating the PLO and strengthening Hamas position.[361] In this vein, with Hamas repeatedly isolated within international interaction, Iranian overt and explicit supports to the organization would help Hamas lift its leverage in international politics since Iran along with its abundant oil and gas resources and very large population, has realized that its strategic position in the region can't be overlooked by the Arab countries which tend to underestimate Hamas' militancy in dealing with the conflict.

For Iran, Hamas founded in 1987 following the first phenomenal Intifadha, has adopted a charter giving emphasis on annihilation and elimination of Israeli existence with military fighting and revolutionary action, making it to be designated by west as terrorist group.[362] Supporting Hamas with its large supporters in Palestine has indicated more prestigious position and leverage for Iranian regime that it finally succeeded to attract Sunni Arab population's sympathy, demonstrating once again that Islamic revolutionary principles Iran has always promoted is also acceptable by Sunni population.

Therefore, Iran has already found much commonality in mechanisms, methods as well as targets within the organization which is currently ruling Gaza strip with a 1.7 million of total population. In the other hand, while facing much pressure internally and externally, both politically and economically, Hamas has sought that keeping cordial relations with Iran would benefit it a lot particularly in searching for political and economical supports, granting it more leverage among Palestinians by undermining the west- supported Fatah, and international community. Yet, in the meantime such a pragmatic relationship often makes Hamas to be more isolated. It can be said that the more Iran gives support to the organization, the more Hamas would face political isolation from international interaction. Yet interestingly, in spite of emerging various polemics and problems, Iran would not stop extending its supports to Hamas as it significantly believes that Hamas organization unflinchingly constitutes an oppressed group Iran shall help as a religious and moral duty, complying with sacred values cited evidently in its basic constitution. Most startlingly, despite much objection and opposition from its own people due to flow of abundant millions dollars amid economic stagnation at home, Iran has been proud to intensively extend financial, and military technological and equipment supports to Hamas organization,

---

[361] Ora Szekely, The Politics of Militant Group Survival in the Middle East, Resources, Relationships and Resistance, Palgrave macmillan, 2017, page 214
[362] Profile : Hamas Palestinian Movement www.bbc.com, 12 May 2017

as what Ali Khamene'i has always urged that he will endorse and help any nation or group who confronts the Zionist regime. [363]

The Hamas charter adopted one year after its formal creation, while identifying the organization to have been inspired by political Ikhwanul Muslimin in Egypt, has significantly called its members to carry out Jihad and martyrdom against Israel to liberate Palestinian land from the illegal occupation. In article 13 of the Charter, it has been stated that sole solution for the conflict is by implementing Jihad. The chapter also explained evidently that Hamas has criticized all kinds of international negotiations and proposals as futile and wasting – time efforts despite their emphasis on humanity and tolerance to other religion followers as long as they stop disputing Islamic sovereignty in the region. [364]

The support of Iran to Hamas by all means has been once stated by Ali Akbar Velayati, Iranian Foreign Minister of the time in 1994 that Iran would pledge to resume its political and emotional support to Palestinian groups which have rejected Declaration of Principles (DoP) between Israel and PLO in 1993, despite his denial on military support for those groups. Yet, with the passage of time, Iran's effort to supply Hamas with the technology to develop Fajr-5 missiles that are able to reach Tel Aviv, Israeli capital was admitted explicitly by the commander of Iranian elite Revolutionary Guards, Mohammad Ali Jafari.[365] In the other hand, alongside with clear pronouncement given by Yehya al-Sinwar, military leader of Hamas of receiving such a military support from Iran in 2017,[366] Hamas leaders have also acknowledged its shared perspectives and visions with Iran in dealing with the conflict which certainly would strengthen Iran's more engagement in the conflict through Hamas. [367]

Historically speaking, since Hamas establishment, Iran has been implicitly demanded to fully concretize and materialize its support to the organization. Yet interestingly, such a tangible support has been carried out by Iranian regime in the aftermath of official founding of Hamas, long after PLO (Palestinian Liberation Organization) and Fatah political party were founded. It indicates more deeply that Iran has lost its trust and hope with PLO and Fatah as the two entities have always preferred soft negotiations and talks with Israel counterpart in dealing with the conflict.

Little wonder In early years of Hashemi Rajsanjani's administration in 1990s, Iran started to approach Hamas organization amid his significant effort to normalize Iranian collapsed economic situation. For the first time in December 1990, Hamas elites were

---

[363] Saeed Kamali Deghan, Iran supplied Hamas with Fajr-5 missile technology, 21 November 2012, https://www.theguardian.com/world/2012/nov/21/iran-supplied-hamas-missile-technology
[364] For further information, please see the charter of Hamas
[365] Opcit.
[366] Andrew Illingworth, Iran and Hamas restore relations, includes major military support, 29 August 2017, https://www.almasdarnews.com/article/iran-hamas-restore-relations-includes-major-military-support/
[367] Kenneth Katzman, Hamas' Foreign Benefactors, the Middle East Quarterly Volume II number 2, June 1995

invited to attend the Islamic conference on Palestine held in Tehran. In November 1993 reportedly the Revolutionary Guard elites successfully met with Hamas officials in Damascus, Syria, that later on at the same year, in order to mark such a special relation, Hamas representative office was opened in Vali Asr street, Tehran, occupying the same building with Lebanese Hezbollah organization representative, that aims at enhancing relations and coordinating multiple concerned agendas of the two entities.[368] In Iranian foreign relations, the cordiality and closeness of the relations between the two entities would implicitly undermine and downplay roles and functions of Palestinian embassy in Tehran that are obviously dominated by Fatah officials, main political rival of Hamas.

As elaborated previously, Iranian supports to Hamas have not been limited to only the holding of several conferences on Palestine and paying official visits. Although official statement from Hamas elites has never been explicitly issued, yet Iran has been accused for years for granting special financial budget of millions dollars to Hamas through Hezbollah organization operating mostly in South Lebanon.[369] This fact was revealed by James Woolsey, former director of CIA, that Hamas has received funds from Iran around US$ 100 million. Accordingly, Itamar Rabinovich, Israeli ambassador to US in the aftermath of the bomb explosion in October 1994, once confirmed that Iran constitutes a premier source for Hamas' funding.

As time went on, amazingly such an accusation was confirmed to be true by Yasser Arafat, legendary former PLO leader by stating in 1992 that Iran had provided Hamas US$ 30 million. Most startlingly, Yaser Arafat's confirmation was also confirmed by Hamas leaders in 1993, saying less than the amount money mentioned.[370] Meanwhile a Lebanon-based magazine once pointed out that since January 2014, the winning political party on 2006 parliamentary election of Hamas has received US$ 10 million as the result of Iranian oil sale in Rotterdam. In December 2008, it is reported that Hamas was granted by Iran US$ 150 million for Hamas rejection to negotiate with Israel in which previously in December 2006, Iran promised Ismail Haniya, Hamas' Prime Minister of the time to receive US$ 250 million to save Gaza from bankruptcy. [371]

According to Mathew Levitt, senior researcher in Washington Institute, Iran would increase financial support to Palestinian radical organizations if terrorism acts are successfully materialized and accomplished. Mathew further unfolded that, based on Palestinian intelligent report in 2000 seized by Israeli authority, Iran had transferred US$ 400.000 directly to Hamas to support military resistance and suicidal attacks. The report also

---

[368] Amy Thomson, the Ties That Bind, Iran and Hamas Principal-Agent Relationship, a thesis made to obtain Master degree in Massey University, New Zealand in 2012 page 3
[369] Matthew Levitt, Iranian State Sponsorship of Terror; Threatening US Security, Global Stability and Regional Peace, the Washington Institute for Near East Policy, 16 February 2005
[370] Opcit page 3
[371] Rachel Brandenburg, Iran and the Palestinians, www.iranprimer.usip.org

discovered an overt meeting held by Iran's Ambassador in Syria with Hamas, Jihad Islam and Hezbollah organization representatives in Iranian embassy in Damascus.

Not only financially, Iran also has given military trainings for Hamas fighters as what Ziyad Abu Amr, Palestinian scholar once revealed. Furthermore in addition, based on an Canadian intelligent, Hamas has training camps in Iran, Lebanon and Sudan as well that are obviously supervised by Iranian military officials.[372] Iran is reported to have provided military equipments to Islamic militant groups in Palestine such as Hamas like what has been advocated by Supreme Leader in November 2014[373] and evidenced heavily by the seizure of Karine A ship that carried military weapons etc by Israel in 2002. As far-reaching consequence, the seizure had prompted George W. Bush to include Iran to the axis of evil, along with Iraq and North Korea.

In diplomatic arena, for the first time in March 1998, Hamas' delegation led by Ahmad Yasin, its founder succeeded to pay visit to Iran and met officially with Ayatollah Ali Khameini, followed by other Hamas' official visits carried out by Khaled Mishal, Head of Hamas political affairs in 2005 and 2007.[374]

Yet howeverhistorically speaking, the special relations between Hamas organization and Iran has also experienced its ups and downs. In August 2011, reportedly that Hamas rejected organizing public demonstrations to show their support to Bashar Assad's leadership whom Iran fully supports. In result of such a rejection, Iran got disappointed with Hamas, assuming the organization that it has no longer a shared vision and standpoint with Iran. Unsurprisingly, Iran decided to cut financial supports to Hamas.[375] Consequently, Hamas officially closed its office in Damascus in 2012 after nearly one decade operation, then moving it to Doha, Qatar. Yet, the worsening of relation, did not necessarily prevent Iran from dispatching military weaponry and equipments to Hamas, shown obviously by the fact that when in clash between Israel and Palestine erupted in November 2012, this Mullah state immediately sent weaponry assistance to Hamas, including Iranian made fajar 5 rockets.

Yet it did not take much longer that in 2014, the relation gradually got improved, evidenced by holding a meeting involving officials from both parties in Ankara and Doha. In addition, in March 2015, Khaled Mishal and Ali Larijani, Head of Iranian parliament held meeting in Doha, pointing out normalization a 3 year-frozen relations.[376] However the relations got deteriorated in 2015 as Hamas tacitly supported Saudi military intervention to curb Yemeni Houthi rebellion and paid official visit to Riyadh, prompting Iran to cancel

---

[372] Ibid
[373] Country Report on Terrorism on Terrorism 2014, www.state.gov
[374] www.bps.org, How Iran Entered the Axis
[375] ibid
[376] Jack Khoury, Hamas and Tehran Boost Ties as Meshal Meets Iran's Larijani in Doha, https://www.haaretz.com/.premium-hamas-and-iran-boost-ties-1.5336165

Hamas' visit to Iran that was supposedly to be held one month after. In July 2015, Hamas elites confirmed that financial support for Iran was totally cut. [377]

Based on my personal observation while I was in Iran for seven years, Palestinian issue did not draw much Iranians' attention. Most Iranians from different backgrounds and social classes, at odds with their government, did little to express sympathy and solidarity to Palestinian struggles against Israeli occupation, asserting that Palestinian cause is the only Arab nation's problem, not Iran's problem. Nevertheless, they opposed human right abuses that Israel often carried out to Palestinians. Furthermore, Iranians tried to avoid discussions on Palestinian Issue, perceiving Hamas organization as a terrorist group by some of those, which doesn't deserve any Iranian assistance as they have thought that Hamas is always associated with extremism and radicalism. Furthermore amid a wide range of economic and social problems, they had hoped that Iranian regime stop funding the group including granting educational scholarships for Hamas and Islamic Jihad young students to continue their educations in Iran.

Such a painful phenomenon was assured by a Hamas friend of mine who happened to study in Tehran by saying that if one person admits to be a Palestinian student, then what soon crosses to Iranians' mind is the uncontrolled flow of million dollars of national oil revenue to the militant group leaders' pockets. So it won't be surprising that slogan **No Gaza, Not Lebanon, I Give My Life for Iran** was used heavily by the public demonstrations in Iran in first week of January 2018. Interestingly, Iranians have never considered Israel as their enemy that may threaten their internal security. Politically they have no problems with Israel, confirming that Arab Saudi, not Israel, is true enemy for Iranian publics. Regrettably, Iranians' disappointment and anger on the Iranian Red Cross Organization aiming at collecting Islamic alms from Iranians, thus distributing them for providing Efthar (fast breaking) for roughly 250.000 Gazans in Palestine during Ramadan month, rather than feeding poor Iranians, has never been blown up by the national media.

Otherwise, in a polling conducted in 2015 was revealed that 57% of the Palestinians had a negative perspective to Iranians. Ironically the percentage was bigger that of other states which don't have direct relations with Iran like Vietnam, Philippines, Peru, Senegal and Ethiopia.[378] Some viral images in June 2017 had shown the burning of gifts by Palestinians sent annually by Iran to them in the occasion of Imam Khomeini's death mourning, by saying that Palestinians want neither bombs which kill their citizens, nor Iranian gifts. They don't like Iran to enter their territory and kill Palestinians.[379]

However as long as Velayat Faqih embodying Islamic Republic of Iran still overshadows Iranian political systems and structures, Iran seemingly would never cease its

---

[377] Rachel Brandenburg, Iran and the Palestinians, www.iranprimer.usip.org
[378] www.tabnak,ir, Negarash 57 dar sad Falestiniha be Iran Manfi ast, 20 Khordad 1394
[379] www.irankhabarnews.com

all sorts of support to Hamas and other militant organizations which own shared vision and perception with Iranian regime, which is annihilation of the Jewish state.

Most startlingly, such a revolutionary policy once again demonstrates evidently that Shia as Iranian formal religion would not be effecting a lot to its foreign policy taking, considering into account that Hamas constitutes a Sunni militant movement that one day may have contradictory stance with Iran, depending on its ability to support the organization financially and militarily.

As already intimated, as long as a nation is considered oppressed by its own oppressive regime, not differently Sunni or Shia, Iran would have a moral and religious duty to offer helps as much as possible. In addition, the amendment of Hamas Charter in May 2017 showing Hamas' moderate approach does not necessarily imply Hamas' recognition to the existence of Israeli state. So in this regard, I can argue that Iran is still in dire need to Hamas, along with Lebanese Hezbollah, in order to accomplish its revolutionary export to the region as an integral part of the mechanisms to create and realize Shia crescent in Middle East region. In turn, undoubtedly, Hamas needs Iran to gain political and economic supports as well increase Hamas leverage in international arena. Therefore, it is no exaggeration to note that Sunnite of Iranian foreign policy, as once portrayed by an official of Hezbollah organization, could simply reflect in Palestinian cause (by establishing good ties with Hamas).[380]

Iranian Pragmatism in Palestine Cause

Historically speaking, Iranian pragmatic approach towards the cause has been applied since early years of its establishment as a strategy taken for temporary. Meaning that with Iran implementing hostile attitude towards Israeli Zionism, on the same time it also reportedly opened good relationship with Israel that obviously violated the principles of Iran's foreign policy. Anti-Zionism and anti-Israeli occupation slogans have been modified precisely so that more exigent goal could be achieved. In this vein, Iran is demanded to flex its strict foreign policy while facing the existential and imminent threat which likely destroy the territory and the survival of the regime as well. As such, it is not surprising Iran would like to apply such pragmatism tacitly due to its sensitiveness, with the aim at safeguarding its international reputation and image as a leading state for Islamic nations. Apart from this, it is open secret that Iran also will not see a big issue to establish closer relations with other countries which prove to have diplomatic and good relations with Israel. Iran will keep silent and not criticize any intimate relations that those countries establish with Israeli state.

---

[380] A report compilation by National Security Research Division on Saudi-Iranian Relations Since the Fall of Saddam, 2009, page 22

In addition to Iran Contra Scandal elaborated previously, military cooperation heavily was established by Iran and Israel in the first years of the revolution in which as a matter of fact that the advance of Israeli technology was mainly acknowledged and materialized through intensive military cooperation by Pahlavi Dynasty, prior to Islamic Revolution itself. For instance, in 1980s after the Hostage Crisis[381] erupted, Ahmad Kashani, the youngest son of Ayatollah Abol Qassem Kashani, a key figure in Iranian oil industry nationalization in 1951, is reported to be the first person who visited Israel to discuss the weapon sale and military cooperation against Iraqi nuclear program in Osirak. In response, Imam Khomeini would allow many Jews who lived in Iran for thousand years to immigrate to other desired countries such as USA and Israel. In countering Saddam Hossein's military threat in Iran-Iraq war, both states were known for having bilateral meetings to discuss military cooperation. For instance In Zurich, Switzerland, Colonel Ben Youssef from Israel and Colonel Zarrabi, director for Iranian military industrial complex, had discussed on the dispatching of Israeli technicians to train Iranian military staffs in the field of weaponry. Ahmad Haydari, Iranian transaction dealer who worked for Imam Khomeini, once said that 80% of military weapons Iran had bought in early years of the war, originated from Israel. [382] Not only that, reportedly between 1980 to 1983, according to Jaffe Institute for Strategic Studies at Tel Aviv University, Iran had bought cutting-edge weapons from Israel for US$ 500 million mostly conducted in the exchange of oil.[383] Last but not least, based on report issued by American officials in Carter's era in August 1981, Israel secretly sold to Iran 250 spare part tyres for American f-4 bombing aircrafts in late 1980. [384]

Seemingly Iranian policy to cease revolutionary anti-Zionism for short term, was taken due to the painful fact that Iraqi aggression threat was on the way to destroy Iran's side. The theocratic state assumed if it had maintained and kept promoting such revolutionary slogan, it would be decisively annihilated. For Iran, fighting against Saddam Hussein's military aggression was much more crucial than that of against Israel. Interestingly according to Iranian hardliners, fighting Iraq as well retaliating it would pave the way to conquer Iraqi territory as main gate for realization of Shia crescent in the Middle East region. This ambition that led Imam Khomeini to declare assuming the war would smoothen to realize supporting Jerusalem through Karbala of Iraq after obtaining a decisive success of Iranian troops in recapturing Khoramshahr city and conquering Kushk territory in Iraq.[385]

Such a policy taking once again displays implicitly that Imam along with his loyalists had always believed that the Palestinian cause must be solved first by Palestinians alone,

---

[381] The longest hostage crisis in modern history involved fifty-two American diplomats and citizens held hostage for 444 days from November 4, 1979, to January 20, 1981, after a group of radical Iranian students who supported the Iranian Revolution, occupied the U.S. Embassy in Tehran.
[382] Trita Parsi, Treacherous Alliance the secret dealings of Israel, Iran and the U.S, yale university press, page 106
[383] Ibid page 107
[384] www.nytimes.com, Iran Said to Get Large-Scale Arms From Israel, Soviet and Europeans, 8 March 1982
[385] Mounir al-Rabih, Hezbollah and Iran in Syiria, 13 November 2017, www.washingtoninstitue.org

then by Arabs in the region, and if necessary Iran and other Muslim states. This is what Ali Reza Alavi Tabar from the reformist political group had assured that Iran has never sought its direct involvement against Israeli occupation and aggression to Palestinians.[386] According to Mohsen Milani, Iranian expert for Middle East affairs, since the creation of Islamic regime, the Iran's engagement in Palestine conflict has been (only) implemented through granting military trainings, particularly to Hezbollah troops in Bekka valley in Lebanon.[387]

Despite Israeli intention to open good relations with the newly born Islamic revolutionary Iran and its continuous denial of Iran to such a transaction military, some facts have emerged reversely. For instance in June 1980, Argentine Cargo aircraft that once had its transit in Israel before heading to Iran with carrying on American spare parts and ammunitions, crushed in Russian and Turkish border.

In sum, although politically and diplomatically Iran and Israel have no relations to date, but it has not prevented both states to develop more tangible and long term relations, mainly in the economic and trade fields. Such acknowledgment to having economic business relations has been commonly stated by Israeli side, not Iranian. Yet a scandalous business relations kept secret tightly emerged to surface when reportedly Israeli Ofer Brothers Group-owned ships have often anchored in Iranian water territory for many years.[388] As usual, such covert business and transactions between the two states have been denied by Iranian officials.

Yet as a matter of fact, Israeli companies tacitly have held business with Iranian counterparts for many years. By considering a wide range of obstacles and restrictions due to the economic sanctions, the millions dollar business deals have been struck through third party such as Uni Emirates Arab, Jordan and Turkey, already registered in Europe and prone to American boycott. During the years, Israeli product exports to Iran would include agricultural equipments; meanwhile Iran would export its own products to Israel, including pistachios and marbles. Not only that, Iran has been interested in security equipments of Israel. In November 2000, Iranian government had asked an Israeli company to pay visit to Iran to make renovation to the 30 year old- waste pipes. Not only that, based on an Israeli official confession, Director General Assistant of the Ministry of Agricultural Affairs paid a visit to Israel secretly and stayed for night in Tel Aviv Hilton Hotel, with an aim at opening relations in the field of irrigation pipes, pesticide and fertilizer purchasing.[389] Furthermore, an article published by Xinhuan News Agency in 12 December 1997 revealed that an

---

[386] opcit
[387] Mohsen Milani, Why Tehran Won't Abandon Assad (ism), the Washington Quarterly Fall edition 2013 page 81
[388] www.haaretz.com
[389] Ofer Petersburg, Israel-Iran trade ties thriving, 31 May 2005, www.ynetnews.com

agricultural expert delegation of Israel secretly visited to Iran and met with Deputy of Iranian Ministry of Agricultural Affairs.[390]

Additionally in humanitarian field, Iran was reported to have invited some Israeli expert in the field of earthquake to visit the most isolated province of Sistani Baluchistan in Iran ruined due to earthquake in April 2006. In fact, Israel is well known for having expertise to reconstruct many destructed infrastructures built by Israeli company since Pahlavi dynasty. Besides, such a quite sensitive measure was taken by Iranian government forcedly as there was a harsh criticism on its slowness in tackling the earthquake.[391]

However the close relationship of many years between the two states has been affirmed by Nader Karimi, Iranian journalist, an expert in Iran and Israeli relations and being detained in Evin prison, Tehran. He even disclosed that both states have succeeded to exploit the role of journalists to manipulate world's public thoughts that they are hostile to each other instead.[392]

Saudi Arabia and the Issue of Palestine

The Kingdom of Saudi Arabia if compared to Iran or other Muslim countries including Indonesia, has possessed more opportunities to be involved actively in finding a proper solution for the issue. One of the reasons is the similarity of Arab ethnicity and the geographical closeness of Saudi, covering 80 % of whole Arab peninsula, to territories of Palestine and Israel. Besides, Arab Saudi is traditionally regarded to have better in terms of economic stability and more importantly has religion (Sunni) and cultural similarity (Arab) with Palestinians. In regional and international diplomacy, due to its moderate approach to the case, Saudi seems to be more legitimized than Iran with its radical and frontal stances. The Arabness of Palestinian issue has been eluded indirectly by Avigdor Lieberman, the Israeli Minister of Defence, that the real conflict that takes place is between Israel and Arab world, given that Palestinian government does not have power to sign any agreement (with Israel).[393] Such privileges which Iran and Indonesia never enjoys are supposed to be exerted by Saudi Arabia to actively contribute more evidently to resolve the conflict. However in fact Iran and Indonesia were never reported to dispatch military personnel directly to help Palestinians struggle against Israeli occupation. Instead, the states preferred to send humanitarian reliefs, financial assistances and some other kinds of assistance. In contrast, Arab Saudi, according to Medea Benjamin, an American peace activist well known to be having good relations with Iranian government, allowed to deploy three thousand Saudi troops to take part in combat against Israel during the 1948 Arab-Israel war. Not only that,

---

[390] Meir Javedanfar, Was Ariel Sharon Israel's Secret Channel to Iran? 22 April 2013 www. Al-monitor.com
[391] ibid
[392] Sayyed Abu Dawud, Tasa'ad Al Madel Irani Fil A'lamil Arabi, Obeikan publisher, first edition, year 2014 page 32
[393] www.aawsat.com, 28 April 2018

the Kingdom also sent two thousand Saudi troops to stand with Syrian troops against Israel in the 1973 Yom Kippur.[394] When partition plan of Palestine by the UN came into surface in 1947, Saudi is also reported to have pursued that Palestine should simply be declared independent.[395]

If we take a look to Saudi foreign policy towards Palestinian case mainly in recent decades, it can be concluded for a while that Saudi stance and position has been softened and even indicated more reconciliatory approach. However Saudi Ministry of Foreign Affairs would invariably support Palestinian struggle both politically economically since the Kingdom has believed that such a measure frames Islamic duty. Accordingly, Saudi's approaches have not been popular in Muslim nations and failed to attract Muslims's sympathy due to their assumption that Saudi could never object and reject politically multiple American controversial Israel interest-biased policies, and Israeli discriminatory policies that certainly endanger Palestinian interests, and downplay their constant struggles.

Many political observers often believe that the soft approach has been taken by Saudi regime to maintain and keep cordial bilateral relations and partnership with USA- known for being pro Israel interests- since the end of the Second World War in 1945, thus discouraging Saudi from giving harsh criticism and condemnation to any Israeli aggression and brutality, reflected explicitly by the Donald Trump's statement in October 2018 that the Saudi wouldn't last for two week without US military backing.

Little wonder that much scepticism and cynicism of Islamic world emerge as Saudi has thwarted to realize its general expectations that Saudi, by considering its huge capacity that any Muslim country would never enjoy, could become a bridge and play more tangible role to resolve the conflict by among other things putting more political pressure to the Israeli side politically and economically. Such a fact is greatly confirmed by the statement of Robert Jordan, former US ambassador in Saudi Arabia that on the international arena, King Abdullah had to implement a balanced attitude of being both pro-Palestinians and pro-America, despite the fact the King once showed his protest on Israeli brutality against Palestinians, by refusing a US invitation in 2001.[396] As latest instance instead of condemning Donald Trump's controversial policy on Jerusalem capital in December 2017, Saudi rather offered the village of Abu Dis as future capital of Palestine and gave Mahmoud Abbas, Palestinian president two months to respond the offer.[397] In sum Saudi credibility deserves to be questioned since it has failed to embrace Hamas and other Palestinian Islamic militant organizations that, rather Saudi seemingly has been trying to keep distance from those

---

[394] Medea Benjamin, Kingdom of the Unjust, OR Books, 2016, page 108

[395] John Quigley, the International Diplomacy of Israel's Founders, Deception at the United Nations in the Quest for Palestine, Cambridge University Press, 2016, page 75

[396] Robert Jordan, with Steve Fiffer, Desert Diplomat, Inside Saudi Arabia Following 9/11, Potomac Books, 2015, Page 45

[397] **Saudi Offers Abu Dis as future capital of Palestine,** 6 December 2017, https://www.middleeastmonitor.com/20171206-saudi-offers-abu-dis-as-future-capital-of-palestine/

organizations, which the Islamic world had never considered those organizations as terrorist groups. Several initiatives suggested by Saudi Arabia since 1980s implicitly pointed out heavily normalization of this monarchy with Israeli government along with several preconditions. Yet in recent years, such normalization between the states has grown more apparent which eventually pushed President Donald Trump to state obviously in recent months that Israel would be in big trouble without Saudi Arabia.

As already intimated that Saudi foreign policy reflects an outcome of Royal family's pure assessment that excludes any further consultation with its clerics whose authorities are greatly granted for dealing with social and religious affairs at home. Accordingly, its foreign policy would not necessarily accommodate Islamic world interests, or it would not be driven to prioritize Muslim countries, despite its Islamic ideology basic constitution. In other words, pragmatism still would be overwhelming its foreign policy implementation.

As a matter of fact, the Kings who ruled before King Fahd bin Abdul-Aziz are reported to have had firm stances towards Israel, even viewing sceptically that Israeli state would generate a plethora of calamities for Arab world. Saudi decisive opposition to Israel is simply reflected by a historical fact on Faisal's anger and disappointment, Saudi Foreign Minister during the time, following the unilateral declaration of Israeli independence in 1948, by attempting hard to convince the Arab state representatives in United Nations to keep a mind that US would not recognize Israeli state.[398] In addition, Islam and Arab are the two key pillars that drove King Abdul Aziz Ibn Saud, the founder of Saudi modern monarchy to have never agreed with the establishment of a Jewish-controlled state in Palestine during his leadership.[399]

However, with the passage of time, the softening of Saudi stance towards the issue has begun to prevail from the era of King Fahd in 1982. Even when he was Saudi crown prince in 1977, he once stated normalization of Arab states with Israel would happen if the latter recognizes Arab Palestinians rights comprehensively. Not only that, the crown prince confirmed such a proposal in a meeting with President Carter, asking him to convince Israeli government to find solution of the conflict as much fairly as possible.[400] It is hardly surprising that such a soft position taken by the Kingdom created PLO's much fear and vacillation that Arab leaders have no longer prioritized Palestinian cause to be the core of their respective foreign policy, making Yasser Arafat, the PLO leader to tilt to support Iraqi Baath party led by Saddam Hussein by saying that Saddam and his people were true Arab nationalists who paid more attention to the Palestinian issues.[401]

---

[398] Robert Lacey, Kerajaan Petrodollar Saudi Arabia, Pustaka Jaya, first edition, 1986, page 357
[399] Matthew Fallon Hinds, The US, The UK and Saudi Arabian in World War II, the Middle East and the Origins of a Special Relationship, IB TAURIS, London, New York, 2016, Page 85
[400] Gregory Kosatchv dan Yelena Milkowiyan, Tathawor Siyasate elKharejiye alSaudiya, Riyadh 2005, *mahadu dirasatu diplomasiyah* page 90
[401] Shibley Telhami, the World Through Arab Eyes, Basic Books, New York, 2013, page 10

Nevertheless, Saudi interaction with the conflict has lasted since its modern Saudi creation in 1932 which according to Madawi Rasheed, prominent expert on Saudi Issues, the founder, King Abdul Aziz began to pay attention much to Palestinian issue in the aftermath of the second world war due to his focus on dealing with King Jordan, Abdullah's ambition, his main rival, in creating the greater Jordan, including Palestine.[402] The most propelling factor for King Abdul Aziz to pay much attention to Palestinian issue was the location of Aqsa mosque as the third holy place and first qibla (direction of a Muslim during his prays) for Muslims, and an integral part of *Waqf* (inalienable charitable endowment under Islamic law). The King's worries and fears appeared due to the intensively massive Jewish immigration into the Palestinian territory, followed by many pathetic incidents inside Palestinian land. The official documents issued by the King in 1930s and 1940s had reaffirmed Saudi decisive stance against Zionism and Israeli unilateral declaration of its independence in 1948. Even according to both King Abdul Aziz and then King Saud, creation of Israel embodied a great betrayal by UK, a country that they had once established a good relation with.[403]

Yet however, some scholars believe the King's efforts to support Palestine issue were underpinned mainly by two things, first King's wish to expand his ideological influence to entire territories that he just conquered, secondly, strengthening his legitimacy as a ruler for Hejaz region, where Mecca and Medina are situated, by replacing Hashemi Dynasty who once ruled the region before the King's amazingly successful conquering. [404]

In fact, despite initially having a soft stance, mainly in response to British Peel Commission in 1938 that planned to divide Palestinian land with Saudi seemingly approving such a proposal,[405] the King's stance got firmer given much political chaos in Palestinian land, starting to condemn and censure the conflict through his letter correspondence with American government by emphasizing his objection to Zionism illegal expansion and UN's plan (Partition Plan) as well as his decisive criticism to American pro-Israel policies. In February 1945, when the issue was discussed during a historically bilateral meeting with President Roosevelt in Suez Canal, Mr. President urged the King to extend his support to Jewish immigration to Palestine and hoped that King could give constructive advices to the issue. In response to such proposals, King Abdul Aziz rather expressed his disapproval to the partition of Palestinian land that could imply unjust treatment to Palestinians. It was also reported that at the same month, King refused the British Prime Minister Winston Churchill's proposal that Saudi exert its leverage to urge Arab world to tolerate Zionism's aspirations. [406]

---

[402] Madawi el-Rasheed, a History of Saudi Arabia, Cambridge University Press, Second Edition, page 98
[403] Jennifer Bond Reed, the Saud Royal Family, Chelsea House Publishers, 2007, page45
[404] Ibid page 92
[405] Ibid page 97
[406] Letter From Roosevelt To King Ibnu Saud, April 5, 1945, 26 November 2010, www.crethiplethi.com

In order to express Saudi great support and solidarity to Palestinian issue, *Mahrejanet al-Jihad* (Jihad festivals) was held in 1947 in which roughly 200.000 Saudis registered themselves to take part in fighting in Palestine despite the fact, no one came to fight in Arab-Israel war in 1948. [407] On the other hand ironically, the King himself suggested that such a war should be waged without any military intervention from other Arab states. However, amid instable economy and politics at home as direct repercussions of a newly born state, the King decided to give financial donations to support Palestinian struggles.[408]

Since 1960s and 1970s, as mentioned earlier that the creation of organization of Islamic Cooperation and Muslim World League initiated by Saudi Arabia, have had aims at, among other things, discussing and supporting the Palestine cause as well. Through Organization of Islamic Cooperation, recognition of PLO as official representative of Palestinian nation has been reached unanimously by the member foreign ministers.[409] Besides, Saudi had often given condemning statements on Israeli aggression which destroyed several Islamic holy sites.[410] Most importantly, King Faisal had urged Muslim countries to hold a summit meeting in Rabat, Morocco. The 1974 meeting attended even by President of Egypt, Gamal Abdul Nasser had declared the leaders' strong aspiration on Palestinian interests,[411] including the declaration that PLO to be sole legitimate representative of the Palestinian people.

Besides, several official meetings have been implemented by both Saudi and Paletinian sides. For instance, in 1952 the Crown Prince had welcomed officially a visit of Palestinian Student Association. In 1967, King Faisal also welcomed Yasser Arafat's arrival, PLO leader, thus allowing Fatah organization (under PLO) to open its office in Riyadh in 1973. The peak of close relations of both sides was reflected obviously by opening Palestinian embassy in Riyadh, attended by Yasser Arafat. However, given PLO's support to Iraqi invasion to Kuwaiti territory in 1990s, the bilateral relations deteriorated, prompting Persian Gulf States to cease annually financial support of around 10 billion dollars, to Palestine.[412]

Following Arab Israel war in 1973, Arab Saudi by using its leverage on world oil market, boycotted oil sale by not sending oil to America and other American-allied states which seemed to be very dependent on Middle Eastern oil supply. Even furthermore, alongside with Kuwait and Libya following Arab's humiliating defeat in 1967, it had a strong commitment as a follow up of the League Arab meeting in Khartoum, Sudan, to finance Egypt, Syria and Jordan, well-known to be front line states, to later resist the Israeli

---

[407] Sherifa Zuhur, Saudi Arabia, ABC CLIO, page 119
[408] Gregory Kosatchv dan Yelena Milkowiyan, Tathawor Siyasate elKhareijye alSaudiya, Riyadh 2005, mahadu dirasatu diplomasiyah page 98
[409] Thomas Hegghammer, Jihad in Saudi Arabia, Violence and Pan-Islamism since 1979, Cambridge, page 19
[410] ibid
[411] Robert Lacey, Kerajaan Petrodollar Saudi Arabia, Pustaka Jaya, first edition, 1986, page 457
[412] Youssef Ibrahim, Confrontationn in the Gulf; Arafat's Support of Iraq Creates Rift in PLO, 14 August 1990, www.nytimes.com

military aggression (1973 war).[413] Such a decisive strategy taken by King Faisal, well-known as the most critical Saudi ruler to American policy towards Israel,[414] proved effective as it had caused economic instability and tension throughout the world that eventually compelled America to change and decline its large support to Israel. In addition due to the pressure created by the oil embargo in 1982, Israel was compelled to withdraw its military troops from west Beirut, rescuing Palestinian citizens from humanitarian tragedy that might occur.

In 1979, alongside other Arab states, Saudi had given harsh criticism to Camp David agreement signed by Egypt and Israel regarded as betraying Palestinians' struggle and Arab world's efforts as it signified first Arab's official recognition to Israel state. For Saudi, the peace deal would definitely encourage Israel to treat Palestinians more brutally.[415] Accordingly, Saudi decided to cut diplomatic relation with Egypt, despite the fact Saudi initially did not object Camp David deal, yet its strong objection came into realization given that Egypt had acted one sided and unilaterally, without further consultation with other Arab states.[416]

In order to materialize its support tangibly, Saudi issued two important initiatives, first Fahd Plan that was presented in Arab Summit in Fez, Morocco in 1982 including eight points which once sparked controversy and suspicion among Muslim community over Saudi sincere intention to further recognize Israeli state.[417] The second one was presented by King Abdullah in Arab's Summit meeting held in Beirut, Lebanon in 2002 that confirmed heavily its official recognition to Israeli state with preconditions of Israeli recognition on Palestine as an independent and sovereign state, returning Palestinian land occupied by Israel since 1967 and ceasing all violent measures taken by Israelis including their government.[418] [419]

---

[413] Madawi el-Rasheed, a History of Saudi Arabia, Cambridge University Press, Second Edition, page 125
[414] For instance, in a remark delivered before Saudi ambassadors in Riyadh, the King pointed out that Saudi won't harm American interests as long as America respects Saudi and other Arab's interests including the issue of Qods. He also reaffirmed Saudi stance in espousing Palestinian cause by his commitment to taking firm position over Israel if it does not respect principles of the two UN resolutions of 242 and 338
[415] Gregory Kosatchv dan Yelena Milkowiyan, Tathawor Siyasate elKharejiye alSaudiya, Riyadh 2005, mahadu dirasatu diplomasiyah page 108
[416] Mehran Kamrava, Mediation and Saudi Foreign Policy, jurnal the Foreign Policy Research Institute, winter edition 2013 page 161
[417] The points of the Fahd Plan are : 1. That Israel would withdraw from all Arab territory occupied in 1967, including Arab Jerusalem 2. That Israeli settlements built on Arab land after 1967 would be dismantled, including those in Arab Jerusalem 3. That freedom of worship would be guaranteed for all religions in the Holy Places 4. That the Palestinian Arab people would have the right to return to their homes, and that those who did not wish to return would be compensated 5. That the West Bank and the Gaza Strip would have a transitional period, administred by the UN, for a period not exceeding a few months 6. That an independent Palestinian state would be established, with Jerusalem as its capital city 7. That all states in the region should be able to live in peace, and 8. That the UN or member states of the UN would guarantee the carrying out of these provisions.
[418] www.mofa.gov.sa,
[419] Rachel Bronson, Thicker Than Oil, America's Uneasy Partnership with Saudi Arabia, Oxford University Press, 2006 page 155

In international level, Saudi has adopted entire resolutions related to Palestinian cause issued by many international organizations. Saudi reportedly has participated actively in attending several international meetings and conferences, including Madrid Conference in 1991 and Road Plan in 2000s. This monarch state often has lobbied other states including America itself to impose pressure to Israel to abide by the international laws. Furthermore to respond illegally racist settlement building carried out by Israel for many years, in 2004 Saudi presented its protest note to ICJ (International Court of Justice).[420]

For Saudi, before reaching and accomplishing an independent state of Palestine, the settlement of internal dispute between Fatah and Hamas the Palestinian, the two largest political parties, shall be processed first. Therefore in 8 December 2007, Arab Saudi initiated mediating the two parties to reach reconciliation in a deal often called Mecca Accord. Under the Accord, they agreed to shape Palestinian national government as a preparation for realizing the ultimate goal, despite much existing pressure on Hamas organization by world community due to its designating as terrorist radical organization, particularly after the party had won parliament election held in January 2006.[421] However in spite of various Saudi supportive approaches in dealing such an issue, Rachel Bronson, in her book Thicker than Oil, assessed that Saudi role in resolving Palestine conflict was once regarded not too essential by President Bill Clinton who assumed that Saudi is just an instrument used for a while to help bridging Israel and Palestine, not a key player.[422] It is long believed that Saudi would prefer to choose economic mechanisms and financial contribution in settling the conflict, rather than exerting its influence and leverage to push the feuding parties, of Hamas and Fatah, and more widely between Palestine and Israel.

In discussing how much Saudi has already given financial contribution for the issue, then Islamic nations would ostensibly agree that Saudi has been a main strategic donor which ceaselessly and regularly grants billions of dollars for Palestinian project reconstructions and infrastructure building. Arguably, Saudi's nonstop contribution to settle the issue has been mostly dominated by economic aids in funding, not political ones, with the state attempting at preserving good ties with the US government as the outstanding patron for Israeli interest. In this vein, Saudi Arabia views that supporting Palestine economically rather than developing political mechanisms constitutes the best strategy to maintain amicable relationships with Arab region which sought the Arabness of Palestine issue, and the US in the meantime. Perhaps such a strategy is taken by Saudi policy makers as seeing frustratingly that whole political efforts given to resolve the conflict did not bear any fruit. Therefore, Saudi financial assistance to Palestine would hopefully fill the vacuum to accomplish Palestinian short-term goals that encompass reconstruction and rebuilding of

---

[420] www.mofa.gov.sa
[421] Gregory Kosatchv dan Yelena Milkowiyan, Tathawor Siyasate elKharejiye alSaudiya, Riyadh 2005, mahadu dirasatu diplomasiyah page 108
[422] Rachel Bronson, Thicker Than Oil, America's Uneasy Partnership with Saudi Arabia, Oxford University Press, 2006 page 229

the destructed infrastructures, and preventing economic stagnation within the territory as a plausible outcome of non-payment of the government employees' salary. Unlike Iran which often takes confrontational approach in engaging with the cause, Arab Saudi with its enormous financial aids to Palestine would reflect a perception to the international community including Muslim states that its approach to the issue is reconciliatory rather than revolutionary.

For many decades mainly following Arab Summit in Khartoum, Sudan in 1967, Saudi has been the largest donor for Palestine cause ever since. Following Palestinian delegation's official visit to Saudi Arabia in 1968, King Faisal agreed to establish a Committee to collect donation for Palestine and cull 7% of the salaries of Palestinian workers in Saudi Arabia as taxes to be paid to the Palestinian Liberation Organization (PLO).[423] In a summit meeting held in Baghdad in 1978, Saudi pledged to grant donation as much US$ 2 billion for ten years. One decade after, it also pledged to give its donation US $ 6 million annually etc.[424] Even in 2018 following soft stance of Saudi over Donald Trump's controversial policy on Jerusalem capital for Israel, King Salman once again pledged at the Arab Summit $ 200 million of donation, in which $ 150 million would be granted for preserving Islamic sites in Jerusalem and another $ 50 million for Gaza reconstruction.[425] It can be said to date Saudi financial assistance for Palestinian is countless.

In Refugee problem, since *Nakhba* event (massive expulsion of Palestinians from their hometown by Israel brutal troops and militias) in 1947, Arab Saudi reportedly has been trying significantly to convince the UN regarding Palestinian refugees' rights and find more appropriate solution. As can be gleaned from the above, Saudi has often presented the problem through its initiatives and breakthroughs, demonstrating its deep concern over such a matter.[426] The latest Saudi effort is framed obviously by giving its perspective on the problem and polemics surrounding it before the UN's Special Committee of Politics and Decolonization in November 2017.

Just for information, like Jordanian, Lebanon and Syria, Saudi has also hosted over 240.000 Palestinian refugees (according to CIA, around 125.000 in 2008) in its territory despite the fact they are not allowed to gain Saudi citizenship unless by having marriage

---

[423] Ora Szekly, the Politics of Militant Group Survival in the Middle East : Resources, Relationships and Resistance, Palgrave Macmillan, 2017, page 65
[424] www.mofa.gov.sa

[425] Bruce Riedel, Saudi king uses Arab Summit to adjust Riyadh's stance toward Trump, 16 April 2018

Read more: http://www.al-monitor.com/pulse/originals/2018/04/saudi-king-salman-arab-summit-posture-trump.html#ixzz5TsSzcQEB
[426] Sherifa Zuhur, Saudi Arabia, ABC CLIO, page 119

with Saudi citizens.[427] Historically speaking, Ibn Saud once shared his willingness to ARAMCO Company to employ at least one thousand Palestinian refugees that eventually was approved.[428]

Yet the more concrete Saudi support over the case has been reflected obviously by its ceaseless donation granting through UNRWA (the United Nations Relief and Works Agency for Palestine Refugees in the Near East). Such a Saudi significant contribution to humanitarian reliefs in Gaza and West Bank was confirmed by its Commissioner during his visit to Saudi on March 2014 that Saudi has been one of the three greatest donors for the organization ever since.[429] Not only within Palestinian territory, Saudi Arabia also has made significant contribution by giving its abundant financial assistance to Palestinian refugees who are living in Syria and Lebanon. [430]

Seeds of Relation Normalization of the Kingdom with Israel

As an Islamic state which always claims its endless supportive standing with Palestinian nation, the Saudi Kingdom has been alleged widely of having secret relations with the Jewish state, despite its strong denials of such normalization. In this vein, just like Iran, Saudi apparently might have applied strategic and pragmatic approach to achieve its own short-term goals.

For Islamic world, the establishment of good relation with Israel would be no longer shocking and stunning as many Muslim countries have already applied cordial relations with Israel, particularly in business and trade sectors. In this vein, for many decades Saudi has been regarded as allied state for US in which Israel and US has already succeeded to convince the Kingdom over Iran as common enemy and existential threat for regional stability and security. Arguably such normalization between the Kingdom and Israel has just appeared more deeply in some recent years due to the fact that both Saudi and Israel have mutual commitments and shared perspectives to curb spilling over of Iranian influence an ambition over the region. So little wonder that framed the reason why in November 2017, Saudi government surprisingly did neither confirm nor deny allegation that Saudi has been establishing its cooperation with Israel to fight against the Iranian-supported Hezbollah

---

[427] www.arabnews.com, 14 February 2005. Meanwhile, according to CIA report, the number of Palestinians in Saudi Arabia in 2008 is around 125.0000 of total 550.000 who existed in Gulf territory, https://www.cia.gov/library/readingroom/docs/CIA-RDP84S00556R000300070003-4.pdf
[428] Madawi el-Rasheed, a History of Saudi Arabia, Cambridge University Press, Second Edition, page 99

[429] Saudi contribution until now is estimated to more than $550 million.
https://www.unrwa.org/newsroom/press-releases/kingdom-saudi-arabia-contributes-us-59-million-unrwa-support-projects
[430] www.aljazeera.com, 21 November 2017

militant organization.[431] For Israel alone, by electing Donald Trump as new President who visited Saudi before any other countries right after his presidential inauguration, would pave the way to open good relations with Saudi. In this regard, Donald Trump has given Israeli more self-confidence to approach the monarch state.[432]

In November 2017, a famous Saudi website had published an interview with Israeli army officer who pointed out closer relationship between the two countries with aims at resisting Iranian influence in the region. In another occasion, Israeli Lieutenant General Gad Eisenkot also expressed his readiness to cooperate with Saudi in information sharing to face Iranian threats. On the same month, reportedly Ayoub Kara, Israeli Minister of Communication Affairs once invited Abdul Aziz Sheikh, senior Mufti to pay visit to Israel.[433] even in June before, Yisrael Katz, Israeli Minister for Intelligence and Transportation urged King Salman to invite Benyamin Netanyahu to visit Riyadh to discuss on the feasibility of diplomatic relation opening.[434]

As mentioned earlier, a rumour of Mohammad bin Salman's secret visit to Tel Aviv in September 2017 had became viral despite Saudi continues denial. However in October 2017, Prince Turki bin Faisal, Saudi former head of Intelligence once acknowledged that he had been co-speaker on Iran with Efram Haley, Israeli former Director of Intelligence Mosad, in one synagogue in New York.[435]

In fact, such efforts of both countries toward normalization of relationship have taken place for over one decade. For instance, Israeli media reported in 2006 that there were secret meetings between Olmert, Israeli Prime Minister with Saudi senior elites in Jordan. Additionally, it was reported some meetings held between Israel officials with Prince Bandar, Saudi Ambassador for US. Saudi oppositions, headquartered in London, once reported secret meetings between Turki al-Faisal, former Saudi Ambassador with Meir Dagan, head of Israeli Mosad, in Washington in December 2006.[436]

In sum, an intelligent analysis source in USA stated that Arab Saudi has given at least $ 16 billion for 2.5 years to fund Israeli infrastructure development, mainly in West Bank, by transferring the money via third country into Israeli account in Europe. The source had

---

[431] Analysts: Saudi Arabia calling on 'ally' Israel to fight a war in Lebanon , 10 November 2017,
https://www.middleeastmonitor.com/20171110-analysts-saudi-arabia-calling-on-ally-israel-to-fight-a-war-in-lebanon/
[432] www.aljazeera.com, 17 November 2017
[433] Linah alsafin, What is behind the covert Israeli-Saudi relations? 21 November 2017,
https://www.aljazeera.com/news/2017/11/covert-israeli-saudi-arabia-relations-171120142229835.html
[434] opcit
[435] Choirul Aminuddin, 4 Fakta Hubungan Terselubung Arab Saudi dan Israel,
https://dunia.tempo.co/read/1035421/4-fakta-hubungan-terselubung-israel-dan-arab-saudi 20 November 2017
[436] Sarah Yizraeil,i, Saudi-Israel Dialogue ; What Lies Ahead, Journal Strategic Assesment, Volume 10 nomor 2 Agustus 2007 page 72o

called the bank account "Netanyahu Slush Fund", instead of mentioning "Israeli Slush Fund" due to its sensitive issue.[437]

Based on Israeli media report, some of the Israeli companies have assisted Gulf states including Arab Saudi through security consultation, military training as well as sophisticate weaponry transaction. Israel also has an access to the Gulf territory to sell its potential products as long as they are not branded to be Israeli products, avoiding boycott policy taken by many Arab states. [438] Not only that, in 2009 Saudi has been accused of testing air defence to evaluate Israeli ability to exert Saudi territory in launching military attack to Iranian nuclear facilities.[439]

Most surprisingly, in October 2016 the number one Saudi lobbyist in USA, also founder SAPRAC (Saudi American Public Relations Affairs Committee), Salman al-Ansari had advised the Kingdom to establish cooperation alliance with Israel in a bid to bring benefits for the region and create profitable economic partnership.[440] However Saudi in January 2018 reportedly has detained Naha Balwa, a female activist due to her critics on Saudi normalization effort with Israel. [441]

Apparently if such normalization happened, it would not necessarily create tensions and repercussions within Saudi society. Evidently, based on an report issued by the Associated Press in 2015, it was revealed that 53% Saudis perceive Iran as main opponent to Saudi, compared with only 18% who perceive Israel as the biggest threat for Saudi. This also reflected strongly my seven year research in Iran that the biggest foe for Iranians is actually neither Israel nor America, but Saudi Arabia.

Indonesia and the Issue of Palestine

As a reflection of its free and active foreign policy that shall be implemented through creative, active and anticipatory diplomacy as well as flexible and rational in approach, elucidated in detail in the earlier chapter, Indonesia has actively played roles in seeking a best solution for the conflict. Its position on the issue is palpable and constantly stable, supporting Palestinian Independence state by promoting relentlessly the two state solution approach based on international law and human rights principles. In Indonesian legal context, such a noteworthy support, Indonesian foreign policy on Palestine is invariable based on the first paragraph of the 1945 basic constitution preamble stating that in the

---

[437] Robert Parry, Did Money Seal Israeli-Saudi Alliance?, special report, page 1
[438] Udi Dekel and Yoel Guzanksy, Israel and Saudi Arabia : Is the Enemy of my Enemy My Friend?, INSS Insight No. 500, 22 Desember 2013, page 2
[439] www.huffingtonpost.com, 13 September 2017
[440] Saudi lobbyist calls for 'collaborative alliance' with Israel, 13 October 2016, https://www.middleeasteye.net/news/saudi-lobbyist-calls-collaborative-alliance-israel-1007577915
[441] Naha Balwa, Shaghiga va Shagigatuha rahnel al-eteghal, 14 February 2018http://www.aljazeera.net/programs/newsreports/2018/2/14/الاعتقال-رهن-وشقيقتها-شقيقها-البلوي-نهى

reality, independence is a genuine right of all nations and any form of alien occupation should thus be erased from the earth as not in conformity with humanity and justice.[442]

As a matter of fact, its foreign policy towards Palestine was implemented profoundly by the Indonesian first President, Soekarno by opposing vehemently illegal occupation carried out by Israel, which among of his policies in 1953 he banned travelling to Israel for any Indonesian citizen. Soekarno is believed to have prevented Israel from taking part in Asian African conference in Bandung, west Java in 1955.[443] Indonesia also rejected Israeli participation in Asian Games in 1962 hosted for the first time by Indonesia that accordingly led expelling Indonesia from membership of International Olympic Committee. President Soekarno even once stated that as long as Palestinians do not gain their independence, so Indonesian will stand against Israeli occupation.[444]

Therefore arguably since Indonesia's independence, its foreign policy towards the conflict has never been guided to perceive that Palestine cause is an integral part of Islamic world. Indonesia always attempts at refraining to associate profoundly the issue with Indonesian Muslims' problem that may lead policies into more frontal ones. Rather, it would underscore deeply that giving support and sometimes putting the issue into the top priority is only because that Israel has been practicing illegal occupation and implementing human rights abuses, the reason that is also held by almost all Muslim countries. This regard of accentuating non-religious identity for the case has been evidently noted by President Soeharto that Palestine issue is a manifestation of the irreversible global movement against colonial rule and alien domination.[445] Indonesia further believes that injustice and colonialism will not be automatically justified by any religion, not only by Islam, meaning that enforcing justice and respecting to the human rights principles are the sacred concepts that all religions including Islam itself have to uphold in order to create order and stability in the world. In Indonesian context, to pursue the case precisely would reflect automatically Indonesian Muslims' interests who often carry out massive demonstrations in several parts of the country to express their sincere solidarity with the oppressed Palestinians. In addition the 'peripheral' image of Indonesia of being not Arab and distant geographical location has helped the state carry out unimpeded opposition towards Israel.

Furthermore, Indonesia depicts that the Palestine issue constitutes the core of its own integral foreign policy. Such a policy was then well reflected by Indonesia's insistence to establish its own honorary council in Ramallah Palestine in 2016 for the first time in the history of the bilateral cooperation despite Israel's strong rejection. Indonesia has always insisted that as long as Israel does not recognize the establishment of Palestine state, it

---

[442] For further information, please refer to remark delivered by vice chairman of Indonesian parliament in 23 April 2018, www.aspacpalestine.com
[443] Arbia Soemandoyo, 21 September 2015, https://www.merdeka.com/khas/jejak-mesra-hubungan-jakarta-tel-aviv-perdagangan-indonesia-israel.html
[444] www.liputan6.com, 8 December 2017
[445] Rizal Sukma, Islam in Indonesian Foreign Policy, Routledge Curzon, London and New York Page 48

would not recognize Israel as an independent state by opening new chapter of diplomatic relation. As recently elected as a non permanent member of the UN Security Council in 2018 for the next two year, would put the top priority to the Palestinian issues as highly urged by the Indonesian President himself, Joko Widodo. [446]

In spite of not explicitly imposing critical position to America- biased approach on pursuing the peace process, Indonesia would give emphasis on the necessity of international community to engage the case impartially. In addition, despite the fact that Indonesia is not a key partner for UNRWA (United Nations Relief and Works Agency for Palestine Refugees in the Near East) and not even the first eleven donor states,[447] yet the state would support the sustainable works of the Agency and international community's involvement to deal with a wide array of Palestinian refugee problems, evidenced clearly by the latest Indonesian commitment which is exentending its humanitarian assistance $ 2 million to the agency during the regional meeting of Conference on Cooperation among East Asian Countries for Palestinian Development (CEAPAD) III in Bangkok, Thailand 27 June 2018.[448] In the same token, Indonesia has promised to consistently materialize its firm commitment to help settle the long running dispute between Israel and Palestine.[449]

Therefore, it is hardly suprising for many years Indonesia has offered hundreds of technical trainings that aim at improving Palestinians' capacity as preparation for establishing Palestine state in the future, interalia offering training programs for 1.338 palestinians divided into 128 programs that would be extended up to 2019, not to mention other assistance forms that are provided regularly by Indonesian non state stakeholders such as granting many scholarships for Palestinian students.[450] In 2016, the government has planned to provide capacity building program for Palestinian policemen and civil servants.[451] In addition, Indonesia has trainned over 1400 Palestinians for the period 2008-2013 covering strategic sectors such as agriculture, industry, diplomacy, law enforcement and tourism. In the field of humanitarian assistance, during 2008-2016 the state has granted over $ 10 million to Palestinians, apart from the building of a hospital in Bait Lahiya Gaza which was realized by the Indonesian people donation. Not only that, since December 2017 Indonesia has implemented a zero tariff policy for any Palestinian products such as dates

---

[446] Ray Jordan, Jokowi: Isu Palestina Jadi Prioritas RI dalam DK PBB, 12 June 2018, https://news.detik.com/berita/4065800/jokowi-isu-palestina-jadi-prioritas-ri-dalam-dk-pbb
[447] AS donatur terbesar untuk Palestina di PBB, sejauh mana sumbangsih Indonesia? 10 January 2018, https://www.bbc.com/indonesia/indonesia-42622307
[448] Teddy Tri Setio Betti, Indonesia Beri Bantuan Rp 28,5 Miliar untuk Program Penguatan Kapasitas di Palestina, 1 July 2018, https://www.liputan6.com/global/read/3574749/indonesia-beri-bantuan-rp-285-miliar-untuk-program-penguatan-kapasitas-di-palestina
[449] www.kemlu.go.id, 20 January 2016
[450] For many years, some of the Indonesian universities provide scholarships for Palestinians. Most currently, 10 scholarships have been offered to Palestinians to study on aviation science in the School Penerbang Angkasa, m.republika.co.id, 2 July 2018
[451] ibid

and olive oil. In 2018, Indonesia has also had a program to provide clean water for Palestinian citizens. [452]

As a matter of fact, not only bilaterally and regionally, Indonesia has also played significant roles to consistently echo Palestinian interests in various international forums, mainly in the UN and Non-Alligned Movement. For instance, as a non permanent member of the UN Security Council for 2007-2008, Indonesia continuosly voiced on Palestinian's rights including the establishment of independent and democratic Palestine state, and often encouraged the UN Security Council to issue resolutions related to the Palestine issue. In result, Indonesia was among the main initiators to convene special meeting of UN General Assembly in January 2009 that yielded in its resolution containing particularly the support for the implementation of the Security Council resolution no 1860 and the call on international community to help lift humanitarian crisis in Gaza strip. Additionally, as a member of Human Right Council of the UN, Indonesia had urged holding the special session in January 2009 that resulted in ratifying the resolution draft on "the Grave Violation of Human Rights in the Occupied Palestinian Territory, particularly due to the recent Israel military attacks against the Occupied Gaza Strip. In the Asian African Conference hosted by Indonesia in April 2015, the member states have successfully adopted Declaration on Palestine which highlights their support on the Palestinian's struggles to achieve the long dreamed Palestine state, their reaffirmation on the two state solution. In sum, the Conference also issued a declaration to strengthen New Asia Africa Strategic Partnership, accordingly showing their firm commitment to extending assistance for Palestinian capacity building enhancement until 2019.[453] Last but not least, in October 2018, Indonesia for the first time held Solidarity Week for Palestine which involved various stakeholders and resulted in the inauguration of Palestine Walk : Road to Freedom in Bandung as well as the first bilateral consultation which emphasizes Indonesia's commitment to granting financial assistance US$ 7 million to Palestine.[454]

In addition, one of the reflections of its strong commitment, Indonesia has hosted several international conferences on Palestine, and has actively participated in numerous international meetings and conferences concerning the conflict including the most recent emergency OIC meetings in Turkey held to condemn the so-called the century's deal US unilateral decision to move its own embassy from Tel Aviv to Jerusalem. As it was predicted previously, Indonesia explicitly denounced the US policy by attempting to give several recommendations in the summit meeting.

---

[452] Minyak Zaitun dan Kurma Asal Palestina Bebas Tarif Impor Berlaku September, 6 Agustus 2018, https://www.liputan6.com/bisnis/read/3611535/minyak-zaitun-dan-kurma-asal-palestina-bebas-tarif-impor-berlaku-september www.bbc.com, 10 January 2018
[453] ibid
[454] Azis Rahardyan, 17 October 2018, http://kabar24.bisnis.com/read/20181017/15/850309/solidarity-week-for-palestine-kisah-persahabatan-indonesia-palestina-sejak-1944

Historically speaking, when Palestine National Council proclaimed a Palestine state in Alger in 16 November 1988, Indonesia soon officially recognized the proclamation, then followed up it by the signing of joint communiqué in 19 October 1989 between Palestinian Foreign Minister Farouk Kaddoumi and Indonesian Foreign Minister Ali Alatas, marking the opening of diplomatic relation of both countries in ambassadorial level. In fact, at the same date, Mr. Kaddoumi officially inaugurated the opening of Palestinian embassy in Jakarta while Indonesia was assigning its ambassador in Tunis to be accredited to Palestine.[455] Nevertheless, the seeds of the both states' willingness to open diplomatic relation was preceded incredibly by the first official visit of PLO leader Yasser Arafat to Indonesia in July 1984, welcomed warmly by Soeharto who emphasized once again its support on Palestinian's struggles to gain their independence.[456] The two leaders also had met in the sidelines of the 10th Non Alignment Movement Summit Meeting that was held in Jakarta in 1992.

As a matter of fact, supporting the Palestinian cause is a domain monopolized only by the state including its parliament that also actively has played prominent role to support Palestinian National Parliamentary in several international meetings, but also Indonesian people. Arguably almost all Indonesians from diverse backgrounds including Islamic preachers would support and approve the government's firm position by among others, donating their belongings to help lift economic crisis facing Palestinians. At least Indonesians would hold numerous peacefully massive demonstrations and protests when any humanitarian event takes place in Palestine. The roles of Indonesians non-governmental organizations and initiatives such as ACT (Immediate and Quick Action) and PKPU Human Initiative are highly undeniable which regularly send various much humanitarian assistance to Palestinians amid Israeli continuous efforts of blockading.

However with the passage of time a few important Indonesian figures have advocated normalization relation with Israel.[457] In the Abdurrahman Wahid's (Gusdur) presidential period (1999-2001), discourse of establishing relationship in economic and trade sectors with Israel significantly emerged with an ultimate goal that Indonesia could learn on economy and democracy from Israeli experience. Such a discourse to open commercial and trade ties with Israel was affirmed by Alwi Sihab, the foreign Minister of Indonesia of the time[458] sparking much debate and outrage among Muslim militants albeit interestingly President Yasser Arafat did not express his objection to this Indonesian desire.[459] Definitely the economic consideration had prompted Indonesia with its

---

[455] Boer Mauna, Hukum Internasional, Pengertian, Peranan dan Fungsi dalam Era Dinamika Global, PT. Alumni Bandung, 2005 second edition, page 81
[456] Soeharto.co
[457] As what was once implicitly advocated by Effendi Choirie, a Parliament member from National Awakening Party in 2007 that Indonesia has to revise its position towards Israeli occupation in Palestine, m.merdeka.com, 15 July 2007
[458] www.nu.or.id, 10 February 2017
[459] Rizal Sukma, Islam in Indonesian Foreign Policy, Routledge Curzon, London and New York, Page 112

predominantly economic improvement and growth agenda to scale back its deep antipathy with Israel, particularly with regard to attracting foreign investors to Indonesia. For Indonesia, Israel could be an appropriate bridge linking its economic policy to the outside world that having closer economic ties with Israel will not contravene Indonesian foreign policy principles as evidently stipulated in its 1945 basic constitution, rather it would undoubtedly help accomplish national interest gradually. In addition, Indonesia did realize that several Muslim Arab countries also do not mind having such economic relations, not diplomatic, with Israel as their view on Israeli importance as key player in economic terrain in the Middle East region. In this vein, Indonesian government once again had to face democracy dilemma in which the Islamic militant organizations expressed their vehement objection and opposition to any gesture and measure that give wider space in creating such a relation.

By taking into historical account four decades ago Indonesia, as what Iran practiced for the purpose of military engagement against Iraq under Saddam Hussein leadership which Indonesia was a neutral party, was alleged to have unofficial relations in trade sector with Israel when it agreed to purchase fourteen A-4 Skyhawk ground fighter aircraft and two TA-4 Skyhawk trainers from Israel.[460] Other news version noted that it was the purchasing of over 30 Skyhawk aircrafts, carried out through a covert operation called Alpha operation. Not only that reportedly several Indonesian pilots had also received aviation training in Israel given by Israeli instructors.[461]

Moreover, the shockingly initial secret visit of Israeli Prime Minister Yitzhak Rabin in 1993 to Indonesia to meet with Soeharto had also prompted controversy and speculation that Indonesia was likely to normalize its relation with Israel. In this vein, Israeli much willingness to open good relationship with Indonesia has been reflected well since the early period of Indonesia's independence in 1945 by sending congratulatory telegrams and its pledge to recognize Indonesia's sovereignty to Indonesian Vice President Mohammad Hatta.[462] However it is also worth mentioning that Indonesian pragmatism by accepting the Prime Minister in Jakarta after his visit to China and Singapore, had successfully prevented US from imposing military sanction to Indonesia that Israel would take over US role as military equipments supplier to Indonesia.[463]

---

[460] Ibid page 48
[461] Heder Affan, Hubungan rahasia Indonesia-Israel: Operasi Alpha, temu Suharto-Rabin, pembelian pesawat tempur, 12 December 2017, https://www.bbc.com/indonesia/indonesia-42305112
[462] Arbi Sumandoyo, Jejak mesra hubungan Jakarta-Tel Aviv, 21 September 2015,
https://www.merdeka.com/khas/jejak-mesra-hubungan-jakarta-tel-aviv-perdagangan-indonesia-israel.html
[463] ibid

2. Combating on Global Terrorism

In Britannica encyclopaedia, terrorism could be defined as the use of systematic violence to raise fear generally in one society that commonly has a certain political goal. Noam Chomsky defined it as the calculated use of violence or threat of violence to attain goals that are political, religious, or ideological in nature through intimidation, coercion, or instilling fear.[464]

In fact, terrorism has been practiced by political organizations with leftist and rightist hand objectives, by nationalistic and religious groups, by revolutionaries, and even by state institution.[465] Nevertheless, the definition of terrorism usually contains complexity elements and controversy as violent elements would be defined ambiguously. For instance, terrorism for the first time was popularized in 1790s to indicate terror actions carried out by revolutionaries to curb their oppositions in French Revolution so they would think twice before continuing their actions. Maximillien Robespierre from Jacobin party had spread terrors by imposing brutal punishment including guillotine used for massive execution. The fact implied that the terrorism definition was initially used to refer to all violent actions carried out by a state to silent and crush its oppositions. Yet as time went on, mainly since 20th century, the definition of terrorism has expanded to include all kinds of terrorism which aims at, either directly or not, to influence policies or eliminate ruling regimes.[466] For instance, the declaration of Helsinki Summit in 1992 defines terrorism as threat to security, democracy and human rights,[467] whereas OIC organization in which the three countries are the active members, defines it as violence or threat thereof against persons, property, environment, resources, stability of state.[468]

In practice, such an ambivalent definition with no internationally-acknowledged clear standards of terrorism, would be more apparent depending on point of view and interest surrounding both perpetrators and victims of terror acts. Commonly no thorough standardization of terrorism definition would absolutely hinder further country's efforts to identify and determine humanly rational steps and strategies to counter terrorism. For instance ratification of Indonesian law on counter terrorism was to be suspended as the parliament members had their distinctive interpretations and definitions on terrorism.[469] In addition, terrorism triggered by radicalization and extremism can happen to any person, group or nation. For instance, US government may define terrorism to be all kinds of action regarded as threatening its own interests, internally, regionally and globally. On the other

---

[464] Charles Webel and Mark Tomass, Assessing the War on Terror, Western and Middle Eastern Perspective, Taylor & Francis Group, first edition, 2017, page 20
[465] www.britannica.com
[466] ibid
[467] Alexander R. Dawoody, Eradicating Terrorism from the Middle East, Public Administration, Governance and Globalization, Springer, 2016, page 92
[468] Natasha Underhill, Countering Global Terrorism and Insurgency, Palgrave Macmillan, 2014 page 2
[469] Fathiyah Wardah, RUU Antiterorisme Terganjal Perdebatan Soal Definisi, 15 Mei 2018, https://www.voaindonesia.com/a/ruu-antiterorisme-terganjal-perdebatan-soal-definisi/4393625.html

side, the Middle Eastern leaders including Iran and Saudi Arabia would encompass terrorism as any effort perpetuated by a group or organization that aims at toppling the long - entrenched ruling systems and structures. In this vein, Iran would assume that Islam militant organizations and movements it regularly supports by all means like Palestinian Hamas and Lebanese Hezbollah are not considered terrorist groups as many western states have already designated, but liberation and resistance ones.[470] Another instance, while Arab Saudi and Egypt designate Ikhwanul Muslimin organization as terrorist group, but Turkey and some other Arab states not. Moreover for Sunni groups, all actions taken intentionally and systematically by Shia radical organizations that endeavour to crush Sunnis in the region could be considered terrorism; in turn revolutionary shia groups would regard Sunni Takfiri Jihadi groups targeting Shia community as terrorist groups. Moreover Saudi Arabia, based on its anti-terror law accentuates that any peaceful protesters and actions which defame Saudi reputation can be considered a terrorism act.[471] It is hardly surprising, people are confused to brand which one terrorist is, is it who protests or ruling regime protested? Furthermore, Saudi even labels all atheists as terrorists.[472] Defining terrorism by a state would be also problematic as it is obliged to take into account human rights enforcement in implementing counter terrorism measures. Nevertheless, most states seemingly agree to brand terror acts which could threaten domestic stability and security, engendering fears and worries of the societies along with purpose to intimidate any target government so as to change its undesired policies in order to comply with the terrorist groups' aspirations.

Despite the fact that scholars seemed to agree that generally a religion is unlikely to teach and urge violent principles and values to its adherents since any religious will be tied up with spreading virtues and preventing evils. Yet however a religion could be misused and misinterpreted, along with any political and economic aspects to prompt its fanatic followers to target civilians through terror acts.[473] In recent years, by harnessing cutting edge technologic advance at large, the terrorist networking could handily recruit individuals throughout the world by manipulating and hijacking religious symbols to entice their sympathy and then join the groups.

Furthermore, experts on terrorism affairs also have the shared standpoint and perspective that other non-religious factors such as economic frustration and racism could be two important factors propelling individuals to carry out terrorism acts.[474] Moreover Fahd Al-Shafi, former extremist, admitted that Saudi young men who joined al-Qaeda group

---

[470] Opcit page 220
[471] Simon Mabon, Kingdom in Crisis? The Arab Spring and Instability in Saudi Arabia, Contemporary Security Policy Journal, 30 Oktober 2012 page 543
[472] Adam Whitnall, www.independent.co.uk,1 April 2014,
https://www.independent.co.uk/news/world/middle-east/saudi-arabia-declares-all-atheists-are-terrorists-in-new-law-to-crack-down-on-political-dissidents-9228389.html
[473] www.huffngtonpost.com, 31 August 2011
[474] Scott Shane, Saudis and Extremism : Both the Arsonists and the Firefighters, 25 August 2016 www.nytimes.com

were encouraged and persuaded mostly by existing frustration on unemployment problem, reaffirming that loyalty to the terrorist group is not the main factor, in which that Saudi educational system and curricula have failed to create and provide skilled individuals to fulfil work opportunities.[475] However, terrorism challenges generated by radical jihadists who support vigorously Usama bin Laden's ideas on Global Jihad has threatened Kingdom's territory since the end of 1990s.[476]

Nevertheless based on Global Terrorism Index report, in recent years, religious extremism has been propelling factor in creating terrorism. For instance, the report obviously noted over 18.000 dead victims because of terrorism in 2013 were dominated (60 %) by four religious extremist groups namely ISIS, Boko Haram Nigeria, Taliban Afghanistan and al-Qaeda, which in previous years terrorism was often perpetuated by separatist and nationalist groups such as IRA and Chechen rebels. In fact, dead victims of terrorism became five folds since tragedy 9/11.[477]

As a matter of fact, terrorism issue in past recent decades has become rampant, often discussed by many stakeholders to mutually identify and determine strategies in combating radicalism and extremism of religious thoughts and interpretations which may engender terrorism. They are fully aware that the issue has posed an existential threat domestic stability, so they often promulgate anti terrorism propaganda through convening various conferences and seminars, discussing the issue in bilateral, regional and international meetings, conducting information disseminations over the dangers of terrorism via electronic and paper media including social media, etc. In their views, the roots and causes of terrorism must be found precisely because terrorism could occur anywhere and anytime, regardless of the levels of economic prosperity and literacy of the nations. States deeply realize that the issue has become one of the most crucial concerns that would guide their domestic and foreign policies to engage in. For decades states despite their profound propaganda on being secure and safe places, have been potential victims and targets by global terrorism which eventually thwarts the assumption that terrorism and radicalism take place only in failed states. In this vein, Saudi and Iran, unlikely to be terrorist actors, have been mainly accused of sponsoring global terrorism among other things by spreading radical and revolutionary ideas to target individuals. [478]

Tragedy 11 September 2001 which left thousands of the civilians killed appears to be a turning point for many states in dealing with global terrorism more aggressively. The tragedy also further displayed that threats of terrorism could be simply triggered by a

---

[475] Fatemeh Syayan, Security in the Persian Gulf Region, Palgrave Macmillan, page 143
[476] Paul Aarts and Gerd Nonneman, Ideology, Economy, Foreign Policy and the Outlook for the Saudi Polity, A Triple Nexus, page 436
[477] Religious extremism main cause of terrorism, according to report, 18 November 2014, https://www.theguardian.com/news/datablog/2014/nov/18/religious-extremism-main-cause-of-terrorism-according-to-report
[478] Natasha Underhill, Countering Global Terrorism and Insurgency, Palgrave Macmillan, 2014 page 12

misguided religious interpretations which led into extremism and radicalism as potential seeds for terror acts to emerge. Additionally the devastating tragedy perpetuated by Sunni militants has led world to pay more attention and concentration to Sunni radical movements. As a matter of fact, in the previous years, considerable international focus was given to Shia radical groups, mainly Lebanese Hezbollah, as the implication of Islamic Iran's establishment. However, 9/11 tragedy has also prompted emerging of a wide array of other terrorism acts based on manipulated Islamic interpretation, that made Islam to be viewed as a potential source for creating the actions. In nutshell, there has been sceptical perception in international community's minds that Islam encourages and persuades its staunch adherents to spread fear and terror within the society

In fact, war on global terror, a jargon intensively developed in the aftermath of 9/11 tragedy has already become an international framework and standard for any state to engage with such a issue, whether it seriously carries out efforts to fight terrorism or otherwise, supports terrorist organizations by all means and mechanisms including financing, recruiting, military weaponry transferring and extreme religious interpretation spreading, etc. For those not committed in eradicating terrorism, US government could put both economic and military sanctions to give more pressure on the states so as to alter their terrorism supportive policies.

Nevertheless it is not surprising in order to avoid such 'punishments', all states would claim definitely to stand with fighting on terrorism, including Saudi Arabia, Iran and Indonesia. Particularly, the two former states, all this time have been often alleged by the world to have supported international terrorist organizations by all means despite their claim on leading states for Muslim nations. Since 1970s, Saudi Arabia along with Sunni rigid Wahhabi ideology has been regarded to have popularized radicalism and extremism that inspired several terrorist groups to spread terrorism in the name of religion, imposing dilemma for Saudi in dealing with counter terrorism in the following decades. Moreover, Robert Jordan, former US ambassador in Saudi Arabia once said that Saudi Arabia was considered to be a breeding ground for the rigid ideology of Wahhabi to grow, and a home to several Jihadists who already returned from Afghanistan. [479] Apparently some observers even find any resemblance between the first Saudi-Wahhabi state and ISIS group in the term of bloodshed and brutality in conquering and expanding their distinct and rigid beliefs.[480]

Meanwhile Iran with radically and revolutionary political Shia interpretation, has been well-known for supporting financially and militarily various radical militia movements in the region mainly in Lebanon, Iraq, Yemen and Palestine. Moreover, Iranian Revolutionary Guard, often engaged actively in Middle Eastern disputes by extending incessant support to

---

[479] Robert Jordan, with Steve Fiffer, Desert Diplomat, Inside Saudi Arabia Following 9/11, Potomac Books, 2015, Page 29
[480] Frederic Wehrey, Beyond Sunni and Shia, the Roots of Sectarianism in a Changing Middle East, Oxford University Press, 2107, page 245

those militias, has been branded as terrorist group by USA which accordingly has imposed various economic sanctions to the organization for years.

Therefore, the governments of both states have unceasingly attempted to convince international community they also encourage and promote moderate Islam, among others by dispatching their military troops to annihilate terrorist groups. Iran's intensive engagement in Syrian and Iraq, despite many allegations that Iran has its own hidden agenda in the region, has been arguably endorsed by its strong commitment to annihilate ISIS group, whereas Saudi Arabia's military involvement in Bahrain in 2011 was under the pretext to help Bahraini rulers crush "terrorist" civilian protesters.

Ironically, due to tight political rivalry in the region, the two states, Saudi Arabia and Iran, have invariably accused one another for supporting global terrorism which endeavours to destabilize the region and spread extremist sectarian ideology to other communities. While Saudi officials have never put Shia teaching to hold responsibility for growing seeds of terrorism but rather revolutionary exporting agenda of Iranian government, Iranian officials would further blame on Wahhabi doctrine supported and disseminated by Saudi government to have inspired the emergence of terrorist groups in the region. Even Dr. Javad Zareef, current Iranian foreign minister has once wrote that some terrorist attacks in Europe can't be ignored the existence of the toxic threat of Wahhabism.[481]

As frequently cited earlier, Iran has been significantly regarded to have successfully support various militant militias and political state rebels in many regions. The latest evidence in May 2018, Morocco government has strongly accused that Iran and its proxy Hezbollah organization have trained and armed Polisario Front fighters, a Western Saharan independence movement, causing diplomatic crises between Iran and Morocco.[482] In the other hand, Saudi Arabia has been also accused for helping cultivate and promote extremism and radicalism by supporting Jihadi movements. For example, in 1996 Arab Saudi along with Pakistan and United Emirates Arab had supported Taliban radical organization which succeeded to unseat and replace the legitimate Afghanistan President Burhanuddin Rabani who was supported by Iranian regime.[483] Even reportedly that between 1980 and 1990, the Kingdom gave almost $ 4 billion officially to Jihadist in Afghanistan.[484]

In the other hand, Indonesia has never been accused for supporting such militant and extremist groups, yet unluckily for many years the country has become the victim of such trans-national and border terrorisms since 1980s that I would like to highlight further later on. Interestingly, the terrorism in Indonesia has increased in the aftermath of reform age in 1998 that leads into simple conclusion that the more democratic Indonesian is the

---
[481] Mohammad Javad Zarif, Let US Rid the World of Wahhabism, www.nytimes.com, 13 September 2016
[482] Morocco cuts diplomatic ties with Iran over Western Sahara feud, www.aljazeera.com, 2 May 2018
[483] Banafsheh Keynoush, Saudi Arabia and Iran, Friend or Foes, Palgrave macmillan, page 146
[484] Madawi Al-Rasheed, Constesting the Saudi State, Islamic Voices from a New Generation, Cambridge University Press, page 107

more rampant terror acts both quantitatively and qualitatively. In Indonesia, it is estimated that terror acts caused by religious misinterpretation ranging from 2000 to 2009 have left 286 killed and 700 wounded. [485]

With an effort to popularize moderate Islam to other nations both in rhetoric and practice, it is almost hard to brand the state as a terrorism sponsor in the region. However, the transitional period following the collapse of Soeharto's authoritarian administration in 1998 had attracted the world's attention on numerous terrorism activities in Indonesia including terrorist recruitment and operation, creating much fear among international community that Indonesia has already became a fertile breeding ground for new generations of terrorists. Nevertheless, after the first Bali Bombing, dubbed the worst terror attack in its modern history, Indonesian government has been preoccupied with multiple terrorism threats emanating from small groups with little central coordination or leadership, which not only target innocent civilians, but also security forces, [486] and often have strong ties with ISIS organization. However it is undeniable that each state of the three always attempts significantly at identifying and implementing strategies and formulas to curb and eliminate all sorts of terrorism including extreme Islamic interpretation alleged to be inspiring for terrorism. They endeavour considerably to restrict, amid their deep understanding on improbability of total annihilation of Islamic radical minds, spreading such a radical Islamic ideology by using moderate identity of Islam.

As a matter of fact, since 1984, Ali Akbar Velayati, the Iranian foreign minister in that period, is reported to have tried to eliminate radical elements affiliating to the Revolutionary Guards within Iranian embassies abroad. Furthermore, in 1992 in his letter to European community, he reasserted on his defiance to all kinds of terrorism and foreign intervention to one state's domestic issues.[487] In the other side, in order to give support to anti-terrorism policies taken by Saudi government, Wahhabi clerics were asked to endorse such policies through issuing various fatwas on condemnation of al-Qaeda terrorist acts and consideration of the perpetrators as heretics, besides fatwas on condemnation of suicidal bombing attacks and banning Saudi young men to join jihadist groups in Iraq or anywhere else following American invasion to Iraqi territory in 2003.[488]

Interestingly as intimated earlier, discourse on global terrorism for many decades has been often associated with Islamic radicalism and extremism repeatedly brought by Wahhabi and revolutionary Shia. Meaning that a Muslim substantively could be radical and extremist if he follows Wahhabi but not Shia. In substance, Shia does not cause a Muslim to

---

[485] Muhammad A.S. Hikam, Deradikalisasi, Peran Masyarakat Sipil Indonesia Membendung Radikalisme, Kompas, 2016, Page 69

[486] Vedi R.Hadiz, Islamic Populism in Indonesia and the Middle East, Cambridge University Press, first published in 2016, page 326

[487] Christin Marchall, Iran's Persian Gulf Policy, From Khomeini to Khatami, Routledge Curzon Taylor and Francis Group, page 45

[488] Nabil Mouline, The Clerics of Islam Religious Authority And Political Power in Saudi Arabia, Yale University Press page 158

be radical, yet when the religion is used as an effective means to propagate revolutionary principles as what Iran has been carrying out, that Muslim could become radical.

Shia and Root of Its Extremism

In order to give the root of extremism in Shia teaching, I would like to emphasize on it by referring to two books. The first is in Persian titled *Hezbollah, Khate Mashi, Gozashte va Ayandeye On* (Hezbollah, Strategic Direction, Past and Present) written by Sheikh Naim Qasim, prominent Lebanese cleric and former Secretary General of the organization, also co-founder of the organization in 1982. The phenomenal book, originally written in Arabic, was claimed to have been translated into various languages. The second is titled *Hezbollah, al-Tarekhul Ideoloji wa Siyasi*, written by Yosef Al-Agha, lecturer of Islamic Studies in American University in Beirut. Although the contents of books have focussed on Lebanese political Hezbollah organization as study case, yet however in order to understand the genesis and background of foundation of the organization would give us a comprehensive depiction over Shia extremism roots which was able to inspire the entire Shia movements in the region apart from Hezbollah. Besides in fact Hezbollah has been one of the first Shia organizations to adopt extremism of human bombing often assumed it as Jehad practice, to give its resistance against Israeli aggression in early 1980s, much earlier than Palestinians (Hamas group) ever did. Not only that, historically speaking, the Iranian Shias are believed to have been the first Muslims to employ it during war with Iraq in 1980.[489]

In his book, Sheikh Naim Qasim (SNQ) suggests that the establishment of Islamic government constitutes a religious proposal that reflects natural responsibility of a Muslim. He claims in Islamic government, the justice aspect expected highly by humankind as a positive outcome of an Islamic government would be undoubtedly embodied. Therefore, establishing it is likely to be accepted by even non-Shia followers as viewed to be a proper mechanism to achieve the ultimate goal of achieving happiness for humankind.

Yet however, the idea of Islamic government establishment is not allowed to be based on coercion from one group to another. Here SNQ seemingly realises that strong aspiration of Hezbollah to implement Islamic government in Lebanon was impeded by reality that total Shia population in Lebanon (27%) is much less than Sunni and Christian populations. Additionally, not all Shia followers in Lebanon were Hezbollah members, thus evincing their approval with the implementation of Islamic government.

SNQ also reasserts that the function of Jihad covers fighting not only against God's enemies, but also against personal lust. In regard to practicing Jihad against enemies, Shia jurists have broken it into two parts, first, Jihad *Ibdtida'i* is carried out while expanding military efforts to other territories to spread Islam. This type of Jihad, according to most

---

[489] Azam Tamimi, Dying For Faith, Religiously Motivated Violence in the Contemporary World, Edited by Madawi Al-Rasheed and Marat Shterin, I.B Tauris Page 122

jurists only prevails in the age of the Prophet Mohammad and twelve infallible Imams. Second, Jihad Defa'i which each Muslim is obliged to make self-defence by all means to face occupation and aggression by alien powers. The second jihad was equally stated by Imam Khomeini that self defence for each Muslim is obligatory. Furthermore according to SNQ, Jihad implementation is suggested not only by God and His Prophet, but also by the infallible Imams, which Imam Ali bin Abi Thalib once said faith has four strong pillars namely patience, belief, justice, and Jihad. In this regard, Imam Jafar al-Shadeg narrated that Jihad poses the most important duty for a Muslim. In the modern era, Hassan Nasrullah, Hezbollah leader, also highly underscored that only the culture of jihad is capable of bringing about victory.[490]

SNQ in his book also reveals his passion to become Syahid (martyr) in Jihad which according to Shia's belief martyrdom embodies the highest testament to faith.[491] Historically speaking such a strong faith has been exemplified by Imam Hossein's martyrdom in Karbala, Iraq in 680 AD in his showing of resistance to despotic ruler, Yazid bin Muawiyah. SNQ obviously believes that Karbala spirit must inspire subsequent Muslim generations anywhere and anytime to fight the tyranny of ruling regimes under a renowned slogan *Kullu Yaumin Asshura wa Kullu Ardhin Karbala* (every day is Ashura and every land is Karbala).

In this vein, Imam Khomeini once stated that Muharram (the first month of the Islamic calendar) constitutes a month of the prevailing blood over sword seen to have inspired the outbreak of Islamic revolution in 1979. In fact, Karbala tragedy also inspired Ashura commemoration held by Shia followers around the world which sometimes is featured by hitting their foreheads with swords and beating themselves until bleeding. Ali Shariati even believed that all Shia history begun in Karbala and would end with an Iranian Revolution as portraying Imam Husein as a seventh-century Che Guevara and Karbala as a revolutionary drama.[492] Furthermore, Sheikh Abdul Wahab Hussain, Bahraini prominent cleric, once explained that the difference between Sunni and Shia is difference between *al-fatih* and *al-maftuh* (conqueror and conquered) that often overshadowed the phases of Shia history which was rife of Shia opposition to Sunni ruling regimes.[493] To him, in the future, Karbala battle might inspire Shia's defiance to Sunni political leaders under the division of the two camps, Hossein camp as oppressed ones and Yazid camp as oppressors.[494] However, interestingly, according to Mehdi Khalaji, Iranian prominent scholar, the founding fathers of Islamic Iran in promoting and developing widely on Jihad and martyrdom, apart from establishing Islamic ideology, were undoubtedly inspired by Sunni political activists and

---

[490] Ibid page 119
[491] Vali Nasr, the Shia Revival How Conflicts Within Islam Will Shape the Future, W.W. Norton Company New York London, Page 43
[492] Ibid page 97
[493] Lawrence G.Potter, Sectarian Politicas in the Persian Gulf, Oxford University Press and Georgetown University's Center for International and Regional Studies, School of Foreign Servisc in Qatar, page 55
[494] Ibid, page 64

scholars, particularly Said Qotb from Sunni Ikhwanul Muslimin organization whose book was translated into Persian by the current Supreme Leader. [495]

According to SNQ, owning small number of personnel shall not be a significant obstacle to realize Jihad because in Karbala battle, Imam Hossein was accompanied by only 70 persons, mostly his family and relatives. Moreover the fighters killed in Jihad could not be regarded as suicides. To him, slogan *Kullu Yaumin Asshura wa Kullu Ardhin Karbala* repeatedly promulgated by Iranian regime would have a remarkable impact to Shia militants anywhere else where they exist given various interpretations of the slogan, justifying Shia followers to resist and oppose both peacefully and violently to their rulers who proved to have oppressed to their populace. Or, such an opposition could be taken against the just rulers due to the fact however, based on Shia faith, entire government systems after Mahdi's major occultation are definitely illegitimate.

However SNQ affirms a central role of Velayat Faqih that covers all human's life including political and security affairs. It is hardly surprising Vali Faqih (Supreme Leader) has special authority to decide various matters concerning war and peace through consultation with other related stake holders. As such when dissent among the jurists appears, Supreme Leader's opinion must prevail. Interestingly the implementation of Supreme Leader's authority is not limited for Iran per se, but also for any Shia individual or groups outside Iran who expressed their loyalty to him. Consequently, they may de facto recognize their own rulers but not de jure due to their devotion to Supreme Leader shall prevail over their own national leaders in all aspects with no exception. Such an ironic fact was once elucidated by Hosni Mobarak, Egyptian former President in April 2006 that most Shia community are loyal to Iran (Supreme Leader) and not to their own leaders where they reside.[496] Moreover this fact, according to Morteza Nabavi, Risalat Newspaper editorial staff, has been confirmed historically which Imam Hossein once reportedly abrogated his pilgrimage due to his unwillingness to acknowledge Yazid as legal ruler. This event implies that pilgrimage, five time prayer, and any other Islamic duties would not be beneficial if the ruling regime is not Supreme Leader.[497] Additionally, because a Supreme Leader has to be *Marja'e Taqleed* (Source of Emulation), so his authority to issue legal matters would automatically encompass each Shia follower throughout the world who already has expressed his allegiance and loyalty to him.

According to Yosef el-Agha, a Supreme Leader will do no wrongs just as twelve infallible Imams due to the fact that he indeed represents God, in which according to Imam Khomeini, his order would be absolute and undeniable. Eventually, the theory of Velayat Faqih will eliminate national borders and sovereignty of the states as well as nationalism principles that likely inspire Shia militants outside Iran to resist and oppose as a reflection of

---

[495] www.hudson.org, Mehdi Khalaji, The Dilemma of Pan Islamic Unity
[496] Ibid page 16
[497] Christin Marchall, Iran's Persian Gulf Policy, From Khomeini to Khatami, Routledge Curzon Taylor and Francis Group, halaman page 49

their loyalty to the Supreme Leader (Vali Faqih). Such a process to shape loyalty and devotion for non-Iranian Shia followers is being made by Iranian regime by exerting soft diplomacy as a main tool to spread Shia ideology that I would like to underscore it further in the next chapter.

In sum, Yosef el-Agha in his book, elaborates in detail the theory of Taqiya as an important principle for Shia ideology that originated from the belief of Imamate concept. Taqiya means the practice of denying one's religion, permissible when one is faced with persecution, especially by Sunnis: regarded as a means of protecting the religion. The concept, integral part of Shia faith, is commonly practiced when Shia community embodies a minority group who live in politically Sunnis-dominated territory. To Shia, the practice is obliged firmly by the religion, which Imam Jafar al-Sadeg even had denounced Shia followers who do not implement the concept by regarding them as the ones who have no religion, that Taqiya was historically practiced by past prophets. Moreover, due to its significance, Ibnu Babawiyah Ali, a prominent Sha cleric, once concluded that any Shia follower who does not implement Taqiya before the re-emerging of Imam Mahdi could be regarded apostates and violating God, Prophet and Imams' commands. However, according to Nabil el-Haydari, a vocal critic on Shia, in his book *Tashayyo al-Arabi wa Tasyayyu Farsi, Dawrul Farsi Tarikhi fi Inherafi Tashayyu*, (Shia Arab and Shia Persia, the Historical Role of Persian in Fabricating Shia) highlighted that some of Shia followers regard Taqiya as an Islamic duty which can't be ignored until the judgement day under any excuse that neglecting such a practice definitely equals to neglecting five time prayer.[498]

In fact, the concept of Taqiya has a very significant impact to the Shia followers in their society anywhere else they live. This concept could imply indirectly that minority Shia groups who peacefully within Sunni dominated- political rulers, would have a feeling of fear and intimidation despite amid political stability. For Shia followers, as mentioned earlier, in spite of Sunni just and fair rulers, as long as state is not ruled politically by the twelve Imams, so their ruling must be illegal and unlawful, that shall be transformed into a political system that at least shows its allegiance to Supreme Leader in Iran, if not similar to the Islamic Republic of Iran. Therefore, Taqiya invariably would view that all Sunni regimes in the entire world are unlawful, which accordingly leads Shia followers to have imaginative threats as manifestation of these 'illegal regimes.' As such, it is obligatory to them to implement Taqiya by hiding their real religious identity and faith to salvage their personal lives, mainly in Sunni-dominated societies. Meanwhile, Imam Khomeini has allowed Taqiya by doing illegal acts under the framework of exigency. In result, Imam banned Taqiya for

---

[498] Nabil el Haydari, Tasyayu al Arabi wa Tasyayyu Farsi, Dawrul Farsi Tarikhi fi Inherafi Tasyayyu, Darul Hikmah, London, page 272

Shia followers in Iran following the 1979-Revolution victory given the fact that no longer need to hide their beliefs under the newly born Islamic state. [499]

With regard to Taqiya practice, Saudi Arabia felt compelled to pay more attention to Shia minority group who mostly live in the eastern part of Saudi, which it often has accused the community of the fifth column of Iranian regime that probably generate their resistance to the Royal family amid their pretention of being loyal to the Kingdom. Along with this reason, Hasan al-Safar, a prominent Saudi Shia cleric, just like Imam Khomeini, had called obviously that Taqiya shall be practiced in the urgent situations, as suggested by Imam Ali bin Abi Thalib.[500] Therefore small wonder that Iraqi Shia followers felt compelled to welcome and approve foreign troops in Iraq in 2003 US invasion, whereas their deep heart would express otherwise by condemning the presence of the foreign national troops.[501]

As a matter of fact, the core function of Supreme Leader is to pave a way for Imam Mahdi to re-emerge that will be accomplished among other things by accentuating endlessly Taqiya and Jihad to Shia followers around the globe. The term of "Paving the path" to accelerate the long waited Imam's advent would be more ambiguous to elaborate. Meaning that it would give implicitly a legal justification for Supreme Leader to take efforts to pave the way by creating political chaos and instability within the existing political systems, so as injustice and imbalance could be embodied that accordingly would accelerate the advent of Imam Mahdi who is adamantly believed to create justice and balance for mankind. Thus, it is hardly shocking that Hasan Rahempour Azgadi, a well-known Iranian theorist, also a member of High Revolutionary Council for Cultural Affairs, once unfolded that Imam Khomeini was the central factor of the World' tensions, so he would not let the world be kept in peace and tranquillity.[502]

Most startlingly, the faith of Imam Mahdi's advent has arguably imbued the President Ahmadinejad's radical and frontal stances toward West, including Israel by highlighting constantly that Iran has become a base for His re-emerging[503] and attempting to pave the way for His re-appearance by carrying out resistance against the rulers' tyranny in the entire world.[504] The great significance of Imam Mahdi faith for Shia followers, although such a strong faith nowadays among Iranians seemingly has declined as implication of their scepticism to clerical rulers, had prompted even Ali Larijani, head of Iranian parliament, to declare during the international conference on Imam Mahdi in Tehran, October 2014 that

---

[499] DR. Amal Hamade, al-Khebratel al-Iraniyah al-Intighal min al-Tsaurati lla Daulat, Arab Network For Research and Publishing, page 91
[500] Mamnon Fandy, From confrontation to creative resistance : Theb Shia's oppositional discourse in Saudi Arabia, page 9
[501] Banafshes Keynoush, Saudi Arabia and Iran, Friends or Foes? Palgrave Macmillan page 181
[502] For further information, please listen to the lecture delivered by Hasan Rahempour Azgadi mengenai Imam Khomeini in Persian language
[503] www1.cbn.com
[504] Mehdi Khalaji, Apocalyptic Poltics, On the Rationality of Iranian Policy, the Washington Institute for Near East Policy, page 25

faith to Imam Mahdi's advent is of the great importance that inspired revolutionary actions Iranian leaders.[505]

According to Yosef al-Egha, Imam Khomeini affirmed that it has become an obligation for all Muslims to obey Supreme Leader's commands in all terrains, including to defend Islam and Islamic Ummah from the unbelievers and oppressors, even Muslim rulers. Such an obligation to be loyal to Vali Faqih has been also confirmed by several fatwas issued by Iranian Shia clerics. In addition, as mentioned earlier, such a loyalty must be expressed without any objection and questioning on his power absoluteness.[506] However, many contemporary Shia clerics have been sceptical to role played by Ayatullah Khamene'i as current Supreme Leader, in which they almost agreed that he proved not to own high capability and capacity in Islamic law and jurisprudence, unlike Imam Khomeini.[507]

In this vein, Imam Khomeini has accentuated the word *Istishad* which means doing (asking) everything to become Shahid (martyr) that poses a grace and honour promised with victory by God in hereafter. Interestingly, Imam Khomeini has been the first Shia cleric who allowed *Istishad* for both male and female, that constitutes a highest peak of self-sacrifice in God's path.

According to Nabil Heydari, a prominent critics on Iranian Shia, radicalism of Shia, mainly Persian Shia, has stemmed from the Imamate concept as a faith pillar that classifies a Sunni as unbeliever due to his denial to Imamate who pretends to act as a Muslim by hiding his real faith (Taqiya). In sum he notes that according to Shia faith, claiming of guardianship for Imams is better than all prophets, even Prophet Mohammad, and Islamic pillars, in which it has become obligatory for all Muslims to believe and follow the Imams, with no exception, otherwise they would be regarded as unbelievers who deserve to enter the hell everlastingly. [508]

---

[505] www.isna.ir, 14 October 2014

[506] Questioning and criticizing Velayat Faqih is extremely a taboo in Iran. based on my observation, people may talk in various political and economic issues and then criticize the wrong policies of government, but not the authority of Velayat Faqih. Mohsen Kadivar and Abdul Karim Soroush, the two prominent Iranian scholars, questioned his authority, were forced to leave Iran. the most recent example is In March 2018, Ayatollah Hossein Shirazi, the Grand Ayatollah's son was arrested after a speech that criticized Velayat Faqih, sparking numerous demonstrations both in Iran and Iraq by the supporters of the Grand Ayatollah

[507] Ayatollah Khamenei admitted before the Assembly of Experts in 1989 his incapability and inability in Islamic law understanding, in which he was not the right person to hold the position of next Supreme Leader

[508] Nabil el Haydari, Tasyayu al Arabi wa Tasyayyu Farsi, Dawrul Farsi Tarikhi fi Inherafi Tasyayyu, Darul Hikmah, London, page 203, 209, 215

Radicalization of Shia Politics in Iran

Historically speaking, shia radicalism was mostly triggered by political dynamics during the time, particularly concerning resistance against the despotic rulers who proved to be tyrannical and repressive to their peoples. For Shia, it has been firmly recommended to make opposition and protest to such regimes until they change their own false policies or otherwise to be toppled down. Asef Bayat, a prominent Iranian scholar has once noted that Shia group, also called religion of protest, is more prone to having revolution than Sunni, which means that many ideas and principles of becoming revolutionary protesters are evidently reflected in Shia history. Furthermore the writings of Ali Shariati has given a scientific legitimization to the revolutionary Shia concept which accentuates a modern concept on class, conflict among classes, and revolution, absorbed into Shia thoughts with the inspiration of the Karbala battle.[509]

As a matter of fact, Shia, while being still considered as a minority group in Islamic world, has gained its golden opportunity to express its political and religious existence when Islamic Republic of Iran was born in 1979. For the first time in modern history, Shia ideology brought by the fanatical Shia clerics was able to politically inspire for creation of a state, thus entering its political domain. As such, this newly born state engendered a plethora of expectations and hopes among Shia followers, which Iran would accommodate more Shia world's interests by taking policies beneficial to Shia community.

As time went on, in recent decades, internationally Shia radical resistance has been more reflected under the manifestation of anti-imperialism and global arrogance, represented by USA and its allied states, mainly Israel.[510] In reality, anti US slogan has been long popularized by Imam Khomeini himself, often branding it as a Great Satan and accusing it as it was trying adamantly to pollute and destroy Islamic ethics and norms. Therefore, due to the Islamic Iranian ideal, the regime would like to call unabashedly "unbeliever or *Munafiq* (hypocrite)" for any individual or group who proved to undermine the Islamic state.[511]

Meanwhile domestically, the interpretation of Shia radicalism in the political terrain in Iran, could be mirrored in the concept of allegiance and submission to God beyond nationalism principles and trans-national borders. Meaning that Iran has viewed that modern concept on national borders and sovereignty as a result of Westphalia concept in 17th century, is not necessarily right and ideal, despite the fact that with the passage of time,

---

[509] Asef Bayat, Life as Politics, How Ordinary People Change the Middle East, Amsterdam University Press, page 229
[510] Farhad Khosrokhavar, Radicalization : Why Some People Choose the Path of Violence, the New Press
[511] Iran-American Forum, Youtube Channel broadcasted in 2 May 2017

Iran still has tolerated the creation of new world order resulted from such a concept.[512] Moreover it believes the only right system of all is the one which keeps preserving Islamic ummah that can bypass geographical, ethnical and national borders and restrictions. Therefore, as a theocratic state, Iran always maintains that any national interest and sovereignty which accordingly emphasize on secular principles will automatically lose their values and thus not to be acceptable as they simply ignore God's authority.

As a state based on Velayat Faqih concept, the Iranian governmental system and structure would be dominated automatically by Shia Imamate clerics who mostly graduate from Islamic Hawzes (religious seminaries) in Qom and Mashhad cities, long believed to be also having a expertise on state administration. In consequence, most decisions and policies taken by them would have spiritual values and dimensions that must be accepted by the society as they would definitely constitute clerical interpretations.

Having no partition and distinction between political and religious authorities in Islamic republic would prompt its own uniqueness in taking such policies. It differs from any political system commonly taken in Saudi Arabia and other Muslim states, including Indonesia which tend to split the authority on political matters and from that of the religious ones whose authority would be often given to a governmental special institution. Yet in Iran, many fatwas can be issued by Supreme Leader as central figure of government system and by other competent Shia clerics who reached the level of *Marja'e Tagleed* (source of emulation). Like Saudi Arabia, fatwas issued by Iranian Shia clerics may function to endorse and justify government policies, and thus they are unlikely to contradict the government policies.

In fact some of the political, economic and cultural policies taken by the Iranian government, commonly secular and liberal in nature and character, would highly and automatically contain their spirituality that having such a perception sometimes compels the government to adjust his policies in order to pursue the goals and interests of Islam. Moreover, little wonder that some Iranian fundamentalist hardliners strongly perceive that all government's policies constitute measures and actions that would be approved by God as the government (Supreme Leader) has been long regarded as a bridge to make communication and interaction with the hidden Imam Mahdi.

Nevertheless, there is an essential difference between fatwas issued by Supreme Leader (Vali Faqih) and non-Supreme Leader clerics, which the fatwas taken and issued by him would be absolute and general in nature that must be followed by all Iranian society, or non-Iranians who have already expressed their allegiance and devotion to him. In addition, such fatwas/legal opinions also bring political force that shall be implemented both in

---

[512] Ahmad Sadeghi, Genealogy of Iranian Foreign Policy : Identity, Culture and History, the Iranian Journal of International Affairs, IPIS, page 17

internal and external policies and will not accept any significant objection from other Shia clerics despite having more competency and capability in issuing legal opinions.

Because of such a confusing perception as a consequence of non partition between political and religious authorities, Iran has often exploited people's perplexity by accentuating religious jargons and slogans in order to espouse and justify vehemently their policies which seem contradictory with national interests.

Not only that, as time went on, Iran has often used Islam as a sacred shield to fortify its own policies which appear to be opposing to public aspirations. For instance, crushing repeatedly many political activists, writers, journalists, bloggers and demonstrators as well and jailing them without single specific charge have been taken due to an existing religious perception that they were truly opposing God's commands and laws. As intimated earlier that objecting laws issued by Supreme Leader would be equivalent to that of God's commands.

In addition, Iran also proved to have executed brutally thousands of political oppositions who were accused to have had intentions to dissolve the Islamic regime, often labelling them as unbelievers and hypocrites as well as terrorists. The regime has religious justification that any brutal punishment carried out by its officers would be blessed definitely by God, in order to prevent such an action from mushrooming that could lead the overthrowing of the regime. Most startlingly, such devastating facts were once confirmed not only by several human rights associations, but also numerous Iranian political elites through their shocking confession. Ayatollah Khalkhali, former head of Revolutionary court for instance had confessed that in early years of Islamic Revolution, he had issued execution sentence for over 2000 political dissents who some of the executed probably were innocent.[513]

In this vein, Mehdi Khalaji, Iranian scholar on Shia affairs, elucidated that the theory of Velayat Faqih in fact was not designed to implement Islamic laws and rules, but to grant legitimacy to the authority of Vali Faqih to ignore the implementation of Islamic laws. In short words, it could mean that Imam Khomeini created religious justifications to disregard Islamic rules with aim at safeguarding the survival of the Islamic regime although they would probably violate Islamic standardization. For instance, Imam Khomeini reportedly had re-legalized practices that were once banned by himself prior to the Revolution, such as women's right to vote in general elections and Caviar trade. In sum, Imam Khomeini also re-legalized even obliged Iranians to pay tax to the state, in which before the outbreak of the revolution, such a practice was banned by himself vehemently as he believed there was no longer need to support financially the Pahlavi despotic ruler.[514]

---

[513] www.awsath.com, 28 November 2003
[514] Mehdi Khalaji, Apocalyptic Poltics, On the Rationality of Iranian Policy, the Washington Institute for Near East Policy, page 29

Additionally, the foundation of Basiji organization in 1980, offshoot of the Iranian Revolutionary Guards, indicates spreading more radical and militant crackdowns of the regime, carried out by young members who seem to be loyal to the regime. In recent years, this group of paramilitary volunteer militia has engendered so much fear and worry among Iranian publics, mainly for those who are suspected to threatening Vilayat Faqih concept and acting incompatibly with the Islamic values. Under the supervision of Supreme Leader, Basiji organization, mobilized anytime if deemed necessary, has succeeded to help realize the Islamic regime's objectives which is creating more Islamic public atmosphere and guarantying the survival of the regime. Like *Mothawa* (Sharia police) organization in Saudi Arabia, Basiji often functions in supervising and monitoring behaviours and ethics of the Iranians in public area that sometimes are carried out with violence.

Several violent acid attacks on women in Esfahan, allegedly conducted by Basiji organization, were triggered due to the improper headscarf wearing. The mobilized attacks to British embassy in 2011 and Arab Saudi embassy in 2016 in Tehran and its Consulate General in Mashhad that accordingly ruptured the diplomatic relations, triggered by politically and religiously sentiments, carried out vigorously by the organization. The successful yet violent crushing of the demonstrators in the Green Movement in 2009, deemed the largest one in Iranian modern history since 1979, in Tehran had involved significantly Basiji roles.

Numerous Iranian Shia hardliner clerics like Ayatollah Misbah Yazdi, Ahmad Jannati, Nasser Makarim Shirazi have been well-known for having 'unusual' opinions/fatawa which often contravene the reformist group thoughts. For instance, Ayatollah Misbah Yazdi has likened political reformist group with the community who revives the unbeliever 2500 year Persian culture. The cleric, arguably the most conservative and authoritative in religious seminary of Qom, had issued fatwas, endorsing violent and radical mechanisms in serial killing tragedy which killed dozens of intellectual dissents in Iran (1988-1998). The 83 year old cleric reportedly has also expressed disagreement with democracy principles, suggesting that such principles are against God and the religion. [515]

Interestingly in Iran, although government institutions such as parliament and presidency are dominated by moderate reformist group, yet radical and conservative group seemingly dominates policy takings in both domestic and foreign issues, etc. Such a fact once again strengthened the indication that conservative Vali Faqih's role in Iranian political administration is extremely central. For many years, it has been viewed broadly that despite the existence of executive, legislative and judicative authorities, all of this could not function effectively as they are under control and supervision of Supreme Leader who tends to be conservative and fundamentalist.

---

[515] Web.archive.org, 10 Agustus 2017, based on controversial confession of Akbar Ganji, an Iranian dissent journalist

In fact, since many years ago, the indoctrination of Shia radical politics has been arranged by a school name Hagghani School, headed by Ayatollah Mesbah Yazdi and found in 1964 in Qom, aiming at first to counter left-thoughts rampantly used by the youths. When the cleric served as a head of the judiciary, he recruited the alumni of the school to hold positions in special court for the clerics, the Centre for Islamic Propagation, and several intelligence community branches. It is well known that its alumni have been also responsible actively to shut down newspapers, accuse progressive and reformist clerics, as well as shape the Violence Commission against reformist group. During Ahmadinejad's administration, its two alumni named Ghulam Husayn Muhsinizi and Mostafa Pour Mohammadi, well known for being radical and notorious, have once held positions as minister of Intelligence and ministry of Internal Affairs. The former official in 2009 had instructed his intelligence agents to carry out arresting, torturing and forcing confessions of hundreds of the detained political activists, journalists and reformist politicians. While the latter, since the early years of the revolution, has been involved in brutal crushing the regime oppositions, mass killing of political activists and carrying out terror to Iranian dissidents who lived in abroad. [516]

As alluded before, many fatwas issued by the Iranian Shia clerics, mainly in political and security affairs have been often associated with the efforts of Shia radicalization. Meaning that, in dealing with the two terrains which apparently would pose an existential threat to the survival of the Islamic regime, the clerics, most frontally the Supreme Leader often issue radical fatwas as spiritual vantage point which justify various violent crackdowns by the regime. The fatwas, particularly issued by him, would have political clouts and powers that must be implemented by all government officials as a general guideline, as he is deemed profoundly to represent Imam Mahdi. So it is hardly astonishing that the allegations of politicized religion by the clerics in order to guaranty and maintain their vested interests, have been often addressed. For instance, in 1979 Imam Khomeini issued a fatwa that likened Sunni Kurd minority group who opposed the regime, as unbelievers who deserved to be fought via Jihad due to their refusal to Velayat Faqih system.[517] In 1988, the mass killings of more or less 30.000 detained political activists around Iran, mostly the radical members of Mojaheden Khalq organization, was triggered by Imam Khomeini's political fatwa which equated them with Hypocrites who were inflaming war against God. [518] Additionally in February 1989, Imam Khomeini also issued a fatwa of death sentence to Salman Rushdie, a famous British novelist of controversial Satanic Verses, and anybody who involved with the publishing of the novel, as he was accused to have insulted Islam. Most startlingly, such a death fatwa was not automatically abrogated in spite of Imam' passing away, even the reward for the assassin of the novelist has been added

---

[516] Ray Takeyh, Guardians of the Revolution, Iran and The World in the Age of the Ayatollahs, Oxford University Press tahun 2009, page 226
[517] Ahmed Eskandari, Islamic Republic of Iran's atrocities against civilian disobedience in Kurdistan, ekurd.net, 19 August 1979
[518] Christina Lamb, 4 February 2001,
https://www.telegraph.co.uk/news/worldnews/middleeast/iran/1321090/Khomeini-fatwa-led-to-killing-of-30000-in-Iran.html

from $ 2.8 million to $ 3.3 million by Iranian government in 2012.[519] During Iran Iraq war that lasted over eight years, Imam had also exerted religious ideas and thoughts to burn Iranians spirits to make Jihad against Saddam Hussein. As Imam Khomeini who labelled the war as holy war, his successor, Ali Khamene'i has viewed that the recent Syrian war joined by Shia militants is a holy war. Furthermore, both of them unabashedly branded those were killed as martyrs.

Nevertheless, due to the sensitive issue of Syrian case, the clerics seemingly refrained from issuing direct fatwas for making Jihad in God's paths. In fact, the same sensitivity with the Green Movement in 2009 had prompted Ali Khamenei to be cautious to issue a religious fatwa in crushing and arresting vehemently yet brutally the Iranian protesters. Not having issued such a fatwa, rather labelling the event as fitnah (sedition), was perhaps due to his view that the political clashes between conservative rulers and reformist protesters were not essential, which he was fully aware that the protesters did not seek to topple the Islamic regime, yet only to question and denounce the fraud of the Presidential election.

It must be borne in mind that radicalization of Shia teaching is also framed in passing several laws that seem unreasonable and exaggerating. Such an implementation of the law often draws the worries of international human rights activists as Iran is already ranked the second most state following China in the term of death penalty implementation. For instance, in penal code ratified in 2012/2013 regarding the destruction on the earth, mainly in article number 286 mentioned that any person massively does criminal acts to individuals' physics and crimes who threaten internal and external securities as well as other acts including spreading lies, paralyzing state economy, burning and making sabotage, distributing poisonous and dangerous materials and microbes, managing and helping build non-ethic centres which cause huge paralysis to public stability and inconvenience or huge detriment to individuals' physics or public and private properties, or cause moral degradation significantly, all of this would be deemed destroyers on the earth with death sentence as their punishment. [520]

As elucidated previously, the authority to issue religious fatwas in Iran is not restricted only to Vali Faqih. Other Shia competent clerics, some trying not to get involved in political affairs, have an authority to issue fatwas concerning the burgeoning issues of the time. For instance, in Keyhan newspaper controlled strictly by Iranian radical political elites in 20 September 1981, had published a political fatwa of Mosavi Tabrizi, former head of Revolutionary Court and Shia clergyman, noting that one of the laws of Islamic Republic is whoever stands against the just Imam government, it would become obligatory that he be assassinated or if he gets hurt, he must be wounded more vehemently until he faces his

---

[519] Iranians revive, boost fatwa for Salman Rushdie, 16 September 2012,
https://www.cbsnews.com/news/iranians-revive-boost-fatwa-for-salman-rushdie/
[520] www.yjc.ir, 5 October 2015

death.[521] Another example showing that a fatwa from other clerics could also prevail is when Syrian conflict started to erupt in 2011 in the wake of Arab Spring, some of competent Shia clerics in Qom such as Ayatollah Sayed Kazem Haeri and Ayatollah Mohammad Sadegh Rouhani had issued a jihad fatwa for all volunteers who join the war under a pretext for defending Sayyedah Zainab's (Prophet's granddaughter) holy Shrine in Damascus, Syria from terrorist /*Takfiri* militant groups. [522]

Wahhabism and Root of Its Extremism

As mentioned earlier, Wahhabism was initiated and developed well by its founder, Mohammad ibn Abdul Wahab, two centuries before the modern kingdom was established in 1932 by King Abdul Aziz ibn Saud. In early periods of its spread, this radical thought was not welcomed warmly by the vast majority of Arab society as it has opposed to any growing traditions that have been practiced for years inside the region. Furthermore Wahhabism significantly advocates a return to the age of Salafiyya (the first three generations of Islam) and pursuing purification of the religion by condemning any type of innovation (bid'ah) Despite its strict interpretation of Islam that various analysts believe to be inspiring the actions of terrorist groups and other extremist groups. Such a unique thought eventually succeeded to influence deeply Arab tribal societies, particularly those who lived in the newly conquered territories, thanks to political support tremendously given by Al Saud, the founder of first Saudi Kingdom, to Wahhabism in 18th century. Al Saud ambitiously attempted to expand his political power to other regions by exerting Wahhabism along with its significant accentuation on the obligatory duty to obey a political ruler, as effective tool to unify the annexed territory under the flagship of El –Saud family. Mohammad bin Abdul Wahab, the founder of Wahhabism, deeply sought to support Ibnu Saud's efforts in expanding his political power into the conquered territories due to the shared view and vision concerning Jihad and typically conservative reading of Islamic law. As time went on, Ibnu Abdul Wahab himself further tremendously called his adherents to express their blind loyalty and obedience to Saudi rulers. [523]

Not only did it adopt Hanbali fiqh school for its jurisprudence (the forth Sunni school with smallest followers and very literal interpretation), Wahhabism has been arguably influenced well by the teachings of Ibnu Taymiyah (1263-1328) although to some extent he posed the opposite opinion to that of Mohammad ibn Abdul Wahab in particular issues such as the tradition of reciting prayers together for dead persons etc. With the passage of time, Saudi elite rulers as I will much elaborate later reportedly have supported spreading this

---

[521] For further information, please see Hassan Daei's statement, Iranian human rights activist, broadcasted in Youtube channel regularly. He owns a critical youtube channel named Iranian American Forum.
[522] Ali Mammouri, 29 July 2013, https://www.al-monitor.com/pulse/originals/2013/07/syria--jihad-fatwas-shiite-clergy-iran-iraq.html
[523] Sherifa Zuhur, Saudi Arabia, Greenwood Publishing Group, 2011, page 82

ideology throughout the world by financing Islamic activities and building facilities which bring its ideology. For the first time since its establishment, Wahhabism succeeded to bypass Arab peninsula with its Arab ethnicity, crossing continents and oceans, often along with a fundamental aim to curb Iranian Shia influence in the globe.

In truth, there are a wide range of books and articles could be referred to in writing this sub-chapter. Yet, here I have finally decided to choose two English books, first book is "Wahhabism : A Critical Essay," written by Hamid Algar, an British American professor in Persian studies. The second is "Wahhabi Mission and Saudi Arabia" written by David Commins, an expert on Arab Saudi and also a professor in History field.

In his book published around early 2000s, Hamid Algar gives an empashis that Wahhabi teaching, first introduced and popularized by Mohammad bin Abdul Wahab, its founder, in 18th century, has defined *Tawhid* (oneness of God) into three parts, al Tawhid - Rububiya (acknowledgement that God is the creator of mankind), *Tawhid al-Asma wa Sifat* (Affirmation on the God's names mentioned in al-Qor'an), *Tawhid al-Ibada* (submission and worship only to God). From this broader definition, acknowledgement to Tawhid is not sufficient to be made only by uttering it as what once took place in the Prophetic age when idol worshippers of Arab already admitted that God is the Creator. Still they were regarded as pagans who accordingly were threatened with entering to the hell. In result, Wahhabi teaching has paid more attention to the third type of Tawhid which principally prevails over other Islamic obligations of five pillars. Therefore, based on this third definition, a Muslim would be deemed imperfect in carrying out those obligations if such a Tawhed is infringed too. The purity of the only God worshipping has been one of the main concern of the Wahhabi ideology that sprouted initially in Najd territory of Saudi Arabia. Little wonder Wahhabi forbids saying prayers with using the words such as *bi-hurmati, isti'ana*, and *istighasa* to indicate the existence of a mediator and linking bridge between him and God. Wahhabi denounces to take any kinds of mediation that prompt the refusal and rejection of a Muslim's good deeds. In sum, Wahhabi also bans and even views it as Shirk (greatest sin of practicing idolatry and polytheism) to any innovative ritual commonly practiced by Muslim society of the world such as *Tawassol, Shafa'at, Tabarrok* during grave visits, which according to Wahhabi all this portrays the existence of a mediator (third party) for all kinds of worshipping.

According to Wahhabi followers, Muslim society for centuries have been living in Jahilliya age (ignorance age/ refers to a period before Islam was born) because Muslims have often mixed the Islamic practices with the matters that did not exist in the Prophetic and *Salafussaleh*[524] ages, that would disgrace Islamic purity and authenticity instead, leading Wahhabi adherents to destroy numerous historical religious sites in Hejaz including the

---

[524] that is the generations of the Islamic Prophet Muhammad and his companions (the Sahabah), their successors (the Tabi'un), and the successors of the successors (the Taba Tabi'in)

prophet's home in Mecca.[525] Wahhabism also believes that their way of life shall be an inspiration and model and revived profoundly for the next Muslim generations.

As a result of the implementation of such a principle, it encourages Wahhabi followers to identify that non-Wahhabi Muslims could be regarded as Mushriks (polytheists) who must be fought with, in which Wahhabi believes that blood of Mushriks is halal (permissible to shed), their property could be annihilated, their women and children could be taken as slaves. Based on this faith, then the Jihad is justified. The events occurred in Karbala, Iraq and Thaif, Arab Saudi in 1803, had witnessed Wahhabi brutality when conquering the areas. In short words, that the implementation of Jihad practice for Wahhabi followers, would be applied not only against unbelievers, but also against Muslims who are deemed to have been deviated from Islamic purity and authenticity based on Wahhabi interpretation. Such a strict implementation will certainly justify and condone Jihad practice against Shia followers and other Islamic sects.

Hamid Alghari in his book unfolds that apart from the concept of the aforementioned Tawhid, the concept of heresy (bid'ah) has been accentuated persistently by the sect. The concept has taken commonly one hadith saying that Muslims are required firmly not to create new matters as they are considered to be heretic and thus, every heretic practice would be misleading. According to Wahhabi, the concept gives emphasis on new innovations that were not well-known in Prophetic period and the third century after. In fact, while four Sunni sects, like Izz al-Din bin Abdussalam, has broken heresy into five laws namely *wajib* (obligatory), *Sunah* (desirable), *Halal* (permissible), *Makruh* (discouraged), *Haram* (forbidden), Wahhabi generalizes every innovative practice and tradition is forbidden. In this vein, Wahhabi will never acknowledge such a division of laws for heresy introduced profoundly by those four prominent Sunni schools, generating a great challenge for Wahhabism by Muslim world society. In addition to the religious innovations cited above, Wahhabi also includes Zikir recital, usually developed Sufi communities, as bid'ah (heresy).

Ironically, for Wahhabi, bid'ah is not restricted to Zikir recital per se, other Islamic celebrations regularly held by Muslims such as eyd Fitr and Eyd Adha, Prophet's birthday etc could be deemed Bid'ah. In addition, Wahhabi would encourage the destruction of Muslim clerics' graves and forbid reading Qonot in Sobh prayer, Al-Qor'an and Zikr reading together on the dead for 40 days and praying in the graves.[526] Not only that, Wahhabi has proven that it would oppose the use of modern technology. For instance, when modern car, radio and television were introduced for the first time in Saudi Arabia several decades ago, Wahhabi clerics expressed their objections and criticisms as they believed such things were not invented and used by the Prophet. However, as time went on, since the creation of

---

[525] Mark A. Caudill, Twilight in the Kingdom : Understanding the Saudis, Praeger Security International, 2006, page 100
[526] www.metroislam.com, 14 March 2016

modern Saudi in 1932, Wahhabi movement was compelled to transform itself from a pure Jihad movement into a movement submitting its loyalty and allegiance to the Kingdom.[527]

In his book titled the Wahhabi Mission and Saudi Arabia, David Commins elaborates that Mohammad bin Abdul Wahab, founder of Wahhabism, in his book at-Tawhed, once had revealed that he lived in the period when Islam was deemed strange. His conclusion has been taken from three Hadith, stating that believers will follow the paths of Jews and Christians; that Prophet would express his fear more to misguided leaders who would rekindle paganism, and the advent of false prophets, rather than the unbeliever enemies who defeat the believers. In sum there is also a prophecy stating that there will a group from the believers who have steady stance on their faith and who do not fall into the false prophets and the misguided leaders. Here, the founder of Wahhabism apparently concluded paganism would be revived among the unbelievers, which in turn there will be only one group who keeps remaining in God's real path.

In dealing with Jihad polemic, Ibnu Wahab interpreted two hadiths taken mainly as a justification for applying Jihad against each who rejects Islam. First Hadits states that when the Prophet gave a legal advice to the expedition leader to Yemen to call on Yemeni people (Jews and Christians) to make five time prayers and pay Islamic alms (zakat), He affirmed if they agree, so they would gain security. The second hadith is when the Prophet told Ali bin Abi Thalib (his cousin) in a war against the Jews in Khaybar, He asked him to invite them into Islam. Nevertheless, many ulemas have already given respond the two hadits mentioned, were indeed addressed to non-Muslims, not to Muslims.

Furthermore, in his book Tawhid, the Wahhabism founder once gave an analogy to justify Jihad, as follows, the unbelievers in the Prophetic age still believed that God is the Creator and Director for all. They had paid Islamic alms, went for Hajj and refrained from doing all the forbidden. Yet it was not sufficient to call them true Muslims. They were still subject to Jihad as they failed to submit all of their deeds solely to Allah. For instance, they slaughtered animals and help each other and swore, yet not in the name of Allah, prompting the Prophet to allow fighting with them and seizing their properties as well as taking women as slaves. The unbelievers may have acknowledged the oneness of God as the Creator of mankind, yet when they took angels, Prophet Jesus and other saints in order to get them more closely to God, but still they were regarded as unbelievers despite the fact that they persistently did five time prayers each day and continuously gave help for needy people along their life. Nevertheless, Ibnu Abdul Wahab did not support to apply Jihad before 'the unbelievers' accept the invitation to Islam, understand it and then reject it, because for him, the unbeliever society where he lived was being afflicted by *Jahilliya* age (ignorance age/before the birth of Prophet Mohammad), that has to be called first to the authentic and true Islam.

---

[527] Michael Dillon, Wahhabism is it a factor in the spreade of global terrorisme? Dudley Knox Library , Calhoun : the NPS Institutional Archieve, page 24

According to Wahhabism, there are three conditions in applying Jihad, first, when Muslim troops inevitably face their enemies. Secondly, when enemy troops have reached Muslim territory, and thirdly, when the political leader (Imam) assumes that Jihad shall be declared. An 'unreal Muslim' who was detained by Ibnu Saud's troop would be automatically regarded as pagan who had to be called to convert to true Islam. So after he converted to Islam, he was permitted to leave, or he could pay Jizya (tax imposed to non-Muslims). If he denied such offers, then he deserved a death penalty. However, on Wahhabi interpretation, it must be borne in mind that the Jihad practice can be implemented when Imam (political leader) declares it, meaning that as long as Jihad is not yet declared by the leader, Jihad could not be implemented. In this vein, Wahhabi maintains to exhibit its loyalty to Saudi regime by still considering final decision taken obviously by the kings. Such an interesting fact could be the main reason why the Kingdom's relations with Wahhabi clerics have survived well until current days, despite their numerous objections to the regimes' policies. In practice, Wahhabi always believes that the loyalty and allegiance to its rulers would occupy the third place after to God and His Prophet, as suggested explicitly by the Qoranic verse.

Suleyman bin Abdullah, one of the most prominent Wahhabi clerics in 19th century had issued a fatwa that all Muslims must demonstrate their hostile stances toward the unbelievers (including non-Wahhabi Muslims). The true Muslims shall avoid to have any contact with them. The concept of *Al wala wal bara* (the concept of loving (to believers) for the sake of Allah and hating (unbelievers) for the sake of Allah) must be kept firmly. In addition, the Ideologue cleric also allowed his followers to apply Taqiya by hiding their faiths, only in weak positions. Furthermore he even allowed them to travel to unbelievers' territories with one condition that they can get access to practice their beliefs and faiths. [528]

Iran and Terrorism

When ISIS (the Islamic State of Iraq and Syria) group began launching its terror attacks in both states, Iraq and Syria since 2014, Iran had responded it immediately. This theocratic state reportedly has been launching numerous lethal attacks to the group in Iraq. As many political observers do believe that the constant dispatch of Iranian militia groups to Syria has aimed at assisting Bashar Asad from oppositions' threats despite Iranian regime's insistence that the aim is only to protect Sayyedah Zaynab mosque in Damascus from Jihadis Takfiri movements attacks. In the other hand, particularly in recent years, Iranian national security has been potential target for terror attacks, not only carried out by ISIS by also by several sectarian militant groups.

---

[528] Nabil Mouline, The Clerics of Islam Religious Authority And Political Power in Saudi Arabia, Yale University Press page 73

For instance in the first June 2017 within Iranian territory, an attack occurred inside the Iranian parliament building and Shia holy place, close to Imam Khomeini's shrine in Tehran, allegedly done by ISIS group. In 2016 was also reported that Iranian security officers often called *Sarbazan Gomnam Imam Zaman* (Imam Mahdi troops) had engaged in an armed clash with ISIS sympathizers in Kermansha province, west Iran, located near to the border with Iraqi territory.[529] As a matter of fact, since the establishment of the Islamic states, Iran has been target for many terror attacks, including the attacks carried out by the Iranian political dissidents such as Mojahedin el Khalq, mainly in the first decade of the revolution. Based on statistics, the dissident group once designated a terrorist group by some western countries, had left at least 16.000 killed in addition to enormous material destruction.[530] As the government once claimed, since the outbreak of the revolution in 1979 until now, there are around 17.000 Iranian victims caused solely by terror acts.[531]

Geographically speaking, Iran has direct border with the countries which are so vulnerable and fragile with terrorism acts, as for many years those countries have been fertile grounds for any potential sectarian clashes, aggravated by various militant and rigid religious interpretations by their peoples. In its eastern part, the Mullah state has direct border with Afghanistan and Pakistan. While in its western part, with Iraq and Turkey. With it having geographically strategic situation, in addition to giving many advantages politically and economically, Iran has been prone to many terrorism attacks as well as become a transit location for international drug cartel and human trafficking, mainly from Afghanistan.

Therefore little wonder that terrorism issue constitutes an integral part of Iranian domestic and foreign policies. Iranian stakeholders often affirm that the government would combat firmly the terrorism and its roots, either local terrorism, commonly triggered by internal sectarian rifts, or trans-national and border terrorism. In exhibiting its strong commitment to eradicate terrorism, Iran regularly convenes a wide range of seminars and conferences at national and international levels, and thus disseminating much information to the society regarding the dangers and threats of terrorism with it accentuating the slogans such as anti-radicalism and extremism in religion.[532] As part of its domestic policy in the field of counterterrorism, Iran has adopted an Islamic Penal Code in 1991 relating the prevention and eradication of violence and terrorism-related actions at home. Interestingly, the law has also likened terrorism acts with *Moharabe* (fighting with God and His Prophet) attempts that may lead to death sentencing for its perpetrators. In this vein, the law has

---

[529] Film Jadid az halakat Daeshha dar Kermansha, 16 August 2016, http://namnak.com/-هلاکت-داعشی-ها-در-کرمانشاه.p35128

[530] Alexander R. Dawoody, Eradicating Terrorism from the Middle East, Public Administration, Governance and Globalization, Springer, 2016, page 201

[531] General Report of the 2nd Int'l Congress on 17,000 Iranian Terror Victims, 25 October 2015, http://www.habilian.ir/en/201510252276/news/general-report-of-the-2nd-intl-congress-on-17000-iranian-terror-victims.html

[532] One example of such manifestations is a holding of international conference on Global Fight Against Terrorism in 25-26 June 2011 held in Tehran

defined terrorism as everyone taking up arms to create fear and panic and depriving liberty and security of the people.[533] In sum as time went on, Iran later prepared a bill on terrorism in 2003 that gave wider scope for terrorism definition, not limited only for taking up arms. Most startlingly, amid international community's allegation of financial support for terrorist groups carried out by Iran, Iran has had a bill on the eradication of financial support for terrorist groups, which was ratified one year later. The law signifies Iran's sincere intention to international community in its efforts to prevent financial flows to terrorist groups based on UN Convention in 1999 and UN Security Council no. 1373. Iran also regularly has sent annual reports on its commitment to combating terrorism under the framework of Terrorism Eradication Committee of the UN Security Council, covering information database making on terrorism, and its efforts to deal with the issue of illegal weaponry smuggling to Iran, and to monitor and control the borders of the state, etc.[534]

Not only that, bilaterally Iran has often addressed the issue of cooperation in combating terrorism, intelligent information exchange, joint military operation with other interested states in fighting national security threats imposed by terrorism. In international forum, mainly in UN, Hassan Rouhani, Iranian President has proposed an initiative called World Against Violent Extremism (WAVE) in 2013, fostering greater dialogue between religions and sects to counter Wahhabism.[535]

However, if compared with the internal security of other neighbouring countries, Iranian domestic security is more stable and conducive. It can be said that the efforts to destabilize Iranian security including mainly through bomb explosion and armed attacks, rarely happen within the territory. Due to its strong commitment and success to empowering its own official apparatus as well as robust awareness of the society on terrorism dangers, the frequency of such attacks carried out by terrorist group is considered low, which such an interesting phenomena could be a proper model for other fragile states such as Iraq and Afghanistan in implementing their anti-terrorism agenda. This infrequency of terrorism attack in Iran is even lower than that of Saudi Arabia and Indonesia, leading to an assumption that surrounding geographically by the fragile countries does not necessarily stimulate and give rise to terror acts in its domestic territory. Nevertheless after many years of calmness, the two recent terror attacks in June 2017 that occurred almost in parallel time with a dozen civilians killed and wounded, has awaken profoundly Iranian's consciousness that Takiri Salafi ISIS group has been targeting Iranians who are Shia adherents. For this reason it is deeply believed that Iranian's constant military involvement in Iraq and Syria by deploying Qods force and equipping militarily Iraqi Shia militant in order to combat the ISIS group has eventually provoked the group to make retaliatory actions, added with a fact that

---

[533] Alexander R. Dawoody, Eradicating Terrorism from the Middle East, Public Administration, Governance and Globalization, Springer, 2016, page 212
[534] Ibid, page 217
[535] Mohammad Javad Zarif, Let US Rid the World of Wahhabism, www.nytimes.com, 13 September 2016

the militant group would invariably target Shia followers who are deemed heretics and polytheists.

As mentioned earlier, the terrorism threats in Iran appear not only from outside the state, but also inside given numerous distinctive ethnics and cultures with diverse interpretation on faiths and beliefs. The sentiment of having been treated discriminatively in political, economic and social dimensions has often generated collective and communal disappointments that could unify a perception for the people to carry out violent resistance against the central government. Disapproval and opposition to the political system of Velayat Faqih, triggered by various motivations, could also inflict tremendously the organizations and movements to express their rejection to the system, with Iran regrettably sometimes accusing the intervention of the other feuding states in creating more chaos and instability. Yet in fact in Iran, radicalism and extremism in religious interpretations have proven not to be a real factor propelling local terrorism.

However despite successfully maintaining internal security from terror attacks, based on the report of year 2017, the State Department of US placed Iran as the main sponsor of terrorism in the region,[536] even since 1984 the US government has put the country as terrorism sponsor in the global level.[537] Some Arab states are also convinced that Iran has been engaged significantly in cultivating radicalism and extremism by extending all means of its supports to the Arab militant, particularly Shia militant organizations under the steady concept of Revolution export and the main goal of Iranian revolutionary foreign policy as suggested firmly by Imam Khomeini in the early years of Islamic Revolution.

For the Arab leaders, Iran's more embroilment in the region has proven to have sparked profoundly terrorism acts in the region causing much fear and worry to Arab societies. Such a sceptical perception has been their main concern in multiple Arab's meetings and discussions simply reflected among other things by strongly urging Qatar in 2017 to keep its distance from Iran, and rendering endless efforts by Saudi regime to restrict Iranian influence expansion in the region. According to some Arab leaders, since the Islamic state establishment, Iran has cultivated seeds for regional terrorism to grow as Imam Khomeini kept having an opinion that Monarch and secular Arab systems were un-Islamic.

On the contrary, a shocking report published by a Russian newspaper in the mid-2017 expressed its praise to Iranian policy by placing it as the most active state in combating al-Qaeda and ISIS groups in both Syria and Iraq, if compared with other states.[538] Such a report indicates during the time Iran has been regarded by international community as both terrorism sponsor and annihilator of terrorist groups. According to Habilian Association, an Iranian Research Centre comprising the families of terrorism victims, the West's suspicions over Iran as terrorism sponsor have been concentrated on the issues relating to Revolution

---

[536] Nicole Gaoutte, Iran remains top terror sponsor as global attack decline, 19 Juli 2017, www.cnn.com
[537] www.habilian.ir
[538] www.ion.ir

export; the hostage crisis of US embassy in 1980s; Iran's considerable support on regionally radical movements and its participation in some terror acts; and its willingness to own nuclear energy for peaceful purposes, not for making nuclear weapon as alleged mainly by the West. Due to such reasons, the West often accuses Iran as the main sponsor for terrorism and would cast doubts on Iranian commitment to creating peace and stability in the region, which through its controlled international media, the West succeeded incredibly to create dangerous public opinion portraying that Iranians for many years have been always associated with brutality and violence.[539]

Arguably having no diplomatic relation with US and further expressing hostility and antagonism since the birth of the Islamic state has exacerbated such suspicions and allegations that Iran has to pay significant price for its risks including the imposition of military and economic sanctions as well as international isolation. In this vein, Iran has to be ready to accept various punishments imposed by the super power which tirelessly echoes its efforts against global terrorism. Not only that, the long drawn and intensive negotiations conducted between Iran and western countries on nuclear issue has been mainly prompted by existing scepticism of the countries over the state's good intention regarding transparency and honesty. According to the West, Iran has failed to convince international community that it has strong commitment to help eliminate regional terrorism. Instead, Iran has proven to have carried out some suspicious measures and illogic actions, such as by imposing security threats to its neighbouring states and intensively developing long range ballistic missiles, aggravating such allegations and killing the spirits of the 2015 JCPOA (Joint Comprehensive Plan of Action) deal as Donald Trump often noticed.

However if we take a look more carefully to the Iranian basic constitution, we will find out the existence of other dimensions of Velayat Faqih governance which drives opinions that Iran is obliged to intervene with other states' internal affairs that implicitly leads to be associated with radicalism and extremism, supported largely by the regime, thus making it as one of the foreign policy mechanisms.

The introduction of the constitution stipulates clearly that the constitution shall provide a necessary basis to assure the sustainability of revolution both internally and externally, meaning that Iranian regime has an additional duty to provide all necessary means in order that such revolutionary principles be materialized outside Iranian borders. The words 'necessary basis' has a broader meaning of implementation as it is likely to cover all financial and military assistances as well as trainings and intelligence sharing, depending greatly on which strategy Iran would take as long as it would lead into the realization of Islamic sacred goals.

In addition, the introduction of the constitution also asserted that the Army of the Islamic Republic and the Islamic Pasdaran Revolutionary Guards will undertake the

---

[539] www.habilian.ir

responsibility of not only guarding and protecting the borders, but also internationalizing its ideological mission, i.e, striving (jihad) on the path of God and struggle on the path of expanding the sovereignty of the law of God in the world, in accordance with the Al-Qor'an verse.[540] This article explicitly elaborates the complementary duty of Iranian military (Revolutionary Guards/ Sepah Pasdaran) to bear responsibility outside the borders by intervening and extending assistance to all sorts of resistance and rebellion of militant groups that help realize Iranian revolutionary ideas. Therefore, special budget shall be allocated annually by the regime, amid much harsh criticism by the public due to internally deteriorating economic situation, to support the realization of such Iranian military goals abroad.

Iran has invariably believed that giving as much assistance to oppressed nations who struggle against their repressive rulers constitutes the priority of its foreign policy. Interestingly, Iran will not consider it as an interventionist action to any other states' internal matters. Instead, in international occasions Iran always rejects any intervention of a state to one state's internal affairs, even calls it as illegal manner. While Iran's actions often deemed an intervention to internal affairs by a wide range of the states, Iran in several occasions has urged other countries, in particular the West, not to interfere with Iranian issues including in the cases of human rights and nuclear.

Interestingly according to Mehdi Khaleji, by relying on one verse in the Qoran saying that *"make ready for them whatever force and strings of horses you can, to terrify the enemy of God and your enemy, and others besides them that you know not.."* Iran further found a religious justification to create and develop modern weapons as well as experiment them with abundant financial support viewed as intimidating and frightening "the enemies of God," in which based on the deep interpretation by contemporary *Mofasser* (an Islamic author of a tafsir/interpretation and explanation of Qoran), "strings of horses" could mean a symbol to include all modern military tools and weapons. In this vein, some Shia authors, then obviously suggested by Hossein Ali Montazeri, a top Shia cleric who was supposed to replace Imam Khomeini's position as Supreme Leader, even interpreted it as any means that creates frightening and fear of the enemies would be regarded good, with no necessity to use them in military battle. [541] Yet moreover defensive Jihad under the Supreme Leader administration could be the offensive one if, based on Imam Khomeini's statement, it is ordered by a qualified jurist (Faqih) and it is carried out for the interest of the Islamic Republic of Iran. [542]

---

[540] For further information, please see Iranian basic constitution www.wipo.int
[541] Mehdi Khalaji, Apocyptic Politics, on the Rationality of Iranian Policy, the Washington Institute for Near East Policy, January 2008, page 29
[542] Ibid page 30

Iran and Terrorism, a Victim or Sponsor?

Apart from becoming a potential target for any terror attack as cited earlier, until now Iran has been often branded as a state supporting terrorism by several countries with it extremely exerting its governmental organs to be involved militarily in international political dynamics. Such a branding has been further cemented by the fact that Iran has implemented lack of its cooperation with global community relating to money laundering and cash flow to terrorist groups issues under the framework of Financial Action Task Force (FATF), international organization established in 1989 on the initiative of G7 members). Iran is regarded reluctant to express strong commitment to dealing with mentioned sensitive issues.[543]

However, the definition of terrorism itself has came into debate and controversy whether targeting military forces could be put under scope of terrorism or not since each may agree to cover the targeting of civilians as terrorism.[544]

Here I will list Iranian regime's embroilment in numerous radical measures and terrorism since the creation of the Islamic state until current years. Some of the information was provided by US government, attached by the US Secretary of the State Mike Pompeo through his Tweeter account in July 2018, and Saudi Arabia embassy as well. However, some of which may refer into allegations and accusations.[545]

No	Years	Actions
1	1979	American embassy occupation in Tehran for 444 days by Iranian militant students affiliated to Muslim Student Followers of the Imam's Line
2	1982	Between years 1982-1992, Lebanese Hezbollah supported by Iran, systematically kidnapped 96 foreign citizens, including 25 American citizens during the hostage crisis in Lebanon. William Buckley, CIA agent, was reportedly killed.
3	1983	18 April, Hezbollah attacked US embassy in Beirut by hitting it with a truck, killing 63 including 17 US citizens.
4	1983	23 October, Hezbollah attacked American barracks in Beirut killing 242 US and 58 French peacekeepers and 6 civilians

---

[543] www.irna.ir, 30 June 2018
[544] Natasha Underhill, Countering Global Terrorism and Insurgency, Palgrave Macmillan, 2014 page 5
[545] www.iranprobe.com

5	1983	12 December, Hezbollah and Shia Da'wa Group bombed US embassy in Kuwait, killing 6 people
6	1984	Hezbollah exploded a van which brought explosive materials targeting the US embassy annex in east Beirut, Lebanon, killing 24 people
	1984	Hezbollah hijacked Air France Airline no 747 which flied from Frankfurt to Paris
7	1985	Hezbollah hijacked Trans World Airline no 847 which flied from Cairo, Egypt to San Diego, US
	1986	Series bombings in Paris were allegedly carried out by Hezbollah, killing 12
8	1986	Thwarting a bombing planned by Iranian Guard Revolutionary in Saudi Arabia during the pilgrimage season, as revealed by Akbar Ganji, former member of the organization[546]
9	1987	The attacking of Saudi embassy in Tehran by members of Revolutionary Guards, rupturing the diplomatic relation
	1987	The hijacking of Air Afrique no 56 in Rome, Italia by suspect Hezbollah, killed one
10	1987 and 1988	Hezbollah el – Hejaz, Saudi Shia organization, endorsed by Revolutionary Guards bombed gas facilities in Ras al Juaymah, Saudi Arabi, also in 1988 succeeded to explode the petrochemical factories in Jubail and the oil refinery in Ras Tanura, Saudi Arabia[547]
11	1988	An UN diplomat was kidnapped and killed in South Lebanon
12	1989	Secretary General of the Kurdish Democratic Party of Iran (KDPI) named Dr. Abdul Rahman Ghasemlou, with his two friends who demanded autonomy or separation of Iranian Kurdistan province from Iran, were assassinated in Vienna Austria
13	1991	Shapour Bakhtiar, a politician and last Prime Minister of Pahlavi dynasty was killed through Iranian regime operation
14	1992	17 March, Hezbollah launched suicidal bombing in Israeli embassy in

---

[546] www.thebaghdadpost.com
[547] www.saudiembassy.net

		Buenos Aires, Argentine, killing 29 people
15	1992	17 September, Iranian regime along with Ali Fallahian, then Iranian minister of Intelligence, assassinated four Kurdish political activists in Cafe Mykonos in Berlin, German
16	1994	Iranian regime through Lebanese Hezbollah bombed AMIA Jewish Community Centre in Buenos Aires, Argentine killing 85 people
17	1994	Car bomb explosion outside Israeli embassy in London, 15 were wounded. The suspect was Hezbollah
18	1994	Venezuelan Foreign Ministry announced that four Iranian diplomats were involved in clandestine operation in Simon Bolivar international airport with a purpose of compelling Iranian refugees to come back to Iran[548]
19	1996	14 Saudi- branch Hezbollah supported by Iran, bombed Khabar towers, killing 19 American citizens
20	2000	Lebanese Hezbollah kidnapped 3 Israelis of IDF (Israeli Defence Forces)
21	2003	Bahraini Kingdom arrested cell terrorist members, known as receiving support from Revolutionary Guards and Lebanese Hezbollah in Lebanon, Kuwait and Uni Emirates Arab
22	2003	Iranian regime has supported Political parties and militia groups, loyal to Iranian regime, who killed 4.400 American and ten thousands of civilians, mainly Arab Sunnis[549]
23	2005	Hezbollah Lebanon assassinated Rafeq Hariri former Lebanese Prime President along with 21 others in the bomb explosion in Beirut
24	2006	Lebanese Hezbollah entered Israeli territory and assassinated 7 Israeli Defence Forces members
25	2007	Iraqi militant group Asaib Ahle Haq, driven by Revolutionary Guards launched attack that killed five troops in Karbala, Iraq

---

[548] Opcit
[549] Www.saudiembasy.net

26	2007	The group cited above organized to kidnap five British citizens in Iraq
27	2009	Several Iraqi paramilitary groups such as Kataib Hezbollah, known to have affiliation to Revolutionary Guards have often conducted military attack in Iraq, targeting American interests
28	2011	October, a plan of bombing a restaurant in Washington DC carried out by two dual citizenship Iranians and a Commander of Revolutionary Guard, Gholam Shukri, targeting Adel al-Jubeir, Saudi ambassador for US, was thwarted
29	2011	An assassination of a Saudi diplomat named Hassan el-Qathani in Karachi, Pakistan
30	2011	November, the attack of British embassy in Tehran was carried out by Basiji organization, leading to the rupture of diplomatic relation
31	2012	In February, a Revolutionary Guard member attempted to kill a wife of Israeli diplomat in New Delhi, India
32	2012	March, Azerbaijan security force arrested terrorists supported by Revolutionary Guards, targeting American and Israel officials
33	2012	July, Lebanese Hezbollah bombed a bus in Bulgaria, killing five Israeli tourists and a driver
34	2013	Two Iranian diplomats were expelled from Bosnia Herzegovina due to their link to espionage and terrorism
35	2015	August, Kuwait government thwarted a plan of terrorism by Lebanese Hezbollah, attempting to disturb the region
36	2015	December, Kataib Hezbollah organization supported by Revolutionary Guards, kidnapped 29 Qatari citizens who reportedly were hunting desert falcons
37	2016	Early January, an attack of Saudi embassy conducted by Basiji organization, rupturing the diplomatic relation of both countries until today
38	2017	November, the assassination of Ahmad Nissi, political activist of ASMLA/ the Arab Struggle Movement for the Liberation of Ahwaz in Dutch. Iranian

		regime was allegedly behind such an action
39	2017	January, the seizing of 17 containers of Russian made weaponry and aircraft spare parts in Kiev airport, Ukraine[550]
40	2018	February, the smuggling of type KH 31 missile spare parts was carried out by Revolutionary Guard in Ukraine [551]
41	2018	March, Albania arrested two Iranian operatives on charges of terrorism[552]
42	2018	March, Bahraini Government announced the arrest of 16 members of cell terrorist group, affiliated to Revolutionary Guards[553]
43	2018	In July, an Iranian diplomat Assadullah Asadi was arrested in German, suspected of attempting to bomb the meeting of Mojaheden el-Khalq dissident organization in Paris. Meanwhile, Belgium security force also arrested two Iranians suspected of doing the same. Almost in the meantime, Netherland expelled two Iranian embassy staff in Amsterdam. No further information was provided[554]
44	2018	In October, a Norwegian citizen of Iranian background, also an Iranian government intelligence service, was arrested in Sweden for being suspected to try to carry out a plot of assassination of an Iranian Arab opposition in Denmark[555]

Apart from abovementioned facts, Iran has been a potential target of terrorism actions that occurred right after the establishment of the state[556]

no	Years	
1	1981	The bombing of Hafte Tir square in Tehran during the meeting of the

---

[550] English.alarabiya.net, 22 January 2017
[551] www.amadnews.org, 10 February 2018
[552] Laurence Norman and Matthew Dalton, 3 August 2018, https://www.wsj.com/articles/u-s-pushes-europe-to-abandon-iran-over-terror-plotsbut-meets-resistance-1533301621
[553] Ir.voanews.com, 3 March 2018
[554] www.alkhaleej.ae, 7 July 2017
[555] Emil Gjerding Nielson, Jacob Gronholt-Pederson, 30 October 2018, https://uk.reuters.com/article/uk-denmark-security/iranian-spy-service-suspected-of-assassination-plot-in-denmark-security-chief-idUKKCN1N42FL
[556] Summarized from a number of sources

		party leaders killed 73 including Ayatollah Mohammad Shahed Beheshti (most Iranian political figure after Imam Khomeini)
2	1994	The bombing of Imam Reza mosque (the eighth Shia Imam) in Mashhad city killed 25 people, carried out allegedly by People Mojaheden of Iran (MEK)
3	2005-2006	The bombing series in Ahvaz city was carried out by Ahvaz's separatist movements, killing 28
4	2006	4 day prior to Nouroz (Iranian New Year), Jondollah terrorists closed a road near to Tasooki and killed 21 people
5	2007	The bombing series during three days in Zahedan city, Sistan Balochistan province, was allegedly carried out by militant Jondollah, killing 18 people
6	2008	The bombing of Sayed el-Shuhada in Shiraz city killed 14 people. The perpetrator was known as Iranian loyal militant Anjoman Padeshahi Iran which demanded the toppling of the regime
7	2009	The bombing of Zahedan city in Sistan Baluchistan province was carried out by Jondolah organization that killed 20 people
8	2009	Suicidal bombing attack in Pishin town, Sistani Balochistan province carried out by Jondollah organization killed 43 people including several revolutionary Guards commanders
9	2010	Two suicidal bombings that targeted Shias in Jami mosque in Zahedan city, Sistani Balochistan province was conducted by Jondollah organization, killing more than 27 people
10	2010	A bomb was blasted in military parade in Mahabad city that killed 12 people. The suspect was Ba'atah and PJAK groups
11	2010	Suicidal bombing in Chahabahar town, Sistani Balochistan was carried out by Jondollah, targeting Shia and killing 33
12	2017	Suicidal bombing and shooting in the Iranian Parliament building and holy Shrine of Imam Khomeini in Tehran killed 23 people including five ISIS perpetrators

13	Recent years	The attacks of the Revolutionary Guards and Basiji bases and government buildings have been conducted by Iranians under the endorsement of Sayed Mohammad Hosseini, Re-start leader who is currently residing in US
14	2018	Shooting in a military parade in Ahvaz city, claimed both by Islamic State and Al-Ahvaz separatist group, killed 29 people including children

As a ideological state, it is hardly shocking that Iran has political opponents who have often imposed terror to its important government officials. Below the list was summarized from Iranian website, Aftabnews :

	Years	
1	1979	April, shooting of Sayyed Mohammad Vali Qarni, first Iranian Army Commander
2	1979	May, the shooting of Ayatollah Morteza Motahari, main political figure
3	1979	May, the failed shooting attempt shooting to Hashemi Rajsanjani
4	1979-1983	Terrors that killed five Joma prayer Imams
5	1981	June, the failed shooting attempt to Ayatollah Khamene'i in Abu Zar mosque, Tehran was conducted allegedly by Furqon group
6	1981	August, the blasting bomb occurred in the Prime Minister's office in Tehran, killing President Mohammad Ali Raj'i and Prime Minister Mohammad Javad Bahonar with a number of other important officials
7	1998	A non political terror killed Asadollah Lajordi, a judge of Engelab court
9	1999	Terror to Ali Shayad Shirazi, Army commander was allegedly conducted by Mojaheden Khaleq organization
10	2000	March, the thwarting of shooting terror to Saed Hajariyan, Tehran city council member and former intelligence officer
11	2008 onward	Terrors to Iranian nuclear experts, among others (Ardershir Hoseynpor, Masoud Ali Mohmmadi, Mostafa Ahmadi Roshan, Majid Shahriari, Dariush Rezai Nezhad, Faridun Abasi Dayani and Reza Qasqawi were

		allegedly conducted by Mojaheden al-Khaleg under the support of Israel
12	2015	Physical attack to Ali Motahari, Iranian Parliament member

Iran and Qods Force

Qods force, established following the Iran-Iraqi war, constitutes a military elite wing of Revolutionary Guards that functions to promote and expand Islamic revolutionary influences abroad, mainly by exerting military hard power. Having been endorsed significantly by the regime, this special force has been headed by Major General Ghasem Soleyman born in 1957 since 15 years ago. In order to accomplish three of its main duties of bringing revolution export, conducting special operation and gathering intelligent data, Qods Force is often perceived negatively by many countries, particularly for those becoming area of its operations both overtly and covertly given the fact that its activities and operations are simply associated with anarchy, subversion and terror in target states. With the passage of time following its designation as a terrorist group, little wonder since 2007 the US government has imposed financial and economic sanctions to the Force alongside Revolutionary Guards, Iranian Ministry of Defence and several major banks that allegedly have helped transfer a large amount of money to the terrorist groups in the region.[557]

Until now, reportedly Qods force has been involved in around 120.000 operations including their intensive participation in proxy wars in a number of Arab states by either its direct involvement in the war or giving all sorts of assistance to the loyal non-Iranian groups, as viewed by Iranian regime as strategically conducive location to embark on revolutionary principles expansion. Considering its importance and significance, the Force enjoys a special position to the Supreme Leader, endowed with much economic privileges and a direct access to him who provides guidelines and directions to the force.[558]

In addition, according to the American government, Qods force is well known for having given material assistances to Taliban, Lebanese Hezbollah, Hamas, Palestinian Islamic Jihad and the Popular Front for the Liberation of Palestine-General Command (PFLP-GC). Mainly to Taliban organization, since 2016 the Force is reported to have extended financial assistance and weaponry so as to get rid of American-led coalition troops in Afghanistan. For many years Qods has supported Hezbollah organization by all means, including operating

---

[557] Fact Sheet: Designation of Iranian Entities and Individuals for Proliferation Activities and Support for Terrorism, 25 October 2007, https://www.treasury.gov/press-center/press-releases/Pages/hp644.aspx
[558] www.vsquds.com, please refer to the website in order to know in detail the force's operations available in both Persian and English

the military training camps in Beka'a Valley, Lebanon and giving military training to over 3000 Hezbollah members in Iran. In this vein, reportedly that Qods provides funding annually about $ 100 to 200 million dollars to the organization. In sum, as cited earlier, Qods Force also helped Shia militia groups in Iraq kill foreign coalition troops and Iraqi forces as well as innocent civilians.[559]

Iran and Unit 400

Unit 400 constitutes a special unit of Qods Force with a membership around 10.000 up to 15.000. The tiny unit, emerging to surface since 2012, has focused on planning and executing violent attacks outside Iran, in addition to realizing a duty of transferring Iranian military assistances to terrorist and guerrilla groups throughout the world. Not only that, the group also makes several coordination of operation before launching attacks.

Due to its secret and sensitive natures, the operation of the unit has to gain special mandate from Qods Commander and also approval from Supreme Leader. According to an American official, the Unit conducts multiple sensitive undercover operations outside Iran including terror attacks, assassinations, kidnappings and sabotages.[560]

In this moment, the unit headed by Major General Hamed Abdollahi, has been responsible for several terrors and attacks in some past years including the assassination of Saudi diplomat in Pakistan in May 2011, plotting the assassination of Saudi ambassador in US in September 2011, and several other terror plots in February 2012 in New Delhi, India, Tbilisi, Georgia and Bangkok, Thailand.[561] The illicit weaponry dispatch in 2010 to Nigeria, Senegal, and Gambia were allegedly carried out by the Unit. Even furthermore the bullets used by the Casamance separatists of Senegal, reportedly originated from Iran.[562] Ironically, such routinely illegal sending by Iran, was admitted by Iranian Foreign Minister during his meeting with Senegal President in 19 February 2011 prompting diplomatic relation rupture of the two countries[563] Apart from these facts, the Iranian agents were tremendously believed to have hired Mexican drug cartel agents to conduct assassination, in which FBI had confiscated $ 100.000 that was being transferred to fund assassination efforts in US.[564]

As a matter of fact, the modus operandi of Unit 400 uses a number of methods while keeping the level of secrecy and obscuring Iranian regime's traces. Some of the methods as follow:

---

[559] ibid
[560] Irantruth.org
[561] For Bangkok bombing, an official of the unit 400 named Alavi was reportedly involved, in which he headed to Bangkok in 19 January 2012, using diplomatic passport on the name of Hossein Tehrani. He was believed to have entered Bangkok via Malaysia, www.irantruth.org
[562] Drew Hinshaw, 25 February 2011, https://www.bloomberg.com/news/articles/2011-02-25/senegal-forensic-study-shows-iranian-weapons-used-in-casamance
[563] Anne Look, 22 February 2011, https://www.voanews.com/a/senegal-accuses-iran-of-supplying-weapons-to-rebels-116742984/161641.html
[564] www.irantruth.com

1. The Unit would use a facilitator and third person (usually non-Iranian) to gather intelligence data and to make logistic preparations before the operation begins. Sometimes, the recruited individuals would get operational trainings in Iran including mechanisms in using weapons, exploding, spying etc. The Unit will meet them to make briefings either in abroad or at home, in which they submit the intelligent results including information and data gathering to the Unit until they materialize the operations.

2. The Unit uses commercial companies that help implement the operations while in abroad

3. The Unit sends weaponry and other equipments to the target regions. Another functions of the companies like Arash Zoobin and Aria Navid have been wielded covertly to carry out such a method.

4. The Unit uses religious, cultural and charity institutions that exist in the rest of the world to recruit the third person (facilitator). In sum, Qods force would also recruit Iranian and non-Iranian students who study Islam in the Shia seminaries in Qom city, Iran.[565]

Iran and Al-Qaeda

When International community is in the same line in waging war against global terrorism, including the one repeatedly carried out by al-Qaeda organization, some evidence further implies covert relations between Iran and the organization in past decades. In this regard, the Wikileaks documents released by US State Department in November 2010, unfolded that a Saudi official once complained to Barrack Obama that Iran was hiding and giving sanctuary to al-Qaeda agents who target the monarch.[566] Interestingly such a covert relation between Iran and al-Qaeda was once implicitly expressed by Abu Mohammad al-Adnani in May 2014, ISIS spoke person, that al-Qaeda has intentionally avoided confrontation with Iran and Shia, [567] seemingly to be a reason behind ISIS group's separation from al-Qaeda.

Not only that, a collection of 19 page documents seized by American troops from Osama bin Laden's home in Abbottabad, Pakistan in 2 May 2011, then released by CIA on October 2017 had detailed the arrangement between Iran and al-Qaeda members to carry

---

[565] ibid
[566] Thomas Joscelyn, 1 December 2010, https://www.weeklystandard.com/thomas-joscelyn/wikileaks-the-iran-al-qaeda-connection
[567] Frederic Wehrey, Beyond Sunni and Shia, the Roots of Sectarianism in a Changing Middle East, Oxford University Press, 2107, page 47

out attacks to the American interests in both Saudi Arabia and Gulf territory, with Iran rewarding money, weaponry and military trainings for Sunni militants in Hezbollah camps in Lebanon. In that secret document which implies the relations ranging from 2001-2011,[568] allegedly written by one senior member of al-Qaeda, notes that Iranian intelligence had facilitated several al-Qaeda agents with visa and homes.[569] Mike Pompeo, former Head of CIA, currently the Secretary of the State, in October 2017 took a conclusion that al-Qaeda and Iran have always established both covert and open relations with one same goal which is the West interests as the bigger threat to them.[570]

The Iranian involvement with al-Qaeda mainly prior to 9/11 tragedy has prompted US court to allow its victim families to make charge of compensation against Iranian government as it based its verdict with some found documents that indicate Iranian help to al-qaeda operatives to conduct military training in Afghanistan before the tragedy occurred. In this regard, Iranian government had instructed the border officers not to put Iranian stamp on their passports. In the document reportedly that Emad Moghniye, a senior leader of Hezbollah which has strong affiliation with Iran, had visited those terrorists in October 2000 and made coordination for their travel to Iran with new passports in order to give more flexibility of movement. In addition, the 2016 -found document had mentioned that Osama bin Laden, al-Qaeda leader and his deputy, Ayman Zawahiri, had met with Emad Zawahiri and Iranian officials in Sudan in 1993 to discuss on establishing mutual alliance and support terrorism.[571] Therefore, little wonder that in August 2018 in his twitter, Faeeg Sheikh Ali, former Iraqi parliament member noted that Iran had already invited al-Qaeda terrorists into Iraqi territory in the wake of US invasion to Iraq in 2003. [572]

According to Daniel Byman, professor of Security Study in George Washington university, the document disclosed that such a relation between Iran and the organization was not an alliance with both parties having essentially different ideology each other, in which al-Qaeda always views Shia Iranians as unbelievers and heretics and in turn Iran that Salafi Wahhabi movement like al-Qaeda may be targeting Shia followers. Establishing relations with al-Qaeda which is an extremist Sunni would be a pragmatic approach of Iranian foreign policy that Iran would wield the organization to oppose American presence in Afghanistan that could threaten Iranian eastern borders under the framework of proxy war. However, such a speculation on that relation could not prevent Ayman el Zawahiri, through a clip video posted in 17 December 2007, from denouncing severely Iranian alliance with US in opening good cooperation in the invasions of the American-led coalitions in

---

[568] Barbara Slavin, Expediency and betrayal : Iran's relationship with al-Qaeda, www.al-monitor.com, 7 September 2018
[569] Josie Ensor, 1 November 2017, https://www.telegraph.co.uk/news/2017/11/01/iran-relationship-al-qaeda-revealed-newly-released-trove-bin/amp/
[570] Daniel Byman, Unlikely Alliance, Iran's secretive relationship with Al-Qaeda, IHS Defense, Risk and Security Consulting, July 2012 page 26
[571] www.alarab.co.uk, 2 August 2018

[572] Farsi.alarabiya.net, 11 August 2018

Afghanistan and Iraq in the early 2000s by noting that Iran, with such actions, was betraying Islamic nations.[573]

In a communiqué dated 11 June 2009 and addressed ostensibly to Osama bin Laden, Atiyah, senior member of al-Qaeda, wrote that Iran had released al-Qaeda mid-level agents in May 2009 due to significant pressures including threats posed to Iranian interests (in Afghanistan and Pakistan) and kidnapping an Iranian consul named Hekmatollah Atharzadeh-Nyaki) in Peshawar, Pakistan in November 2008, in which, based on the confiscated documents, Khaled, son of Osama bin Laden, had once written a letter to Supreme Leader regarding the release of the detained al-Qaeda members, yet the letter was never responded. Furthermore, Iranian efforts to detain al-Qaeda operatives in Iran had sparked much speculation that Iran would use the detainees to increase its bargaining position and leverage before the US.

Still according to Daniel Byman, due to deep enmity and intense suspicions, both parties would never find meeting points and strategy clarities that could unify their perspective in dealing with regionally political dynamics. For instance, in 2000 when there was an attack to USS Cole, Iran was attempting to strengthen relation with al-Qaeda, a measure rejected by Osama bin Laden as he was not unwilling to eschew the organization from Saudi supporters.

Yet, the aforementioned facts were implicitly rejected by James Clapper report, Director of National Intelligence in 16 February 2012 by saying that there has been restricted and partial alliance of both sides, in which Iran reportedly helped train al-Qaeda agents in early 90s, facilitate transit al-Qaeda and other Jihadists to Afghanistan before and after 9/11 tragedy, even allow al-Qaeda figures to reside in Iran. According to the Commission 9/11 report, Sudanese government had facilitated a meeting between Iran and al-Qaeda in Sudan that resulted in giving military trainings to the members both in Bekaa Valley, Lebanon and Iran. Even furthermore, the Commission had evidence that 8 up to 10 of 14 Saudis involved in 9/11 attacks had travelled to Iran between October 2000 and February 2001. In an article written by Thomas Joclyn in May 2011, based on a leaked document prepared in Guantanamo Bay prison, revealed that there was a guesthouse built in Iran through Osama's funding. However according to Daniel Byman, there is some evidence implying that Tehran was still allowing al-Qaeda agents to travel to Afghanistan through Iran for transit. For example, Adel Mohammad Mahmood Abdul Khaliq, al-Qaeda agent and Libyan Islamic Fighting Group (LIFG) arrested in United Emirates Arab, reportedly travelled to Iran at least five times (2004-2007). In reality, such evidence would be in compatible with that of Commission 9/11 report which affirmed if a Saudi citizen travelled to Afghanistan to Pakistan, then he went home to Saudi with Pakistani stamp in his passport, he might have had the risk of confiscating his passport. A US Treasury's report identified some figures who played crucial roles to facilitate Jihadist movements to Iran,

---

[573] ibid

noting mainly that in 16 January 2009, four al-Qaeda agents (among others Mustafa Hamed) were mediators of the meeting between Iran and al-Qaeda, which Mustafa Hamed had negotiated with Iranian government to allowing many of al-Qaeda members to have temporary transit in Iran. Another important member, Yasin al-Suri, permitted by Iran to operate in Iran since 2005, was known for being a connector in transferring funds from Middle East to South Asia, and a facilitator of departure for the recruiters from Gulf region to Pakistan and Afghanistan through Iran. Additionally, Ahmad Siddiqui arrested in 2010, had confessed in Germany court that he along with two other agents had once met al-Qaeda leaders in Iran.

It is worth mentioning that in the wake of the military invasion of American- led coalition to Afghanistan, al-Qaeda has been broken into two groups. First group followed Osama and Zawahiri to Pakistan, and the other group fled to Iran, including Sayf, Abu Hafs, al-Mauritani, Sulayman Abu Ghayth and Saad, one of Osama's sons. Initially Iran limited the ability of those members within the territory by imposing house arrest and getting them back to their motherland. Yet when Iran was once labelled as Axis of Evils by President George Bush in January 2002, it embarked on putting more control to al-Qaeda members living in Iran whom allegedly had designed terror attacks targeting Riyadh compounds in May 2003 through coordination between Sayf and Saad bin Laden, also believed to have been involved in Synagogue attack in Tunisia in April 2002.

So it is hardly surprising that according to CNN report in May 2003, the Iranian officials during their meeting with the UN representative for Afghanistan once admitted that it has arrested several al-Qaeda members in which Sayf was one of them. Moreover several evidences showed that Iran had released the al-Qaeda members, in which according to German's report of Der Spiegel in October 2010, Sayf has been released and then returned to Pakistan in April 2010 after his 8 year stay in Iran.[574]

Iran and Taliban Group

When a short-duration clip in Youtube regarding Ali Khamenei's warm welcoming to Maulana Sami'ul Haqq, Taliban's spiritual advisor, in Tehran in the sidelines of Non Aligned Movement meeting was uploaded, small wonder that the clip had generated speculations at home that Iran had concealed its cordial relation with Taliban radical organization with the entities having stark contrast in Islamic ideology and interpretation which each other. In sum, Iran was for several times a victim of violence and terrorism carried out by the organization in past decades including mass-killings of around 2000-5000 Shia minority in Afghanistan and assassination of eight Iranian diplomats and an Iranian correspondent in Maziar e-Syarief in Afghanistan that provoked Iran to deploy 70.000 Iranian armies in its

---

[574] ibid

Eastern border.⁵⁷⁵ In the other hand, apart from his militancy and being a founder of radical Haghani schools in Pakistan, Samiul Haqq has been well known for having outstanding roles in creating chaos and instability in Baluchistan region of Afghanistan. He has been also a mentor for Mola Mohammad Omar, an extremist prominent leader of Taliban.⁵⁷⁶

In fact Iran had claimed that Molana Samiul Haqq structurally has not been a Taliban political leader, yet however his influence and charisma to the group is undeniable. So his presence in the international event does not show necessarily Iranian official recognition to Taliban's existence and its own radical thoughts. Additionally, the meeting was held based on the previous tradition that rightly after the event, the states leaders would have courtesy call to Ali Khamenei.⁵⁷⁷ Also in 2013, the Godfather of Taliban reportedly attended a conference on Ulemas and Islamic Awakening held in Iran. Interestingly his participation in the event was confirmed by an Iranian official stating that his presence would further exhibit tolerance and religious freedom in Iran.⁵⁷⁸

His twice attendance in several International events hosted by Iran has proven that Iran is likely to cultivate a special relation with Taliban despite Iranian constant denial. However, such a relationship was also once confirmed by Mohammad Reza Bahrami, Iranian Ambassador for Afghanistan that Iran was ready to establish cooperation with Taliban group in order to promote peace process in Afghanistan, nonetheless merely limited in controlling and information directing.⁵⁷⁹

Based on The Wall Street Journal's report in June 2015, Iran has increased financial and weaponry supports to the group, and even recruited and given military trainings to its members as suggested by a news website privately owned by Afghanistan. In May 2015, Taliban delegation led by Mohmmad Tayab Agha, close colleague to Mollah Omar reportedly paid visit to Iran and met with Iranian leaders. Moreover a report shockingly cited that the group has opened its office in Zahedan city in Iran in 2012 and the second in Mashhad city in 2014. Previously, Afghani border policemen are reported to have confiscated land mine smuggled allegedly from Iran to Taliban group.⁵⁸⁰ In addition, in May 2016 America shot dead one Taliban leader named Mullah Akhtar Mansour when attempting to cross Iranian border to head Pakistan. ⁵⁸¹ Last but not least, in May 2018 Iran has been strongly accused for supporting financially and providing arms to Taliban's members that left hundreds killed in the western city of Farah, near the border between the

---

⁵⁷⁵ Vali Kouzehgar Kaleji, Ups and Downs in Irani-Pakistan Ties, jurnal Iranian Review of Foreign Affairs, Volume 2 Number 4, winter edition year 2012, page 153
⁵⁷⁶ Pedare Manawi Taliban dar Tehran, 2 May 2013, http://www.afghanpaper.com/nbody.php?id=51254
⁵⁷⁷ Robusi Rahbari ba Maulana Samiul Haq, http://www.siasi.porsemani.ir/content/-روبوسي-رهبري-با-مولانا-سميع-الحق؟
⁵⁷⁸ ibid
⁵⁷⁹ Fawad Nassiri, Iran officially confirms having communication with Taliban in Afghanistan, 9 December 2016, https://ariananews.af/iran-officially-confirms-having-communication-with-taliban-in-afghanistan/
⁵⁸⁰Joshua Levkowitz, 17 May 2017, http://www.mei.edu/content/article/iran-s-taliban-gamble-afghanistan
⁵⁸¹Mohammad Akbar Notezai, 7 June 2016, https://thediplomat.com/2016/06/balochistan-and-the-killing-of-mullah-mansour/

two countries.[582] Last but not least, the Sunday Times in July 2018 has also reported that based on confession by Taliban as well as Afghanistan officials, Iran is giving and facilitating military trainings to hundreds of Taliban fighters in Kermansha Province, west Iran.[583]

According to Niranjan Chandrashekar, a researcher in the Indian Institute for Defence Studies and Analysis, there have been four reasons why Iran intensively supports Taliban as follow :

1. Iran fears the probability of ISIS presence in Khorasan border due to the fact that ISIS has already operated in Afghanistan, previously in Iraq and Syria. Reportedly that some of former Taliban members had expressed their allegiance to the organization. In order to anticipate profoundly the risk of ISIS infiltration to Iranian territory, such a good relationship with Taliban shall need to be established.
2. American military presence in Afghanistan has already engendered Iranian inconvenience despite the previous cooperation of the both states in toppling down Taliban government in early 2000s. Before reaching the JCPOA deal in 2015, there has been worry from Iranian side over the possibility of American attack to Iran's nuclear sites, launched from Afghanistan's border.
3. While investing in the infrastructure projects and having been involved in funding political organizations and their candidates as well as media in Afghanistan, Iran had expectation that Taliban along with other factions be embroiled in the national government, in which if such an expectation comes into realization, Iran would use its influence in Afghanistan through Taliban in the future.
4. In fact, regionally is being marginalized where as other states like Pakistan, Saudi Arabia and China have opened their communication channels with Taliban in secrecy. Iran did not want to miss the moment when Taliban re-appears in the later days. In other hand, the relation between Taliban and Pakistan has been often overwhelmed by suspicions that the group was willing to come out from Pakistan's shadow. Therefore, Iran would be a proper alternative for Taliban to open its relations. [584]

As a matter of fact, cultivating good relation with Taliban has been an Iranian short term strategy which is securing the domestic territory from any existential threat, mainly ISIS since Iran has been deeply aware that Taliban is always associated with radical Takfiri thoughts that invariably view Iran as a Shia state. More interestingly before ISIS came to emerge in Iraq and succeeded to broaden its operation in Afghanistan, Iran used the roles of

---

[582] Eltaf Najafizada, 24 May 2018, https://www.bloomberg.com/news/articles/2018-05-23/iran-blamed-for-afghan-attacks-after-trump-scraps-nuclear-deal
[583] Anthony Loyd, 8 July 2018, https://www.thetimes.co.uk/article/talibans-best-fighters-being-trained-by-iran-bbzc68n3m
[584] Niranjan Chandrashekar, 8 June 2016, https://thediplomat.com/2016/06/whats-between-the-taliban-and-iran/

Taliban to help Iran accomplish its destructive goals within Afghan's territory, rupturing its bilateral ties with Afghanistan. In 2013 for instance, it is revealed that Iran gave financial assistance to a Taliban commander to destroy the Kamal Khan Dam in Nimruz province, Afghanistan, one of the key sources of the conflicts between the countries for many decades.[585]

In this vein, geographically Iranian western and eastern borders are well known to be vulnerable to the infiltration of terrorist groups from the states that could hardly control their own internal security. As the list above indicated, some of terror acts in Iran occurred in Sistani Baluchistan province, situated closely to the Afghanistan and Pakistan's direct borders. Also reportedly in order that the operation to succeed, ISIS has recruited its sympathizers in the Iranian eastern border in which several other militant groups like *al Tauhid Brigade* and *Ansarul Khelafat wal Jehad* have also expressed their loyalty and allegiance to ISIS.[586]

Iran has to grab a moment of the hostility between Taliban and ISIS which feud one another sometimes reflected by bloody armed clashes in Afghanistan. For Iran, ISIS poses the most dangerous threat of any terrorist groups due to its trans-national and border natures, which Iran is always convinced that Taliban will not infiltrate to its own territory, thus targeting Iranian Shia followers.

Arab Saudi and Terrorism, a Victim or a Sponsor?

As a matter of fact, prior to 9/11 tragedy, Arab Saudi had never shown its commitment in combating terrorism whereas the state has been terrorism target in Khaibar towers bombing in 1996. Furthermore, Arab Saudi obviously approved the dispatch of Jihadists to the Muslim conflicting countries such as Bosnia, Afghanistan and Chechnya and funded millions of dollars to espouse their struggles since last 70s that arguably succeeded to implant seeds for shaping both Taliban and al-Qaeda. Nevertheless, with the passage of the time, such financial assistance of Saudi was withdrawn due to the indication that Taliban had its link with al-Qaeda terrorist group which succeeded to bomb US embassies in Kenya and Tanzania in August 1998.[587] Yet in the other hand, when reportedly 15 of 19 terror perpetrators of 9/11 tragedy were Saudi citizens, Saudi government felt uncomfortable despite the fact that such a devastating event ultimately gained its Wahhabi cleric's condemnation. Suddenly international community began to brand the monarch state as a regime which for decades endlessly has been fertilizing doctrines on ideological extremism and radicalism, inspiring the global terrorists, mainly Osama bin Laden who was also a Saudi

---

[585] Srinjoy Bose, Nishank Motwani and William Maley, Afghanistan – Challenges and Prospects, University of Durham, Routledge, Taylor and Francis Group, 2018. page 208
[586] Joshua Levkowitz, 17 May 2017, http://www.mei.edu/content/article/iran-s-taliban-gamble-afghanistan
[587] Natasha Underhill, Countering Global Terrorism and Insurgency, Palgrava Macmillan, 2014, page 45

citizen. Most startlingly, in a shocking interview with President Barack Obama in 2016, he even criticized openly that the Saudi rulers spread an intolerant interpretation of Islam.[588]

However, in August 2002 around 600 American families whose relatives are the victims of the tragedy, brought charges to the court along with a claim that three princes including Sultan bin Abdul Aziz, Saudi Minister of Defence had funded the charity institutions that financially support al-Qaeda organization, indicating indirect involvement in sponsoring the attack.[589] Not only that, based on Jan Schakowsky's assessment from Democrat party of America, almost a half of al-Qaeda members are Saudis.[590]

Based on much deeper study, al-Qaeda does not take Wahhabi ideology as its own thoughtful basis, but rather contemporary radical Islamic interpretation introduced significantly by Sayyed Qotb, political activist of Egyptian Ikhawanul Muslimin. In addition, the doctrines of Wahhabi and al-Qaeda are essentially different with each other, which al-Qaeda invariably keeps attempting to topple the Saudi monarch state, while Wahhabism rather exhibits its absolute allegiance to its political rulers as long as they do not contravene Islamic values and principles. Secondly, a call for Jihad against West often echoed by al-Qaeda, did not gain any tremendous support from Wahhabi since Jihad, according to Wahhabi followers, constitutes a prerogative right of Saudi political rulers in declaring Jihad that must be followed.[591] In this regard, Madhawi Rashed, Saudi historian, noted that Wahhabism does not necessarily reflect global messages of al-Qaeda, due to the fact that some of Osama bin Laden's thoughts were different from those of Wahhabi followers.[592]

Following the 9/11 tragedy, the cordial relation between Saudi and US was ruptured for a while. Consequently Saud al-Faisal, Saudi Minister of Foreign Affairs of the time, once gave a cynical statement that the war on global terror led by US in Iraq in 2003 was a colonial adventure that aims at controlling Iraqi natural resources. In the other hand, the US government was upset that Saudi proved to have failed in preventing its citizens of over 2500 to depart for Jihad to topple down the Iraqi Shia government. In addition, as reported, 60 percent of suicidal bombing practices inside the territory were carried out by Saudis.[593] In July 2004, US government unfolded that private wealth of the royal family still has been prominent source to funding radical Islamic movements amid US undertakings in curbing the money flow to those terrorists. Apart from this, the Kingdom has been well-known for empowering spread Wahhabi principles and values to the rest of the world and

---

[588] Medea Benjamin, Kingdom of the Unjust, Behind the US-Saudi Connection, OR books, page 130
[589] Dore Gold, Mamlakate el Karahiya, Kayfa Daamat al Arabiyat Saudiyah al Irhab el Alami Jadid, translated into Arabic by Mohammad Jalid, published by Mansyurat al Jamal page 8
[590] Fatemeh Shayan, Security in the Persian Gulf Region, Palgrave Macmillan, page 159
[591] David Commins, the Wahhabi Mission and Saudi Arabia, IB Tauris page185
[592] Fatemeh Shayan, Security in the Persian Gulf Region, Palgrave Macmillan, page 140
[593] John R.Bradley, Saudi Arabia Exposed, Inside a Kingdom Crisis, Palgrave Macmillan page 221

accommodating militant Wahhabi to control over domestic affairs such as mosques, courts, educational curricula, Sharia police (Mothawwa) etc.[594]

However, in February 2005, less than two years following suicidal attacks in the foreigners compounds in Riyadh which killed 35 civilians including 9 US citizens, Saudi finally decided to host a conference on combating on terrorism. Such a decision aimed among others at undermining the negative perceptions of international community and proving its own strong commitment to terrorism combating, both domestically and globally, in which Saudi has been aware well that terrorism may take place within its own territory. In addition to such efforts, in April 2004 Saudi Arabian Monetary Authority (SAMA) has been regarded health and cooperative to deal with the issues including money laundering and funding terrorism from the Financial Action Task Force (FATF).[595]

Eventually the Riyadh bombing could regain gradually international community's sympathy. This was once expressed by Frances Fragos Townsend, US Security Adviser, implying on normalization of disrupted bilateral relations, that Washington would stand with Saudi to fight global terrorism.[596] Accordingly, the both states have established cooperation in the intelligence field and information sharing via the establishment of joint operation to curb terrorist funding.[597] In addition, in 2008 they also signed a bilateral agreement on anti-terrorism cooperation, which US would provide its Saudi-funded advisors to help secure Saudi territory, and give training to the Saudi security force.[598]

In order to evince strong commitment on global terror eradication, given much American pressure, Arab Saudi has started taking various measures to control over its own charity organizations, alleged to be an effective mechanism for transferring cash to militant groups, and to deeply monitor all sorts of financial transactions from the Kingdom. Not only that since 2002 onwards, Saudi has also taken strategic steps inter alia issuing a policy that obliges any charity organization willing to operate abroad, must obtain an approval from Saudi Ministry of Foreign Affairs. The steps have also included auditing of those organizations and establishing new government institutions that aim at monitoring them. Since 2004 to 2006, Saudi national budget for materializing its own anti- terrorism measures is estimated to be $ 10 billion dollars.[599]

As a matter of fact, Saudi efforts were not restricted to issue and identify the mentioned policies of limiting cash flow to Islamic militant groups. The Kingdom immediately shut down the office of al-Haramain foundation operating abroad after being

---

[594] Ibid page 222
[595] Mohamed A.Ramady, The Saudi Arabian Economy, Policies, Achievements, and Challenges, Springer, 2010, page 26
[596] Ibid page 222
[597] Fatemeh Shayan, Security in the Persian Gulf Region, Palgrave Macmillan, page 164
[598] Daniel Byman, The US- Saudi Arabia Counterterrorism Relationship, House Committee on Foreign Affairs, page 4
[599] Opcit page 164

alleged for funding extremists, including the two offshoots of the foundation in Bosnia and Somalia. In September 2003, Saudi cabinet had issued new regulations on anti-money laundering, and on allowing the IRS and FBI to open a permanent connecting office in Riyadh to carry out coordination with concerned Saudi officials in monitoring the movements of those charity organizations. [600] Accordingly, Saudi has founded anti money laundering units under the supervision of Saudi Arabia Monetary Agency (SAMA), which bear responsibilities among others to urge Saudi financial institutions to implement measures of anti- money laundering and anti- terrorism funding. Furthermore, collecting of money in mosques and public areas has been banned for anticipation. Reportedly Saudi had shut down an illicit money changer and transfer centre, and imposed sanctions to those involved in terrorism funding.[601] With the passage of time, Saudi security forces have been deployed aggressively to arrest terrorist suspects of al-Qaeda organization that spawned eventually 600 Saudi citizens throughout Saudi arrested.[602]

Furthermore, in May 2003, Saudi Ministry of Religious Affairs had fired the 353 officials and required 1357 of its officials to take courses on Islamic moderation. In December 2003, a source in Saudi embassy in Washington once revealed the Kingdom's intention to invoke diplomatic status from preachers and ulemas sent to abroad, and shut down the Islamic affairs division of each Saudi embassy.[603] In order to espouse Saudi anti-global terrorism policies, in April 2010, Senior Ulema council of Saudi, issued a religious fatwa forbidding any kind of funding for terrorist groups.[604]

In order to convince the international community on Saudi strong commitment of the anti-terrorism implementation, in 2015, Saudi government through Mohammad bin Salman, Saudi Minister of Defence has created a Islamic Military Coalition in Combating Terrorism that has the aim of showing Muslim nations' firm stance against any type of terrorism amid harsh criticisms on reluctant Muslim community in eradicating the roots of terrorism. The coalition, unluckily not joined by all Muslim states, held its first meeting in Riyadh, Arab Saudi in November 2017 in which the Saudi Crown Prince swore to snuff out terrorism vehemently from the earth. [605]

The claim of Saudi success to implement such measures has been triggered by among others sharing intelligent information to US and UE intelligence regarding the undertakings of AQAP group (Al-Qaeda in the Arabian Peninsula headquartered in Yemen)

---

[600] F.Gregory Gause III, Saudi Arabia and the War on Terrorism, Hoover Press; Garfinkle/Terrorisme, page 96
[601] Based on a letter wrote by Mohammad bin Nawaf, Saudi Ambassador in London, please for detail, see www.channel4.com
[602] Nabil Mouline, The Clerics of Islam Religious Authority And Political Power in Saudi Arabia, Yale University Press page 255
[603] opcit
[604] ibid
[605] The coalition is joined by Egypt, UEA, Bahrain, Afghanistan, Uganda, Somalia, Mauretania, Lebanon, Libya, Yemen and Turk, and interestingly includes Qatar

that inserted explosive materials to cargo aircraft routed to US in 2010. Saudi also provided his land as basis for US to launch its attacks to the group in Yemen.[606]

As time went on, the emerging of ISIS in recent years has posed an existential threat for Saudi security with ISIS declaring Saudi as its adversary and calling its Saudi sympathizers to assassinate some of the royal family members and topple down the Jews and US unbelievers-allied monarch state. Not only that, ISIS reportedly attacked some Shia mosques and Saudi security officers. In result, Saudi once again has attempted to exhibit its firm seriousness to eradicate the organization by issuing numerous significant steps inter alia dissuading Saudi citizens to travel abroad to join ISIS, arresting around 1600 of ISIS sympathizers and thwarting the ISIS carried out terror attempts. In addition, once again Saudi and US have expressed their commitment to make cooperation to prevent funds from flowing to the ISIS. Since Riyadh did realise that ISIS has been harnessing technologic advance to spread its messages throughout the world, Riyadh has also actively monitored social media dynamics, viewed obviously as mechanism for ISIS new recruitment. Meanwhile like previous legal opinions in condemning any terror acts, Wahhabi clerics have taken part by issuing religious statements condemning the ISIS group.[607]

Interestingly, it is not restricted only by imprisoning suspect terrorists; the monarch state also founded a rehabilitation centre for getting them back into normal life (de-radicalization) by equipping them with various skills. In that centre, many Saudi Islamic leaders would be involved in providing and emphasizing vigorously on Islamic teaching of anti-terrorism and extremism. Yet ironically, the centre did not necessarily yield an expected result of dismantling radical brains, given that some of the rehabilitees have finally decided to join ISIS again.

Terrorism Actions in Saudi Arabia Since the founding of the Modern State in 1932

Here is the list of several terror attacks occurred within the territory summarized from BBC and other relied sources.

No		
	1960	Series of bomb explosions afflicted Riyadh in last 1966 and first 1967, claimed to be carried out by the People of the Arabian Peninsula in North Yemen
	1979	Hostage crises in Masjid el-Haram, Mecca by radical group led by Johayman al Otaybi, killing 255

---

[606] Daniel Byman, The US- Saudi Arabia Counterterrorism Relationship, House Committee on Foreign Affairs, page 5
[607] Ibid page 6

	1988	The bombing of the tank for saving fuel in Saudi Petrochemical Company Facility in Jubail. Four Shia perpetrators were executed death
	1995	The car bombing in National Guard Office in Riyadh killed 5 US and 2 Indian citizens
	1996	The bombing of apartment compounds of Khaybar Tower in Khaybar, near to Dhahran killed 19 American troops. Al-Qaeda was the suspect
	2002	September, a Germany citizen was killed in a car bombing in Riyadh centre
	2003	February, an American BAE Systems employee was assassinated in his car in Riyadh May, suicidal bombing in Vinnel Compound in Riyadh, killed 35. The incident, claimed by a West report, was the result of collaboration with National Guard May, 2 Saudi officers and a militant were killed June, the ambush of security apparatus in Khalidiya, near to Mecca killed 2 officers and 5 terrorist suspects. 12 of the suspects including on Chadian and one Egyptian were arrested. July, 6 militants (4 Saudis and 2 Chadians) were killed in shooting incident with Saudi security force in farming land outside al-Qassem September, 3 militants and a Saudi police were killed in shooting incident in Riyadh hospital November, two militants self-exploded while being seized by the policemen. The truck bombing in Riyadh houses killed 17 December, a militant was killed in gas station in Riyadh
	2004	January, a shooting incident against an militant in Riyadh killed 5 policemen 5 April, a militant was killed in a car chasing in Riyadh 12 April, an policeman and a militant were killed in armed shooting in Riyadh 13 April, 4 policemen were assassinated by two militants 21 April, a bomb exploded in the gate of traffic and emergency assistance office centre in Riyadh, killing 5 22 April, 3 militants were killed in Jeddah in Al-Fayha district 1 May, 2 US and 2 British along with one Australian, Canadian and Saudi citizens were killed in Yanbo oil company by three brothers. 22 May, a Germany chef was assassinated in Jarir book store in Riyadh 29 May, 22 people including 19 foreign citizens were killed in the bloody assault in Oasis Compound in Khaybar 6 June, a BBC Irish cameraman was killed in an armed shooting in Riyadh

		8 June, a US citizen working in Vinnel Corp, was killed in his villa in Riyadh
13 June, AS citizen was killed and another kidnapped via fake check point in Riyadh
18 June, an American citizen was assassinated brutally by a militant group
July, an armed shooting in Riyadh killed Eisa bin Saad al-Awshan, a most wanted militant while the Saudi offshoot al-Qaeda leader escaped
4 August, an Irish citizen was shot dead in his workplace in Riyadh
30 August, an US official was shot in a bank in Jeddah
11 September, 2 small bombs exploded near to Saudi British and Saudi American Banks in Jeddah. No casualties.
15 September, a British expatriate working Marconi company was shot dead in a Riyadh supermarket
26 September, a French worker of the Defence Electronics Firm was shot dead in his car in Jeddah
9 November a shooting incident took place in Jeddah, carried out by militant group. No casualties.
17 November, an policeman was killed in a shooting incident in Unayzah in Qassem
6 December, the attack to US consulate building in Jeddah was carried out by al-Qaeda group, killing 5 employees
29 December, two suicidal bombings occurred in Riyadh, killing one civilian, one outside the interior ministry complex and another in the training centre of Special Emergency Force
	2005	July, a shooting incident occurred in the eastern Riyadh, killing Younes Mohammad al-Heyari, Moroccan militant activist
	2015	January, the bombing occurred in the border patrol unit, near Arar, killing 3 army officers
May, suicidal bombing took place in an mosque in Qateif, estern part of Saudi, killing 22
May, suicidal bombing occurred in a Shia mosque in Dammam, killing 4
August, a suicidal bombing happened in Abha, southern part of Asir province
	2016	January, suicidal bombing occurred in mosque Imam Ridha in el Hasa, Eastern Province
July, terror attacks took place in three cities including Mecca and Medina, killing 4
August, Houthi group killed 7 Saudis
	2017	January, 2 member ISIS were killed by Saudi police officers in Yasemin area, in

		Riyadh

2 persons exploded themselves during a shooting incident with Saudi security force

March, a police was killed by a ISIS member

May, ISIS attack killed 2 citizens from Pakistan and Saudi

May, ISIS was the suspect for killing an army officer in al-Awwamiya

June, Hezbollah al-Hezab was alleged to be mastermind behind a car bombing in al-Qatef that killed 2, and al-Awamiya killing one army office

Suicidal bombing took place in Mecca

July, a bomb exploded in a city dominated by Shia, killing an police man. Hezbollah al-Hejaz was the suspect

July, the explosion was allegedly carried out by Hezbollah al-Hejaz in el-Awwamiya village, killing a policeman

July, a shooting was allegedly perpetrated by Hezbollah el-Hejaz in Qatef province

Augus, an attack to a bus that killed a Saudi citizen was carried out by Hezbollah al-Hejaz, killing a Saudi

August until today, Arab Saudi has been target for ballistic missiles launched by Houthi in Yemen

Dilemma of Saudi commitment on Terrorism Eradication

In fact, in fighting terrorism carried out among others by curbing cash flow to the militant organizations, Saudi has faced much dilemma which often contravenes its own commitments. It has been well-known that cash flow to the militant groups mainly Sunni including Syria, Iraq and Afghanistan is carried out by Saudi individuals who probably have special ties with the royal family. Their enormous wealth seems to be independent from government, used significantly to achieve a goal of spreading 'true' Islam to the rest of the world. In the other hand, among thousands of the royal family members, some are likely to be secular liberal in thoughts who may tend to continue their studies in Western universities, but some are conservatives who may support financially Sunni radical militant activities throughout the globe.

The second dilemma would be relating to Wahhabi doctrine in which deliberately has been inserted to Saudi educational curricula, sometimes implying on hatred and antipathy towards non-Muslim communities. A wide range of pamphlets, books, or any propaganda tools for Wahhabi spreading has been routinely conducted by Saudi government through its own institutions established largely in abroad.[608] As I will elaborate later, in the entire world, since 80s under Saudi programs, there are approximately 200 high educational institutions, 210 Islamic centres, 1500 mosques and 2000 schools built for Muslim families who reside in non-Muslim territories.[609] Despite given much complaint and criticism from international community to be potential seed for global terrorism to grow significantly, the Kingdom shall make any review and re-evaluate its own educational curricula and other types of propaganda so as to alter them into more moderate and flexible concepts that do not accentuate radicalism and extremism. Regrettably such tireless effort given by the King to revise Wahhabism curricula as one of the effective ways to eliminate roots and mindset of extremism and radicalism, has not yielded positive result since it has been very hard to make reforms as the Kingdom would challenge the entrenched religious-educational bureaucracy at home. [610] Yet interestingly, it did not prevent the kingdom from making revision on the curricula, among other undertakings, by establishing a committee that included government selected religious scholars that aimed at rewriting religion textbooks that encourage tolerance of other religions and discourage spreading hostility and enmity against Jews, Christians, and Shia Muslims.[611] However, as Karen Elliot further argued that not challenging the conservative religious orthodoxies of Wahhabism would be the driving priority for the Kingdom's survival.[612] Nevertheless, she was probably right when the independent federal government commission carried out a study of 22 textbooks published by the Kingdom for the 2017-2018 academic year, it found a very shocking fact that the contents of the books warn students to avoid friendship with members of other religions and encourage both violent and non-violent jihad against non-believers.[613]

However, a Hillary Clinton's email, former US Secretary of State, which leaked to public, has indicated an existing financial link between the Kingdom and ISIS group. Meanwhile Joe Biden, former US Vice President, once accused Saudi and other Gulf states for transferring millions of dollars and weaponry to any group opposing Bashar Assad regime. Additionally, Nouri el-Maliki, well known for having closer ties with Iran and former Iraqi Prime Minister in 2014, has issued a controversial statement that Arab Saudi and Qatar were giving financial supports to terrorist groups.[614] For sure, Iranian government has often issued some statements and comments accusing Saudi role in destabilizing and contributing more chaos and turmoil to the region.

---

[608] Scott Shane, Saudi and Extremism. Both the Arsonists and the Fire fighters, 25 August 2016, https://www.nytimes.com/2016/08/26/world/middleeast/saudi-arabia-islam.html
[609] David Aufhausser, " An Assessment of Current Efforts to Combat Terrorism Financing" a testimony of David Aufhausser, 15 Juni 2004 page 46
[610] Karen Elliott House, Saudi Arabia, Its People, Past, Religion, Fault Lines and Future, Alfred A. Knopf, 2012 page 136
[611] Ibid page 138
[612] Ibid page 219
[613] https://www.al-monitor.com/pulse/originals/2018/11/intel-bigoted-backsliding-saudi-textbooks-mbs.html
[614] Martin Willams, 7 June 2017, https://www.channel4.com/news/factcheck/factcheck-qa-is-saudi-arabia-funding-isis

Meanwhile, the shocking impacts of 9/11 tragedy has been still felt until current days, seemingly does not prevent the victim families from asking compensations to Saudi government. In 2016, thanks to Saudi lobby in Washington, Barrack Obama vetoed the law of the Justice Against Sponsors of Terrorism Act passed by Congress which allows US victim families to charge legally the Kingdom due to allegation of Saudi support to the terrorists of the tragedy. In sum, in September 2017 reportedly that there is strong evidence emphasizing that Saudi embassy in Washington had financed two Saudi citizens in conducting rehearsal before carrying out the terrorism action of 9/11.[615] Interestingly the two Saudi Nationals, namely Mohammad al-Qudhaeein, was allegedly an employee in Saudi Ministry of Islamic Affairs whereas Hamdan al-Sahlawi was an employee for Saudi government in Washington DC.[616]

As a matter of fact, such allegations against Saudi government were self-denied by other US high officials. The Director of US National Intelligence in his a report, concluded that its institution could not find any evidence of Saudi involvement as a state and its government officials in flowing cash to al-Qaeda terrorist group. In addition, CIA and FBI also reported that no such existing proofs could imply Saudi government's and its royal family's involvement in supporting 9/11 tragedy or other terrorism operations both at home and abroad. Moreover, Mike Pompeo, former CIA Director currently Secretary of the State, during his official visit in Saudi Arabia in February 2017 granted the George Tenet Award to Mohammad bin Salman, Crown Prince of Saudi, as an appreciation token to his significant efforts in combating terrorism.[617]

Indonesia and Terrorism

As BBC media pointed out, during one week of May 2018, Indonesia has been recently shocked by the successive terror acts that took place in Java Island that for some months Indonesia was quite safe from any terror threats. The terrorists who targeted detention facility at the paramilitary police's headquarters and churches, believed to be carried out by Jamaah Anshorut Daulah (JAD) which has affiliation to the ISIS terrorist group in 2015, have connection to one another. According to Al Chaidar, Indonesian observer on terrorism from Malikussaleh University, the incident that occurred in the detention facility in 8 May 2018 generated remaining terrorists to call other JAD members in the territory for

---

[615] Saudi Embassy may have funded 9/11 dry run : report, 10 September 2017, https://www.aljazeera.com/news/2017/09/saudi-embassy-funded-911-dry-run-report-170909223532351.html
[616] Rachael Revesz, 10 September 2017, https://www.independent.co.uk/news/world/americas/911-saudi-government-embassy-dry-run-hijacks-lawsuit-cockpit-se,
[617] ibid

making Jihad through social media and other interpersonal communication.[618] However, Aman Abdurrahman, the leader of JAD, detained for Thamrin bombing incident in 2016 was sentenced to death in 22 June 2018. Despite much difference of many aspects in recent years, JAD has been playing prominent role in spreading terror acts in Indonesia and begun replacing the role played significantly by the Afghanistan al-Qaida -affiliated Jamaah Islamiyah Group in 2000s.

As previously mentioned that since the collapse of the Soeharto's authoritarian administration in 1998, marking a new era for Indonesian political system, Indonesia has been the focus of international community's eye in the case of trans-national terrorism, particularly following the Bali Bombing in 2002 perpetrated by Jamaah Islamiah group that killed hundreds of foreign tourists and inevitably tarnished the Indonesian efforts in accentuating progressively the smiling face of moderate and tolerant Islam. For Indonesian government, terrorist act is like a time bomb that could explode anytime it seems appropriate, with regard to existing diverse interpretations of Islam that sprout inevitably in Indonesia.

Interestingly, many of the roots of militancy and radicalism in Indonesia have derived from outside the state, mainly Salafiya interpretation largely brought by rigid Wahhabism of Saudi Arabia and Egyptian militant Ikhwanul Muslimin and last not by least, al-Qaeda in Afghanistan. In 1970s some militant members were well influenced by the translated articles on Tauhid published in Indonesia by the Indonesian Islamic Propagation Council which cooperated significantly with Muslim World League and the International Islamic Federation of Student Organization. Not only that, as a matter of fact, the 1979 Iranian revolution that successfully overthrew Pahlavi dynasty as alluded earlier, had inspired Sungkar's[619] radical Islamic movement which interestingly had opposed Shia teachings in 1980s to plan overthrowing the dictator Soeharto from his New Order administration given anti-Islamic policies including the governmental decision to incorporate Javanese mysticism into the Broad Outlines of State Policy, and a decision to establish Pancasila as the only basis for political parties and mass organizations. [620] For some Indonesian radicals, such an imported Islamic interpretation and ideology could be applied in Indonesia albeit long distance and different culture, as they largely believe on universalism of Islam, regardless of

---

[618] www.bbc.com, 14 May 2018
[619] The founder of Jamaah Islamiyah organization, with Abu Bakar Bashir. Sungkar himself relied heavily on the works of Mohammad bin Abdul Wahab, the founder of Saudi Wahhabism. The ideology had influenced him so well that he often criticised the obligation of flag raising ceremony at schools on Mondays and the playing of the national anthem, viewing the practices as idolatrous. In fact, the two figures, following their establishment of Jamaah Islamiyah in Malaysia in 1993 while they were hiding from Soeharto's regime, had returned to Indonesia in 1999. Interestingly with the passage of the time, the group in 1997 divided territorial administration of its operations into 4 divisions called Mantiqi. Mantiqi ula covered Singapore and peninsular Malaysia; Mantiqi Tsani covered the major parts of Indonesia; Mantiqi Tsalis included Mindanao, Sabah, East Kalimantan and parts of Sulawesi, and Mantiqi ukhro encompassed Australia and Papua
[620] Solahudin, The Roots of Terrorism in Indonesia, translated by Dave McRae, Lowy Institute for International Policy, page 6

nations, states, ethnicities, national borders etc. Indonesia has been arguably believed to fulfilling 5 (five) elements which made it for years a fertile ground for spreading radicalism and terrorism, namely sender or ideologue, receiver or potential recruit, message or ideology, channel or medium of the message and methodology of spread, and the influential context. Regrettably, a survey conducted by university researcher Bambang Pranowo in 2011 had shown that almost half of high senior students around Jakarta approved of the use of violence in the name of religion and morality, while in October in the same year, as warned by one senior officer of BNPT (Indonesian National Agency for Combating Terrorism) that top secular universities like University of Indonesia in Depok and Bandung Institute of Technology were experiencing a massive increase in radicalism. Yet however, there was also positive indication as in 2011 a survey conducted in an Jakarta-based non-governmental organization displayed the declining trend of overall support for radicalism which includes attacking places of worship, staging rallies against groups considered enemies of Islam, and supporting or donating funds to any group that promotes violence.[621]

In fact, the radicalism and extremism of Islamic interpretation in Indonesia were not only developed by the Indonesian Sunni majority, but also Shia minority group despite the fact the Shia minority group in Indonesia was not an initiator of any radical movement. Yet the shared mission and vision among them often ignored the significant difference between Sunni and Shia since some of whom were welcoming warmly the outbreak of Iranian Islamic Revolution during the time. For instance, LP3K (the Presantren Express movement founded by Mursalin Dahlan) which relentlessly sought to overthrow the Soeharto regime in 1980s was compelled to make an alliance with Shia group in Malang under the leadership of Habib Husein bin Abu Bakar al-Habshi. As Solahudin noted in his investigative book, Habib once gave a lecture noting that a civil servant salary was illegal because the government obtained revenue from taxes on vices such as gambling, prostitution and alcohol.[622] In addition, the recent outbreak of Iranian Islamic Revolution had prompted several Indonesian students to continue their study in Qom to study Shia religion. One of them was named Ibrahim Jawad (his real name is Krisna Triwibowo) who, after returning to Indonesia, begun to discuss on the importance of maintaining the spirit of Jihad. He often talked on the threat of Zionism and American imperialism against the Islamic world and issues on Christianisation in Indonesia led by Soeharto. As Imam Khomeini had pointed that all political systems in the world but the one under his leadership were illegal, both Indonesian figures, Al-Habshi and Jawad once noted that Islam in Indonesia shall be achieved only by the sword, not through democratic institution. Further al-Habshi urged that Ayatollah Khomeini should be Indonesia's new Imam.[623] Javad himself started to make a bomb in 1984 with the chosen target the mausoleum of Soeharto family member in Yogyakarta, however there was change

---

[621] Kumar Ramakrishna, Islamist Terrorism and Militancy in Indonesia, the Power of Manichean Mindset, Springer, 2015, page 254
[622] Opcit page 119
[623] Ibid page 121

of the plan which was targeting the churches. In January 1985, both figures also started targeting Borobudur temple, the world's largest Buddhist temple, and then Bali island perceived as the manifestation of strong anti-western views. He himself was indicated to have learned how to make bombs while he was in Iran where he received military training alongside his religious education.[624]

It is true that most Indonesians do not demonstrate any interest in the formalization of Islamic state along with its Sharia implementation, yet threats carried out by radically minor groups are likely to haunt their life. Yet it is also right to note that despite becoming more religious and pious evidenced by some surveys conducted by the Centre for Islamic and Social Welfare Studies[625] and the increasing desire to display more manifestations of their faith such as wearing a headscarf and going to mosque, after years of Soeharto's dictatorship,[626] it does not mean that Indonesian Moslems tend to spread violence and simply implement radicalism in the name of Islam within the society. The 2005 PEW poll showing 39 percent of the respondents identified themselves as Muslim in the first, and Indonesian in the second, does not necessarily show that violence and terrorism on behalf of Islamic radical ideology would be automatically justified and condoned by them since, according to William Liddle and Saiful Mujani, the religiosity of the Indonesian Muslims is more reflected on the returning to the traditional Islamic traditions. [627]

In this vein, Zachary Abuza in his book Political Islam and Violence in Indonesia, attempts to be wisely assessing Indonesian Islamist individuals, thus giving preference to distinguish them into three categories : 1) Islamists, who believe that Indonesia should be governed by Islamic law, but who are willing to work through democratic institutions 2) radical Muslim militants, who tend to use violence but only for a limited and defined political outcome 3) Muslim terrorists, who employ indiscriminate violence for revolutionary change. [628] Such a categorizing, will further brings conclusion that terrorists will never pay much attention to the targets, as long as their acts are viewed as the manifestation of ideological interpretation.

In Indonesia, the seeds of terrorism are not only developed by the suspect Pesantrens with their strong salafiya traditions in their educational curricula, but also by Islamic study group, often called Pengajian which sometimes accommodates the extreme

---

[624] Ibid page 122
[625] Interestingly, according to the surveys, the percent of people who pray five times a day or very often was 77 percent in 2001 and 82 percent in 2004. The surveys also (2001-2002) had implied increase support for Islamic governance : 58 percent and 67 percent in 2001 and 2002.
[626] Historically speaking, the large suppression carried out by Soeharto's regime drove the Islamist student groups to carry out the underground Dakwah (Islamic calls) movement in mosques and campuses. Some of which were carried out by the middle eastern universities alumni, including the DDII, Institute for Islamic and Arabic Studies (LIPIA(, the al Irsyad Foundation, Hizbut Tahrir, Khairul Ummah, Muslim Student Organization and Kammi, for further information, please refer to Zachary Abuza, Political Islam and Violence in Indonesia, Routldge Taylor and Francis Group, first published in 2007, page 19
[627] Ibid page 93
[628] Ibid page 84

dakwah (Islamic calls), depending on the individuals who deliver the lectures. The practice joined mainly by curious participants who sought to know on the 'real Islam,' can be carried out in mosques, other public buildings or in private residences. One of the best examples of the deviated function of pengajian was mirrored by the arrest of Aman Abdurrahman, mentor of a Pengajian in Cimanggis, south Jakarta in 2004. He who openly condemned the disagreeing Muslims as infidels and constantly propagating to make Jihad, was graduated from the Arab Saudi-supported LIPIA (Islamic and Arabic Sciences Institutes) in Jakarta. [629] Nevertheless, Jamhari Makruf has noted that in Indonesia, the young men who study science due to its one track mind is more likely to become radical than those studying social science as it would be very easy to manipulate science students.[630]

Apparently, the seeds of extremism and radicalism in Indonesia have grown significantly in recent years in the strategic places where tolerance is supposed to be dominant. Based on recent survey conducted by Rumah kebangsaan (National Home) in collaboration with Dewan Pengawas Perhimpunan Pengembangan Pesantren dan Masyarakat (Monitoring Board of Association for Developing Pesantren and Society) in July 2018, there are 41 of 100 mosques in government institutions in Jakarta which are regrettably indicated to spread radicalism and extremism of Islam covering hatred and negative demeanour to non-Muslim adherents, revival of Islamic Caliphate, and denouncement to women leadership.[631] Not only that, based on a national survey conducted by the Centre of Islamic Studies and Society, Islamic State University in August-September 2018, has shown a very shocking fact that schoolteachers since kindergarten until High Senior School have high intolerant and radical attitudes, which, based on the survey, 56 percent of the teachers don't agree with a non-Muslim to found a religious school in their vicinities, and 33 percent of the surveyed teachers, would agree to encourage the others to take part in fighting to realize an Islamic state based on their version.[632]

Indonesia as a victim of terrorism

In this vein, I would like to summarize briefly the terror incidents that took place in Indonesia.

No		

---

[629] Greg Fealy and Sally White, Expressing Islam, Religious Life and Politics in Indonesia, Institute of Southeast Asian Studies, first published in Singapore in 2008, page 218
[630] Kumar Ramakrishna, Islamist Terrorism and Militancy in Indonesia, the Power of Manichean Mindset, Springer, 2015, page 239
[631] www.liputan6.com, 8 July 2018
[632] Muhammad Nur Rochmi, 18 October 2018, https://beritagar.id/artikel/berita/6-dari-10-guru-punya-sikap-intoleran

1	1981	The hijacking of Indonesian Garuda Airways carried out by the members of Komando Jihad, killed 1 aeroplane crew, 1 army and 3 terrorists
2	1985	Borobudur temple bombing
3	2000	Philippines embassy bombing in Jakarta, August, killed 2 Malaysian embassy bombing in Jakarta, August. No casualty Indonesian Stock Exchange in Jakarta, September, killed 10 Series of bombings in several cities in Christmas eve, killed 16
4	2001	Santa Ana and Huria Kristen Batak Prostestan churches bombings in Jakarta, July killed 5 Atrium Plaza bombing, September. No casualty Kentucky Fried Chicken restaurant bombing in Makassar, October. No casualty Australian school bombing in Jakarta, in November. No casualty
5	2002	Serial bombings of New Year eve in Ayam Bulungan restaurant in Jakarta killed one, and 4 bomb explosions in some churches in Central Sulawesi. No casualty Bali bombing, October, killed 202 mostly Australian tourists. At the meantime, in Philippine's Consulate General in North Sulawesi was bombed. No casualty McDonald's restaurant bombing, December, killed 3
6	2003	The bombing of the compound of the Headquarters of the Indonesian National Police in February, Jakarta. No casualty Soekarno Hatta Airport bombing in April. No casualty JW Marriot Hotel bombing, August. Killed 11
7	2004	Palopo bombing in South Sulawesi in January, killed 4 Australian embassy bombing, September. Killed 5 Immanuel church bombing, in Central Sulawesi. No casualty
8	2005	Two bombings in Ambon in March Tentena market bombing in Central Sulawesi, March, killed 22 Pamulang bombing in June. No casualty Bali Bombing October. Killed 22 Market Bombing in Palu, Central Sulawesi, killed 8
9	2009	Hotel JW Marriot and Ritz Carlton hotel bombings in Jakarta, killed 9
10	2011	Regional police headquarter's mosque in Cirebon, West Java in April killed a terrorist Suicidal bombing of in Kepunten church in Solo, Central Java in September killed a perpetrator
11	2012	Police security post bombing in Solo, Central Java in August. No casualty
12	2013	Regional Police headquarter's mosque bombing in Poso, Central Sulawesi in June. Killed a perpetrator

| | 2016 | Thamrin bombing in Jakarta in January, killed
Suicidal bombing in regional police in Solo, Central Java in July killed a perpetrator
Suicidal bombing in Stasi Santo Yosef church in Medan, North Sumatera in August. No casualty
Oikumene church in Samarinda, east Kalimantan in November killed one
Vihara Budi Dharma bombing in Singkawang, West Kalimantan in November. No casualty |
|---|---|---|
| | 2017 | A pan bomb exploded in East Jakarta in December, killed 3 policemen and 2 perpetrators |
| | 2018 | -Hostage of the members of Mobile Brigade Corps and Special Detachment 88 in the headquarter in Depok, West Java in May, killed 5 policemen and one prisoner
-Serial bombings in 3 churches in Surabaya, East Java including a bombing in Wonocolo apartment in East Java and a bombing in the headquarter of Regional Police in Surabaya, East Java in May, in Surabaya killed 25. The perpetrators were Jamaah Ansharut Daulah (JAD)
- Terrorist attack of the headquarter of Regional Police in Riau in May, killed one police and 4 perpetrators (Jamaah Ansharut Daulah) |

Strategies of Indonesian Government to combat Terrorism

According to AS Hikam, an Indonesian prominent scholar, eradicating terrorism and its roots would be compatible with the goals stipulated evidently in the preamble of 1945 basic constitution. In the preamble, there are four important goals Indonesian will achieve, most importantly is to protect the whole people of Indonesia and the entire homeland of Indonesia. Therefore, in order to accomplish such a goal, Indonesia is obliged to curb and restrict the growing of radical and extremist movements that would harm integrity and unity of Indonesia. In addition, still according to him, Indonesia is also obliged to protect the people from misleading Islamic interpretation.[633]

Many strategies and further steps have been identified and formulated by Indonesian government to prevent terrorist acts from taking place apart from its declaratory forms of condemnation on terrorist brutality, as what was shown by President Megawati's when she severely condemned 9/11 tragedy and then presented Indonesia's willingness to cooperate with the international community to eradicate terrorism.[634] Nevertheless, during

---

[633] Muhammad A.S. Hikam, Deradikalisasi, Peran Masyarakat Sipil Indonesia Membendung Radikalisme, Kompas, 2016, Page 47
[634] Rizal Sukma, Islam in Indonesian Foreign Policy, Routledge Curzon, London and New York, Page 132

the time, its strong commitment on terrorism combating had to face challenge when it reluctantly dealt with the US demand that all countries be taking necessary measures to freeze financial assets of organizations suspected to have sponsored international terrorism to grow much further, in which such an Indonesian reluctance was seen as Indonesian weak commitment in eliminating the case.

However as Sidney Jones, chief researcher of the International Crisis Group in Southeast Asia, further argued that the state made significant inroads toward identifying, prosecuting, and putting on trial those involved in militant (terror) activities. In this vein, she believed that police training was incredibly changed to include matters such as investigation procedures, the organization of prisons, and programs that emphasize on cultural and religious traditions.[635] For the terror incidents in the mid-year of 2018, she further implicitly urged that Indonesia government implement program to monitor jihadist returnees, curb extremist teachings and protect religious minorities.[636]

In this vein SBY' (2004-2014) (Susilo Bambang Yudhoyono) administration has been praised by West for his significant and firm efforts to eradicate terrorism until its deep roots from Indonesian territory. However, such SBY's firm stance was a little bit different from that of former President Megawati Soekarnoputri who looked reluctant to condemn terrorism even the aftermath of Bali bombing in 2002.[637] Therefore In SBY era, some of the prominent terrorists like Azhari, the Malaysian bomb maker, Zuhroni, latest commander of Jamaah Islamiah and Abu Dujana, a former commander were either arrested or killed. However, along with all complements in eradicating terrorism, SBY administration was also criticized for applying dual standard which some of his Ministers have had strong ties with Islamic radical groups in Indonesia.[638]

The effort of de-radicalising the suspect terrorists has been well developed and conducted by the Indonesian police, along with no guaranty of preventing them to do the same things after their release. Even worse, some of them are reported to have used jails to open wider networking of terrorism among the prisoners. As Ken Ward said, the Indonesian police officers are unlikely to be able to bring enough surveillance to prevent the released terrorists from carrying out all terrorism-related measures.[639] Tito Karnavian, senior Indonesian police officer, even acknowledged in June 2010 that Indonesian prisons remain ineffective in countering terrorist indoctrination, in which out of 100 suspected terrorists arrested in 2010 alone, more than a dozen have repeated their acts once they were

---

[635] Mirjam Kunkler and Alfred Stepan, Democratization and Islam in Indonesia, Columbia University Press, New York, page 31
[636] www.nytimes.com, 22 May 2018
[637] Zachary Abuza, Political Islam and Violence in Indonesia, Routldege Taylor & Francis Group, 2007, Page 95
[638] Abdullah Ubaid & Mohammad Bakir, Nasionalisme dan Islam Nusantara, Kompas, 2015, page 40
[639] Greg Fealy and Sally White, Expressing Islam, Religious Life and Politics in Indonesia, Institute of Southeast Asian Studies, first published in Singapore in 2008, page 213

released.⁶⁴⁰ The country's poor legal system was to be complained as rather creating Indonesia as a haven for terrorists, including granting the short duration of the imprisonment of the suspect terrorist prisoners.

However, according to Zachary Abuza, the most dangerous aspect would be embodied if the NU and Muhammadiyah, the largest Islamic mass-organizations in Indonesia seem reluctant to perceive the threat terrorism carried out by Islamic militant movements as they did to the bombing incidents between 9/11 tragedy and Bali Bombing.⁶⁴¹ In addition, Indonesian government has always emphasized on the importance of mutual cooperation among moderate clerics, NGOs and former militants to eradicate terrorism roots, as well as instilling much awareness of information flows which seem no longer possible to be controlled by the government.

In order to display strong commitment in eradicating terrorism and radicalism, Indonesian government in July 2010, under the Presidential Regulation, the National Counter-Terrorism Agency or BNPT was established which aims at formulating policy, strategy, and national programs in the field of counter-terrorism, coordinating relevant agencies in implementing policies in counter-terrorism, and establishing task forces comprising elements from relevant government agencies in accordance with their respective responsibility, function and authority.⁶⁴² Six years prior to BNPT establishment, Special Detachment 88 or Densus 88 which is part of the Indonesian Police Force that has a specific aim at carrying out counter terrorism was established. As a matter of fact, Densus 88 was formed after the 2002 Bali Bombing and succeeded significantly to curb the Jihadi terrorist cells linked to Jamaah Islamiah group including the shooting of Azahari Husin and Noordin Mohammad Top, two Malaysian figures of the prominent terrorists. Some years ago, BNPT has also established the Forum for Communication and Terrorism Prevention (FKPT) in each province that aims at preventing and curbing radicalism and extremism in the society. The forum is well known of being effective to socializing the counter terrorism programs and giving understanding on the danger of terrorism to the grass roots of the society.

Not only that, due its wide array of success stories in eradicating and annihilating terrorism, BNPT is well known for establishing many progressive bilateral cooperation with other countries, including ASEAN and European countries, that also includes strengthening intelligence function with other countries such as Turkey to monitor Indonesians suspected mainly to join ISIS.⁶⁴³ Not only that, BNPT has also participated in efforts on counter

---

⁶⁴⁰ Kumar Ramakrishna, Islamist Terrorism and Militancy in Indonesia, the Power of Manichean Mindset, Springer, 2015, page 242
⁶⁴¹ Zachary Abuza, Political Islam and Violence in Indonesia, Routldege Taylor & Francis Group, 2007, Page 97
⁶⁴² Recent days since May 2016 the position of BNPT has been strengthened through revision of the law number 15 year 2003, stipulating that the institution nowadays is under the law, not Presidential Regulation, m.republika.co.id, Ini Peran dan Tugas Baru BNPT Usai Revisi UU Terorisme, 25 May 2018
⁶⁴³ Muhammad A.S. Hikam, Deradikalisasi, Peran Masyarakat Sipil Indonesia Membendung Radikalisme, Kompas, 2016, Page 24

terrorism at regional and international levels such as its participation in the UN' conference on Preventing Violent Extremism National Action Plans: Supporting Whole-of-Society Responses to Violent Extremism, 29 June 2018.[644] Indonesian police and army alike have regularly participated in the American programs such as Anti-Terrorism Assistance (ATA) under the Bureau of Diplomatic Security of US and Regional Defence Combating Terrorism Fellowship Program (CTFP) under the Department of Defence of US.

In addition, Indonesia, in cooperation with Australia that regularly provides it with financial assistance, has established in 2004 in Semarang city a very sophisticated international training centre for investigation named Jakarta Centre Law Enforcement Cooperation (JCLEC) that aims at enhancing capacity and ability of law enforcement institutions or individuals in handling the trans-border and trans-national crimes including global terrorism and international security. It is well informed that over 46 states have established cooperation with the centre that regularly holds numerous trainings focusing on intelligence, management, and investigation and forensic.[645]

In multilateral level, Indonesian foreign policy as a reflection of its domestic interest with regard to counter terrorism, has also been geared toward support UN's efforts in the field of counter terrorism, inter alia its support on the establishment of Counter Terrorism Committee based on UN Security Council No.1373 no 2001, which accordingly Indonesia shall convey a annual report on its commitment of eradicating terrorism at home. In addition, Indonesia has already ratified 8 of 16 international conventions and protocols in the issue of terrorism. Indonesia has proven to have actively addressed the solutions on the issue, including emphasizing on soft power approach, and accentuating on terrorism roots eradication as the best effective mechanism.[646] In 2010, Indonesia hosted a workshop on the Regional Implementation of the UN Global Counter-Terrorism Strategy in Southeast Asia in cooperation with UN Counter Terrorism Implementation Task Force. In this vein, Indonesia is reported to have various regional workshops and international conferences involving multiple countries in the fields of information exchange and good practices, and strengthen international cooperation in tackling the issue of Foreign Terrorist Fighters. Furthermore, in Asian Africa conference held in Jakarta 22-23 April 2015, President Jokowi call explicitly all the participating countries to eliminate radical ISIS terrorist group. [647]

Thanks to its incessant diplomatic efforts, in 2015 Indonesia has been excluded by the FATF from the list of the states with strategic weakness in the regime of anti money laundering and eradication of financial flows to terrorism. Furthermore, Indonesia through Indonesian Financial Transaction Reports and Analysis Centre has signed MoU with Financial

---

[644] www.bnpt.go.id,
[645] M.detik.com, 21 November 2010
[646] Ganewati Wuryandari, Indonesian Foreign Policy in Dealing With International Terrorism Issue, Indonesian Institute of Sciences, 2014 page 72
[647] Muhammad A.S. Hikam, Deradikalisasi, Peran Masyarakat Sipil Indonesia Membendung Radikalisme, Kompas, 2016, Page 24

Intelligence Unit from 48 states to consolidate countering money laundering and terrorism finance. In sum, Indonesia has already had a list of terrorist suspects and terrorist organization based on the list of sanctions for Al-Qaeda and Taliban organizations in asset freezing.[648]

Last but not least, in February 2018 in Jakarta, a meeting between former terrorist prisoners and terror victims was held to promote reconciliation and dismiss vengeance as well as erase trauma of the victims. Such an agenda is arguably seen as the first ever held in Indonesia, even in the world and an essential soft power manifestation of de-radicalisation of one of the most successful countries in terrorism eradication. [649]

Concerning the anti terrorism law issued and ratified in 2003,[650] after long debates among the Indonesian high officials to make revision to the law since February 2016 that also prompted President's threat to be issuing a governmental regulation replacing the law, finally in 25 May 2018, the mentioned law has been revised and ratified. The revised law would give broader scope in defining terrorism and more importantly legal justification for Indonesian national police to arrest both members and recruiters of terrorist group, and individuals who participate in terrorism training both at home and abroad. Most startlingly, the new law also stipulates that any terrorist who involves children in operating his agenda, the sentence would be added one third.[651]

---

[648] www.kemlu.go.id
[649] www.goodnewsfromindonesia.id, 1 March 2018
[650] In fact, besides the aforementioned law, there are some laws related implicitly to terrorism eradication in Indonesia such as the law number 34/2004 that gives an authority to the national military to dealing with any existential threats taken by non state actors to the state; the law number 3/2002 on national defence; the law number 17/2013 on banning any social organization to take non-Pancasila ideology
[651] Nasional.kompas.com, 26 May 2018

V. Soft Power of Saudi Arabia, Iran and Indonesia

The Importance of Soft Power

Soft power constitutes a concept commonly used by states to impose their leverage to the others by exerting softer approaches. The concept, developed for years by Joseph Ney, stresses on exploiting cultural and ideological mechanisms, rather than taking military and sanction options simply called hard power, to give influence to a target state behaviour and policy.[652] Soft power is not limited only to ability of persuasion the others, but also more broadly, ability to render self-attraction that would yield a result of approval from the target without any objection, meaning that a country can exert its own potentialities and modalities a target may not have, such as enormous natural sources, diverse cultures and traditions, geographic location, etc in order to create attraction that aims to influence the target to act as what that influential country wants.[653] Soft power often constitutes an overriding pillar of a state's foreign policy when seen that political and diplomatic approaches, not military one, are the best solution in dealing with a wide array of burgeoning issues, as Manmohan Singh former Indian Prime Minister has ever underscored that the Indian influence across much of Asia has been one of culture, language, religion, ideas and values, not of bloody conquest.[654]

In the case of Indonesia, soft power would accommodate obviously all components of the nation with its diverse religions, cultures and traditions, in which the philosophy of Bhineka Tunggal Ika (unity in diversity) has to widely inspire identifying the state's super power. In developing its bilateral and multilateral cooperation, Indonesian government often gives emphasis on its widely diverse potentialities of national background and identity as the best means and tools to affect other states' behaviours. Given its constant designation as the third largest democratic state in the world, Indonesia would bring responsibility to accommodate and absorb all interests of both majority and minority groups impartially. Yet however, an assumption emerges that Indonesian government is unable to deny the reality that roughly 90 percent of its people are Muslims, thus attempting at accommodating the majority's voices before international community. Interestingly in Indonesia such a reality does not necessarily stir jealousy and marginalized feelings among the minority groups who apparently became more aware of the significance of togetherness and unity in diversity. This is due to that the country would try to listen to their basic

---

[652] www.publicdiplomacy.wkia.com
[653] Joseph S. Nye Jr, The Benefits of Soft Power, Harvard Business School, www.hbswk.hbs.edu
[654] www.kemlu.go.id, 11 August 2006

aspirations, then applying them as an impartial policy, like what President Abdurrahman Wahid has once done to Chinese ethnic minority group in Indonesia. In the other hand, becoming a democratic and more open society has been also followed by its own ramifications particularly relating to the significant arising of several radical Islam movements coupled with their diverse goals such as the establishment of an Islamic state and the total application of Islamic law (Sharia).

As frequently elaborated before, given the fact that its basic constitution has not explicitly stipulated Islam as the official religion and legal source, Indonesia would have more room to express and pursue its foreign policy based on its national interest instead of Islamic and Muslims interests. For instance, Indonesia will not necessarily put priority to establish more cordial relations with Muslim countries, chiefly in economic field. The constitution won't behove it to play significant roles only in the domains of Muslim states. Moreover, in many international forums, Indonesia will feel free to present its cultural and traditional diversity to other nations, without being obliged to present Islamic values. Such pluralism and diversity, ostensibly secular, have been underpinning vigorously Indonesian foreign policy takings, presented proudly as paramount weapon and efficacious element to alter one state's vantage points. The principle of pluralism itself has been practiced deeply by the Indonesia's founding fathers since it had entered decolonization period in 1940s. During the time, Jakarta Charter had failed to adopt Sharia as state Ideology as a result of 'a bitter' compromise among the members. However, once again it can be argued that Islam as a long- believed religion of most Indonesians has never been ignored its importance by the government, particularly in the wake of Reformation age following President Suharto's collapse in 1998. The government would be unable to overlook the reality that the country consists of the vast majority of moderate Muslims. Therefore unsurprisingly, by considering Islam as an inseparable identity of Indonesian society, the third Congress of Indonesian Muslims that involved Indonesian Islamic preachers and scholars has been rekindled and reinvigorated held once within five years in 1998 after many years of stagnation since Indonesian Republic's independence.[655]

In this vein, Indonesia would be proud in presenting and promoting moderate Islam upheld by most Indonesians to the world community. Indonesia does realize that Islamic moderation and middle path could be an effective means to counter radicalism and extremism of Islamic interpretation that may lead into the creation of global terrorism. The country always believes that implementing and applying moderate Islam in daily could be an undeniably important tool to fortify the society from any existential threat of disintegration and disunity created by separatists who seem to disapprove of Sharia law implementation in the multicultural society. Unsurprisingly Indonesia seems enthusiastic to host and take part in various agenda at home and abroad regarding interfaith dialogues such as its hosting of Asia Pacific Regional Interfaith Dialogues, International Conference on Islamic Scholars

---

[655] Agung Sasongko, 20 April 2018, https://www.republika.co.id/berita/dunia-islam/islam-nusantara/18/04/20/p7h4qu313-catatan-sejarah-kongres-umat-islam-indonesia

and the New Asia Africa Strategic Partnership (NAASP).[656] To date, since 2014 Indonesia has convened Interfaith Dialogue with more than 25 countries in the world, with aims at giving much understanding and knowledge on Islamic moderate religiosity within Indonesian society.[657] In addition, for the first time in April 2018 Indonesian government has initiated to send dozens of its young diplomats to give more knowledge on moderate Islam to be later promoted in international diplomacy, to one of the most well-known Islamic boarding school, Pesantren Gontor in East Java.[658] In recent months, Indonesia has also succeeded to hold high level consultation of moderate Islam (*Wasthiyah*) in May 2018 in Bogor town, attended by 100 ulema and scholars from many countries that produced a Bogor Message, emphasizing on that Islamic moderateness is not only a solution for world civilization but also a reminder so that they will not deviate from moderate Islam in dealing with a wide array of global issues.[659] Not only that, in order to promote more deeply on moderate Islam, Indonesia had successfully hosted the Trilateral Ulema Conference at Bogor palace involving Indonesian, Afghan and Pakistani clerics, roughly five months following President Jokowi's official visit to Afghanistan in January 2018 which he met with Ashraf Ghani, President of Afghanistan.[660]

However, Indonesia still views that the aforementioned efforts to promote moderate Islam to the world are not sufficient. Little wonder, the country would own its huge ambition to be *qiblat* or centre of Islamic moderation that could attract students of the world to continue their Islamic studies in Indonesia. In this regard, Indonesia wants to affirm implicitly that the country would be the only alternative that offers open-minded, not rigid Islamic studies to the world. Among the efforts is by establishing International Islamic University in West Java, Indonesia, along with tremendous budget allocation, simply attesting that Indonesia has further expectation to be a stage centre for Islamic civilization study and research of the world.[661] However, such an Indonesian effort to promote moderate Islam to the world by establishing the university would be seemingly far less budget than what Saudi Arabia and Iran have been conducting to promote both Wahhabism and Shia to the Muslim's world, given many factors including lack of human and financial resources.

With regard to the above facts, Indonesia seemingly sought to counter various ensuing allegations that Islamic teaching is affiliated with radicalism and extremism, thus

---

[656] M.detik.com, 17 January 2011
[657] www.kemlu.go.id, 28 October 2014
[658] Elik Susanto, 12 April 2018, https://nasional.tempo.co/read/1078948/47-diplomat-kementerian-luar-negeri-nyantri-di-pondok-gontor
[659] Yusril Wijanarko, 1 May 2018, http://www.pikiran-rakyat.com/nasional/2018/05/01/ktt-islam-moderat-dari-bogor-untuk-dunia-423667
[660] Rizal Bomantama, 14 July 2018 http://www.tribunnews.com/internasional/2018/07/14/jadi-tuan-rumah-pertemuan-trilateral-indonesia-diundang-hadiri-forum-icg-di-azerbaijan

[661] Maulandy Rizky Bayu Kencana, 6 June 2018, https://www.liputan6.com/bisnis/read/3551088/dibangun-universitas-islam-internasional-indonesia-telan-biaya-rp-35-triliun

inspiring terror acts and spreading fears and worries in the globe. In other words, Indonesia would ostensibly expect to become a reliable bridge between extremism militancy and secularism which negates altogether the role of religions in human being's aspects. Therefore, with the passage of time, due to significant effort given by Indonesian government along with its national endorsement, international community has begun to acknowledge that Indonesia has been main leading state for Islamic moderation and flexibility, enabling to adapt greatly with all dynamics.

Unlike Indonesia, Arab Saudi and Iran with their own explicit Islamic basic constitutions that believe on universalism and trans- border tenets of the sects (Wahhabi and Shia) are profoundly obliged to spread their Islamic interpretations to the rest of the world. There are unique principles and values beyond the goals of national interest achievement that lead Saudi Arabia and Iran to constantly pursue as a part of their religious duty and responsibility to create a better world based on their respective interpretations to the religion. For both states, such unique interpretations shall not be consumed only by the local citizens, but also all nations of the world, which that true and real Islam that both states invariably portray, must be adopted by other states in order to gain everlasting happiness in this world and hereafter. Both countries, as usual, have much self confidence, apart from their unrelenting claims as leading states for Islamic world, that their lands have become the centres for Islamic studying. In this vein, Iran aggressively and intensively, along with its Shia rivalry with Najaf institution led by Ayatollah Ali Sistani seen as a pure, non-political, Shia institution, introduces itself as another *Ummul Quro* (mother of the villages, mostly refer to Mecca) for Islamic world that should be followed.

Besides, the spread of the doctrines would not be affected by political dynamics at home which whoever of the Kings for Saudi Arabia and Presidents for Iran is ruling, propagating and promulgating the ideologies would be resumed. The situation is also the same with Indonesia that it will keep promoting Islamic moderation to the international audience despite its understanding that moderate Islam as antithesis for Islamic radicalism and extremism would no longer bring an unique character, and is universally accepted and also voiced by most countries of the world.

Historically speaking in the early years of its spread, Wahhabism was limited only to the society who dwindled in the already conquered lands of Arab peninsula. However, according to Salam Hawa, Wahhabism has its own tacit goal which is recreating an Arab Empire in the name of one God, thus making its loyalists to expand the doctrine beyond the Kingdom's current borders.[662] Yet, with the passage of time, the Wahhabism supported by abundant oil income to the Kingdom, has been spread considerably to outside Saudi border and territory for achieving two goals, purification of rampantly deviated Islam and counterweighing and curtailing aggressiveness of Iranian Shia influence in the globe that may threat Saudi's position in front of the international Muslim community.

---

[662] Salam Hawa, The Erasure of Arab Political Identity, Colonialism and Violence, Routledge, 2017, page 168

In the other hand, disseminating and propagating Shia ideology and value throughout the world has been considered as both religious and moral responsibilities and duties as well as logic repercussion of a newly founded Islamic state. As a country which holds constantly self claim of representing Imam Mahdi by its founding father, no wonder, Iran would take the unique principles of revolution export as the most essential of its foreign policy of all the time. In this vein, Iranian regime has always hoped that Shia could be accepted by world's Moslems as the best alternative of all, thus making easier for it to insert revolutionary ideas and principles to their minds. Interestingly, with Iran deeply realizing that most world Muslims are not Shia, but Sunni, in promoting and propagating such agenda, Iran will not take and pursue sectarian issues in its rhetoric in a bid to attract their eagerness to follow such an ideology.

It is hardly shocking that in order to achieve their sacred goals, the two governments would definitely apply soft power concept to draw Muslim nations' attentions to accept and follow sincerely such an interpretation of the two teachings. For Wahhabi clerics with their specific authority to identify and determine educational curricula and develop Wahhabi principles at home,[663] the spread of Wahhabi throughout the world shall be endorsed financially and facilitated by the elite rulers since they have been fully aware that their unique interpretation of Islam would surprise vehemently the target countries that may view it weird. It is open secret that the intense and uncontrolled penetration of Wahabbism could radicalize minds of the society, thus generating horizontal conflicts and clashes, as evidently shown by a historical fact that rigid Wahhabism succeeded to dramatically change the natures of moderate and tolerant Hejazi of Mecca and Medina, when it was conquered in 1920s by the Saudi leader,[664] even triggering Indonesian traditionalist ulemas to create a Hejazi Committee in January 1926 with aims at among other things persuading the King Ibnu Saud to rekindle freedom of religions of other four Islamic sects (Hanafi, Maliki, Shefe'i and Hambali), apart from Wahabi faith.[665]

Yet Saudi government seemingly insists to become the leading state for Arab and Islamic worlds by using the ideology to influence the international community's behaviours. For Saudi, such attempt at spreading the ideology would automatically at least disprove and diminish allegations of human right abuses to the kingdom often imposed by western countries through its proclamation that the ideology instead would encourage the enforcement of human rights,[666] as Islam would respect and endorse the human right issues to be implemented.

As time went on, soft power of Saudi diplomacy ostensibly can't be separated from the achievement of Wahhabi goals, that the root of such a beneficial collaboration dates

---

[663] Sarah N.Stern, Saudi Arabia and the Global Islamic Terrorist Network, palgrave macmillan, page13
[664] John R. Bradley, Saudi Arabia Exposed, Inside a Kingdom in Crisis, Palgrave Macmillan, 2005, page 5
[665] www.nu.or.id
[666] Tim Niblock, Saudi Arabia, Power, Legitimicay and Survival, Routledge Taylor and Francis Group, 2006, Page 112

back to the history of first Saudi establishment in 18th century when Mohammad bin Abdul Wahab, the founder of Wahhabism, was in desperate need of the political role played by Mohamad bin Saud to help spread a newly interpreted Islam of Wahhabism to local citizens in Arabian peninsula he just conquered. Furthermore before the modern Saudi was established in 1932, in 1917 King Abdul Aziz is reported to have ordered printing the Abdul Wahab books regarding the basic educations on faith, three pillars and the proofs, imported from India to be disseminated inside the region. [667] In turn, in order to promote and spread such a ideology any Muslim making hajj in Mecca could be given a free copy of fatwas on Islamic duties including pilgrimage, prayer and fasting and Islamic ethics of visiting Prophet's tomb in Medina in a right way based on Wahhabi clerical interpretation since Wahhabism believes that most growing practices of Muslims relating to tomb visit is misleading.[668] However, the first history of Wahhabi expansionism, coupled with the King's ambition to expand its power by annexing multiple territories within Arab peninsula, was rife with bloodshed and anarchy, as shown well by massacre tragedy taking place in Hejaz, Asir and eastern part of Saudi where many Shia minority group resided. Such a horrible fact is also confirmed by a historian, Said K. Aburish who even claimed that no fewer than 400.000 people were slaughtered during the establishment years of the Saudi state. [669]

Iran may apply the same practices and strategies as much as Saudi does, particularly when both states impose a long running psychological war with each other in a bid to draw more sympathy from Muslim nations. Despite strong commitment from Iranian elite rulers not to interfering internal affairs of one country, it does not mean that Iran has to cease the entire undertakings of exporting the revolutionary principles without direct guidelines of Imam Khomeini. Imam Khomeini alone had once underscored explicitly that the revolution export to other regions shall not be carried out in coercive ways, but through elegant actions and behaviours on the basis of Islamic tenets,[670] although practically the Imam Khomeini's advice has not affected his successor (Ayatollah Ali Khamene'i) to take more rational measures in accomplishing the objective.

In result, according to Hoover Institution, in spreading propaganda abroad, Iran has to adjust its own strategies to the target audience, including by taking into consideration their backdrops, traditions, languages, religions, etc. For instance, if the targets are Islamists, Iran has to present itself as a model of the sole Islamic state on the earth that succeeded to combine religion and politics. On other hand, if the targets are secular groups, Iran would automatically present itself as a friendly state which massively calls on the resistance against Sunni Radical Takfiri groups. [671] For Iran, as elucidated by Mahmood

---

[667] Robert Lacey, Kerajaan Petrodollar Saudi Arabia, Pustaka Jaya, 1986, page 183
[668] Madawi Al-Rasheed, Constesting the Saudi State, Islamic Voices from a New Generation, Cambridge University Press, page 127
[669] John R. Bradley, Saudi Arabia Exposed, Inside a Kingdom in Crisis, Palgrave Macmillan, 2005, page 9
[670] Ahmad Sadeghi, Genealogy of Iranian Foreign Policy : Identity, Culture and History, the Iranian Journal of International Affairs, IPIS, page 23
[671] www.hoover.org, 12 December 2017

Sariolghalam, an outstanding Iranian professor, that ideological underpinning would shadow Iran's foreign policy related to Islamic culture spreading in which it is totally different from political and economic terrains often overwhelmed with pragmatism.[672]

In other words, triggered by only truth claim of its Shia and Wahhabi teachings and excessive self-confidence, both rulers would be surely allocating their specific budgets mostly stemming from oil income to espouse financially their agenda in abroad with no guaranty that the target community would accept the interpretations. The inappropriateness of Shia and Wahhabi teachings to Islamic principles upheld significantly by the vast majority of the world's Muslim community, has created big hurdles and challenges for both states to re-formulate and re-identify numerous strategies and steps so that the newly unique interpretations are able to be well accepted by the majority. One of the most important steps taken by the countries is to avoid explicitly mentioning Shia and Wahhabi respectively given the fact such a mentioning would draw sensitiveness within the target society.

However naturally speaking, the Kingdom of Saudi Arabia has its own privilege more than Iran does due to the fact, according to Elie Kedourie, an historian, that religion of Islam originates from Arab nation, descended as a God's revelation in Arabic (Qoran and Hadith) to an Arab figure Mohammad Peace be Upon Him, in which 70 percent of whole Arab speakers in the world are Sunnis.[673] Besides, due to the fact that Iran is always associated with Persian nation and language with its ancient Zoroastrian religion, Iran is convincingly not considered to be a place of origin of Islam. Apart from the existing two holy lands as the most visited location for Muslim pilgrims, then it is hardly surprising to acknowledge that Saudi, if compared with Iran and Indonesia, would bear heavier responsibility to introduce Islam extremely keenly to other communities in the rest of the world. Worse, as once stated by Naser Ghobadzadeh, the anti democratic polity blended with revolutionary agenda developed by the Iranian founding fathers has failed to find a home in any one land in the Muslim world. [674]

While giving much effort to popularize their respective Islamic interpretations, both states would try to realize their utmost steps to curb the efforts in global context each other, which ultimately leads them to be enmeshed in more religious rivalry. In fact, such a rivalry has been prompted by the different characteristic of Wahhabism which tremendously instructs Muslims to be obedient and submissive to their rulers so as to guaranty them entering the paradise despite imperfect rulers,[675] whereas Shia with its

---

[672] Christin Marchall, Iran's Persian Gulf Policy, From Khomeini to Khatami, Routledge Curzon Taylor and Francis Group, page 19

[673] Lee Smith, The Strong Horse, Power, Politics, and the Clash of Arab Civilizations, Doubleday, page 44

[674] John L. Esposito, Lily Zubaidah Rahim, Naser Ghobadzadeh, The Politics of Islamism, Diverging Visions and Trajectories, Palgrave Macmillan, 2018, page 58

[675] Karen Elliott House, Saudi Arabia, Its People, Past, Religion, Fault Lines and Future, Alfred A. Knopf, 2012 page 31

revolutionary character would largely advocate its adherents to conduct any resistance and objection to any despotic and oppressive ruler. In addition, with its significant efforts to spread and propagate revolutionary Shia, Iran really hopes that target nations to express their loyalty and submission to the existing Supreme Leader in Iran, making it look more enthusiastic to provide multiple assistances including giving scholarships to those fragile and vulnerable nations as they could be easily to be shaped as revolutionary ones. Meanwhile, Saudi Arab with its agenda to spreading Wahhabi has never expected that target nations demonstrate their loyalty to the royal family since the only aim of Wahhabi is to promote purification of Islamic teachings, that still views the Islamic world is polluted by heretic rituals.

Therefore, little wonder, both states seemingly compete each other in abroad to build religious-spirited infrastructures such as mosques, Islamic schools and universities, Islamic cultural centres; publishing books and pamphlets, bulletins; granting many scholarships to non-citizen students; financing research and book translation into several international languages; establishing charity organizations and media networks; and to some extent also funding several concerned traditions and rituals. As elucidated earlier, it is noteworthy to note that Arab Saudi and Iran would never brand their ideological projects with brands of Shia or Wahhabi that may draw antipathy of the targets. Meaning that they would prefer to use only the word 'Islam' in order to obscure their own hidden agenda amid their full understanding over the sensitiveness of the ideologies all this time.

So there is no exaggerating, unlike hard power approach, rivalry of the both states embodied by soft power approach is hardly felt, bestowing them more opportunities to develop and expand the agenda flexibly with no fear of penetrating other national borders and sovereignty, since their target has been limited only to people's perspective and vantage point. In this vein, Saudi Arabia will not find much difficulty as the country, due to its tremendous dependence on foreign workers, has been a main destination for millions of Muslim foreign expatriates who then return home along with new Wahhabi interpretation, apart from hosting millions of world's pilgrims annually who consist of Muslims with different sects. In addition, Iran as Saudi's most rival, has been also main destination for Muslim pilgrims to visit Mashad city as it hosts the holy shrine of Imam Reza, the eighth Imam of Twelver Shiites. Yet, it is restricted only to Shia Muslim minority.

For Iran and Saudi Arabia, obtaining acknowledgement on their spiritual leadership from Islamic world would be extremely important, mainly to Iran which highly perceives that the ideology it brings and promotes, constitutes the minority ideology which is often viewed not to be compatible theologically with the Sunnite of the vast majority of Muslim nations. Some of the countries even undoubtedly would issue Islamic legal opinion/fatwa on digression of the Shia ideology as Muslim society of those states overtly opposes and rejects Shia more evidently and harshly rather than to Wahhabism. Most sadly, even many Shia prominent clerics oppose and reject such spiritual leadership to be associated with

Iranian Supreme Leader whom they believe to be less capable and eligible in understanding Shia law and jurisprudence.

Therefore, historically speaking, the rampant propagation of Wahhabi has been accentuated significantly by Saudi rulers since 70s and 80s due to increasing threats imposed by atheist communism and secular Arab nationalism as well as Shia propagation massively brought by Iran. The Kingdom had viewed that the three deviated ideas and principles would disrupt the unity of Islamic nations and spawn disintegration of Arab region, thus curbing spill over of such thoughts to the region has constituted Saudi's extra religious duty. Unsurprisingly in facing massive Iranian efforts and fortifying the monarch state structure and its legitimacy before the Muslim nations, King Fahd bin Abdul Aziz in 1980s proudly presenting himself as Custodian of two holy mosques, had initiated more aggressive measures to strengthen Wahhabi's position both at home and abroad by founding a wide range of Islamic infrastructures with a support of billion dollars.[676]

It is undeniable that both Shia and Wahhabi require strong financial support generated significantly by their oil sale, yet it is worth mentioning that if oil revenue no longer supports such an effort to spreading the ideologies, Saudi Arabia is more likely to abandon the effort given the fact that the existence of the Kingdom does not simply hinge on Wahhabi ideology. In contrast, Iran would not cease spreading the ideology as it is already an integral part of Iranian political system, profoundly believing that the revolutionary system shall be the best alternative for the entire world's systems. Even arguably Shia has constituted a national identity of Iranian society, yet Wahhabi is not integral identity for both Saudi government and its society since there is an evident power sharing between royal family and Wahhabi clerics as elaborated in the previous chapter.

In addition, in principle Shia and Wahhabi are a little bit different with each other, which Shia faith appears to be more flexible with all new innovations than a rigid Wahhabi.

---

[676] Denis MacEoin, The hijacking of British Islam, How Extremist literature is subverting mosques in UK, Policy Exchange page 25. In this vein, King Fahd had donated billon dollars to accelerate the founding of mosques and Islamic schools in the rest of the world. For instance, between 1982 and 2001, around 1500 mosques, 200 cultural centres, 202 universities, 2000 schools, were founded with Saudi funding in non-Muslim states. Not only that, many cities and towns such as . New York, Washington, London, Toronto, Paris, Roma, Brussels, Tokyo, Buenos Aires, and many others have received regularly King Fahd's donations. Some Islamic universities also were also built Malaysia, Nigeria. King Fahd academy also was established in Washington, London and Africa. Again reportedly Saudi opened around 2000 schools spread in many countries like US, Canada, UK, France, Russia, German, Swiss, Australia, Belgium, New Zealand, Spain, Austria, Italia, Croatia, Bosnia, Hungary, Afghanistan, Pakistan, Egypt, Palestine, Jordan, Lebanon, Yemen, Japan, Indonesia, South Korea, Thailand, Malaysia, Bangladesh, Burundi, Fiji, Azerbaijan, Kurdistan, Algeria, Nigeria, Chad, Kenya, Cameroon, Senegal, Uganda, Mali, Somalia, Sudan ,Brazil, Eritrea and Djibouti. In European continent alone, several Islamic centres were also founded, such as in Brussels, Geneva, Madrid, London, Edinburgh, Rome, Zagreb, Lisbon, Vienna, Aachen, Munich, Budapest, Malmo and Malaga (King Fahd Islamic Centre)

Yet with the passage of the time, when genuine Shia is used as an ideological revolutionary within a political system, no doubt it would undermine and downgrade such a flexibility as it shall be simply conditioned by the aspiration of the regime.

Ironically in early years following the revolution, despite Iranian regime preference to exert more psychological influence, Iranian intensive Shia propagation to the Middle East region as primary gate for exporting its revolution was undeniably reflected by Imam Khomeini's insistence to resume the nearly one year-ceased military war against Iraq under Saddam Hossein. Imam did believe that the Iraqi leader had represented a despotic and repressive ruler. However, as a matter of fact, Iranian soft power was to be realized rightly after the end of the 8 year Iraq-Iran war and Imam Khomeini's death in June 1989. In this vein, Iranian policy makers have acknowledged accordingly that special budget allocated by the Kingdom to propagate Wahhabism in the entire world would be much more that of Iranian regime. For instance, Saudi would donate its wealth unflinchingly to build a twenty million budgeted mosque in a target state, in contrary to Iran due to its own financial constraints as a calculative result of declining oil income chiefly caused by economic sanction imposition.[677] This fact has been emphasized more by Charles Allen in his book Wahhabism that since 1979, Arab Saudi has spent 70 billion dollars to endorse the Wahhabi propagations. [678]

However, each state and Islamic militant militia organizations that Iran supports well by all means and mechanisms do realise that Iran would not relinquish its revolutionary principles from its foreign policy taking at all. Those Iran's allies if any would understand completely as long as they express and promote revolutionary steps in their agenda framework, Iran would be the most likely to support and endorse their interests. Therefore, they would harness such a fact in a good way to grab a plethora of economic profits and advantages from Iran's wealth and investment. Accordingly, little wonder when Iran faces economic problems at home in tandem with the emerging of more profitable offers from other rival countries like Saudi Arabia, those states and militant organizations would no doubt start to abandon Iran and keep distance from it by decreasing the intensity of relations gradually. In turn, Iran would have another hidden agenda when establishing ties with other states in which if such an agenda is not able to be implemented in the target countries, Iran would decrease the intensity of relations. Howsoever, economic interests and benefits constitute the most prominent factor for any entity or party to establish more cordial relation with Iran. Interestingly this thing has been the most prominent element that is understood by the US to impose multiple economic sanctions to Iran. In the other hand, as frequently intimated before, the Kingdom has no necessity to give much effort to attract alignment and inclination from Muslim countries given the fact that they would be automatically in dire need of conducting Hajj and Umra (lesser hajj) to Mecca and Medina of

---

[677] www.hawzah.net
[678] Denis MacEoin, The hijacking of British Islam, How Extremist literature is subverting mosques in UK, Policy Exchange

the Kingdom, the only reason why Saudi Arabia repeatedly rejects other rival countries' efforts to internationalize hajj affairs.

Propagating and promoting its Shia and revolutionary political agenda have been further generated by Iranian mentality of self portraying as superior nation among others that could be traced back into thousand years ago long before military invasion by the second caliph, Omar bin Khattab in the 7th century to Persian territory under Sasanian empire ruling. An ancient Persian empire that once ruled many parts of the world in addition to outstanding economic and military achievements in Pahlavi Dynasty has embodied extraordinary pride to Iranians, thus giving over self confidence, including founding fathers of Iran who further believe that with Islam, Iran would take over back the ruling and controlling of the world. Furthermore, the Iranian rulers always claim that its religiously-combined political system is the only one on the earth that God would prefer.

Additionally, despite the strict radicalism of its interpretation, Wahhabi is still seen as part of Sunni sect, with Hanbali as its Fiqh reference, in which theologically does not have any difference from that of majority of world Sunni followers. Meanwhile Shia is theologically different from Sunnis which many of those still view its adherents as heretics and even unbelievers. Therefore, apart from the reasons of the politically isolated Iranian position due to significant labelling as sponsor state for terrorism, and the internationally more-welcomed Saudi Arabia, dispatching Wahhabi missionaries to the target states usually would not face any obstacle of permission from local governments if compared with Iranian Shia missionaries, particularly prior to 9/11 tragedy.[679] While the west's more awareness of the fact that Wahhabi is not solely a factor propelling radical groups to spread much terror, Iran still enjoys its internationally negative branding as sponsor state for terrorism.

In practice, the local governments of target states have proven to have rendered considerably restrictions of both Shia and Wahhabi propagations that might lead into security instability and internal chaos, despite their deep understanding that the two states would harness the functions of diplomatic mechanisms to help spread the doctrines to the societies. In this vein, the host governments would exert the whole necessary ways to limit the free movements and latitudes of those propagators, in order not to radicalize the internal situations and snuff out and deconstruct the moderation of Islamic point of view. Most interestingly, in order to anticipate the strict measures taken by the host countries, many of the propagators, by holding diplomatic passports, often exploit diplomatic rights and privileges of immunity to smoothen and obstruct their agenda. Both countries usually rely on prominent roles played by their Religious or Cultural Attaches in the respective embassies to introduce, promulgate, and attract the host society to get familiar with such

---

[679] ibid

ideologies through a wide range of tempting programs including offering a wide range of educational scholarships. [680]

For instance, Malaysian government has been well known for having restricted Shia followers to practice their Shia rituals and traditions, and even since 1996 officially banned Shia propagation in Malaysia, seen to be creating domestic tension and turmoil as well as national disintegration. In Pakistan, Shia gatherings have for quite some time become bombing target perpetuated by militant groups. The burning of Iranian Culture House Library in Lahore, Pakistan in 1997 and the attack of Iranian Cultural House alongside the assassination of its 7 members in Multan, Pakistan in February 1997 have shown that Iranian efforts to spread the agenda would face obstacles and challenges.[681] Much defiance and resistance of Sunni people in North Africa and entire Africa often hamper Iranian hidden agenda undertakings through charity and Islamic activities in those states.[682] [683] In Indonesia in 2012, Indonesia Ulema Council of East Java even issued an fatwa of anti-Shia. Moreover In Bogor in 2016, a town of Indonesia, the Mayor also banned Ashhura festival. Not only that, labelling as Shia is often granted to any anti regime movements, like what took place in Nigeria in which in 1998 the Nigerian government Sani Abacha accused the Muslim Brotherhood leader Sheikh Ibrahim al-Zak Zaki of being a Shia due to his anti government activism. In 90s, in Bahrain the movement requiring reform in the governmental system was accused as Shia.[684] In October 2018, France government has frozen asset of Shia center in France affiliated to Iranian government for six months named Markaze Zahra, with an accusation of promoting terrorism and supporting terrorist organizations like Hamas Palestine and Lebanese Hezbollah organization.[685] Worst, revolutionary Shia continuously propagated and promoted by Iran has been also rejected and opposed tremendously by Shia followers in the globe, most recently showed in September 2018 by chaos and turmoil in Basra city in Iraq whose Shia population opposed vehemently Iranian intervention in Iraq.

Meanwhile for Wahhabi, Muslim civil society including moderate Sunnis has often defied severely the spreading of the sect into the community. Muslims civil society often associate inherently Wahabbism with extremism in Islamic practices. For instance, a very important conference was held for the first time after 50 years of vacuum in Grozny, capital of Chechnya August 2016 attended by around 200 Sunni moderate ulemas, directly

---

[680] Krithika Varagur, 17 January 2017, https://www.voanews.com/a/saudi-arabia-quietly-spreads-its-brand-of-puritanical-islam-in-indonesia-/3679287.html
[681] Vali Kouzehgar Kaleji, Ups and Downs in Irani-Pakistan Ties, jurnal Iranian Review of Foreign Affairs, Volume 2 Nomer 4, winter edition 2012 page 152
[682] Ahmad Majidyar, 8 June 2018, http://www.trackpersia.com/iranian-embassy-algeria-accused-promoting-sectarianism-north-africa/
[683] www.thetower.org
[684] *Vali Nasr, the Shia Revival How Conflicts Within Islam Will Shape the Future, W.W. Norton Company New York London, Page 118*
[685] Faransa tuthleq hamlatan wasiatan liqhasghasafi ajnihati Iran, www.rawabetcenter.com, 2 October 2018

criticizing Wahhabism Salafi Takfiri concept viewed as not part of Sunni world.[686] For many years, Wahhabism has been concern of Central Asian governments that could be an inspiration to Islamist militants in dominating political spheres. In addition, it was also reported that the groups in Egypt, Jordan, Syria, Pakistan, Algeria etc have opposed vigorously the legitimate governments.[687] Western prominent figures such as Bill Maher and Fareed Zakaria once issued their critical statements on dangerous Wahhabi for the world, even Farah pandit, first US diplomat assigned for 80 Muslim states, took conclusion that Saudi has to cease its agenda of Wahhabi spreading that would affect accordingly diplomatic, cultural and economic implications. [688]

Most startlingly, despite much defiance and resistance of local ulemas and Muslim communities due to significant danger it may pose, Islamic world never has officially and overtly issued any fatwa banning Wahhabism, even in several countries well-known of following moderate Islam such as Indonesia and Malaysia.[689] [690]Ulemas are very careful to issue such a fatwa on Wahhabi digression due to affinity of five Islamic and six faith pillars between Wahhabism doctrine and Sunni sects, thus viewing that the doctrine is a part of Sunni world.

Whereas in Indonesia alone, the idea of Wahhabism brought first by some Moslem modernists after they returned from pilgrimage in the 19th century long before the declaration of Indonesia's independence, has created much challenge for the Moslem conservatives to deal with all purification efforts promoted largely by them who begun to denounce some of the religious rituals and practices they viewed as heretics within the community.[691] The Kingdom of Saudi Arabia itself, for almost all Indonesian Islamists who intensively advocate the formalization of Islamic state to Indonesia, is not a ideal model for Islamic states, rather they apparently have referred to some western states as proper model for Islamic states due to their successful stories in joining in the same time between religious plurality, economic welfare and political stability.[692] Furthermore according to Sidney Jones, Director of Institute for Policy Analysis of Conflict in Jakarta, ever believed that Saudi purposely funds anti Shia and Ahmadiyah campaign in Indonesia.[693]

However in nature, Wahhabism as evidently experienced by Saudi Arabia, will not endanger the host government as it remains aloof from any political issues. In this vein,

---

[686] Crescent.icit-digital.org
[687] www.islamicsupremecouncil.org
[688] Scott Shane, 25 August 2016, https://www.nytimes.com/2016/08/26/world/middleeast/saudi-arabia-islam.html
[689] MUI Pusat: Tidak Ada Fatwa Pelarangan Wahhabi Salafi, 5 December 2015 https://www.kiblat.net/2015/12/05/mui-pusat-tidak-ada-fatwa-pelarangan-Wahhabi-salafi/
[690] www.themailyonline.com
[691] Luthfi Assyaukanie, Ideologi Islam dan Utopia, TIga Model Negara Demokrasi di Indoesia, Freedom Institute, first edition, August 2011, page 45
[692] Ibid 83
[693] Scott Shane, 25 August 2016, https://www.nytimes.com/2016/08/26/world/middleeast/saudi-arabia-islam.html

Wahhabism seemingly radicalize only horizontal ties among individuals in the society by giving much effort to purify 'deviated' Islam. In the other hand, revolutionary Shia would apparently radicalize vertical ties between society and its political government. Therefore, apart from the proximity of faith between Wahhabism and Sunni teaching most international Muslims follow, host countries have a little suspicion to the spreading of it, rather than Shia ideology. The radicalizing Wahhabi is more likely to be opposed and rejected by the civil societies of host countries, rather than by governments. Most startlingly, less acceptable Shia is also exacerbated by the weak position of Iran in international arena along with economic sanctions imposed intermittently to the theocratic state, if compared with Saudi Arabia.

Based on a poling carried out by PEW Research Centre in winter 2015 regarding the level of Shia and Wahhabi influences on Middle East's communities obviously developed by Iran and Saudi, shows that Wahhabism dominates 78 percent of Jordanians, Shia only 8 %. In Palestine, Wahhabism affects 51 % of Palestinians, Iran Shia only 34 %. In Turkey, Wahhabism 21 % and Shia 17%. Even in Lebanon where Hezbollah organization mainly exists, Wahhabi gives influence to 48 % of its citizens, more slightly than Shia Iran with 41 %.[694] Not only that, based on a polling conducted by the same research centre in 2015, shows that average world communities do not have good/positive opinions to Iran, including the ones living in Middle East region.[695]

Numerous countries with their full-fledged democracy often do not regard the spread of Wahhabi and Shia within their territories as problems but rather should be restricted as long as their activities are still under the domestic law and regulation corridor which mainly do not prove to radicalize the local citizens. In US alone, there are several Shia Islamic culture and education centres founded in Houston, Maryland, New York, Virginia etc.[696] Moreover in Caribbean and Latin America, there are approximately 80 Iranian culture centres which are affiliated to al-Mostafa University in Qom, Iran.[697]

Nevertheless, based on long standing field observation, the propagations of Wahhabi Salafi carried out by Saudi would face tremendously obstacles by a society with Islam as minority religion. In the target states along with high awareness on terrorism danger and radicalization of thinking, their civil societies, mainly in European Union and US would give their resistance and protest over Saudi undertakings, by imposing significant pressures that Saudi has to revise the violence and extremism nuanced materials it purposely exerts to influence the societies.[698] Yet as time went on, as mentioned earlier, West society has begun realizing that Wahhabism concept constitutes one of many existing radical Islamic

---

[694] For more detail, please see PEW Research Centre, winter edition in 2015
[695] ibid
[696] ISICRG.org
[697] Counterjihad.report.com, 6 April 2015
[698] Denis MacEoin, The hijacking of British Islam, How Extremist literature is subverting mosques in UK, Policy Exchange

thoughts in the world, which it is not fair to associate terror acts with Wahhabism per se. Hind Fraihi, a senior journalist embroiled in numerous researches on terrorism in Europe, came into conclusion that it is extremely hard to relate terrorism acts with Saudi Wahhabism given various factors propelling such actions.[699]

Interestingly, the spread of the ideology to either state often stirred bilateral ties rupture. The concept of revolution export accentuated considerably by Imam Khomeini by the year 1980s, had spawned the resurrection of Saudi Minority Shia group to oppose the repression and discriminative treatment done constantly by the royal family. In the other hand, Iran has also often accused Saudi of having funded Sunni Militant Madrassa (Islamic schools) in Pakistan and Iranian Baluchistan province to propagate actively Wahhabi Salafi ideology within Iran.[700] Not only that, Iran has once accused Saudi Arabia along with UK and Israel of provoking security upheavals in Iranian Khuzestan province in mid-2015, also accused it for being involved in the shooting tragedy in Ahvaz military parade on September 2018 that killed at least 29 and wounded 70 people.

In truth, the success of soft power implementation will depend mainly on financial ability of the states to materialize mechanisms and means of the propagation, including the recruitment of human resources, which help smooth out to gain the payoffs. The credibility and reputation of the states in international arena would also affect the success of soft power approach, in which global communities may assess and evaluate the states' commitments on terrorism combating and their track records. All of these assessments will certainly affect the target governments in allowing such propagated ideologies and concepts to be operated within their sovereign borders.

With the passage of time, not only through founding various Islamic and charity centres and mosques, both states have for years actively played in establishing Satellite based station TV and Radio, newspapers, websites and etc. Public diplomacy among others reflected by establishing such media eventually 'compels' both states to broadcast and publish their propagations as objectively as possible so as not to plunge into false propaganda as public diplomacy shall contains only facts and truths.[701]

In Iran, a burden for cultural identification in abroad would be mainly endured by an organization named Organization of Cultural and Islamic Relations (ICRO) founded in 1995, which is a merged organization among the Department of International Affairs of the Ministry of Islamic Culture and Guidance, the Department of International Affairs of Islamic Propagation Organization, the Secretariat of Ahle Bayt Council, the World Forum Secretariat for Proximity of Islamic Schools and the Council for Dissemination of Persian Language and

---

[699] Scott Shane, 25 August 2016, https://www.nytimes.com/2016/08/26/world/middleeast/saudi-arabia-islam.html
[700] Rasmus Christian Elling, Minorities In Iran, Nationalism and Ethnicity after Khomeini
[701] Anna Tiedeman, Islamic Republic of Iran Broadcasting : Public Diplomacy or Propaganda, the Fletcher School page 5

Literature. ICRO organization constitutes a legal and independent entity affiliated to the Ministry of Islamic Culture and Guidance with direct supervision from Supreme Leader, based on Iranian foreign policy and rules and regulations established by the Iranian basic constitution.[702] Meanwhile, all arrangement and management of Television and radio stations would be greatly monopolized by a state institution named Islamic Republic of Iran Broadcasting (IRIB) in which Supreme Leader has authority to appoint directly its head.

In the other hand in the Kingdom, the duty to deal with Islamic matters, thus propagating them both at home and abroad has been granted to the Ministry of Islamic Affairs, Endowment, Propagation and Guidance along with the Ministry of Education and the Ministry of Higher Education, Senior Ulema Council, High Judiciary Councils and some private enterprises.[703] even within the Senior Ulema Council, there is a board named the General Presidency of Scientific Research with the aims at, among other things, promoting and propagating Wahhabi thoughts, both at home and abroad.[704]

Islam Nusantara (Islam of the Archipelago)

In recent years, amid fully-budgeted religious competition and clash between Iran and Saudi Arabia in attracting sympathy of World's Muslim community, both Indonesian government and its people, particularly NU (Nadhatul Ulama) organization, the largest non-state Muslim organization both in Indonesia and the world, seemed to be self-confident to introduce a new concept called Islam Nusantara (Islam of the Archipelago) to the world.[705] The controversial concept, incredibly introduced by NU organization and long before promoted intensively by one of its charismatic leaders, Abdurrahman Wahid (Gusdur) as the concept of Pribumisasi Islam (indigenisation of Islam) frames an understanding and implementing human's relations and transactions with one another (Muamala) under Islamic legality, as a dialectical result between Islamic sources (al-Qoran and Hadits) and local traditions in archipelagic state of Indonesia (Nusantara), without promoting any hatred and antipathy to other nations and cultures, mainly to Arab Saudi widely known as the birthplace of Islamic civilization.[706]

At the same token, Mostafa Bishri, Indonesian prominent cleric of NU (Nahdatul Ulama), has once affirmed that for the time being the world is looking at carefully to

---

[702] Encro.ir
[703] Denis MacEoin, The hijacking of British Islam, How Extremist literature is subverting mosques in UK, Policy Exchange
[704] Nabil Mouline, The Clerics of Islam Religious Authority And Political Power in Saudi Arabia, Yale University Press page 156
[705] Historically speaking, Islam Nusantara is not a new concept, yet it begun to be popularized by Said Aqil Siradj in a NU agenda in 14 June 2015 in Esteglal mosque in Jakarta. Ever since, this concept came into surface more often and even was the main topic for the most important NU meeting (Muktamar) held in East Java in August 2015 by titling "Cementing Islam Nusantara for Indonesian and World's Civilizations"
[706] www.nu.or.id

Indonesia as Islamic reference and perhaps a new alternative of all sorts of Islamic interpretation, rather than to 'Middle Eastern Islam' which ironically proved for centuries to have galvanized much chaos and instability in the region. He then promulgated that Islam Nusantara would like to give emphasis on peace and harmony, as taught deeply by Wali Songo (nine saints who played initially significant role in spreading Islam in Indonesia) who had called non-Muslim local Javanese citizens not only by oral propagation but also deeds, putting priority to Islamic substances rather than formality.[707] Furthermore, President Joko Widodo defines the concept as Islam which accentuates politeness, good manners and tolerance, while Said Aqil Siradj, current general head of NU, noted that the concept poses a friendly Islamic character, anti-radical, inclusive and tolerant, not Arab's Islam which is often associated with sectarian conflicts and civil war.[708]

According to the concept, many decades ago Islam as a new belief for local Indonesian inhabitants that was introduced and propagated ceaselessly by the nine saints often called the Nine Saints, did not necessarily deconstruct local cultures and dismantle long entrenched traditions of the target local people. Wali Songo had attempted to embrace local traditions by preserving them with gentle and humane approaches, aiming at influencing their behaviours gradually as preparation to accept a new religion of Islam they introduced. Therefore, the substance of Islam slowly yet surely was introduced to these local people unwittingly without any significant opposition. In this vein, furthermore, Nurcholis Majid even argued that the efficient strategy that succeeded in bringing peaceful and tolerant Islam to Indonesia was brought largely in a way to involve esoteric of Islam (Sufi), stronger than the exoteric one.[709] For instance, Wali Songo initiated to harness Wayang Kulit (Javanese puppet theatre art) as an effective means to introduce Islamic theology to the local people, placing gradually Buddha and Hindu cultures. They also inserted slowly Islamic teaching to the narratives of Mahabarata and Ramayana books, very popular among Buddha followers, with a great hope to preventing sudden cultural shock to them.[710] However with the passage of time, the acculturation of Islamic teachings to Javanese ancient and authentic culture had faced numerous challenges by some Javanese who seemed critical of Islam, viewing it as a catastrophic civilisation mistake, evidenced largely by the 1870s three books from priyayi secular families in Kediri. The meant books are Babad Kediri, Suluk Gatholoco and Serat Dermagandhul, underscoring that the true Javanese culture was pre-Islamic, that it had been corrupted by Islam. [711]

---

[707] www.sarkub.com, 19 July 2018
[708] Mohamad Guntur Romli and Ciputat School Team, Islam Kita Islam Nusantara, Ciputat School, first edition February 2016, page 17
[709] Jajat Burhanuddin and Kees van Dijk, Islam in Indonesia, Constrasting Images and Interpretations, Amesterdam University Press, page 41
[710] Al-ma'aref, Islam Nusantara : Studi Epistemologis Dan Kritis, Journal of Studi Keislaman, Volume 15, No 2, December 2015, Page 278
[711] Greg Fealy and Sally White, Expressing Islam, Religious Life and Politics in Indonesia, Institute of Southeast Asian Studies, Singapore, Seng Lee Press Pte Ltd, Page 119

As time went on, Islam Nusantara, as Lukman Saifudin, Indonesian Minister for Religious Affairs, reiterated despite his fear that such a concept would be rather used as mechanism to promote sectarian fragmentation, has become a hot topic in international arena as if the world nowadays is placing Islam in Indonesia as a model for modern Islamic civilization, thus becoming a focus of various discussions of many scholars in European and American universities.[712] Even Saifuddin Abdullah, Malaysian Minister of Foreign Affair during his visit to NU organization in Jakarta last July 2018 was much impressed with the concept of Islam Nusantara that could be a concrete contribution of Islamic tolerant call at international level. [713]

By promoting Islam Nusantara to international community, Indonesia has sought to give implicitly a reactionary stance to Wahhabi and Shia teachings brought by both Saudi Arabia and Iran respectively. In this vein in contrast to Wahhabi teaching which tries to dismantle local cultures and traditions, Islam Nusantara evidently accepts local acculturation that has grown in indigenous society for many centuries such as Tahlilan (zikir and Al-Qor'an verses recital for the dead persons), Selametan (celebration of an important event), Mauludan (celebration of Prophet's birthday), etc. Islam Nusantara, in contrast with revolutionary Shia that tries to undermine national boundaries and sovereignty, has been attempting to emphasize on the importance of nationalism for Muslims. Besides, in contrast to Revolutionary Shia that often provokes the society to carry out resistance to their governments, Islam Nusantara in Indonesian modern history has never required Muslims to express their resistance against their legal governments as the resistance would mean betrayal to the state that was legally founded.[714] More broadly, Islam Nusantara would challenge and question the passive roles played by Middle Eastern clerics to bring reconciliation and mediation to the sectarian feuding parties of the society, unlike the active roles of Indonesian clerics who prove to have given concrete contributions in making peace and stability at home.[715]

Interestingly, as largely highlighted by Guntur Romli, young Moslem scholar from NU organization, the uniqueness of Islam Nusantara will try to curtail the Arabization attempts brought by the Indonesian Islamists as well as to prevent sectarian Shia-Sunni conflicts promoted significantly by Iran and Saudi Arabia in the region from spreading their influences to Indonesia. As a matter of fact that any conflict in the Middle Eastern region would affect the vantage point of Indonesian Muslims, which accordingly, by holding much to Islam Nusantara, Indonesians will not be interested in embroiling themselves in such military

---

[712] Opcit page 20, one of the most outstanding examples for this exhilarating fact is Islam Nusantara concept was welcomed deeply by Muslim community in US who held discussion with Islamic scholars, observers, diplomats and noble society in the head office of UN in New York
[713] Novita Intan, 21 July 2018, https://www.republika.co.id/berita/dunia-islam/islam-nusantara/18/07/21/pc7nef384-pbnu-dan-menlu-malaysia-suarakan-islam-nusantara
[714] Abdullah Ubaid & Mohammad Bakir, Nasionalisme dan Islam Nusantara, Kompas, 2015, page x
[715] Ibid, page 6

conflicts. [716] In this vein furthermore the concept implicitly makes only simple generalization that Islam currently being promoted and developed by those Middle Eastern states is no longer a genuine Islam as it is often associated with violence and brutality shown simply by the ensuing bloody conflicts that take place to date. Under the spectrum of Islam Nusantara, Islam of the Middle East as an authentic and original source of the religion itself has already lost its peaceful contour and reconciliatory character. Yet still weirdly, thousands of the alumni of those Pesantrens which affiliate to NU organization have regularly been sent to study Islam in various universities in Middle East region, mainly al-Azhar University in Egypt.

Not only that, the concept has also given rise to much accusation and allegation at home that Islam Nusantara would further justify for Javanization/localisation to many of the Arabic/Islamic identities as what it was once displayed in reciting Al-Qor'an verses by using Javanese style, in the Presidential palace in May 2015, sparking much debate and controversy among Islamic clerics.

Nevertheless, the moderate face of Islam in Nusantara has to face numerous challenges given by some radical Islamic movements which sprang up largely in the late 1990s in the transitional period after Soeharto's administration collapse in 1998. Bloody Muslim Christian conflicts took place in some parts of Indonesia- mainly in Ambon and Halmahera in Maluku and in Poso in Central Sulawesi that killed thousands of civilians and destructed worship places, forcing some of the citizens to leave out the conflict areas. The emerging of militant Islamic groups such as Laskar Jihad and Laskar Jundullah as well as Islamic Defenders Front (FPI) and Hizbut Tahrir in that period also indirectly re-questioned the essence of moderate Islam that Indonesia has always developed. Regrettably, some of radical Islamic movements are reported to be an effective means used by the government to achieve its own specific goals.

In fact, those radical Islamic minority groups that have existed dating back into the early years of Indonesian independence declaration such as DI/TII (Islamic State/the Army of Islam in Indonesia) in 1950s and Komando Jihad (Jihad Command) in Soeharto's era, could tarnish significantly the pluralism and diversity of Indonesia the majority has been attempting to preserve, as alluded by Robert Hefner, an American anthropologist in 2000, on the growing strength of uncivil Islam and concomitant threat to Indonesia's pluralist Islamic culture. [717] Yet attacking minority religious groups like Shia and Ahmadiya in several areas in Indonesia, sometimes indirectly endorsed by MUI (Indonesian Ulema Council) Fatwa issuing, has already dwarfed the democracy values in Indonesia, and killed gradually the freedom of expression, in addition to the aggressiveness of vigilant FPI members who have been often involved in recent years in destructing places viewed as the resources of the evils. However, the significant rise of the militant radical Islamic movements in

---

[716] Mohamad Guntur Romli and Ciputat School Team, Islam Kita Islam Nusantara, Ciputat School, first edition February 2016, page 73
[717] Greg Fealy and Sally White, Expressing Islam, Religious Life and Politics in Indonesia, Institute of Southeast Asian Studies, Singapore, Seng Lee Press Pte Ltd, Page 1

Indonesia has been an inevitable result of democratization process that requires accommodating the aspirations of all Indonesian segments, which was seemingly restricted under the Soeharto's administration.

For the time being, in fact Islam Nusantara is well promoted solely for domestic consumption. The concept, supposed to entice the attention of the broader international audience, has not been developed yet more deeply by Indonesian policymakers. One of the reasons, the concept is being truly accentuated only by NU organization which once selected the topic of cementing Islam Nusantara towards Indonesian and World's civilizations for its 33th conference in East Java in 2015. In this vein, seemingly the roles of Ministry of Foreign Affairs in collaboration with Ministry of Religious Affairs and Islamic non-state organizations would be very significant to develop and promote the concept to the international community.[718]

Building up Capacity of Foreign Students

Of the most efficacious strategies to achieve the goals of soft power approach is by developing human resources through granting educational scholarships to non-citizens to continue their studies in several Islamic universities in Saudi and Iran. For the hegemonic states like Iran and Saudi Arabia, it seems crucial to create emotional closeness to any foreign student who is interested in continuing his study in these countries, with a significant hope, after returning home, he could promulgate and propagate the certain ideologies within the target societies, as well as give regular reports on the internal conditions so the states would identify and take more strategic steps in promoting their own ideologies. Therefore, to smoothen the agenda, the concerned institutions of the states would usually give complete facilities that support educational systems that students are able to focus only to studying. Such tantalizing offers, mostly given under the framework of bilateral cooperation, often galvanize their passions to decide continuing their study in the countries. Interestingly, the both states, implementing massively the program as an immediate impact of the outbreak of Islamic Iranian Revolution that shook the world, would prefer to give scholarships to those living in the least developed countries or in countries that likely go through worsening political and economic situations. Therefore, it is undeniable, financial consideration is often the most significant factor for a foreign student to grab such an opportunity.

Meanwhile Indonesian government also has been providing scholarships to foreign students, yet however it does not give any emphasis to them to study in specific Islamic universities in Indonesia. In this vein, Indonesian government has done little to promote moderate Islam it is always proud of, through its Islamic universities or any other effective

---

[718] Abdullah Ubaid & Mohammad Bakir, Nasionalisme dan Islam Nusantara, Kompas Publisher , 2015, page 65

means and mechanisms. Therefore in recent years, for the first time Indonesia, due to existing high consciousness of Indonesian stakeholders to disseminating Islamic moderate message to the world that Islam is a religion full of mercy, has planned to build International Islamic University in Depok town, not far from the capital Jakarta. The university would be operated in last 2019, and definitely accept foreign Muslim students to study in six faculties namely Economy, History, Education, Politics, Islamic Study and Islamic Science. [719]

Based on my own observation during my stay in Iran, the average Indonesian students who received fully Iranian governmental scholarships, have come from ordinary or less fortunate families economically. As a matter of fact, they are not necessarily Indonesian Shia followers, but Sunnis who look interested in understanding and exploring Shia theology and jurisprudence in Iran. Although their total number approximately 200 is not as much as in Saudi, yet Iran has ostensibly succeeded to infiltrate its revolutionary ideology -covered Shia teachings to those students.

Therefore, once they finish their studies, they are simply expected to propagate and popularize Iranian revolutionary Shia and Wahhabi ideologies in their respective countries. They are hoped to introduce the uniqueness of such Islamic interpretations to the target societies, and defend totally the 'truth' of the ideologies from any possible objection and opposition. To achieve the coveted goals and considering obstacles and challenges that may emerge, Saudi Arabia and Iran would often support them financially and establish places for them to make further coordination and arrangement for operating. Often, such an existing vehement objection from the target society will prompt them to found small exclusive communities that organize the ideological agenda tacitly.

According Sayyed Mohammad Hoseini, Iranian prominent opposition and a former famous TV actor, Iranian regime would undoubtedly give millions dollars to hire "its agents," regardless of uncertain economic condition.[720] Therefore, due to their significant and central roles in echoing their interests, after coming back home, the graduates would often be empowered by the two states to manage and develop their Islamic institutions in respective countries. In this vein, according to Vali Nasr, expert on Shia modern world, has once highlighted that the International Saudi Islamic Universities progressively built in Malaysia and Pakistan are staffed by men who were trained in the Kingdom.[721]

However it is also no guaranty that the graduates would be willing to make cooperation with the sponsor countries (Saudi Arabia and Iran) to echo the states' interests which include the promotion of Shia and Wahhabi ideologies throughout the world. For Wahhabi alone, the students will not necessarily mean they tend to spread Wahhabism

---

[719] Universitas Islam Indonesia akan dibangun di Depok, begini Konsepnya, 17 December 2017, http://wartakota.tribunnews.com/2017/12/17/universitas-islam-internasional-akan-dibangun-di-depok-begini-konsepnya
[720] Please see his interview in Farsi in 8 February 2018 broadcasted by Kalame TV station
[721] *Vali Nasr, the Shia Revival How Conflicts Within Islam Will Shape the Future, W.W. Norton Company New York London, Page 118*

ideas while returning to their hometowns. In this vein, they could be more radical than they are supposed to become, which according to Stephen Lacroix, Middle East expert, in the 1970s, the Saudi universities were well known of becoming the two centres of attraction and influence : Wahhabism with creed as its bastion and a Muslim Brotherhood which focused on Islamic culture that even covered most other departments, [722] or they could be moderate and often reject to the rigidity of Wahhabism, so they would not eagerly promote and promulgate the ideology in their own states.

Among the Islamic educational institutions well known for granting many scholarships to the foreign students, as follow:

1. **Al-Musthafa University in Qom, Iran**

Under the framework of export revolution concept, Supreme Leader has significantly acknowledged the importance of building several Islamic boarding schools (universities) to educate and train potential human resources so as to bring Iranian revolutionary messages throughout the world. The most effective and long standing educational institution that has been much hoped to accomplish and realize such a valuable aim is Al-Mustafha University in Qom, Iran[723], often called *Hawze Ilmiyah Qom*. The city itself is situated around 150 km from Tehran.

The university previously a traditional Shia seminary school was founded in 2007 with its headquarter in 2007. It has been claimed to having around 50.000 from 122 countries. It was estimated that over 25.000 foreign students have graduated from the university/Hawza.[724] The university also has 170 branches in which 60 are situated in countries such as South Africa, Albania, German, Afghanistan, Indonesia, UK, Uganda, Brazil, Bulgaria, Bangladesh, Burkina Faso, Bosnia Herzegovina, Benin, Pakistan, Tanzania, Thailand, Togo, Denmark, Japan, Ivory Coast, Sweden, Senegal, Syria, Sierra Leon, Iraq, Ghana, Philippines, Kirghizstan, Kazakhstan, Cameroon, Kosovo, Congo Democratic, Comoro, Gambia, Georgia, Guyana, Guinea, Lebanon, Madagascar, Malawi, Malaysia, Mali, Myanmar, Norwegian, Niger, Nigeria and India.

The university has 150 study groups for science and research and 90 scientific institutions with 2500 researchers and 60 libraries of around 500.000 book collection. Additionally, the university is also active in writing and translation, reviewing 12.000 books, 4000 thesis and 200 scientific magazines and journals, 500 school books, and 83 scientific sites. The university also has translated around 35.000 articles into over 20 international languages. Not only that, the university achievements are reflected in publishing books, brochures, bulletins, pamphlets written in various languages such as Persia, Arab, English,

---

[722] Stephane Lacroix, Awakening Islam, the Politics of Religious Dissent in Contemporary Saudi Arabia, translated by George Holoch, Harvard University Press, Cambridge, Massachusetts, London, UK, 2011, page 48
[723] Mehdi Khalji, Nazhme Novin Rouhaniyat Dar Iran, Aida Orient Book, first edition 2010, page 49
[724] www.ar.miu.ac.ir

French, German, Russia, Urdu, Azeri, Turkish Istanbul, Hausa, Sawahili, Benggal, Tajiki etc which later printed and distributed to all of its international publication divisions that lie in Qom, Mashhad, Tehran, Esfahan and abroad like UK, Indonesia, Malaysia, Lebanon, India, Pakistan, Afghanistan, Thailand.[725]

In order to increase research ties and scientific exchanges, the university also intensively holds regular numerous international conferences, research collaborations, scientific visits, international competitions, both at home and abroad, sometimes conducted through collaboration with other countries. The university often invites international researchers to come to Iran to conduct a specific research and broadens the scopes of the cooperation by signing a wide range of MoUs with hundreds of foreign universities and scientific studies. Until now, there are 15 times of international Sheikh Toosi research festival held by the university with it receiving around 4000 scientific articles from global researchers. In this vein, it has succeeded to operate several specialization centres and 220 cultural institutions comprising 40 countries with their own experts, holding about 7000 cultural visits, 5000 cultural and religious ceremonies and 18 international Al-Qor'an and Hadist competitions, etc. Accordingly, the university has created around 2000 Al-Qor'an memorizers, including foreign students.

As mentioned earlier, more than 25.000 non-Iranian students have graduated from the university, who later, albeit not all, manage and supervise Islamic institutions affiliated with the university in their respective countries, often under Iranian embassies' auspice. Until today reportedly there are about 40 alumni association clubs in 40 countries, aiming at coordination and information sharing and experience with other alumni, highly supported by the university that also routinely invites its best alumni around the globe to gather in on a specific location to share the report the actual situations of the target countries, giving recommendations and points of view. All these measures are carried out to create significant improvement in identifying and programming the next steps and strategies.

Therefore, considering the strategic roles played by al-Mustafa university, Ayatollah Sayyed Yousef Thabatabi, representative of the Supreme Leader, once noted that the graduates would have very important roles to spread and propagate Shia and Iranian revolutionary values to the rest of the world, apart from its role to be a golden opportunity to call Sunni followers into Shia. [726]

---

[725] Ibid
[726] Rasanews.ir, 31 January 2015

2. Islamic University of Medina, Saudi Arabia

The university founded by Saudi government through a royal decree in 1961 in Medina city currently has 6000 until 7000 students, another version 12.0000, predominantly foreign students. [727]Unlike university of al-Mustafa in Iran, Medina university receives only male students.[728] No sufficient information regarding the university caused the difficulty to describe comprehensively the university, yet guessed that it routinely provides scholarships for non-Saudi of various states to continue their studies for Bachelor up to doctoral degrees. However, the educational syllabus and curricula have designed on the basis of Salafi interpreted Al-Qor'an and Hadist.[729]

The university, situated near to al-Haram mosque, also constantly holds the national and international levelled conferences which discuss on contemporary polemics. Besides, it routinely publishes 4 times each year scientific journals named Majalate al-Jamiatul Islamiyah. A newsletter is also published to highlight the university's activities at home and abroad, including reports on student's activities and conference holdings, scientific projects and so on.[730]

Some alumni of the university were reported to having strategic positions in governmental and religious institutions scattered in some countries including Indonesia. Meanwhile, fundamentalist followers of Juhayman el-Otaybi, including himself who once conducted bloody occupation of Haram mosque in Mecca in 1979 were well known for having graduated from the university.[731]

3. The Islamic Boarding School (Pesantren)[732] in Indonesia

It has been estimated that for years Pesantrens, estimated to have grown up since 700 years ago, have accepted thousands of foreign students, mostly originating from ASEAN countries like Malaysia, Thailand, Philippines and Myanmar,[733] in which assumedly most of those are not covered by Indonesian government scholarship. Unlike the universities developed by Iran and Saudi with their own revolutionary and theological agenda as mentioned above, Pesantren would have emphasis on creating students, often called santri,

---

[727] www.madinahstudent.co.uk
[728] www.4icu.org
[729] opcit
[730] Enweb.iu.edu.sa
[731] Rachel Bronson, Thicker Than Oil, America's Uneasy Partnership with Saudi Arabia, Oxford University Press, 2006 page 147
[732] A word Pesantren derives from word Santri (religious student), which with us of prefix and suffix Pe and an, pesantren could mean place for many santris (religious students).
[733] Regional.kompas, 10 March 2017

to completely 'humanize' them and equip them with local culture so as to be able to contribute positively to the society where they live. In Indonesia where the vast majority of Pesantren have culturally and ideologically to moderate and inclusive NU (Nahdatul Ulama, largest independent Islamic organization in Indonesia and even in the world with membership of 40 million in 2003),[734] the existence of Pesantren for years has become the most important core for Indonesian Islamic education, invariably associated with simplicity and humbleness.

Historically speaking, the structure and system of today's pesantren dates back into 18th century, yet the first establishment can be traced to the first days of Islamic propagation in Indonesia, mainly in Java Island in which Maulana Malik Ibrahim (died 1419), well known as the first of Wali Songo (nine men generally believed to have introduced Islam in Java island), had exerted deeply mosque and Pesantren to disseminate Islam teaching to local communities who previously believed in animism and dynamism or followed Buddha and Hindu since thousand years.[735] During the time, Pesantren in Java Island had become important destination besides Mecca if possible, for other santris from Sulawesi. Lombok and Kalimantan islands to study Islamic subjects.[736] Pesantren that was developed initially by Indonesian Islamic reformers, according to government reports had significant number of 94.000 students in 1863. At first years of its establishment, many of the students were taught more on reading Al-Qor'an by rote, they were not taught practical subjects, nor Javanese script or literature.[737]

Tellingly the most privilege of Pesantrens' educational system that entices many young people to choose Pesantrens is that the offered educational curriculum does not provide any material advantage, but stresses exemplary in teaching process that constitutes an integral part from Islamic call and propagation (dakwa). In Pesantren, the students would have direct contacts 24 hours with Kyai (clerics) in which under their guidelines,[738] the students, aside learning Islamic studies, would learn many social things that are likely not to be taught in common schools, such as experiencing simple life including gardening and farming that will automatically create solidarity, togetherness and mutual respect among them in facing various social problems. in Pesantren, Santris are taught to be independent of their parents by self- producing financial income In this vein, Lukman Hakim Saifuddin, Indonesian Minister for Religious Affairs even furthermore believes that Pesantren could provide santris with the concept of how to interact with other cultures, thus appreciating and learning about differences and pluralism.

---

[734] As time went on, Pesantren is no longer exclusive for NU, but also many Islamic non state organizations such as Muhammadiyah, Persis, Al-Irsyad which ideologically may be affected slightly by Wahhabi principle, www.al-Khoirot.com, 15 July 2015
[735] www.pontianakpost.co.id, 13 August 2016
[736] ibid
[737] Greg Fealy and Sally White, Expressing Islam, Religious Life and Politics in Indonesia, Institute of Southeast Asian Studies, Singapore, Seng Lee Press Pte Ltd, Page 118
[738] Hariya Toni, Pesantren Sebagai Potensi Pengembangan Dawah Islam, Journal of Dawah dan Komunikasi, Volume 1, no 1, 2016 page 98

According to Azyumardi Azra, Santri has played significant role in reviving and rekindling Islamization tendency that the result could be seen in two last decades. The revival of Indonesian Islamization would be reflected in increasing number of new mosques and other ritual places (like mushalla), growing number of the pilgrims to Arab Saudi, and more establishment of Islamic organizations and institutions like Islamic Bank and Islamic Assurance. [739]

In short words, the function of Pesantren would cover religious, social and educational functions.

In Pesantrens, there are five elements should be fulfilled as follow :

1. Kyai (Cleric), constitutes the most essential element in a Pesantren that functions as founder, manager, leader as well as teacher. All matters and affairs within Pesantren must be affiliated with the Kyai who is regarded as the most charismatic figure one which whose policies and decisions shall be obeyed.
2. Dormitory for santri (students in Pesantren) that functions not only as home but also as location for developing social skills.
3. Mosque, that functions not only for holding prayers, but also teaching process and other Islamic rituals such as Zikir (together prayer citing), Itikaf (staying all night commonly in the last ten days tenth days of Ramadan month) and reading on classical books (kitab Kuning/ yellow book)[740] written by prominent scholars
4. Santri, that could be divided into Santri Muqim, a santri who comes from very distant area that prefers to stay all days in Pesantren, and Santri Kalong, a santri due to its near location, would rather stay in his home, not in Pesantren
5. Classical books reading, that refers to traditional books which contain various Islamic subjects. The books are often called Kitab gundul (bald book) given that most of which have been written without putting any harakat (vowel marks).[741] Accordingly such a fact would create much challenge for a santri to stay years in Pesantren, only to understand the whole contents of the books. [742]

Nowadays, some of Pesantrens in Indonesia are well managed and operated in modern ways which highly attempted to rule out many burgeoning perceptions in society that Pesantren is traditionally old fashioned that could no longer respond to any

---

[739] Azyumardi Azra, Pendidikan Islam, Tradisi and Modernisasi Menuju Millenium Baru, Kalimah Publishing, Jakarta Page 70
[740] The reason why classical books widely used in Indonesian Pesantrens are often called yellow books is due to most of the books were written in papers with yellow colour
[741] www.republika.co.id, 3 March 2018
[742] Ziemak and Mafred, Pesantren Dalam Perubahan Sosial, (Jakarta : P3M 1986) page 157

contemporary issues, a criticism also imposed by Nurcholis Madjid, an Indonesian prominent scholar.[743]

Pesantren and Terrorism

With the passage of time, amid Indonesia's undertakings to eradicate terrorism and its roots, among others by popularizing the role of Pesantren as a symbol of Islamic moderation and making 22 October as Santri day since 2015, regrettably several pesantrens have allegedly supported spreading terrorism by endorsing militancy and radicalism in the curricula albeit not formally. Some pesantrens failed to materialize their goals in humanizing their santris to be more tolerant to religious difference, rather accentuating fundamentalism and extremism foundations within their cultures. Therefore, some santris, instead of introducing moderate Islam they've learned in Pesantren to their societies, are involved deeply in terrorism cases both at home and abroad. Many schools/Pesantren in Indonesia have been transformed heavily into safe haven for radical minded students, in which according a survey arranged by Setara Institute in 2016 revealed that 35,7 of the students displayed a tendency to intolerance in their minds. Although, the survey involved only 760 students in High schools (not Pesantren) in Jakarta and Bandung,[744] yet it is no exaggeration to note that some Pesantrens could be proper places for the extremists to receive radicalized Islamic teachings.

In addition, some of Pesantrens have been also simply alleged to have supplied most of the Jamaah Islamiyah members, which by 2000 alone, the organization operated over twenty schools, whereas many pesantrens were to open in the next years. Among the suspected Pesantrens were al Mukmin in Ngruki central Java, al-Mutaqien school in Jepara, central Java, and Darusshahadah in Boyolali, central Java.[745] In 2011, a tiny Pesantren of Umar bin Khattab in West Nusa Tenggara province is known to have stored bomb ammunition.[746] In those Pesantrens, santris would feel as if they lived in an environment resembling a miniature Islamic government, interpreted rigidly by Salafiya radical movement, indoctrinating them not to view that whole Indonesia is an ideal state. They were asked not to use modern devices like television, and not to practice singing and playing music.[747] In nutshell, the sense of moderate Islam the santris uphold gradually disappeared, replaced by the feeling of making Jihad, given such a rigid practice that was conditioned significantly by the Pesantrens managers and teachers. Even Nur Huda Ismail, Ngruki Pesantren graduate, had once guaranteed that roughly 100 of the 15000 graduates of the

---

[743] Abdullah Ubaid & Mohammad Bakir, Nasionalisme dan Islam Nusantara, Kompas, 2015, page 45
[744] www.jakartapost.com, 18 May 2018
[745] Solahudin, The Roots of Terrorism in Indonesia, translated into English by Dave McRae, Lowy Institute for International Policy, page 161
[746] Abdullah Ubaid & Mohammad Bakir, Nasionalisme dan Islam Nusantara, Kompas, 2015, page 28
[747] Ibid page 162

Pesantren have been involved in terrorism.[748] Nevertheless with the passage of time, such allegation of producing terrorist alumni was denied vehemently by Pesantren al Mukmin, underscoring that there is no specific relation between terrorism act with its own educational curriculum. Even Hamzah Has, Indonesian Vice President, before the Bali Bombing tragedy, had paid visits to the Pesantren to meet with Abu Bakar Bashir, highlighting that the Pesantren does not produce any terrorist, thus challenging the security apparatus to arrest himself instead of Abu Bakar Bashir.[749]

One of the most recent alleged pesantrens was Ibnu Masud in Bogor town, whose a 13 year old santri named Hatf Saiful Rasul is reported to have been killed in Syria by joining ISIS. Moreover Pesantren also has ties with Hari Budiman, a suspect of military training case in Aceh province in 2010. Not only that, according to Reuters, Ibnu Masud pesantren is also associated with 31 terror acts, with it having relations with other terrorists such as Dulmatin, Bali bombing initiator, Dian Juni Kurniadi, Thamrin bombing perpetrator, and Gusti Adam, Samarinda's church bomber.[750]

However, according to Indonesian Ministry of Religious Affairs whose one of its functions in dealing with Pesantren affairs, the total number of radical Pesantren in Indonesia is too few roughly 20 out of total 70.000 pesantrens, in which accordingly the Ministry will not grant the licence to those pesantrens to operate. However, in the meantime the government has no right to impose any sanction given no single law passed, rather asking Indonesian society to have more awareness on the natures of the pesantrens in their areas. Taufik Andre, Indonesian terrorism observer, furthermore believes that emotional approach taken by the Ministry has been proven to be effectively applicable to reduce radicalism and extremism in Pesantrens.[751]

Meanwhile arguably santri terrorists are not merely produced by the extreme curricula of pesantrens, but their militant and violent approaches could be influenced altogether by their experience during their stay in some countries like Afghanistan, Pakistan and even Malaysia and South Philippines mainly Mindanao. The existing direct interaction among those radical Muslims has prompted the exchange of new idea and experience. Besides, they also accept inspiration from several terrorist networks such as Afghanistan veteran network.[752]

In fact, besides the presence of Pesantrens influenced slightly by Wahhabism, commonly affiliated to non NU-Islamic mass organizations which often attack some NU's rituals deemed heretics by them, some of the pesantrens have attempted significantly to

---

[748] Kumar Ramakrishna, Islamist Terrorism and Militancy in Indonesia, the Power of Manichean Mindset, Springer, 2015, page 232
[749] Zachary Abuza, Political Islam and Violence in Indonesia, Routldege Taylor & Francis Group, 2007, Page 96
[750] Abraham Utama, 15 September 2017, https://www.bbc.com/indonesia/indonesia-41268665
[751] Sekitar 20 Pesantren Ajarkan Radikalisme, 28 August 2014,
https://www.bbc.com/indonesia/berita_indonesia/2014/08/140828_kemenag
[752] Bambang Hermanto, MA, Terrorisme and Akar Fundamentalisme Pesantren, page 15

propagate Islamic purity as much as Saudi Wahhabism promulgated. Furthermore, Said Agil Siroj, former head of Nahdhatul Ulama organization implicitly believes that many Pesantrens with Arabic names in Indonesia, and not using local region names where the pesantrens are located, have significant radical and puritan roots which indirectly reject the principles of nationalism. [753]

Generally, the managers and directors of such pesantrens are the alumni of Saudi sponsored Islamic universities such as Islamic University of Medina, Ummul Quro university in Mecca, Ibnu Saud university, LIPIA Jakarta etc, which have been often accused for propagating radicalism and extremism in Indonesia such as their denials to Pancasila, not Islamic Sharia, as basic foundation of the state, and promoting vehemently Jihad anywhere else. Some of the directors/founders even named their pesantrens with radical Islamic figures such as Pesantren Ibnu Taimiyah, Pesantren Abdullah bin Baz (most prominent Saudi cleric) and Pesantren Firqah Najiyah (safe group). [754] Furthermore, Ulil Abshar Abdalla, the liberal Indonesian Muslim scholar, also alumnus of LIPIA, once stated that LIPIA's graduates would adapt an hostile attitude to the local Indonesia culture and Muslim practices, in which, according to Australian scholars Greg Fealy and Anthony Bubalo, LIPIA constitutes the most influential institution in Indonesia that propagates significantly contemporary forms of Wahhabism within Indonesian society.[755]

The Establishment of Non Governmental Organizations

Apart from building the universities, in order to espouse the expansion of Wahhabism ideas to the corners of the world, Saudi has also initiated to establish some non-Governmental Organizations, among others :

1. **Muslim World League**

This non- governmental organization founded in 1961 with its headquarter in Mecca, has main objective of spreading the truth message on Islam. The organization established based on a decision taken during Islamic General Conference has engaged in spreading Islamic calls, explaining Islamic principles and rejecting false allegations made to discredit Islam. It also has opened its office in many countries. However, in the early years of its founding, the organization targeted only immigrant workers in Saudi oil company,[756] to counter the spread of pan Secular Arabism considerably popularized by Egyptian President, Gamal Abdul Nasser and reject atheist communism concept brought mainly by Soviet Union.

---

[753] Abdullah Ubaid & Mohammad Bakir, Nasionalisme dan Islam Nusantara, Kompas, 2015, Page 5
[754] www.al-Khoirot.com, 15 July 2015
[755] Kumar Ramakrishna, Islamist Terrorism and Militancy in Indonesia, the Power of Manichean Mindset, Springer, 2015, page 163
[756] Muslim World League and World Assembly of Muslim Youth, 15 September 2010
http://www.pewforum.org/2010/09/15/muslim-networks-and-movements-in-western-europe-muslim-world-league-and-world-assembly-of-muslim-youth/

The organization founded by Crown Prince Faisal and funded millions of dollars by the Kingdom since its establishment, has given much effort to extend aids to Muslim nations by attempting to solve their own problems and providing reliefs for victims of natural disasters and war under an affiliated organization, called the International Islamic Relief Organization. Not only that, the organization often engages in building various projects in propagation, education and culture sectors. Interestingly, it affirms its rejection on all sorts of violence and rather promotion on dialogue with diversely cultural societies.[757] More interestingly, the organization is not exclusively dominated by Wahhabi clerics, but by those with different Sunni theologies, claimed by Wahhabi as heretics like Ash'ariya, Maturidiya and Tasawuf. Moreover the senior mufti handed over the presidential position in the first meeting of the organization to an Indian Maturidi cleric named Abu al Hasan al-Nadawi.

In implementing and realizing its goals, claimed mainly to promoting tolerance and harmony, the organization often dispatches missionaries to various continents including Africa, Asia, Europe, North and South America to propagate true and humane Islam based on Hanbali traditions, with emphasis on anti violence, terrorism and extremism. Besides, the organization has also engaged in building mosques, schools and centres for cultural and women affairs, as well as giving much undertaking to improve the educational and societal quality of Muslim nations.[758]

Apart from aforementioned above, the organization plays actively its role to improve the function of Islamic mass media as a means for Islamic calls, and to advocate the implementation of Islamic law (Sharia) and organize many events and symposiums, as well as Arabic language learning. In sum, the organization with its observer status in UN ECOSOC (Economic and Social Council), reportedly provides much information on Islam to non-Muslim citizens or those who just converted to Islam.[759]

With the passage of time, to counter many allegations of spreading radicalism and extremism addressed to the organization based on the fact that the head of the organization is being held by Saudi senior cleric whereas its board has been filled by several fundamentalist Abu Ala Maududi sympathizers,[760] the organization often has held conferences on anti terrorism and extremism both at home and abroad such as in New York, London and Pakistan. Interestingly such conferences are regularly held regardless of opposing Muslim European citizens as they seemingly prefer more moderate local Islamic organizations like Muslim UK and European Council for Fatwa and Research. Their opposition to the organization has come into surface as they view that that the organization

---

[757] www.britannica.com
[758] ibid
[759] Muslim World League and World Assembly of Muslim Youth, 15 September 2010
http://www.pewforum.org/2010/09/15/muslim-networks-and-movements-in-western-europe-muslim-world-league-and-world-assembly-of-muslim-youth/
[760] Denis MacEoin, The Hijacking of British Islam, How extremist literature is subverting mosques in the UK, Policy Exchange page 13

could no longer respond to the ongoing challenges and does not represent Islam as a religion of mercy and affection.[761]

Not only that, in order to demonstrate more attention to the efforts of terrorism combating and extremism eradicating, the organization, relying so much on Saudi's funding and other donations, has also announced its vehement support on the publication of 59 figure and institution names issued officially by four Arab states in June 2017 who allegedly have endorsed new terrorism for years, including the most Egyptian prominent Sunni scholar, Dr. Yosef Qardhawi.[762]

However, in order to manifest its goals more broadly, the organization reportedly has established its branch offices such as in Brazil, Spain, Denmark, Geneva, Nigeria, Dutch, Venezuela etc. In Indonesia, the office of the organization is situated in East Jakarta,[763] yet however the organization seemingly has never had willingness to open its branch in Tehran, Iran. In addition, the organization is reported to actively exert social media like Facebook and Twitter to propagate its own vision and missions.[764]

Nevertheless, the organization would not necessarily have responsibility to spread the ideas of Saudi Wahhabism per se. This conclusion was taken as historically speaking, the organization was once controlled by the Ikhwanul Muslimin group in Hejaz in the early years of its establishment.[765] In Indonesian context, the organization, through DDII or Islamic Propagation Council established in 1967 by Indonesian Islamist activists, has routinely granted scholarships to Indonesian students to complete their study in the Middle East. In this vein, DDII, which often operated in numerous social activities as well as Islamic propagation in Indonesia revealed a fused Wahhabi-Islamist or neo-Wahhabi orientation.[766]

2. The World Supreme Council for Mosques

The non-governmental organization was founded through a resolution adopted in the conference on Message of Mosque in Mecca in by September 1975 under the auspice of Muslim World League. This independent organization aims at revitalizing the functions of the mosque as focal point for Islamic activities that resembles that of in prophetic age. In addition, the organization consisting of 40 voluntary members from the globe attempts to protect mosques from any deviated faiths as well as to maintain the sanctity of the mosques in the entire world. Therefore, the organization has several missions, as follows:

---

[761] Opcit
[762] Following the Qatar's blockade by Saudi Arabia, UEA, Bahrain and Egypt in June 2017, www.arabnews.com
[763] En.thewml.org
[764] opcit
[765] Stephane Lacroix, Awakening Islam, the Politics of Religious Dissent in Contemporary Saudi Arabia, translated by George Holoch, Harvard University Press, Cambridge, Massachusetts, London, UK, 2011, page 129
[766] Kumar Ramakrishna, Islamist Terrorism and Militancy in Indonesia, the Power of Manichean Mindset, Springer, 2015, page 162

a. Planning various agenda to revive the mosque function for guiding, educating, propagating
b. Publishing a mosque message periodically in order to find a right mechanism to improve technical ability of prayer Imams and preachers
c. Making surveys comprehensively to the globe's mosques and publishing much information through books and bulletins printing
d. Making selections and assigning qualified preachers to the entire mosques in the globe
e. Holding courses to enrich cultural knowledge for Imams and preachers
f. Forming a board to monitor all affairs of the mosques
g. Understanding ideas and behaviours which contradict Islamic teaching
h. Helping rehabilitate and train Imams and preachers assigned later in order to be able to identify right practices in leading prayers, delivering sermons and studying the religion. [767]

3. World Assembly of Muslim Youth (WAMY)

The WAMY organization founded in 1972 is funded by Saudi government, also relying on donations from Saudi philanthropists. The largest Muslim youth organization has several goals including:

1. Keeping identity of Muslim youth and helping them overcome their own problems while dealing with modern life
2. Educating and training them in order to become active citizens in their respective countries
3. Introducing the pure and genuine Islam to non Muslims as comprehensive way of their life
4. Building up ties with dialogue and mutual understanding and respect
5. Providing assistance to Muslim and non-Muslims to reach the mentioned goals through training and cooperation[768]

In order to reach the mentioned goals, the organization, headquartered in the Kingdom, routinely holds camping for young Muslims domestically and regionally, and help shaping Muslim scout groups. It also publishes books, brochures, reports and other materials containing introduction on Islam to non-Muslims. In addition, the organization affiliated with 500 young Muslims in five continents, has roles of organizing visit exchanges, hajj and Umrah, of providing support and training to Muslim organizations throughout the

---

[767] ibid
[768] www.wamy.co.za

world. The organization is also actively embroiled in many social and educational activities, among other things by granting thousands of scholarships for young Muslims to study in several famous Islamic universities in the world,[769] and establishing orphanages and Islamic schools and mosques, organizing various events to find solutions for humanitarian issues like Afghanistan crisis,[770] in which accordingly the organization has received various awards from several countries and once been appointed by UN as an organization which deals with humanity and relief contribution. Not only that, WAMY also actively participates in many international youth conferences and has established ties with UN organs such as FAO (Food and Agriculture Organization), WFP (World Food Programme), UNHCR (United Nations High Commissioner for Refugees), WHO (World Health Organization) and UNICEF (the United Nation's Children Fund).

As a matter of fact, in order to promote the true Islam to international communities with diverse cultural backgrounds, the organization also often convenes programs involving foreign diplomats in Saudi. For instance, the agenda Annual *Ifthar* Party (breaking Ramadan fast) would be commonly attended by foreign ambassadors and diplomats, businessmen, volunteers, media representatives and etc. In that agenda, the diplomats would be asked kindly to present their vantage points regarding the role of WAMY as a reliable charity organization. The organization that often provides dowry assistance for young Saudis since 1992[771] also routinely holds once in 4 years a large conference with youth related topics, which is usually joined by prominent Muslim scholars. The capital Jakarta[772] was once chosen as a venue for holding the 11th conference from 2 to 4 October 2010 with a topic Youth and Social Responsibility.[773]

The Allegation of WAMY's Involvement in Terrorism Issue

WAMY has obviously claimed that in implementing and accomplishing its vision and mission would put priority to Islamic moderation, anti-extremism and radicalism to Muslim youth. However, like World League Muslim, the organization has been often associated with terrorism and radicalism support in the rest of the world.[774] In Canada for instance, based on an intensive investigation, the organization was well known of having violated the standards of a charity organization and having linkage to some funding organizations of al-

---

[769] www.globalmbwatch.com
[770] In Afghanistan crisis, the organization established collaboration with the UN Food Program under the project called Hospital Feeding, providing food logistic for patients in Afghanistan's hospitals
[771] Mark A Caudill, Twilight in The Kingdom, Understanding the Saudis, Praeger Security International, London, page 4
[772] WAMY also opened its branch office in Jagakarsa area, south Jakarta and actively holds Islamic social activities such as joint fast breaking in Ramadan month, slaughtering animals during the period of Eid ul Adha, donations gathering for orphanages etc
[773] World Assembly of Muslim Youth, Leading Organization for the Distinctive Youth, page 13
[774] IPT News, WAMY Canada Loses Charitable Status, 7 March 2012, https://www.investigativeproject.org/3476/wamy-canada-loses-charitable-status

Qaeda group in the globe. In 2003, Steven Emerson, executive director for investigative project on terrorism, stated that WAMY actively has opened its link to several Jihadist members by granting educational programs, funding and other financial assistances. According to the report, WAMY reportedly had invited Khaled Meshal, head of political affairs, Palestinian Hamas organization as honorary guest in the conference of Muslim Youth and Globalization in 2002 in Riyadh, Saudi, and then granted donation millions of dollars to Hamas in the wake of second Palestinian Intifada since 2000 till 2005.[775]

In sum, still according to the report, Pakistani branch WAMY was also once known for having offered military trainings to Jihadists group in fighting against USSR occupation in Afghanistan, and engaged in many conflicts like Kashmir, Bosnia, Kosovo and South Philippines. Apart from this, WAMY reportedly had issued educational materials full of Jihad and violence endorsement against Jews and other unbelievers, disseminated incessantly in 6 continents. A WAMY document titled 'Military Lessons in the Jihad Against the Tyrants' was ever found in the hands of a 1993 World Trade Centre bombing perpetrator and a two US embassies in Africa bombing perpetrator, named Khalied al-Fawwaz, in his apartment in London. The document affirmed the establishment of a globally Islamic state, formed not by peaceful mechanisms, but by written words and guns. [776]

As a matter of fact, the organization reportedly has funded its students to study in numerous Islamic schools in Pakistan and Arab Saudi, and published books containing much hatred on unbelievers and a Jews discrediting encyclopaedia. In 2004 alone, the organization also reportedly granted donation around $ 200.000 to fund the fighters against US troops in Iraq, in which it had close ties with radical Anshar al-Islam in northern Iraq. Not only that, the organization allegedly flowed its cash to the perpetrators of 9/11 tragedy, in which Dr. Al Badr al-Hamza, a radiologist, whose his credit card was found among the perpetrators, had received fund from WAMY. Based on the report of 9/11 Commission, the organization overtly has supported terrorism under the name of Islam and had allegedly ties with the perpetrators of the tragedy. [777]

Apart from WAMY denials on such baseless allegations, WAMY has affirmed that the organization has already become target for monitoring and auditing carried out by Saudi financial institutions such as Saudi Arabian Monetary Agency (SAMA/ Saudi Central Bank), the Saudi Ministry of Finance, and other committee that is charge on monitoring the cash flows for various charity organizations, which have issued concerned regulations on financial controlling and often involved international auditors to audit their bank accounts. Not only making transparency, WAMY also gives routinely reports to the donators on fund use, in

---

[775] ibid
[776] ibid
[777] World Assembly of Muslim Youth (WAMY), https://www.discoverthenetworks.org/organizations/world-assembly-of-muslim-youth-wamy/

which all financial transactions would be kept in administrational archives along with copies of the cheques.[778]

In Indonesian context, the organization was accused of funding the Islamic Youth Movement in Indonesia, the group that successfully recruited and dispatched 300 members to go to Afghanistan to fight alongside the Taliban against the US attack in 2001 and was suspected for being as a talent scout for Jamaah Islamiah organization.[779]

Establishing and Empowering the functions of Iranian and Saudi Political Lobbies in Abroad

In order to build their positive images politically in international arena, both states are in dire need of establishing and empowering political lobbies in abroad, to help strengthen the function of soft diplomacy. The role of lobby is very important to blow their own leverages to the targeted governmental stakeholders and publics for the sake of the short and long term goals achievement. In US, Iran and Saudi have been well known for years for having established their political and economic lobbyists as an effective mechanism to echo their national interests in abroad. They would allocate millions dollars to exert the functions of their own lobbyists to preserve and maintain their interests by influencing US behaviour.

In recent decades, for Saudi it is extremely vital to maintain and keep its close bilateral relations with USA despite changing presidency and administration. On the other hand, for Iran, the role played by its lobby in Washington is of great importance to prevent re-imposing economic sanctions and materializing military threats by USA government which inevitably will harm Iranian interests. Nevertheless such an economic sanction lifting would be expected automatically to attracting foreign investors to invest their wealth in Iranian territory.

In fact, Arab Saudi reportedly has paid significant price for hiring non-Saudi lawyers, firms, professionals who conduct political approaches, by exerting their own leverage, to the concerned US government. For instance, in 2015 Arab Saudi had hired lobbyist firms such Podesta Group, BGR Government Affairs, DLA Piper and Pilssbury Winthrop to carry out much coordination of meetings between Saudi officials and US business and media leaders and to make promotion on Saudi domestic economy to numerous potential investors, as well as to arrange public policy generally and give legal advices to Saudi ambassador along

---

[778] World Assembly of Muslim Youth, Leading Organization for the Distinctive Youth, page 20
[779] Zachary Abuza, Political Islam and Violence in Indonesia, Routldge Taylor and Francis Group, first published in 2007, page 72

with the embassy in Washington. Not only that, the lobbyists would have functions to assist Saudi embassy to enhance its ties with US in security terrains. Even furthermore, some of them would be assigned to formulate writing many contents for Saudi official Social media like Twitter and Youtube. As an example in 2014, the consultants in Qorvis firm have created Twitter account for Syrian coalition opposition, supported by Saudi Arabia.[780] Not only that, in February 2018 Saudi Arabia reportedly had hired Winthrop Shaw Pittman Company to lobby US government regarding Saudi government willingness to develop nuclear energy for peaceful purposes.[781] Furthermore, in order to identify new strategies of enhancing the more closely bilateral relations following the election of Donald Trump, Arab Saudi was known to have hired 6 American lobbyist firms, in which Saudi ministry of interior hired Sonora Policy Group in Arizona in May 2017 as trade sector consultant prior to Donald Trump's arrival in Saudi.[782]

Other Saudi prominent lobbyist organization in US is named SAPRAC (the Saudi American Public Relation Affairs Committee) founded by Salman al-Anshari, Saudi businessman and political analyst in March 2016.[783] Headquartered in Washington, apart from presenting Saudi positive credibility and image to US public, SAPRAC for several times has been embroiled in creating propaganda to discredit Qatari position related to its activities as global terrorism sponsor, helping Saudi government along with Bahrain, UEA and Egypt isolate Qatar following the issued policy with regard to economic blockade to Qatar in mid-2017. For instance, in July 2017 the organization had been involved in anti-Qatar campaign for $ 138.000.[784]

Interestingly, in addition to the aforementioned facts, according to Medea Benjamin, the Kingdom has also donated to various think tanks, universities, and nonprofits, including the Atlantic Council, the Middle East Policy Council, the Smithsonian Freer Museum of Art and the Arab Gulf States Institute. Moreover, as she writes, the Royal Embassy of Saudi and Saudi Aramco have been top sponsors of the Middle East Institute in Washington D.C since 2005. It is reported that in 2005 Saudi Prince Al-Waleed bin Talal donated $20 million each to Harvard University and Georgetown University to advance Islamic studies and further understanding of the Muslim World, in addition to donation of $ 10 million by a Saudi

---

[780] Catherine Ho, 20 April 2016, https://www.washingtonpost.com/news/powerpost/wp/2016/04/20/saudi-government-has-vast-network-of-pr-lobby-firms-in-u-s/?noredirect=on&utm_term=.8c4e447c728f

[781] Bryant Harris, 22 February 2018, https://www.al-monitor.com/pulse/originals/2018/02/saudi-arabia-recruit-legal-muscle-leverage-us-nuclear.html

[782] Thomas Frank, 2 June 2017, https://edition.cnn.com/2017/06/01/politics/saudi-arabia-lobbyists-trump/index.html

[783] Faisal J Abbas, 16 March 2016, https://english.alarabiya.net/en/perspective/features/2016/03/16/Saudi-lobby-group-SAPRAC-launches-in-the-US.html

[784] Creede Newton, 25 July 2017, https://www.aljazeera.com/news/2017/07/saudi-lobby-pays-138000-anti-qatar-ads-170725041529752.html

billionaire banker to Yale University and Yale Law School to establish a Center of Islamic Law and Civilization, etc. [785]

Meanwhile Iranian government willingness to establish its lobbyists in US has been confirmed by incumbent President Hassan Rouhani and his foreign Minister, Javad Zareef viewed as effective tool to display its moderate foreign policy and friendly gesture to the West. Amid constant rejection by the Iranian Supreme Leader to normalize ties with US, the Iranian government does realize that such an incessant hostility would yield in negative repercussions for Iranian interests globally. At least, the governments would try to minimize the negative impacts of such long entrenched hostility by exerting elegant mechanisms. Apparently, Ayatollah Ali Khamenei does not oppose establishing Iranian lobbyists in US whereas interestingly in the meantime he still maintains and advocates his loyalists to yell out revolutionary jargons of anti-US. The Iranian dual policy and inconsistency may affect the outcome of Iranian lobbyists in US, thus facing multiple failures to contain US from imposing economic sanctions to Iran successively. Furthermore, Iranian lobbyists abroad chiefly in US, differently from its ruling elites at who tend to take revolutionary and antagonistic steps, would act more professionally and elegantly, with putting much respect to the prevailing rules and regulations at abroad. Interestingly the lobbyists who often have access to many both former and incumbent high officials of the US would also have an extra duty that shall not been overlooked its significance, which is the lobbyists would do everything to undermine and downgrade the echoes of Iranian opposition abroad that may influence the US policy against Iran. As such, the lobbyists may seem critical to the unpopular Iranian government and its mismanaged policy in various meetings and discussions, in order to obscure and blur its ultimate and true goal which is shaping the wide public opinion that Iranian regime is still good for peace and stability in the region, and cordial friendship between US and Iran is likely to be established.

As open secret, hostile and antagonist attitudes toward western countries developed mainly by Ahmadinejad, former ultra-conservative Iranian president for years, had disgraced Iranian position and image in international arena, in particular West, thus evidently thwarting all steps and strategies taken out by the lobbyists who attempted to frame Iran otherwise. Certainly, anti-western policy promoted by his administration has destroyed the entire constructive and reconciliatory steps taken by earlier President, Mohammad Khatami who developed profoundly principles of dialogue among nations.

The institution like NIAC (National Iranian American Council) headed by an Iranian Trita Parsi until 2018, despite no clear indication on whether it has received financial assistance from Iranian government or not, has become the most outstanding Iranian lobbyist in US, mainly with regard to significant efforts to encourage US investors and traders to explore Iranian potentialities. The organization, mainly aiming at strengthening dual Iranian-American citizens' voices and promoting mutual understanding of friendly and

---

[785] Medea Benjamin, the Kingdom of the Unjust, Behind the US-Saudi Connection, OR books 2016 page 104

open Iran to the local people, has been reported to have organized successfully and intensively over 30 meetings between Iranian former diplomats including pro-Iran political activists with several White House officials in Barrack Obama period, in which such meetings had undeniably resulted in softening US stances toward Iran, particularly related to nuclear issue.[786] According to Hassan Da'ei, prominent Iranian political analyst and human right activist, the organization founded in 2002, is well known to be coordinating numerous meetings between Iranian leaders and Iranian citizens in US in the sidelines of summit meeting of UN General Assembly, held annually in September. To him, NIAC furthermore has been accused to have manipulated many pro-Iranian regime polls, thus presenting the results to American audiences in seminars. [787]

As a matter of fact, long before NIAC establishment, in 1991 an Iranian lobbyist organization called AIC (the American Iranian Council) was founded. Similar to NIAC, the organization reportedly had succeeded to issue various initiatives of meetings between Iranian and US officials, and to considerably influence them to put more attention to Iranian issues in a friendly way. Some of AIC's significant achievements were among others, organizing a meeting between Mahdi Karoubi, former head of Iranian parliament, with his US counterpart in New York, helping persuade Madeleine Albright, former US Secretary of the state regarding Iran and her apology expression of 1953 Coup d'état carried out by CIA, toppling down Mosaddegh, Iranian nationalist prime minister, helping persuade issuing the proposals of Joe Biden, former Vice President and senator John Kerry in holding dialogue between US congress and Iranian parliament, exonerating American mountain hikers from Iranian jail, promoting the Shield Iranian-American From Sanction (SIAS).[788] In recent years, the role of AIC lobbyist began to diminish, replaced by more dominant role played by NIAC organization.

In sum, if Saudi Arabia is seemingly inclined to establish its political lobby through giving financial donation to some US famous universities as elucidated earlier, Iran has been well known for actively inserting some of its lobbyists to become researcher and lecturer in several universities in US. The most phenomenal instance has ever existed is the appointment of Sayyed Hossein Mousavian as a Middle East Security and Nuclear Specialist in Princeton University.[789] He previously was Iranian senior negotiator in nuclear issue in 2003 and ambassador for German in 1990. While holding an ambassadorial position in German, he was alleged to have involved in shocking assassination targeting four Iranian dissidents in Berlin.

---

[786] Kayhan.london, 24 January 2017
[787] For further information, please see Hassan Daei presentation on NiAC role through Youtube channel
[788] www.us-iran.org
[789] Seyed Hossein Mosavian, www.princeton.edu

Establishing Television and Radio Stations

As elaborated earlier, in order to propagate, introduce and influence international target audience, the establishment of satellite television and radio stations constitutes a vital strategy carried out by the two governments for many years. It further shows that electronic and print media have played pivotal roles to promulgate and echo both states' perspective and standpoint usually supported with enormously incessant funding of the governments, believing that due to the satellite technological function, the whole agenda would grant access more easily to people, including those living in very remote areas with no fear of violating sovereign boundaries of other states. Therefore, it looks necessary to find out more effective and up-dated strategies that the programs would attract target audience as many as possible, among other things by broadcasting widely the offered programs with various languages.

Unsurprisingly the Iranian owned- Arabic TV station al-Alam has succeeded to entice Arab viewers in the Middle East region, evidenced clearly by 6 millions of 'like' in facebook page, despite their understanding that al-Alam belongs to Iranian government. In this vein, al-Alam could draw sympathy to Arab people, commonly by 'selling' the issue of suffered Palestinians against the Israeli Zionists and how the US government has proved to be a partial advocate for settling the issue, rather than a honest mediator. In this vein, according to Hoover Institute, al-Alam, has been able to shape Arab's public opinion and vantage point regarding conspiracy theory of Western countries and Israel, by diminishing US influence in the region.[790]

Yet furthermore, as far as my personal observation, in such an effort, Iran has been moving one more step forward in compared with Saudi Arabia. The theocratic country proves to have been more aggressive and consistent in harnessing intensively the broadcast stations than Saudi Arabia, but all any other states in Gulf territory. By assessing its politically isolated position before the international audience, Iran has deliberately taken such a step to prove that the international publics are different in opinions and stances from their own leaders. In this vein, Iran is convinced that all programs it offers would be compatible with the perspectives of all international public, but not with their rulers. As intimated earlier, Issues like anti Zionism and global arrogance of the US which tends to dominate and rule the world could be the strategic selling points for Iran in order to gradually shape further opinion that Iran is the pioneer for enforcing justice and spearhead for defending suppressed nations around the globe.

In order to accomplish its ultimate goals, Iran has succeeded to build a wide array of television and radio stations, hundreds of internet websites deliberately broadcasted in various international languages. Due to its paramount significance for Iran in voicing its agenda under the framework of exporting the revolution to many regions, Supreme Leader

---

[790] www.hoover.org, 12 December 2017

will have the exclusive authority to appoint directly heads of the IRIB (the Islamic Republic of Iran Broadcasting), despite his pleading that he won't have any right to intervene with its management and operation.[791] Meanwhile the vast majority of Saudi television and radio stations are broadcasted predominantly in Arabic, with Saudi having only one English channel news network namely KSA 2 that mostly focuses on political, economic and cultural news coverage, along with its widespread correspondents not only in Middle East, but also US and UK.[792] As mentioned previously, Saudi Arabia seemingly doesn't focus on taking roles and functions of the broadcast stations, if compared to Iran as it does believe there could more effective ways and mechanisms, rather than harnessing the broadcast stations, to influence the target states. Apparently some factors could prevail that encourage the Kingdom not to exert the broadcast stations profoundly, although the role of Saudi media shall not be ignored to undermine and downplay any state and person who evidently oppose the policy of the Kingdom. In this regards, to counterweight the Arabic -broadcast Iranian television such as al-Alam, a Persian TV was founded and funded by the Kingdom of Saudi Arabia targeting obviously Iranian citizens since May 2017 as a realization of Mohammad bin Salman's previous statement on Saudi readiness to move the battle to inside the Iranian territory.[793]

Iranian government through IRIB has the authority to manage and operate widespread broadcast of television and radio stations with often using various international languages by employing its foreign native correspondents. The institution has been well known to have special enormous budget annually and seen significantly to be the most reliable means to voice Iranian agenda against the stations of the "enemies."

In this vein, Iran has been estimated to own at least 200 television and radio stations operated both at home and abroad, many of which broadcast outside Iran, have affiliation with Iranian government. The TV stations meant among others are Press TV (English), al-Alam (Arabic), al-Kawthar TV (Arabic), Hispan TV (Spanish), and Arabic television stations broadcasted outside Iranian borders chiefly in Middle East such as al-Manar and al-Mayadeen Arabic TV stations (owned by Lebanese Hezbollah), al-Masirah TV (belong to Ansharullah group in Yemen yet broadcasted from Beirut), al-Naba TV (Beirut), al-Ghader TV (Iraqi Badr organization), el-Ettejah TV (Kata'ib Hezbollah in Iraq), al-Ahd TV (owned by Shia Asa'ib ahl al-Haq in Iraq), al-Forat TV (owned by Ammar Hakim, Iraqi Shia prominent cleric), al-Nujaba TV (owned by Harakat Hezbollah al-Nujaba in Iraq), Afagh TV and Biladi TV (Shia Da'wa political party), al-Masar TV (affiliated to Shia political party of Da'wa), Palestine Today TV and Qods Tv, al-Agsha TV (owned by Hamas organization in Palestine).[794]

---

[791] Khamenei : Modereyet Seda Sima va Quwwa Qadhaiye Ba Rahbary nist, www.dw.com, 29 May 2018.
[792] Wwitf.com
[793] https://alarab.co.uk/السعودية-تشن-حربا-إعلامية-موجهة-للداخل-الإيراني, 1 November 2018
[794] Iranian-American Forum, Iranian regime's Media Empire in the Middle East, Youtube Channel

As mentioned previously, IRIB institution has also established various radio stations, broadcasted in 32 international languages, including Indonesia.[795] Among the radio stations, English Radio consistently broadcasted from Tehran, has reached all listeners in European, American and Australian countries. The station founded in July 2003, has a controversial program namely the Voice of Justice, containing a campaign of anti- US interventionist policy in the global arena. Iranian government also has been involved in operating English newspapers such Tehran Times and Iran Daily, apart from four English national news agencies namely Islamic Republic News Agency (IRNA), Iranian Students News Agency (ISNA), Fars News Agency and Mehr News Agency,[796] targeting foreign expatriates, businessmen as well as diplomats.

Challenges for Iranian Propagandist Media

With the passage of time, Iranian media have been going through their own obstacles and challenges, disgracing gradually their credibility and reputation in the world. The media which often echo and encourage maintaining the Islamic principles and values within the society, rather proved to have ironically contradicted Islamic values, in which Islam invariably promotes the great importance of human right issues comprising the freedom of speech and expression. It is open secret, Iranian media has been often accused by the Iranian society to manipulate and fabricate the information and data that don't signify the reality. In this regard, the paradoxical situation often appears that Iran has been striving hard to safeguard the implementation of the Islamic tenets in operating and controlling its own national and international media, claiming that its non-Persian broadcast stations reflect the realization of its Islamic-nuanced soft power.

Therefore manipulating and fabricating news coverage conducted by IRIB, mainly in political affairs, only to achieve the aim of displaying the perfectness of Islamic Republic to the world, thus shaping wider public perspective that Iran is the true ruler of the world. Such a biased coverage of the Iranian media could be seen through its largely intensive coverage on bad economic and political situations in both Europe and America. In this vein, Iran puts a hidden goal to demonstrate a perception to the Iranian society at home, that not only was Iran the victim of uncertain economic global crisis. Worst, Iranian media, also Saudi media, would deliberately bring public opinion that any action taken by opposition to dismiss any ruler it supports would be illegal. Media in both countries, Iran and Saudi Arabia, don't often eagerly cover humanitarian tragedies and human right abuses caused by their supported regimes.

---

[795] The languages used including Albania, Arab, Aran, Armenia, Azerbaijan, Bengali, Bosnia, Chine, Dari, English, French, Georgia, Germany, Hausa, Hebrew India, Indonesia, Italia, Japan, Kazakh, Kurdish, Pashto, Russia, Spanish, Swahili, Tajik, Tallish, Turkish, Turkmen, Urdu and Uzbek
[796] English.irib.ir

Most startlingly such a fact of manipulating and fabricating has been once affirmed recently by Hassan Mohadesi, Iranian sociology expert and lecturer when appeared in a discussion and debate in the aftermath of 2018 massive demonstration held by an Iranian national television station broadcasted live, when he lamented on IRIB institution that systematically has disseminated lies to Iranian public, mainly in political issues. In addition, the incredibility of IRIB has been also the main concern of Jafarzade, Iranian parliament member, who criticized the institution not to be objective in reporting and covering Iranian public voices and aspirations. [797]

Therefore small wonder, based on International News Monitoring Agencies evaluation, Iran consistently constitutes one of the countries with lowest media reliance. In a report issued by Radio Free/Radio Liberty in 2003, much news covered by Iranian televisions and radios are biased to pro regime, and not accurate in which many programs offered would no longer entice Iranian viewers/listeners.[798] Additionally, based on a survey conducted by Freedom House in 2017, it was stated that Iran gains not free status in press and media, while NGO Reporters Without Borders in 2017 plunged this theocratic state into 165th position regarding the press freedom. [799]

In fact since 2013, IRIB itself has faced economic sanction imposed by Washington which had accused that it endorsed widely the human rights violations taking place considerably in Iran in 2009 green movement, by broadcasting coerced confessions of several Iranian political activists during their stay in jails. Even furthermore, European Union in March 2012 had given sanction to Ezzatollah Zarghami, the head of IRIB of the time.[800] Such a fact has been once revealed by Freedomhouse.org, saying that many political dissidents put to the jails, have been asked to conduct interview broadcasted by TV station under severe pressure, which aims at discrediting and destroying their reputation and credibility.[801]

As a whole, the Economist in 2016 also placed Iran as a country with extremely bad treatment in implementing democratic values.[802] Anna Tiedeman further believes, given the fact of Iranian media's inability to accommodating and understanding public interests, this fact has led IRIB to become no more an Iranian regime propagandist tool. In sum, tight censoring of Iranian national media almost fully controlled by the regime has become a

---

[797] Jafarzade Kash mitonestim raes sedaye sema estezah konim, 7 July 2018, http://www.entekhab.ir/fa/news/417693/جعفرزاده-کاش-می%E2%80%8Cتوانستیم-رئیس-صداوسیما-را-استیضاح-کنیم-کنند-آن-صدایی-که-به-نام-صدای-مردم-پخش-می%E2%80%8Cگیرند-اما-کار-حزبی-می%E2%80%8Cبودجه-را-به-نام-رسانه-ملی-می%E2%80%8Cشود-کاملا-تقطیع-و-تحریف-شده-می%E2%80%8C
[798] Anna Tiedeman, Islamic Republic of Iran Broadcasting : Public Diplomacy or Propaganda, the Fletcher School, page 6
[799] Rsf.org
[800] Treasury Announces Sanctions Against Iran, 2 June 2013, https://www.treasury.gov/press-center/press-releases/Pages/tg1847.aspx
[801] www.freedomhouse.com
[802] For further information, please refer into democracy index issued by the Economist in 2016

great challenge for those media to offer objective and honest news programs on the basis of reality.

However according to a report by the Committee to Protect Journalist (CPJ), many Iranian journalists and writers have been indeed granted freedoms and latitudes to echo reform agendas reflected more by censuring wrong government policies and its mismanagement that causes multiple bureaucratic and financial corruption by state officials, yet unfortunately they have no longer such a courage to write on Iranian political elites issues or any issues later to be perceived as threatening national security and stability.[803] More evidently, there is no standardized measure for the government to prosecute the local journalist and writers who report on something the government perceives to be opposing it, thus galvanizing assumption among the society that the degrees of the prosecution imposed those dissident journalists and writers may depend on who is ruling and who is the President. Yet generally the Iranian society has no longer much expectation that any president elected will bring brighter future for press freedom despite their intensive promises in the presidential campaigns. All of these devastating facts prompted Freedomhouse to single out Iran as an unfriendly state for journalists.

In this regard, Hassan Daei, Iranian political observer residing in US, has once presented an example of the Iranian nuclear dossier. He assumed that Iranian national media had deliberately agreed to only report Iranian public opinions supporting vehemently their government effort to have nuclear energy for peaceful purposes. Yet ironically, opposing voices to such a giant agenda given wasting large amount of money and posing much threat for the environmental sustainability, were never deliberately presented, thus implying Iranian unanimously supportive opinions regarding the issue,[804] in which according to Akbar Ganji, Iranian dissident journalist, such a policy of tight censorship on specific nuclear issue was issued by an Iranian governmental board namely the Supreme National Security Council (SNSC).[805]

In fact, the multiple arrests of Iranian journalists and social media activists have been no longer a new phenomenon in Iran, rampantly occurred since the eruption of the Green Movement 2009. In 2017 alone, some of the journalists who worked for Iranian newspapers were arrested and put to the jails, such as Ehsan Mazandarani, Saman Safarzade, Afarin Chitsaz, Sadra Mohaghegh and Yashar Soltani, along with Jason Rezaeiyan, American-Iranian Washington post journalist.[806] The curbing of the journalists would sometimes be followed by the dissolving of the newspapers, mainly owned by moderate reformists. For instance in

---

[803] www.pressreference.com
[804] Hassan Da'e, American-Iranian forum
[805] Akbar Ganji, Foreign Affairs, the Latter Day Sultan, translated from Persia by Farhad Abdollia, published in www.abdolian.com, 19 November 2008
[806] Persian.humanrights.org, 8 February 2018

June 2016, Ghanoon newspaper was compelled to be shut down due to its critical report on the inhuman conditions of the prison facility in Tehran.[807]

Not only that, some figures engaged in polling following the widespread demonstrations in over 100 cities/towns in 2017/2018 which the result did not embolden the regime, have also been arrested.[808] Apart from web blogs, gigantic social media like Youtube, Facebook, Twittter and recently Telegram which attracted 40 millions of the Iranian accounts have been constantly subject for restriction and blocking.

However as elucidated previously, silencing press freedom in Iran seems to be very obscure, meaning that the right definition of what kind of news provoking stability and security threats is unclear and ambiguous. For instance, an Iranian journalist who reports corruption case evolving in one government institution probably wouldn't face arrest and interrogation that ultimately put him to jail whereas the other who reveals the same case could be put to prison.

Nevertheless, most of the journalists, reporters and bloggers know deeply about the unwritten redlines, an element that Saudi journalists and bloggers uphold with regard to the royal family. They almost agree that critical questioning of Supreme Leader and its absolute authority would constitute the most essential taboo they strive to avoid in writing. An Iranian journalist named Issa Saharkhiz was arrested and jailed under the accusation of insulting the Supreme Leader and disseminating anti regime propaganda.[809]

With the passage of time, credibility and impartiality of the government institution of IRIB once was questioned and doubted due to deliberately wrong translating carried out by its translator/interpreter. For instance, when an Iranian television station deliberately translated from Arabic into Persian and replaced the words "Syria state" with "Bahrain state" during the official remark delivered by Egypt's president, Mohammad Morsi in Non-Aligned Movement (NAM) summit held in Tehran in 2012 in which Mr President rigorously denounced Iranian allied Bashar Assad's brutality and repression, such an unethical action not surprisingly sparked much controversy and bullying. Not only that in 2017, an IRIB translator named Nima Chitsaz eventually confessed his deliberate improper translating while he was interpreting Donald Trump remark on Iran in the UN General Assembly in September 2017. For example, when Trump severely criticized Iran as "a depleted rogue state whose chief exports are violence, bloodshed and chaos," he simply translated the sentence into Persian "Iran speaks of destroying Israel. When later Trump said that "Other than the vast military power of the United States, Iran's people are what their leaders fear the most," the young man comfortably translated it as "The US Army is a very strong nation."

---

[807] www.rferl.org
[808] ibid
[809] Persian.humanrights.org, 8 February 2018

As time went on, IRIB's credibility has been undermined by un-Islamic attitude of its presenter named Azadeh Namdari when in July 2017 a short video showed her drinking beer and not wearing her headscarf while on holiday in Switzerland. Ironically the presenter who was always seen wearing Chador (a dress code which covers women from head to toe and leaves only the face exposed) while appearing on the television, often called the Iranian women audience to wear proper Islamic headscarf.[810] Accordingly Iranian public then labelled her as a hypocrite.

Press TV, famous Iranian government owned English TV station in 2012 has been banned in UK and fined as it was seen not to abide by the proposal issued by UK broadcasting stakeholders on UK's willingness that Press TV shall be under the editorial control of the same company which enjoys broadcasting right in London. Such an proposal was deeply triggered by an arrest incident of Iranian News Week journalist by Iranian security authority during his coverage of Iranian Presidential general Election in 2009 named Maziar Bahari, in which he admitted that during his stay in jail, he was severely tortured and put pressure physically and psychologically, thus giving false statement ironically broadcasted by Press TV.[811] Not only that, Press TV was reported to have granted $ 27.000 to Jeremy Corbin, UK politician for his appearance in Press TV show from 2009 until 20012,[812] defending significantly human rights issues amid ironically many critics on Iranian policies that often violated human rights.[813] Also becoming viral in social media was in 2016, a director of Press TV station named Hamed Reza Emadi was involved in sexual abuse scandal carried out through his vulgar phone conversation with Sheena Shirani, the Press TV news anchor.[814]

In July 2013, Hispan TV and some other Iranian government's channels have been dismissed by American and European satellites due to economic sanctions and their allegations on Iranian propaganda of anti Semitism and hatred toward Jews offered by those stations. Besides, such threats of curbing Iranian government's stations imposed by Western countries was also admitted by the trans border IRIB director who advocated deeply to rather broadcast the programs through social media like Youtube channel.[815]

Last but not least, Iran has been also much involved in cyber crime including cyber attacks to institution sites in US such as Banks and government departments. Besides, in March 2018, it is reported that nine Iranians were charged as they tried to steal academic

---

[810] Shoma : Inteshare Aksahaye Azade Namdari, Harim Khususi yo Nafe Umumi, 25 July 2017, http://www.bbc.com/persian/interactivity-40720858
[811] David Blair, 20 January 2012, https://www.telegraph.co.uk/news/worldnews/middleeast/iran/9028435/Britain-bans-Irans-Press-TV-from-airwaves.html
[812] Adam Payne, 2 July 2016, http://uk.businessinsider.com/jeremy-corbyn-paid-iran-press-tv-tortured-journalist-2016-6/?IR=T
[813] ibid
[814] Press TV's News Director Caught on Tape Asking Anchor to Have Sex With Him, 2 August 2016, https://www.thedailybeast.com/press-tvs-news-director-caught-on-tape-asking-anchor-to-have-sex-with-him
[815] www.isna.ir, 17 February 2018

data of many US colleges and attempted to get acces to E-mail accounts of US government employees and citizens.[816]

The lack of credibility of Iranian television has also been experienced by myself when in several years ago during my one week trip to Kehgoleye va Boyer Ahmad province, about 800 km from Tehran, in the location called Balqis spring water, most favourite tourism destination of the area, I was asked to have short interview using Persian by a local television station. I agreed as it would be my first interview of Iranian national television. Then I was shocked when before interview, I saw the reporter censuring harshly the current Iranian regime for not well preserving touristic locations, contradictory to what Pahlavi dynasty had done. During the interview, the reported seemed by using his body language, to put little pressure on me that I shall say that I have already visited religious sites in the area in which I have not. One month later, one of my friends phoned me, congratulating for my appearance in the interview television. What shocked him a lot and me as well, the television mentioned that I was coming from Japan, whereas before starting the interview, I deeply introduced myself as Indonesian student, not Japanese.

Therefore since many years, various Persian language television and radio stations operated by Iranian political dissidents in US and Europe emerged rampantly, contesting those Iranian regime's stations mentioned above. The satellite stations funded by both local government and Iranian donators give much effort to broadcast real Iran to Iranian public at home and abroad who are exhausted of many monotonous and strictly censored programs offered by the regime. Those TV and Radio stations often claimed by the regime as continuously having opposed its policies and even further advocating the regime change, have already become prominent alternatives for Iranian audience to fill the vacuum. Therefore many of their presenters and reporters would not have any courage to come back to Iran as they are fully aware on the security risks facing them, evidenced by the arrest of some employees of the stations by Iranian authority.

The rise of Persian language TV and radio stations like BBC, VOA, Manoto, Simaye Azadi, Radio farda, Iran International etc are deemed to be blowing fresh air for Iranians, mainly living at home despite much restriction on owning satellite dishes, in a way that those television stations often present Iranian political and economic analysts often calling for Iranian regime change, in order to discuss and talk on a wide array of issues that mostly mirror the realities and facts, in contrary with Iranian regime's stations. For them, the Iranian regime's television offers only news covering the failures of western countries in administering their governance, and rather presenting heavily revolutionary jargons and slogans. However in public areas including in restaurants and cafes, Iranians, due to much fear of sealing, are forced to display only Iranian governmental television programs.

---

[816] U.S Expects Iranian Cyber Attacks in Retaliation to New Sanctions, Experts say, David Brennan, 8 August 2018, www.newsweek.com

Again based on my personal observation inside Iran, there has been a pretty interesting fact since one decade ago, in which that almost all Iranians have satellite dishes at their homes, seen illegal by the Iranian government. More interestingly when I visited a very remote area close to Sanandaj city, Kordestan capital province, I was shocked heavily with no exaggerating that whole small and humble homes of the Iranian Kurdish farmers had parabola for accessing trans border television programs offered in both Persian and Kurdish languages. Such an interesting phenomenon within Iranian society has also been re-affirmed by a survey in 2015 conducted by an Iranian news site called asriran. The survey showed explicitly that 64 percent of Iranians do not watch Iranian television at all or less than one hour for each day. Furthermore the survey also indicated that only 4 percent of Iranians watch Iranian television more than 5 hours each day.[817]

According to Narges Bajoghly, Iranian anthropologist, for many years the decline of Iranian loyalty to their regime has been well understood by the Islamic Revolutionary Guard Corps, particularly following the 2009 green movement, that Iranian young generations no longer understand religious languages offered by governmental media and have been exhausted of all types of the regime's propaganda. Such a conclusion finally led the government to identify new strategies that accommodate more youth's aspirations including calling Amir Tataloo, controversially famous Iranian rap singer, to collaborate in making clip video on "Iranians indispensable right of nuclear possession." Additionally, Hawze Honary, the Iranian largest art centre under the direct supervision of Supreme Leader, has released the most expensive clip video in Iranian history that spent $ 385.000 with only 7 minute duration. The clip was titled "we are standing until the last drop of blood" in which interestingly its song lyric did not contain any spiritual values.[818]

In addition, some of Iranian dissidents abroad, equipped well with religious Shia knowledge, often give critical statements on the concept of Velayat Faqih and some other concerned issues, which deemed no longer compatible in responding the world's dynamics and meeting contemporary requirements. Accordingly, in order to spread their message to the rest of the world, they also established Shia teaching-based television stations such as el-Marjiye TV, Khadijah TV, el-Zahra TV, el-Anwar TV, Imam SHadeq TV that Iranian regime has deeply claimed as being supported financially by British M16 intelligence that aims at creating schism and disunity among Muslim nations. In Iran alone, those figures are branded as British Shia given that their opposition is controlled from UK and constitutes a branch of US Islam.[819] For instance, Persian Ahle Bayt TV station established in 2009 by Shia cleric from Afghanistan named Hassan Allahyari, had once been aired from Qom and Esfahan cities and moved to San Diego, California, US. Through the station, the controversial Shia

---

[817] http://www.asriran.com/fa/news/438206/33-درصد-4-تلویزیون-های-مشتری-ببینند-نمی-را-ایران-تلویزیون-اصلاً-درصد هستند, 16 December 2015

[818] Narges Bajoghly, 14 December 2017, https://www.al-monitor.com/pulse/originals/2017/12/iran-new-nationalism-religion-politics-trump-saudi-isis.html

[819] www.mashregnews.ir, 22 September 2016

cleric has undoubtedly singled out Iranian clerical politicians as Dajjal group, criticizing harshly the concept of Velayat Faqih and denouncing heavily the Shia competency of both Imam Khomeini and his successor Ali Khamene'i. The cleric also censured the concept as it has played significant role in distributing chaos and stability in many regions and discrediting Shia followers position in international arena.[820]

Last but not least, one of the most likely concern for Iranian government in propagating its ideas and opinions is removal of hundreds of accounts linked to an alleged Iranian propaganda operation by social medias like Facebook and Twitter as well as Alphabet Inc's Google. Such accounts had targeted international audience in US, UK, Latin America and the Middle East. [821]

Challenges of Saudi Arabia's Propagandist Media

As mentioned earlier, Arab Saudi, unlike Iran, has focused more in spreading Wahhabism through the establishment of many Islamic institutions and independent charity organizations rather than founding Television and radio stations. However, the monarch state has also its own newspapers published at home in abroad with English and Arabic editions such as Syarqh el-Awsath centred in London. Not only that, since 1975, the General Presidency of senior ulema board has published a magazine called the Islamic Research Review that aims at promoting theology and law research based on Wahhabism, apart from its own website. The institution also has exclusive right to publish Al-Qor'an massively and has authority to censor foreign books.[822]

As a matter of fact, due to vehement repression on freedom press and expression within Saudi carried out by the Saudi rulers, Saudi critical opposition movements have emerged since recent years, mostly by those living abroad. There is so much evidence to present. For instance in Yemeni conflict which Saudi has been involved in military intervention, the government attempted to control opposition writers and even restrict foreign journalists to get access to cover on Yemeni situation.[823] In August 2017, hundreds of social media activists, prominent dozens of independent clerics and around 30 judges were put into prisons without any charge.[824] Last but not least, Saudi authority had arrested Saleh Sheikhi, a writer and also journalist of al-Watan newspaper just because he criticized

---

[820] www.ahlebiat.com, for further information, please watch Hassan Allahyari's discussion broadcasted periodically in Youtube channel
[821] Google removes several blogs, Youtube accounts linked to Iran, www.reuters.com, 24 August 2018
[822] Nabil Mouline, The Clerics of Islam Religious Authority And Political Power in Saudi Arabia, Yale University Press page 155
[823] www.freedomhouse.org
[824] www.alaraby.co.uk, the case has atrracted attention of international audience given that such massive arrest contradicted Mohammad bin Salman's, the Crown Prince, efforts to impose much reform in domestic policies. Y

corruption within royal family who were proven to have distribute lands illegally to many individuals.[825]

They have often criticized Saudi government as it has engaged much in silencing many critics by among other things, putting them into jails. Therefore in general, the Economist placed Arab Saudi as one of the worst countries in the term of democratic values implementation.[826] According to freedomhous.org in 2016, similar with Iran, Saudi was placed not free status in the term of press freedom, and even until now Saudi has become one of the most countries which restrict media latitude in the world. Meanwhile NGO Reporters Without Borders in 2017 placed Saudi into rank 168 of 180 states in the term of press freedom.[827]

Although theoretically, the 1992 Saudi basic constitution mainly article 139 mentioned its respect to rights of opinion expressing via media and other publications as long as the opinions or other expressions are still in law corridors, yet with the passage of time, some laws which restrict the latitude of Saudi media and press more deeply, began to emerge such as law on printing and publishing in 2003, royal decree in 2005, law on cyber crime in 2009, royal decree in 2011 and the Penal Law for Crimes of Terrorism and Its Financing in 2014, and lastly a law in 2015 that requires online websites be registered and to get the licence first. Most ominously, under the Saudi anti terrorism laws, those critics and protesters are even likened to those disobeying the ruler, undermining the integrity of the state and inciting public opinion against the authorities.[828]

Therefore, the implication of the mentioned laws and decrees is very huge reflecting Saudi regime's war on cyber freedom, in which some activists like Raif Badawi (a blogger), Zuhair al Kutbi (reformist writer), Abdulkarim al-Khodr (founder of ACPRA, the Saudi Civil and Political Rights Association), Omar al-Saeed and Mikhlaf al-Shammari (writer and Human rights activist), Naha al-Balwa and the others have been put into jail. Not only that, twitter accounts proven to criticize Saudi government have to be blocked accordingly. And since 2013 until 2017, in order to prevent demonstrations and protest by Saudi public to spill over, the government also banned phone calls in Skype and Whatsapp and etc.[829] in February 2016, the Saudi commission of Communication and Information Technology was reported to have blocked 40 newly local websites that operated underground. Saudi also had also fired some critical newspapers editors despite the fact that they were appointed by the government, which interestingly the editors alone had authority to conduct censorship before articles are published. Even furthermore, the Saudi Ministry of Information also sometimes undertakes its intervention and give specific guidelines to the editors with regard to the articles publishing. In this vein, David Bradleys, a former editor in Arab News

---

[825] www.ajazeera.net, 3 January 2018
[826] For further information, please see democracy index in 2006 issued by the Economist
[827] Rsf.org
[828] Medea Benjamin, Kingdom of the Unjust, Behind the US-Saudi Connection, Or Books, 2016, page 38
[829] www.telegraph.co.uk, 20 September 2017

and author of Saudi Arabia Exposed, Inside a Kingdom in Crisis had exemplified that based on Saudi Information Ministry's guidelines, news on one year tragedy 9/11 commemoration was not published in the national newspapers. Not only that, even news on the historical meeting between prince Abdullah, and Shia minority group could not be published either due to its sensitivity of Shia rights discussion.[830]

Just like in Iran, owning satellite dishes is legally forbidden, that Saudis would have parabola covertly as they have deeply assumed, based on my personal observation during my five month stay in Saudi Arabia, that many programs offered by the national TV channels looked boring and monotonous.

As cited previously, the opposition movements emerged that could be broken simply into two entrenchments, Islamic religious and secular academicians. Aside their constant appearance in several Arabic and English TV stations like Aljazeera, the Islamic religious opposition such as Dr. Saad al-Faqih periodically appears in Islah (reformation) channel TV broadcasted from London by his organization of Movement for Islamic Reforms in Arabia (MIRA), analyzing and criticizing the regime's policies, that consequently he several times has been threaten by terrors. In addition, Hamza Hassan, Saudi shia figure now living in London, also announced the creation of the Salvation Movement in the Arabian Peninsula) which often call many Saudi at home to express self determination.[831] Earlier than this, we may have heard regarding a very controversial Saudi opposition figure named Mohammad al-Massari who leads Committee for the Defence of Legitimate Right (CDLR).

Other oppositions who came from academic atmosphere such as Dr. Madawi Rashed and Yahya Assiri had participated in an opposition conference held for the first time in Dublin September 2017 titled on demands on reformation and human right enforcement within Saudi Arabia, apart from their activities to write a wide array of articles and several books denouncing policies issued by royal family. The conference alone had succeeded to form a movement called the Mu'aridika that aims at enriching information on political activists and their detainees through internet websites.[832] Most interestingly the second entrenchment was also represented by some royal family members who escaped to abroad due to their critical stances.[833]

In fact, the opposition figures just often lament on the repressive government in dealing with political dissidents, without no further intention to call on dismissal of the kingdom. According to them, Saudi rulers would take unreasonable crackdowns simply because they are upset by those political and religious issues -unrelated criticisms. For instance, Essam al Zamel was arrested because he called Saudi government to carry out

---

[830] John R. Bradley, Saudi Arabia Exposed, Inside a Kingdom in Crisis, Palgrave Macmillan, page 193
[831] www.carnegiendownment.org, 14 June 2013
[832] www.middleastmonitor, 29 September 2017
[833] Documentary clip in BBC titled House of Saud, Family at War the first episode in January 2018 could be watched in Youtube Channel

economic reform in his Twitter account.[834] Not only that, Dawood al-Shirian, a well known Saudi columnist was asked to stop writing for months, just because he wrote regarding hand phones and Saudi Ministry of Health. [835] Last but not least, the assassination of a Saudi senior journalist, Jamal Kashoggi often criticizing Saudi policy, in the Saudi Consulate in Istanbul, Turkey, in October 2018 was allegedly carried out by Saudi government and according to the CIA report, ordered by Mohammad bin Salman, the Saudi crown prince.

---

[834] www.amnesty.org, 15 September 2017
[835] Opcit page 204

Chapter VI

Pragmatism in Foreign Policy in Islamic Sunni Perspective

Since Islamic scholars have agreed unanimously that establishing leadership constitutes one of the most important Islamic duties in order to create and accomplish Muslim's benefits and interests that can be achieved through collective gatherings,[836] no matter such a leadership is accomplished through Bay'at (pledging allegiance) or holding general elections or other creative mechanisms. Interestingly, both in al-Qoran and Hadist, any detail legal evidence on could not be found that Islam has obliged establishing a state based Islamic teachings along with its mechanisms and methods of such an establishment, rather the two legal resources have just given emphasis on general principles and common standards in societal living.[837] In addition, Islam has also never postulated one specific form and concept for an Islamic state to be established, whether it is monarch, secular, theocratic or the kinds.[838] In this vein, Ali Abdu al-Raziq, the first Muslim scholar in 19th century moved forward by stating that Islam grants absolute freedom to its followers to manage the state based on prevailing intellectual, social and economic conditions by considering social developments and the requirements of the time.[839] Furthermore, Abu al Hasan al-Mawardi, Sunni scholar and philosopher in his magnum opus *Al-Ahkam Sulthoniya* (Political and governmental laws) explained that any system for any political government would be accepted by Islam as long as principles of humanity and public interests are implemented and accomplished by its political government or leader.[840]

Furthermore, it could be argued that as long as Islam is adopted to inspire lawmakers of the states to prescribe and create their respective national laws, the states would be regarded as Islamic states, and not secular ones. Such a conclusion doesn't undermine the fact that none of the countries would not totally adopt Islam as their laws because however, there must be a wide range of new issues that perhaps differ in their forms from the previous ones. Therefore, unsurprisingly, in order to tie these new phenomenon that may arise in the future to be based on Islamic law, the Islamic jurists have long introduced a concept of Qiyas to extract legality from those issues. Qiyas, according to Oxford Islamic Studies, emphasizes on the deduction of legal prescriptions from the al –

---

[836] Yousef Qardawi, Min Figh Daulah fil Islam, Darusshuruq , third edition, 2001, Page 18
[837837] M.republika.co.id, 22 October 2012
[838] www.nu.or.id, 20 March 2014
[839] John L. Esposito, Lily Zubaidah Rahim, Naser Ghobadzadeh, The Politics of Islamism, Diverging Visions and Trajectories, Palgrave Macmillan, 2018, page 49
[840] Reno Muhammad, ISIS Mengungkap Fakta Terorisme Berlabel Islam, Noura Books, 2015, page 71

Qor'an or Sunnah by analogical reasoning stipulating that precedent (asl) and the new issue (far') share the same operative or effective cause (illat).[841]

In this vein, Dr. Yosef Qardhawi even argued that Medina state established by the Prophet PBUH has been role model for an Islamic state which accommodates all aspects that relate to enforcement Islamic laws and embroil much participation of civil society in taking policies. He even significantly rejected the theory of theocracy that grant much authority to Islamic jurists in dealing with political (non-religious) issues, which however in parallel state will require the existence of ulemas in order to give ruling elites legal advices.[842] Moreover, by referring into Yosef Qardawi's definition, any state which is underpinned by legacy and inheritance currently in monarchy form would not be automatically considered Islamic state given the absence of democratic principles which significantly persuade participation of all citizens to elect their rulers. [843]

As much elucidated earlier, that pragmatism is commonly used and practiced by the entire states of the world including Muslim states whose Islam is a religion of the majority, and Islamic states which explicitly introduce al-Qoran and Sunna as the main basis for their constitutions. Such pragmatic approaches are usually taken by the governments of the states in order to accomplish and achieve assorted national interests despite contradictive with ideologies they deeply uphold. In shorter words, contrary to conservatism, pragmatism reflects a flexibility of mind and seeking efforts of any practical solution instead of giving emphasis on inflexibility of ideologies,[844] as it would be framed in achieving short term goals of the countries as effective mechanisms to realize long term goals.

As Islam is always constant and consistent, while politics could change, so it means that political Islam implicitly 'compel' Islam to accept such a change, so as Islam would be compatible with any changing situation and condition. According to Islamic perspective, foreign policy could be included one of the three of Fiqh siyasi (political Islamic Jurispudence) elements that deals with relations and interactions between Muslim states with non-Muslim states, and relations between those countries in warfare and peace periods.[845] As such, in practice, the implementation and guiding of the element would automatically acknowledge and accept possible flexibility if deems necessary since al-Qoran and Hadits did not grant specific guidelines and strategies on how foreign policy of a country shall be conducted. However, Wahbah Zuhaili, an Islamic prominent scholar on Islamic law

---

[841] Qiyas, http://www.oxfordislamicstudies.com/article/opr/t125/e1936. Islamic law is based upon four main sources, al-Qor'an, Sunnah, Ijma (Consensus of the Islamic Jurists), Qiyas.
[842] Yousef Qardawi, Min Figh Daulah fil Islam, Darusshuruq , third edition, 2001, Page 32
[843] Ibid page 40
[844] www.tutor2ku.net
[845] Ibid, in general Fiqh Siyasi (political Islamic jurisprudence is broken into four parts. First, legal politics which includes legal adoption, court, administration, and its implementation. Second, foreign policy as cited earlier. Third, monetary and finance politics which deals with management of state's finance, trade, state's vital sources, and banking systems. Fourth, strategic politics in dealing with warfare that includes guarantying security for detainees and loots, as well as efforts to realize peace

and jurisprudence has attempted to make list of the Islamic main principles of international relations based on al-Qoran and Sunnah teaching, which include seven points. 1) human brotherhood 2) Honouring the human being and preserving human rights 3) Commitment to the rules of the ethics and morality 4) Justice and equality in rights and duties 5) Mercy in peace and war 6) Honouring covenants and commitments, as long as the other party is faithful to its own pledges 7) Reciprocity unless contrary to the fundamental principles of virtue and ethics.[846]

Furthermore pragmatism in foreign policy could be included as part of practical politics brought by political rulers, that could be right and wrong, akin to Ijtihad (independent reasoning carried out by only capable Ulemas) in the term of perception that granting one reward if a decision proves wrong, and two if it proves right.[847] as a matter of fact, Islamic Sharia along with universal dimension (*kulliyah*) that includes faith, ethic and some Islamic laws, will be constant and steady, which means that such laws would not accept flexibility and changing, while Fiqh (Islamic Jurisprudence) would be changeable. Islamic jurists even believe that Fiqh shall be deducted with flexibility, thus further demonstrating that Islam could be applied and implemented anytime and anywhere, not restricted only in certain situations and conditions as long as that resulted law does not contravene al-Qoran and Sunnah. Because politics poses an integral part of Fiqh that has to take various aspects into considerations, so foreign policy would be changed flexibly depending current situations and conditions.

To describe best on how Fiqh could be changed is Imam Shefei's (whose mostly adherents are Muslims in Southeast Asian Countries, Egypt, Yemen, etc) personal experience as he had to change his most of legal opinions, often called *Qaul Jadid* (new opinion) and much compiled in his famous book named al-Umm, while he moved to Egypt for living, considering Egyptian local cultures and traditions that differed from where he originated in Baghdad and Mecca.

As a matter of fact, international relations that also covers foreign policy had been well practiced by Prophet Mohammad when He ruled Medina as political and religious leader. The only aim of such an establishment was to promote and spread new Islamic messages to other rulers outside Arab peninsula, in which interestingly the Prophet prioritized in proselytizing to regional kingdom/neighbouring territories through sending letters before reaching wider global audience. In the aftermath of Prophet's passing away, most of political rulers in Muslim countries until current days have not associated with their character to be religious leaders (exceptionally Supreme Leader/Vali Faqih of Iran) who ostensibly still require legal opinions issued by competent and capable ulemas at home.

---

[846] Eka An Aqimuddin, Islam Sebagai Sumber Hukum Internasional, Masalah-Masalah Hukum, volume 45 number 4, October 2016, page 323
[847] www.alhikmah.ac.id, 10 October 2011

With the passage of time, the Fiqih concept of *Siyasah Syariah* that deals much with political affairs whose regulations and laws are not explicitly mentioned in al-Qoran and Hadist was significantly introduced by Islamic scholars. In this vein, by formulating and constructing the theory, they did realize that various phenomena and human inventions that largely did not exist in prophetic age, have began to arise due to more intensive human's interactions and assimilations prompted tremendously by more cutting-edge technology and communication means. Furthermore, when the two legal sources are consistent and constant, not subject to change and revision, yet multiple interpretations from the sources by competent Mujtahids/Islamic jurists, that are demanded to be applicable until the judgement day, would change and diverse to adapt with continuously changing human's life. In this vein, sometimes, re-opening other interpretations would enable some mujtahids to misuse their interpretation and deduction to comply with their own vested and political rulers' interests, not for public interests. Therefore, dozens of principles of Islamic jurisprudence first initiated by Imam Shafe'i in 8th century, were formulated so as to restrict and curtail such reckless interpretations that could tarnish Sharia initial purposes.

By promoting the concept of Siyasah Syariah, Islam is hoped to be inspiring force for any ruler to identify its both domestic and foreign policies which certainly do not contradict Islamic principles and values. In the short word, Islamic scholars would further believe that Islam as the last religion must be applicable despite changing situations and conditions to bring humankind to happiness both in the world and hereafter.

In order to explain on concrete application of the concept in more detail, Djazuli has been trying to elaborate definition of the concept reflected within three points, first; such governmental policy is devoted for public interests. Second, the policy shall be regarded an alternative that apparently close to mutual interest by preventing corruptions and evils. Third; the policy shall be taken given that its legality is not mentioned explicitly in two premier legal sources, al-Qoran and Hadist, thus generating to further use *qiyas* (the mechanisms of deductive analogy applied in the interpretation of Islamic laws not explicitly cited in al-Qoran and Hadist) and *maslahat mursalah*.[848] Therefore, the concept explicitly depicts that its implementation can't be associated with the pursuit of the regime's vested interests or specific groups, but instead to pursue public interests that do not contradict Islamic teachings. Nevertheless, the concept implicitly denies such a pursuit for achieving regime's interests, albeit by exerting Islamic identities and symbols, which are not a goal for adopting the concept. However, in realizing such a concept, Sharia implementation must be superior and inspirational element for making political ijtihad by a ruling elite. As such, in order to issue and make any policy based on Siyasah Syar'iyah concept, rulers with lack of ability in knowing Islamic laws, would be in dire need of the presence of competent ulemas who give them legal advices.

---

[848] A.Djazuli, Fiqh Siyasah, Kencana Prenada Media Group, Jakarta. 2003, revised edition page 29

The theory of Maslahah Mursalah itself could be defined as any ruler policy that consider benefits and interests of its ruled society, which laws for issuing such policies are not mentioned explicitly in al-Qoran and Hadist. In this vein, one of the most important principle of Islamic jurisprudence that allows political ruler to issue policies by taking into account public interest is *tasharofful Imam alar ra'iyyah manuthun bil maslahah*, which means any ruler's measure to his people shall be based on Maslahah. It further shows that an authority for ruling and Maslahah are two intertwined components that shall be an inspirational force in issuing multiple domestic and foreign policies.[849]

In fact the theory constitutes a result of Siyasah Syar'iah which deals with collective matters, which covers only Muamala (human interaction) and public interest-related issues is viewed by most ulemas as a legal source given much consideration of the abovementioned needs. Interestingly such policy taking that reflect the implementation of Maslahat Mursalah theory was deeply implemented and practiced by Muslim rulers since the early years of Islam birth in Arab peninsula. For instance, Abu Bakar's policy, first Caliph after the Prophet's passing away according to Sunni school, to collect verses of al-Qoran and compile them in one manuscript despite no direct guideline from al-Qoran and hadist to issue such an initiative. In addition, Umar bin Khatab, the second Caliph, has proved not to undergo hand cutting for thieves as certain punishment, despite explicit mentioning in al-Qoran and Hadits, during famine period. As a matter of fact, Umar alone if compared with other Caliphs, was the most Caliph who implemented Siyasah Syar'iyah by issuing multiple public policies in almost all fields including economics and international relations. For instance, he had issued some policies regarding tariffs, taxation for land and property, regulations on exports and imports, dividing power into executive, legislative and judicative, and foreign policy and international relations, that all these were not guided explicitly by the Prophet and not mentioned evidently in the two legal resources, and even not practiced by his former Caliph, Abu Bakar ibn Shiddiq.[850]

In this vein, even Imam Shatibi, most prominent theorist of Principles of Islamic jurisprudence, even argued that imposing punishment of hand cutting by a ruler for a thief is not meant to destroy parts of body, but to maintain and safeguard other's properties,[851] further implying that any measurement and action can be imposed as long as the main purpose of safeguarding and realizing humankind's benefits and interests persist, which include safeguarding religion (*dien*), soul (*nafs*), offspring (*nasl*), property (*mal*) and mind (*aql*) as basic purpose that all of which is required to be fulfilled at once. As such, a ruler must take these five elements into consideration before he identifies and applies his policy, so as not to contravene each of them. Nevertheless Imam Shatibi did not explicitly further if those elements are applied sequentially or not, meaning that whether religion shall be put

---

[849] www.nu.or.id
[850] Abdul Mukti Thabrani, Ijtihad Politik Umar Ibn Al-Khatattab, Nuansa Jurnal IAIN Madura, volume 12 no 2, 2015, page 263
[851] Imam Syatibi, al-Muwafagat fi Ushul al-Shariah, first part, Beirut, Darul Kutub Ilmiyah, page 94

first over offspring and property, whether safeguarding offspring shall prevail over property, and so on. Indeed such an ambiguous and unclear preference has constituted Islamic jurists's concern that make it disputable. In fact there is no consensus among Islamic jurists which element shall be taken first over the others. While Yousef Qardhawi put preference based on recently mentioned sequence which means that religion must be put in first priority rather than the others and so forth.[852]

Therefore, it would implicitly reflect that the preference would be applied depends on dynamics of situations and conditions on which one of the elements more required and necessary (dharuriyat) is. In fact, there are so many examples of such practises and implementation in our daily life that keeping soul alive is so much suggested, even obliged according to Islamic perspective before carrying out other duties. For instance, to rescue a dying person when drowning is preferable than practicing an obligatory prayer in the meantime. Eating forbidden things is permissible when there is no longer option, in order to preclude him from losing his life. An ailing person is allowed not to fast in Ramadhan month, replacing it at other time, etc.

In short words, pragmatism in foreign policy could be somewhat common and usual reflected tremendously through Islamic past history and practiced largely by Muslim rulers. In this vein, pragmatism of foreign policy which is a part of Siyasah Syariah implementation would be religiously legalized as long as it encompass public interest and does not contravene Islamic principles. The two conditions surely must be taken into account by any Muslim rulers while taking decisions and issuing policies, which means, however, the religious element shall be inspirational force for the action so as to accomplish the goals of the establishment of the states.

In addition, foreign policy conduct based on Islamic perspective must take several principles into consideration that is largely covered by so-called priority Fiqh (Fiqh Aulawiyat) as well as reality fiqh (fiqh Waqhe'eyat) In this vein, Yosef Qardhawi has put some Fiqh opinions and rules that priority must be given into something certain in legality over uncertain and ambiguous. Moreover priority must be given into social public/larger interests over individual/less, and priority to accomplish constant and long standing interests over temporary and incidental. Therefore, the principles of Fiqh that should be taken into account would include the formula of gaining lesser Mafsadah (damage/destruction) would be tolerated to gain greater Maslahah, and temporary Mafsadah would be tolerated to gain more sustainable Maslahah.[853]

In this vein, Islamic scholars often refer to the Prophet Muhammad's decision when He had undoubtedly replaced words "Muhammad Rasulllah" (Muhammad, Messenger of Allah), with words "Muhammad bin Abdullah" (Mohammad, son of Abdullah), in Hudaibiya

---

[852] Dr. Yosef Qardlawi, Fiqh Prioritas, Sebuah Kajian Baru Berdasarkan al-Quran dan Sunna, translated into Indonesia, Rabbani Press, Jakarta, page 30
[853] Ibid page 32

treaty in March 628 AD between Muslims in Medina and unbelievers of Quraish tribe in Mecca. Not only that, in the same treaty the Prophet also changed words Bismillah (in the name of Allah), replacing them with words *"bismikaallahumma"*(in the name of you, O Allah) as tactical response on their strong objections on things and words associated with Islamic identity. Startlingly, all this was deeply done by the Prophet in order to create peace and stability in the region as political priority by deeply realizing on very recent Islamic state foundation, thus enabling the Prophet to continuously promote Islam as new religion to many kings and leaders outside borders.[854] Indeed, other examples on that could be certainly found in Prophet's life.

Therefore arguably, pragmatism in foreign policy substantially is not anathema to Islam, and it would be parallel and compatible with Islamic principles if it significantly put notice on those formulas of priority and theory of *Maslahah Mursalah* (Siyasah Syar'iyah), which means that according Fiqih perspective and theory, the religion element shall be put into the top priority of any other aforementioned elements in taking and driving foreign policy by any Muslim country. However, if we refer and take more notice on the Prophet's and His companions practices, we would understand that in order to achieve greater *Maslahah*, they tended to put aside Islamic identity for a while. Indeed such political Ijtihad has arguably never contravened Islamic teachings and principles, along with their strong beliefs that Islam element shall constitute first priority for all Muslim life dimensions, including certainly foreign policy taking by Muslim rulers. In nutshell, by taking regional and global dynamics and developments into consideration, pragmatism in foreign policy, in order to achieve and accomplish larger *Maslahah* that relates to national interest, is religiously somewhat allowed, even obliged if *Mafsadah* turned into imminent threat that destroys and demolishes Muslim community life of one country. A wide arrays of examples of such pragmatic foreign policy obviously applied by the three countries (Saudi Arabia, Iran and Indonesia) were given in previous chapter.

A polemic then emerges if cited *Maslahah* is not associated and linked to national interest of the states, but rather, to *Maslahah* of the regimes to be a guarantor of their survival. Meaning that instead of for achieving Maslahah of greater public community, the pragmatism of foreign policy is taken and practiced to realize interest of certain individuals, which sometimes not compatible with national interest. Ruling elites, mainly undemocratic and authoritarian ones, intentionally put aside Islamic identity and spirit by exerting any effective mechanisms and ways only to put guaranty their survival and sustainability in leadership. Worse, in several states, ruling elites often legalize and justify any action and policy that does not reflect Islamic spirits so as their political ambition has significant continuation despite much opposition and objection of the ruled people. Therefore they seemingly attempt at obscuring and blurring discrepancies between regime's and national interests by further claiming that their own interest would simply echo national interest.

---

[854] Ibid page 30

Ominously, such an intense claim is often supported through manipulating and misusing Islamic legal sources in order to make further justification that regimes and peoples' interests are significantly intertwined. Most often, regimes in Muslim countries would co-opt numerous competent Islamic jurists to issue legal opinions that comply tremendously with regime's willingness, thus undermining gradually their independent status and eliminating honesty and objectivity.

Therefore, pragmatism in both in domestic and foreign policies of authoritarian and undemocratic states would not be meaningful at all as it is still not clear if such a pragmatic approach is taken to accomplish their national interests or prolong survival duration of the regimes. Nevertheless, those countries would certainly exert the most effective means to conceal their political weakness and declining legitimacy, inter alia by exploiting functions of governmental clerics and pursuing popular economic policies by allocating enormous budgets such as granting subsidy for premier necessities, reducing taxes, recruiting massively unemployed persons to fulfil job vacations in state sectors, etc. The states fully understand that if such popular policies are not realized, little wonder it would trigger public backlash against their governments by carrying out massive protests and demonstrations, both held peacefully and radically, that may lead into overthrowing the regimes who intentionally overlook main public aspirations. In sum, such a long standing public frustration and dissatisfaction could prompt them to turn around their minds from religiosity and spirituality.

More interestingly, the states often pursue pro-Islamic and Muslim world interests in their foreign policy, only to cement and consolidate their political legitimacy at home. In this vein, the Fiqh concepts of *Maslahah* and *Mafsadah* interpreted by those authoritarian regimes would undermine and downgrade their significant importance as Islamic legal source, which means that *Maslahah* for a regime is not necessarily a *Maslahah* for its public, and the case is the same with *Mafsadah*. The concepts would also lose their credibility and reliability given states policies no longer comply with the aforementioned seven points. Worse, in authoritarian and undemocratic states as intimated considerably earlier, roles of the clerics could not function well as they would lose their independency to issue fatwas as their fatwas shall be designed to be compatible with the government's interests.

In addition, pragmatism in foreign policy is well reflected by the countries to take relentless reluctance, not to condemn and criticize other states which seemingly are involved in carrying out crimes to their own people. Such a awkward position has been commonly adopted by considering the fact that maintaining and keeping cordial relations with those countries look to be more preferable as achieving national interests are the most important of all. Certainly, such a pragmatic approach to keep silent by not expressing furher reactions of objecting and opposing would be seen to be contradictory to the Islamic teachings encouraging Muslims to change an evil with their hands (power), or if they are unable to do so, then with their tongues (speech), and if again they are unable to do so, then with their hearts. [855]

---

[855] The hadist was narrated by Muslim.

VII. Conclusion

Islam as the last religion to come down mostly the people of Saudi Arabia, Iran and Indonesia hold to date is an integral part and identity incredibly understood by the rulers of the three countries. In addition, the role of the religion in founding the three countries shall not been overlooked as the religion, in varying degrees, has been admittedly the main element for unifying their people's distinct aspirations under the flagship of the newly born countries. In this vein, Saudi Arabia exerted Islamic spirits of Wahhabism to expand its territorial control in Arabian peninsula in 1900s, Iran used Islamic Shia spirits to topple down the long entrenched Pahlavi dynasty in 1970s, whereas Indonesia used Islam to galvanize Jihad spirits to its adherents in expelling the foreign occupiers in 1940s.

Therefore, the rulers would attempt at identifying and implementing both domestic and foreign policies under the consideration of such a fact which however, Islam, is still a main and essential element in the society. The rulers do realize total secularization of many aspects are somewhat opposed and rejected by the societies, thus pursuing secular policies would bring the sustainability of the rulers into peril.

The implementation of foreign policy which is believed to be achieving national interest of a country could be significant impetus for the rulers of the three countries to take Islamic foreign policy into account. They are automatically demanded to be engaged in many global issues that are related to both Islamic characters/identities and Muslim world. The rulers understand in such a modern world where Muslim countries appear inferior to the western world, that pursuing Islamic characters like establishing Caliphate, struggling Sharia laws to be one of the main legal sources for international laws, etc in their own foreign policy must be much harder than pursuing the interests of Muslim world. Little wonder, the countries are much eager in playing out their prominent roles in pursuing the world's Muslim nations. The best evidence for this is Palestinian case.

However, the degree of compulsion and duty to pursue such a goal among the three countries would vary. Saudi Arabia and Iran overtly claim, considerably expressed in their own basic constitutions, that Islam is their state identity and Sharia is the main legal source. Meanwhile, Indonesia since its establishment in 1945 to date has never claimed that Islam is the official religion of the state, accordingly Sharia wouldn't be its main legal source. Yet, the country further believes that Pancasila it views as its ideological philosophy doesn't contradict the principles and values of Islam. However, Indonesian rulers wouldn't undermine the fact that Islam still constitutes the religion of the majority (90%). As a result, Saudi Arabia and Iran shall automatically have more duty than Indonesia, in attempting to realize the goals of Muslim world even often viewed as religious duty.

To accomplish the goals of Muslim world, the degree of inclination and tendency would also vary, depending on various aspects including ongoing situations and eagerness of the rulers. If compared with Indonesia, both Saudi Arabia and Iran shall have more stable attitude to accomplish the goals of Muslim nations due to the fact that final says in their foreign policy must be rendered to the Saudi King and Iranian Supreme Leader (Vali Faqih). However, in reality, many possible changes would overshadow the foreign policy implementation of the two latter countries as pragmatic approaches shall eventually prevail, more than just insisting and maintaining the objection of pursuing Muslim nation interests. In this vein, Saudi Arabia and Iran, like practices of any other countries, would take pragmatism putting aside their Islamic ideology, as the temporary strategy to guaranty the survival of the rulers, also well known as authoritarian and undemocratic states, and to some extent, their public interests. Regrettably, it seems that pragmatism of Saudi Arabia and Iran in foreign policy has been taken for long and unspecific time, that eventually leads to a dangerous assumption of Muslim world that both states are no longer viewed as the Islamic states. In nutshell, arguably the countries are Islamic in theory, but secular in practice.

Interestingly, so often, due to incessant claim to be leading states of Muslim world, Saudi Arabia and Iran have been involved in political and religious clashes in dealing with global issues, in order to draw more attention and sympathy of Muslim world which still feel weird on accepting the doctrines that both countries strive to propagate and promote as the doctrines are often viewed to contradict the pathway of Islam most Muslims uphold. Unsurprisingly, Iran, along with revolutionary Shia Islam, and Saudi Arabia, along with radical takfiri Wahhabi, will be significant challenges for both policy makers to identify and implement a wide array of strategies so the doctrines would be acceptable by the target nations. Meanwhile, Indonesia, along with its low profile, seems not to be interested in embroiling itself in such rivalry, but rather, Indonesia would identify and implement its own foreign policy to only achieve its national goals. In this regard, Indonesia is very confident to note, its foreign policy implementation would automatically aim at realizing its Muslim people, despite the fact it has never claimed explicitly that its foreign policy should be based on adopting and bringing Islamic identities and characters. Therefore, in recent years, Islamic flavour of Indonesian foreign policy has been felt more obvious since the policymakers do realize that the religious conservativeness and fervencies of Indonesian society has grown significantly, showed by much empirical evidence within the society. However, in Indonesia, the presence of religious passion and zeal does not necessarily mean that Indonesian society has already become radical and extreme which tends to pursue the establishment of an Islamic state along with the implementation of Sharia laws, rather than "secular/Pancasila" one.

In Islamic perspective, taking pragmatic stances in foreign policy is permissible, evidenced by several cases that took place in the early Islamic history. But however, the implementation of such a policy should meet criteria that Islam introduces, among other things, to accommodate and accomplish public interests rather than ruler's interests. in this regard, Islam also gives respect to the independency and honest Ijtihad of competent Islamic clerics, whose fatwas are not issued based on their ruler's interests.

Glossary of Terms

Ayatollah : Means sign of God, high ranking title given to Shia clerics

Bayt Rahbar : House of Leader (Supreme Leader/Vali Faqih)

Bebas Aktif Policy : The Independent and active policy, commonly used to describe a mechanism how Indonesian foreign policy should be taken

Caliphate : The political-religious state following the death of the Prophet Muhammad in 631 M

Caliph : Ruler of Caliphate

Darul Islam : The land which is governed by the laws of Islam

Dar al-harb : The land is ruled not by Islamic laws

Ijtihad : independent reasoning in seeking Islamic laws carried out by competent Islamic Jurists

Islam Nusantara : Islam of the archipelago, promoted largely by Indonesian NU organization, the largest Islamic organisation in Indonesia requiring peaceful and tolerant Islam, somehow refers into local and genuine-characterized Islam

Mafsadah : Damage/destruction

Marja'e taqleed : Source of Emulation, highest ranking authorities of Twelver Shia followers whose authority is followed

Maslahat Mursalah : unregulated/unattested public interest for which there is no textual authority/reference to judge it as valid or invalid

Pancasila : the five principles underlying the state ideology of Indonesia, Believe in the one Supreme God; Just and civilized humanity; the Unity of Indonesia; Democracy led by the wisdom of deliberations among representatives; Social justice for the whole of the people of Indonesia

Salafiyya : the first three generations of Islam

Qaul Qadim : Sunni legal opinion of Imam Shafe'i when he lived in Baghdad, and before he moved to Egypt

Qaul Jadid : Sunni legal opinion of Imam Shafe'i after he moved to Egypt

Qiyas : the deduction of legal prescriptions from the al –Qor'an or Sunnah by analogical reasoning stipulating that precedent (*asl*) and the new issue *(far')* share the same operative or effective cause (*illat*)

Taqiya : one of the basic principles of the Shia twelvers, which is presenting outwardly something that is different from what one believes inwardly, for self-protection

Takfiri Muslim : Pronouncement that someone is an unbeliever (kafir) and no longer Muslim

Velayat Faqih : Governance/Guardianship of the Jurist, the central axis of Iranian contemporary Shia political thought.

Vali Faqih ; an individual who owns the authority of Velayat Faqih

Wali Songo : nine saints, Islamic scholars and well known for the spread of Islam in Indonesia. they are Maulana Malik Ibrahim, Sunan Ampel, Sunan Bonang, Sunan Giri, Sunan Drajat, Sunan Kalijaga, Sunan Kudus, Sunan Muria, Sunan Gunung Jati.

Bibliography

A. Caudill, Mark, Twilight in the Kingdom: Understanding the Saudis, Praeger Security International, 2006

A.Djazuli, Fiqh Siyasah, Kencana Prenada Media Group, Jakarta. 2003, revised edition

A. Ramady, Mohamed, The Saudi Arabian Economy, Policies, Achievements, and Challenges, Springer, 2010

Aarts, Paul and Gerd Nonneman, Ideology, Economy, Foreign Policy and the Outlook for the Saudi Polity, A Triple Nexus

Abuza, Zachary, Political Islam and Violence in Indonesia, Routldge Taylor and Francis Group, first published in 2007

Abu Dawud, Sayyed, Tasa'ad Al Madel Irani Fil A'lamil Arabi, Obeikan publisher, first edition, year

Adib-Moghaddam, Arshid, the International Politics of the Persian Gulf, A cultural genealogy, Roudledge Taylor & Francis Group

Akbar Velayati, Ali, Jomhoriye Islami Iran va Tahavolat Palestin (1979-2006), markaze esnade va tarekhe diplomasi, Tehran 1386

Al-Atawneh, Muhammad, Wahhabi Islam Facing the Challenges of Modernity, Leiden, Boston, 2010

Allison, Marissa, Militants Seize Mecca : The Effects of the 1979 Siege of Mecca Revisited, University of Mary Washington

Alfoneh,Ali, Iran Unveiled, How the Revolutionary Guards is Turning Theocracy Into Military Dictatorship, the AEI Press, 2013

Assyaukanie, Luthfi, Ideologi Islam dan Utopia, TIga Model Negara Demokrasi di Indoesia, Freedom Institute, first edition, August 2011

A.S. Hikam, Muhammad, Deradikalisasi, Peran Masyarakat Sipil Indonesia Membendung Radikalisme, Kompas, 2016

Azra, Azyumardi, Pendidikan Islam, Tradisi and Modernisasi Menuju Millenium Baru, Kalimah Publishing, Jakarta

Bahgat, Gawdat, Anoushiravan Ehteshami & Neil Quilliam, Security and Bilateral Issues Between Iran and Its Arab Neighbours, Palgrave Macmillan

Bayat, Asef, Life as Politics, How Ordinary People Change the Middle East, Amsterdam University Press

Benjamin, Medea, The Unjust Kingdom, Behind the US-Saudi Connection, OR books 2016

Bond Reed, Jennifer, The Saud Royal Family, Chelsea House Publishers, 2007

Bose, Srinjoy, Nishank Motwani and William Maley, Afghanistan – Challenges and Prospects, University of Durham, Routledge, Taylor and Francis Group

Bronson, Rachel, Thicker Than Oil, America's Uneasy Partnership with Saudi Arabia, Oxford University Press, 2006

Brunner, Rainner, Islamic Ecumenism in the 20th Century, the Azhar and Shiism between Rapprochment and Restraint, Brill Leiden Boston, 2004.

Buehler, Michael, the Politics of Shari'a Law, Islamist Activists and the State in Democratizing Indonesia, Cambridge University Press, first published in 2016

Burhanuddin, Jajat and Kees van Dijk, Islam in Indonesia, Contrasting Images and Interpretations, Amesterdam University Press

Byman, Daniel, The US- Saudi Arabia Counterterrorism Relationship, House Committee on Foreign Affairs

Commins, David, The Wahhabi Mission and Arab Saudi, IB Tauris

Cowan, David the Coming Economic Implosion of Saudi Arabia, A Behavioural Perspective, Palgrave Macmillan, 2018

Dillon, Michael, Wahhabism is it a factor in the spreade of global terrorisme? Dudley Knox Library, Calhoun : the NPS Institutional Archieve

D. Kirkpatrick, David, Into the Hands of the Soldiers, Viking, 2018

Elliott House, Karen, Saudi Arabia, Its People, Past, Religion, Fault Lines and Future, Alfred A. Knopf, 2012

El-Rasheed, Madawi, a History of Saudi Arabia, Cambridge University Press, Second Edition

-------------------------Constesting the Saudi State, Islamic Voices from a New Generation, Cambridge University Press

El Haydari, Nabil, *Tasyayu al Arabi wa Tasyayyu Farsi, Dawrul Farsi Tarikhi fi Inherafi Tasyayyu*, Darul Hikmah, London

Fandy, Mamnon, From confrontation to creative resistance : Theb Shia's oppositional discourse in Saudi Arabia

Fallon Hinds, Matthew, The US, The UK and Saudi Arabian in World War II, the Middle East and the Origins of a Special Relationship, IB TAURIS, London, New York

Fealy, Greg, and Sally White, Expressing Islam, Religious Life and Politics in Indonesia, Institute of Southeast Asian Studies, Singapore, Seng Lee Press Pte Ltd

Firozi, Alireza, dan Sayyed Jalal Dehgani Firozabadi, Diplomasi Umumi Jumhuri Islami Iran dar Dorene Usulgharayi, Jurnal Ravabethe Khareji, 4th year, 2 summer edition, 1391

G.Potter, Lawrence, Sectarian Politicas in the Persian Gulf, Oxford University Press and Georgetown University's Center for International and Regional Studies, School of Foreign Service in Qatar

Gause III, F.Gregory, Saudi Arabia and the War on Terrorism, Hoover Press; Garfinkle/Terrorisme,

Geertz, Clifford, the Religion of Java, the University of Chicago Press

Gold, Dore, Mamlakate el Karahiya, Kayfa Daamat al Arabiyat Saudiyah al Irhab el Alami Jadid, translated into Arabic by Mohammad Jalid, published by Mansyurat al Jamal

Guntur Romli, Mohamad, and Ciputat School Team, Islam Kita Islam Nusantara, Ciputat School, first edition February 2016

Hamade, Amal, Al-Khebratel al-Iraniyah al-Intighal min al-Tsaurati Ila Daulat, Arab Network For Research and Publishing

Hawa, Salam, The Erasure of Arab Political Identity, Colonialism and Violence, Routledge, 2017

Hasehmi, Nader & Danny Postel, Sectarianization, Mapping the New Politics of the Middle East, Oxford University Press

Hegghammer, Thomas, Jihad in Saudi Arabia, Violence and Pan-Islamism since 1979, Cambridge Middle East Studies

Hinnesbuch, Raymond & Anoushirvan Ehteshami, translate by Dr. Mohammad Qahremenpour dan Morteza Mesah, Siyasate Khareji Keshvarhaye Khavarmiyane, Tarbiyat Islami Marjeyeat ilmi, tahun 2002

Ibrahim Amini, Ayatollah, Foreign Policy of an Islamic State, Islam and Muslims, el-Tauhid Islamic Journal volume 2 no.4

Ibrahim, Badar, Muhammad Sadeq, Al-Harake Syi'i Fi Saudiyah Tasisel Mazhab wa Mazhabate Siyasi, Arab Network For Research and Publishing

Imanpour, Abbas, Jayegeye Farayandeye Solhe Khavarmiyane dar Siyasate Khareji Iran va Amrika, three monthly journal of Middle Eastern Region, Center of Research and Strategic Study of Middle East Region year 11, No 2, Summer edition, 1383

Ikhwani Kazemi, Bahram, *Vagereyaha va Hamgrayeha dar ravabithe Iran va Arabistan*, a three month periodical journal of Middle east, Centre for Research, Science and Strategic Studies of the Middle East, the seventh year, summer edition 1379

Ismail, Faisal, Islam, Politics and Ideology in Indonesia : A Study of The Process of Muslim Acceptance of the Pancasila, a doctoral dissertation for Institute of Islamic Studies in McGill University Montreal in December 1995

Ismail, Raihan, Saudi Clerics and Shia Islam, Oxford University Press

Jalal Dehgani Firozabadi, Sayyed, Siyasat Khareji Jomhori Islam Iran, Markaz tahqeq va to'see olome insane

Jordan, Robert, with Steve Fiffer, Desert Diplomat, Inside Saudi Arabia Following 9/11, Potomac Books, 2015

Kadivar, Mohsen, Wilayat Alfaqih and Democracy, The first draft of this paper was presented in 36th Annual Conference of Middle East Studies Association of North America (MESA), Washington DC, November 2002

Katzman, Kenneth, Hamas' Foreign Benefactors, the Middle East Quarterly Volume II number 2, June 1995

Kamrava, Mehran, Mediation and Saudi Foreign Policy, journal the Foreign Policy Research Institute, winter edition 2013 page 161

Khalaji, Mehdi, Apocyptic Politics, on the Rationality of Iranian Policy, the Washington Institute for Near East Policy, January 2008

_____Nazhme Novin Rouhaniyat Dar Iran, Aida Orient Book, first edition 2010

_____The Future of Leadership in the Shiite Community, the Washington Institute For Near East Policy, year 2017

_____Tightening the Reins, How Khamenei Makes Decisions, the Washington Institute for Near East Policy, March 2014

Kersten, Carool , Islam in Indonesia the Contest for Society, Ideas and Values, Oxford University Press

Kusach, Gregorry, Yelena Milkomian, *Tathawwaru Siyasate al-Kharijiye Saudiya Min Tasis daulat ila bidayatil islahat,* Riyadh 1426 H/ 2005 M#

Keynoush, Banafsheh, Saudi Arabia and Iran, Friend or Foes, Palgrave macMillan

Khosrokhavar, Farhad, Radicalization : Why Some People Choose the Path of Violence, the New Press

Kouzehgar Kaleji, Vali, Ups and Downs in Irani-Pakistan Ties, jurnal Iranian Review of Foreign Affairs, Volume 2 Number 4, winter edition year 2012

K. Ramezani, Rouhollah, Reflections of Iran's Foreign Policy : Spiritual Pragmatism, Journal of Iranian Review of Foreign Affairs, Volume 1 No.1, spring edition year 2010

Lacey, Robert, Kerajaan Petrodollar Saudi Arabia, Pustaka Jaya, first edition, 1986

_____ Inside the Kingdom, Kings, Clerics, Modernists, Terrorists, and the Struggle for Saudi Arabia, Viking,

Lapidus, Eram, Tarekhe Jawame Islami, Ettelaat publishing, Tehran, 1387, second edition

Lacroix, Stephane, Awakening Islam, the Politics of Religious Dissent in Contemporary Saudi Arabia, translated from French to English by George Holoch, Harvard University Press, 2011

Latif, Yudi, Inteligensia Muslim dan Kuasa, Democracy Project, Yayasan Abad Demokrasi, Jakarta 2012

Lindholm, Charles, The Islamic Middle East: Tradition and Change. John Wiley & Sons.

L. Esposito, John, Lily Zubaidah Rahim, Naser Ghobadzadeh, The Politics of Islamism, Diverging Visions and Trajectories, Palgrave Macmillan, 2018

Mabon, Simon, Kingdom in Crisis? The Arab Spring and Instability in Saudi Arabia, Contemporary Security Policy Journal, 30 October 2012

Marchall, Christin, Iran's Persian Gulf Policy, From Khomeini to Khatami, Routledge Curzon Taylor and Francis Group

Matthiesen, Toby, the Domestic sources of Saudi Foreign Policy : Islamists and the state in the wake of the Arab Uprisings, Working Paper

Mauna, Boer, Hukum Internasional, Pengertian, Peranan dan Fungsi dalam Era Dinamika Global, PT. Alumni Bandung, 2005 second edition

McMillan, M.E., From the First World War to the Arab Spring, Palgrave Macmillan

Milani, Mohsen, Why Tehran Won't Abandon Assad (ism), the Washington Quarterly, Fall season 2013

Moaddel, Mansor, and Julie De Jong, Values, Political Action, and Change in the Middle East and the Arab Spring, Oxford University Press, 2017

Mohammadi, Manocheher, *Ayendeye Nezame Baynal Melali Va Siyasate Khareji Jomhoriye Islami Iran*, Ministry of Foreign Affairs, Tehran, Summer 1387

Mouline, Nabil, The Clerics of Islam Religious Authority And Political Power in Saudi Arabia, Yale University Press

Muhammad, Reno, ISIS Mengungkap Fakta Terorisme Berlabel Islam, Noura Books, 2015

M. Alsultan, Fahad, the Saudi King : Power and Limitation in the Saudi Arabian Foregin Policy Making, International Journal of Social Science and Humanity, Volume 3, No. 5 September 2013

N.Stern, Sarah, Saudi Arabia and the Global Islamic Terrorist Network, America and The West's Fatal Embrace, Palgrave Macmillan

Nasr, Vali, the Shia Revival How Conflicts Within Islam Will Shape the Future, W.W. Norton Company New York London

Niblock, Tim, Saudi Arabia, Power, Legitimacy and Survival, Routledge Taylor and Francis Group, 2006

Noori, Vahid, Status Seeking and Iranian Foreing Policy : The Speeches of th e President at the United Nations, Iranian Review of Foreign Affairs, Volume 3 No 1, spring edition, 2012

N.Hosein, Imran, the Caliphate the Hejaz and the Saudi-Wahhabi Nation-State, Masjid Darul Qur'an, Long Islam, New York

Parsi, Trita, Treacherous Alliance, The Secret dealings of Israel, Iran and the US, Yale University Press/New Haven London

-------------- Losing an Enemy, Obama, Iran, and the Triumph of Diplomacy, Yale University Press/New Haven & London, 2017

Pollack, Kenneth, Unthinkable, Iran, the Bomb, and American Streagy, Simon & Schuster, Page 24

Prifti, Bledar, US Foreign Policy in the Middle East, the Case for Continuity, Palgrave Macmillan, 2017

Qardawi, Yousef, Min Figh Daulah fil Islam, Darusshuruq , third edition, 2001

Quigley, John, the International Diplomacy of Israel's Founders, Deception at the United Nations in the Quest for Palestine, Cambridge University Press, 2016

Ramakrishna, Kumar, Islamist Terrorism and Militancy in Indonesia, the Power of Manichean Mindset, Springer, 2015

Rubin, Barry, the Arab States and the Palestine Conflict, Syracuse University Press, first edition

R.Bradley, John, Saudi Arabia Exposed, Inside a Kingdom Crisis, Palgrave Macmillan

R.Wald, Ellen, Saudi Inc, the Arabian Kingdom's Pursuit of Profit and Power, Pegasus Book, New York London

R. Dawoody, Alexander, Eradicating Terrorism from the Middle East, Public Administration, Governance and Globalization, Springer

R.Wald, Ellen, Saudi Inc, the Arabian Kingdom's Pursuit of Profit and Power, Pegasus Book, New York London

R.Hadiz, Vedi, Islamic Populism in Indonesia and the Middle East, Cambridge University Press, first published in 2016

Sadeghi, Ahmad, Genealogy of Iranian Foreign Policy : Identity, Culture and History, the Iranian Journal of International Affairs, IPIS

Salim, Arskal, Challenging the Secular State, the Islamization of Law in Modern Indonesia, University of Hawa'i Press, Honolulu

Sadjadpour, Karim, Reading Khamenei : The World View of Iran's Most Powerful Leader, Carnegie Endowment for International Peace

Shayan, Fatemeh, Security in the Persian Gulf Region, Palgrave Macmillan

Syatibi, Imam, al-Muwafagat fi Ushul al-Shariah, first part, Beirut, Darul Kutub Ilmiyah

Solahudin, The Roots of Terrorism in Indonesia, translated by Dave McRae, Lowy Institute for International Policy

Soltani, Fakhreddin, dan Reza Ekhtiari Amiri, Foreign Policy of Iran after Islamic Revolution, research gate Januari 2010

Smith, Lee, The Strong Horse, Power, Politics, and the Clash of Arab Civilizations, Doubleday

Sukma, Rizal, Islam in Indonesian Foreign Policy, Routledge Curzon, London and New York

Sunarto, Andi, Hukum Islam di Indonesia, Fakultas Hukum Universitas Hassanudin, Makassar 2011

Szekely, Ora, The Politics of Militant Group Survival in the Middle East, Resources, Relationships and Resistance, Palgrave macmillan, 2017

Kunkler, Mirjam, and Alfred Stepan, Democratization and Islam in Indonesia, Columbia University Press, New York

Tamer, Yasin, Basic Changes in Iranian Education System Before and After Islamic Revolution, December 2010

Tamimi, Azam, Dying For Faith, Religiously Motivated Violence in the Contemporary World, Edited by Madawi Al-Rasheed and Marat Shterin, I.B Tauris

Takeyh, Ray, Guardian of the Revolution, Iran and The World in the Age of the Ayatollahs, A Council on Foreign Relations Book, Oxford University Press 2009

Telhami, Shibley, The World Through Arab Eyes, Basic Books, New York, 2013

Thomsoon, Amy, The Ties that Bind Iran and Hamas Principal Agent Relationship, a thesis written as precondition to obtain master degree in Masey University New Zealand, 2012

Ubaid, Abdullah & Mohammad Bakir, Nasionalisme dan Islam Nusantara, Kompas, 2015,

Underhill, Natasha, Countering Global Terrorism and Insurgency, Palgrave Macmillan, 2014

Wright, Lawrence, the Looming Tower, al-Qaeda and the Road to 9/11, Alfred A. Knopt, New York 2006

Vahabzadeh, Peyman, Iran' struggle for Social Justice, Economics, Agency, Justice and Activism, Palgrave Macmillan, 2017

Webel, Charles and Mark Tomass, Assessing the War on Terror, Western and Middle Eastern Perspective, Taylor & Francis Group, first edition, 2017

Wehrey, Frederic, Beyond Sunni and Shia, the Roots of Sectarianism in a Changing Middle East, Oxford University Press, 2107

Yambert, Karl, the Contemporary Middle East, A West View Reader, Third Edition, Westview Press, 2013

Yungui, Wu, the Influence of Islam over the Foreign Policies of Contemporary Islamic Countries, Journal of Middle Eastern and Islamic Studies (in Asia) Volume 5, No 3, 2011

Ziemak and Mafred, Pesantren Dalam Perubahan Sosial, Jakarta : P3M 1986

Zuhur, Sherifa, Saudi Arabia, Greenwood Publishing Group, 2011

INDEX

Abbasid 20

Abu Bakar Bashir 21, 214,250

Ahmadiya 46,51,235,241,

AQAP 296

Assembly of Experts 79, 82

Bayt Rahbar 85,86

Bebas Aktif 90,92,96

BPUPKI 56

BNPT 214, 220

Camp David 102,103,149

Council of Guardian 82

Gulf Cooperation Council 16

Haghani school 201

High Revolutionary Council for Cultural Affairs 170

Houthi 69,83,117,139,209,210

Iranian Cultural House 234

Indonesian Ulema Council 45,48,98,241

Iran Contra 115, 142

Islam Development Bank 67

Jamaah Islamiah 21,213,219,220,257

Letter of Demand 118

Madrid Conference 129, 150

Majlis Shura 41

Marja'e taqleed 77,168, 173

Masyumi 47,94

Muhammadiyah 55, 220

Nahdatul Ulama 55,238,247

New Order era 95,96

Nimr el Bagher Nimr 17

Ngruki 21, 249

Organization of the Islamic Conference 67

Revolutionary Court and Shia clergyman 174,177

Road Plan 150

Safavid 27

Santri 41,47,246-250

Sasanian 20, 21,81,233

Supreme National Security Council 82,265

The High Council for Islamic Affairs 63

The Council of Senior Ulemas 62,63,65,66

Ummul Quro 11,226,251

Printed in Great
Britain
by Amazon